Mentor Linguistics

# 전공영어
# 멘토영어학

LSI 영어연구소 앤드류 채 편저

**교원임용시험 전공영어 대비**

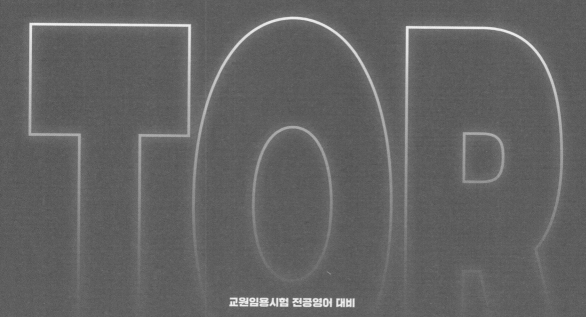

2014학년도부터 임용시험이 서답형으로 전환됨에 따라 시험을 효과적이고 효율적으로 대비하기 위해서는 출제 가능성이 높은 원서들을 잘 선별해서 체계적으로 학습하는 것이 필요하다.

문제는 영어학은 필수로 공부해야 할 원서의 양이 방대하다는 것이다.

따라서 이 책의 내용은 출제가 자주 되는 원서들을 토대로 다양한 이론과 개념들이 이해하기 쉽게 순차적 접근 방식으로 구성되어 있다.

수험생 여러분의 학습 시간 단축에 도움이 될 것이다.

### Keep it simple & smart!

이 책은 영어학의 다양한 이론과 개념들을 이해한 후에 문제에 적용할 수 있는 능력을 요구하는 최근 임용시험의 경향에 대비할 수 있도록 도움을 줄 것이다.

영어학은 단순 암기 과목이 아니다.

영어학을 공부할 때 한 가지 염두에 둘 점은 영미권 국가들의 이론에 대한 접근 방식이다. 어떤 이론이든 이론은 이론일 뿐이다.

즉, 이 책에 소개된 이론들은 말 그대로 하나의 이론일 뿐 어떤 통사 현상에 대한 정답이 아니다.

우리나라 학생들이 통사론을 처음 접하면서 어려워하는 점은 한 가지 현상에 대한 다양한 의견과 주장이 존재할 수 있다는 사실을 받아들이기 힘들어 하는 데 있으며, 정답 찾기 식의 교육에 익숙한 나머지 사고의 폭이 좁다는 점이다.

사고의 폭을 넓히지 않으면 실제 시험에서 자신이 배운 이론을 적용해 문제를 해결하기가 매우 어렵다.

이러한 문제점은 수업을 통해 그 해결 방법을 제시하고자 하며 함께 해결해 나갈 것이다.

이 책이 영어학이 어렵고 까다로운 과목이라는 생각을 넘어 극복할 수 있다는 자신감을 가지는 데 도움이 되길 바랍니다.

합격을 기원하며

*Andrew Chai*

# CONTENTS

## MEN TOR

CHAPTER **01**

Syntax

CHAPTER
02

Grammar

CONTENTS

MEN
TOR

CHAPTER
**03**

Phonetics and
Phonology

CONTENTS

MEN
TOR

**Chapter 01**

# Syntax

MEN
TOR

# Preliminaries

## 1.1. Grammar & Syntax

The linguistic ingredients that language is made up of are arranged in accordance with a set of rules. This set of rules we call the ***grammar*** of a language. Grammar is a vast domain of inquiry and it will be necessary to limit ourselves to a subdomain. In this book we will only be concerned with the part of grammar that concerns itself with the structure of sentences. This is called *syntax*.

Let's now see what kinds of issues syntax deals with. First of all, one of the principal concerns of syntax is the ***order*** of the units that make up sentences. In English we cannot string words into a sentence randomly. For example, we can have (1), but not (2) or (3):

(1) The President ate a doughnut.
(2) *The President a doughnut ate.
(3) *Doughnut President the ate a.

**NOTE** An asterisk (*) placed before a sentence indicates that it is not a possible structure in English.

It seems that *the* and *President* together form a unit, in the same way that *a* and *doughnut* do. Our syntactic framework will have to be able to explain why it is that words group themselves together. We will use the term **constituent** for strings of one or more words that syntactically and semantically behave as units. In other words, we can carve up sentences into smaller constituent parts which consist of single words or of larger units of two or more words, and the way in which these units can be combined and/or rearranged.

Let us look at some further simple sentences and see how we can analyse them in terms of their constituent parts. Consider (4) below. How could we plausibly subdivide this sentence into constituents?

(4) The President blushed.

One possible subdivision is to separate the sentence into words:

(5) The - President - blushed

However, clearly (5) is not a particularly enlightening way to analyse (4), because such a dissection tells us nothing about the relationships between the individual words. **Intuitively** the words *the* and *President* together form a unit, while *blushed* is a second unit that stands alone, as in (6):

(6) [The President] - [blushed]

We will use square brackets to indicate groups of words that belong together. One way in which we can also show that **the string *the President* is a unit is by replacing it with *he:***

(7) [He] - [blushed]

The subdivision in (6) makes good sense from the point of view of meaning too: the word-group *the President* has a specific function in that it refers (in a particular context of utterance) to an individual whose job is Head of State. Similarly, the word *blushed* has a clear function in that it tells us what happened to the President.

## 1.2. Syntax as Science − The Scientific Method

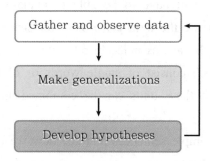

In syntax, we apply this methodology to sentence structure. Syntacticians start by observing data about the language they are studying, then they make generalizations about patterns in the data (e.g., in simple English declarative sentences, the subject precedes the verb). They then generate a hypothesis and test the hypothesis against more syntactic data, and if necessary go back and re-evaluate their hypotheses.

Hypotheses are only useful to the extent that they make *predictions*. A hypothesis that makes no predictions (or worse yet, predicts everything) is useless from a scientific perspective. In particular, the hypothesis must be *falsifiable*. That is, we must in principle be able to look for some data, which, if true, show that the hypothesis is wrong. This means that we are often looking for the cases where our hypotheses predict that a sentence will be grammatical (and it is not), or the cases where they predict that the sentence will be ungrammatical (contra to fact).

In syntax, hypotheses are called *rules*, and the group of hypotheses that describe a language's syntax is called a *grammar*.

The term *grammar* strikes terror into the hearts of many people. But you should note that there are two ways to go about writing grammatical rules. One is to tell people how they should speak (this is of course the domain of English teachers and copy-editors); we call these kinds of rule *prescriptive rules* (as they prescribe how people should speak according to some standard). Some examples of prescriptive rules include "never end a sentence with a preposition," "use *whom* not *who*," "don't split infinitives." These rules tell us how we are supposed to use our language. The other approach is to write rules that describe how people actually speak, whether or not they are speaking "correctly." These are called *descriptive rules*.

## 1.3. Function: Subject and Predicate

Consider the pair of sentences below:

(1) The cat devoured the rat.
(2) The rat devoured the cat.

The structure of these sentences can be represented as in (3) and (4) below using brackets:

(3) [The cat] [devoured [the rat]]
(4) [The rat] [devoured [the cat]]

As we have already seen, these sentences contain exactly the same words, but differ quite radically in meaning. This meaning difference comes about as a result of the different roles played by the various constituents. In (3) and (4) distinct entities, namely *the cat* and *the rat*, respectively, carry out the action denoted by the word *devoured*. We will call words that denote actions *verbs*. Also, notice that we could say that (3) is concerned with telling us more about the cat, while (4) is concerned with telling us more about the rat. We can now define the **function *Subject*** of a sentence as the constituent that on the one hand tells us who performs the action denoted by the verb, and on the other hand tells us who or what the sentence is about.

In (3) the Subject (*the cat*) was engaged in eating a rat, whereas in (4) the Subject (*the rat*) was engaged in eating a cat. We will use the term ***Predicate*** for the unit in a sentence whose typical function is to specify what the Subject is engaged in doing. The notion *Predicate* is therefore a second type of grammatical function. In any given sentence the Predicate is everything in the sentence except the Subject.

## 1.4. Form

In this book we will be using a system of word classification that goes back to the ancient grammarians. It groups the words of languages into ***word classes*** (also called ***parts of speech***). We will make use of the following word classes:

*noun*

*determinative*

*adjective*

*verb*

*preposition*

*adverb*

*conjunction*

*interjection*

The word classes are notions of *form*, as opposed to the functional notions.

## 1.5. Function-Form Relationships

Remember that '**function**' refers to notions such as Subject, Direct Object, Adjunct, etc., and '**form**' refers to word classes (noun, adjective, verb, etc.), phrases (NP, AP, VP, etc.), clauses (matrix clause, subordinate clause) or sentences.

Before turning to a discussion of the linguistic notions of function and form, let's first consider the general notion 'function' in connection with ordinary three-dimensional objects. Rather superficially, an observation we can make is that most objects perform a certain practical function. Consider, for example, a personal computer. What is its function? There is no uniform answer. We can use a computer for word processing, for making calculations, for sending e-mail messages, etc. Notice that as regards objects and the functions we can carry out with them, the reverse situation also holds: for most functions that we may want to perform a variety of objects can be used. For example, the function 'transportation' can be performed by a car, a train, a bus, a boat, a bicycle, etc. The point is that there is no one-to-one relationship between a particular function (writing, drawing, etc.) and the object used (pencil, computer) to carry out that function.

For present purposes it is important for you to see that **in language too there is a lack of a one-to-one relationship between the various forms we encounter and the functions they perform**. The converse also holds: a particular function may be performed by different forms.

## 1.5.1. Realisations of the Subject

### • NPs functioning as Subject

Consider following examples:

(1) [NP *The hedgehog*] ate the carrot.

(2) [NP *A rat*] bit my toe.

(3) [NP *This shoe*] hurts me.

(4) [NP *Teachers*] never lie.

### • PPs functioning as Subject

In (5)-(8) the Subjects are realised as prepositional phrases:

(5) [PP *Under the stairs*] was a safe area to be during the war.

(6) [PP *Outside the fridge*] is a bad place to keep milk.

(7) [PP *After Saturday*] would be a good time to go away for a few days.

(8) [PP *Between eleven and midnight*] suits him.

There are some restrictions on PPs as Subjects in English. Firstly, they are usually phrases that specify a location, as in (5) and (6), or a time interval, as in (7) and (8). Secondly, the main verb of the sentence is often, though not exclusively (cf. (8)), a form of the verb *be*.

### • Finite clauses functioning as Subject

Consider next some examples of finite clauses functioning as Subject.

(9) [*That he will go to New York soon*] is obvious.

(10) [*That this policy is ludicrous*] doesn't need to be demonstrated.

(11) [*What the terrorists said*] puzzled the police.

### • Non-finite clauses functioning as Subject

Nonfinite clauses too can perform the function of subject.

(12) [*For us to understand the issues*] requires a major mental effort.

(13) [*To be a good teacher*] is more difficult than people think.

## 1.5.2. Realisations of the Direct Object

• **NPs functioning as Direct Object**

Let's start with some simple examples of NPs as Direct Objects:

(14) Monica admires [<sub>NP</sub> *the President*].

(15) Ralph enjoys [<sub>NP</sub> *her company*].

(16) Nina described [<sub>NP</sub> *the event*].

• **PPs functioning as Direct Object**

Consider the following conversation:

(17) Speaker A: Where will the new discotheque be built?

Speaker B: I don't know, but the council rejected [<sub>PP</sub> *behind the church*].

(18) Speaker A: Are you going on holiday before or after Easter?

Speaker B: I prefer [<sub>PP</sub> *before Easter*].

Like PPs as Subjects, PPs as Direct Objects tend to be locative phrases or phrases specifying a time span.

• **Finite clauses functioning as Direct Object**

(19) The government believes [*that the voters are stupid*].

(20) Maggie doubts [*that her boyfriend will ever change*].

(21) He knows [*what she means*].

(22) They finally decided [*where they will send their child to school*].

The central concern of this section has been to demonstrate the fact that there exists no one-to-one relationship between function and form in language, and this is why the two notions need to be kept apart.

Consider following two sentences:

(23) *The cat* devoured the rat.

It is possible to rearrange the words in this sentence as follows:

(24) The rat devoured *the cat*.

The NP *the cat* functions as the Subject in (23), and the same NP *the cat* functions as the Object in (24).

A sentence like (25) can be represented as follows at the three levels of description:

(25) David smashed the window.

| | | *David* | *smashed* | *the window* |
|---|---|---|---|---|
| syntax | function level | Subject | Predicator | Direct Object |
| | form level | [s [NP N] | [VP V | [NP Det N ]]] |
| semantics | thematic level | Agent | predicate | Patient |

## 1.6. The Structure of English

### 1.6.1. The rank scale & Tree diagrams

Every sentence can be analysed at four distinct form levels: the word-level, the phrase-level, the clause-level and the sentence-level. (I am disregarding the morphological level.) This is called the ***rank scale***. The representation in (1) below uses so-called *labelled bracketings* to show the rank scale of the given sentence. This is a notation method where words that belong together in a constituent are enclosed in square brackets. The formal status of the constituent is indicated by attaching a subscript label to the leftmost bracket:

(1) Tim thought that Kate believed the story.

**word level**

[N Tim] [V thought] [Comp that] [N Kate] [V believed] [Det the] [N story]

**phrase level**

[NP [N Tim]] [VP [V thought] [Comp that] [NP [N Kate]] [VP [V believed] [NP [Det the] [N story]]]]

## clause level

[$_{MC}$ [$_{NP}$ [$_N$ Tim]] [$_{VP}$ [$_V$ thought] [$_{SubC}$ [$_{Comp}$ that] [$_{NP}$ [$_N$ Kate]] [$_{VP}$ [$_V$ believed] [$_{NP}$ [$_{Det}$ the] [$_N$ story]]]]]]

## sentence level

[$_{S/MC}$ [$_{NP}$ [$_N$ Tim]] [$_{VP}$ [$_V$ thought] [$_{SubC}$ [$_{Comp}$ that] [$_{NP}$ [$_N$ Kate]] [$_{VP}$ [$_V$ believed] [$_{NP}$ [$_{Det}$ the] [$_N$ story]]]]]]

[S = Sentence, N(P) = Noun (Phrase), V(P) = Verb (Phrase), Det = Determinative, A(P) = Adjective (Phrase), Comp = Complementiser, MC = Main Clause, SubC = Subordinate Clause]

Observe that each time lower levels have been included in higher levels. You will no doubt have struggled trying to read the clause and sentence-levels, because of the many details contained in them. It is for this reason that linguists have devised a method of representing syntactic structures in the form of so-called *tree diagrams* (also called simply *trees* or *phrase markers*). Using a tree diagram we can obtain a much clearer representation of (1):

(2)

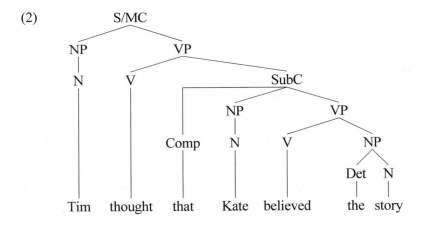

### 1.6.2. Phrase Structure Rules (PS rules)

What kind of rules could we devise which would generate Phrase-markers? For the sake of concreteness, let's consider how we might generate a tree diagram such as (3) below:

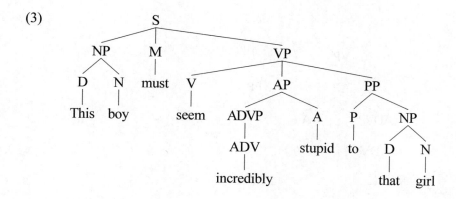

(3)

[Abbreviations: S = Clause/Sentence; M = Modal; D = Determiner; ADVP = Adverbial Phrase; ADV = Adverb; P = Preposition, PP = Prepositional Phrase; N = Noun, NP = Noun Phrase; V = Verb, VP = Verb Phrase; A = Adjective; AP = Adjectival Phrase]

The suggestion we shall put forward here is that structures such as (3) could be generated by a set of Phrase Structure Rules (= PS rules)—so called because they specify how sentences are structured out of phrases, and phrases out of words. Consider, for example, the following set of Phrase Structure Rules (abbreviations as in (3) above, with [X → Y Z] to be interpreted as specifying that 'X can have a Y immediately followed by a Z as its immediate constituents' more informally 'You can form an X by taking a Y immediately followed by a Z'):

(4) ( i ) S → NP M VP

   ( ii ) VP → V AP PP

   (iii) AP → ADVP A

   ( iv) ADVP → ADV

   ( v ) PP → P NP

   ( vi) NP → D N

(5)

(6)

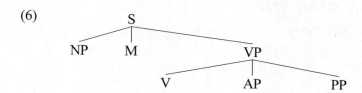

(7)

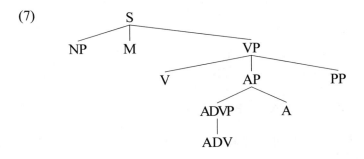

(8)

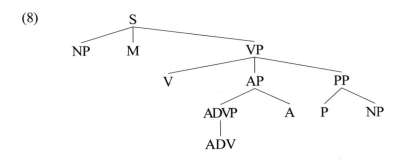

(9)

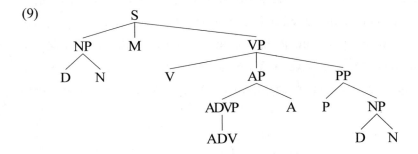

## 1.7. Transformational Generative Grammar

- Standard Theory (ST 1965)
- Extended Standard Theory (EST 1975)
- Revised Extended Standard Theory (REST 1977)
- Government and Binding Theory (GB 1981)

> **GB Theory**
>
> • X-bar Theory (Projection Principle)
> • Government Theory
> • Binding Theory
> • Case Theory
> • Control Theory
> • Bounding Theory
> • Θ-Theory

Let us now turn to a slightly more complex example. Consider the sentence below:

(1) a. Julio is easy to please.

    b. Julio is eager to please.

We have sentences that look exactly the same in terms of word order and differ only in the adjective phrases *easy* and *eager*. We interpret these sentences quite differently, however, as illustrated here:

(2) a. Julio is easy [Δ to please Δ].

    b. Julio is easy (for someone) to please (Julio).

(3) a. Julio is eager [Δ to please Δ].

    b. Julio is eager (for Julio) to please (someone).

In order to interpret this sentence, we must assume that there is an unpronounced subject of the (infinitival) verb *please* and also an unpronounced complement of that verb. These two "invisible" NPs are represented by the delta symbol, Δ. We can't explain the different interpretations of these sentences unless we propose that they include phrase structure that we understand to be there, even though those understood elements are not pronounced.

## 1.8. Deep and Surface Structure

Originally, Chomsky proposed that the base order of the sentence is the **deep structure** and that derived orders (derived by the application of rules) are **surface structures**. The ways in which we can rearrange phrases and words in a sentence are part of our knowledge of syntax beyond our knowledge of phrase structure rules. Phrase structure rules provide a roadmap of the basic orders and structures of the language, but they don't explain how these orders can be rearranged.

The deep and surface structure model, or theory (illustrated schematically below) captures the generalization that acquiring a language involves acquiring rules rather than memorizing a (vast and limitless) list of sentences:

DEEP STRUCTURE

↓

Application of rules (Transformational Rules)

↓

SURFACE STRUCTURE

• **Movement**

Movement is syntactic operation by which phrases can be rearranged in a sentence under specific conditions or constraints.

Deep Structure: John **picked up** the book

↓

Surface Structure: John **picked** the book **up**

• **NP Raising (*Tough* movement)**

Deep Structure: _____ is easy to please Julio

↓

Surface Structure: Julio is easy to please

## 1.9. More on Tree Diagrams

We've already come across the concept of tree diagrams as visual representations of hierarchical linguistic structures. We now need some **terminology** to talk about them in a more precise way. Consider first (1) below:

(1)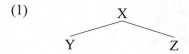

In this abstract tree we call X, Y and Z *nodes*. We will say that X *dominates* Y and Z. What this means is that we can draw a line from the higher position X in the tree to the lower positions Y and Z. Furthermore, Y *precedes* Z. This means simply that Y occurs to the left of Z in the tree structure. Consider next the tree in (2):

(2)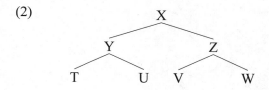

The relationships between X, Y and Z are the same, except that we can be a little more precise. In (2) X still dominates Y and Z, but it also dominates T, U, V and W. To distinguish the dominance relationship between X and Y/Z from that between X and T/U/V/W let us draw a distinction between dominance and *immediate dominance*: X dominates all the nodes below it, but immediately dominates only Y and Z. Using family terminology, we say that X is the *mother* of Y and Z, and, conversely, that Y and Z are the *daughters* of X. Furthermore, Y and Z are *sisters* of each other. Analogous to the terminology concerning dominance, we say T precedes U, V and W, but *immediately precedes* only U.

The new terminology allows us to be more precise about the notion *constituent*. We defined **constituents** in section 1.1 as **strings of one or more words that syntactically and semantically behave as a unit**. Formally we now define a constituent as follows:

### Constituent

Y is a constituent of X if and only if X dominates Y.

Thus in (2) all of Y, Z, T, U, V and W are constituents of X. Notice in addition that the nodes T and U make up the constituent Y, and that V and W make up the constituent Z. We define *immediate constituents* as follows:

### Immediate Constituent

Y is an immediate constituent of X if and only if X immediately dominates Y.

Thus Y and Z are immediate constituents of X, T and U are immediate constituents of Y, and V and W are immediate constituents of Z.

In addition, consider (3) below:

(3)

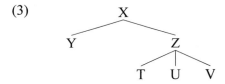

Here T, U and V together form the constituent Z, but T and U do not form a constituent. The reason for this is that:

A set of nodes A forms a constituent B, if B dominates *all and only* the nodes of A.

## 1.10. C-command

*C-command* is a conventional abbreviation of *constituent-command*: only the abbreviated form is normally used. This we might define as follows:

(1) X c-commands Y iff (= if and only if) the first branching node dominating X dominates Y, and X does not dominate Y, nor Y dominate X (*a branching node* is a node which branches into two or more immediate constituents)

Consider a structure such as (2) below:

(2)

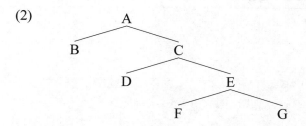

By way of illustration, let's try and work out what the node D c-commands in this structure. The first branching node above D is C: so, by the definition in (1), any other node dominated by C will be c-commanded by D. Now, since C dominates E, F and G (but not A or B), it follows that D c-commands E, F, and G (but not A or B). Since E is the *sister* of D, and since F and G are *nieces* of D (in an obvious sense), then it follows that:

(3) A node c-commands its sisters, and nieces (and indeed its great nieces, great great nieces, etc.)

Or, more generally:

(4) A node c-commands its sisters and their descendants (X is a *descendant* of Y if X is dominated by Y)

In more formal terms, what we mean by saying that X c-commands Y is that X is higher up than Y in the tree, or at the same level as Y. Or, if you like, to say that X c-commands Y is to say that X is not *subordinate* to Y, so that X does not occur at a lower level in the tree than Y. You should now be able to work out for yourself what node(s)—if any—each of the nodes in (2) c-commands: namely A c-commands nothing, B c-commands [C, D, E, F, G], C c-commands B, D c-commands [E, F, G], E c-commands D, F c-commands G, and G c-commands F. The relation c-command plays an important role in the proper description of a number of syntactic and semantic phenomena.

# Predicates, Arguments and Thematic Roles

---

**KEY CONCEPT IN THIS CHAPTER**

- **Predicate**
  - one-place predicate
  - two-place predicate
  - three-place predicate
- **Argument**
  - internal argument
  - external argument
- **Argument structure**
- **Thematic structure**
- **Thematic roles**
  - Agent Patient Theme, etc.
- **Selectional restrictions**

---

## 2.1. Predicates and Arguments

In this chapter we will look at an area of grammar where syntax interacts with semantics. Consider (1) below:

(1) The crocodile devoured a doughnut.

The verb *devour* cannot form a sentence on its own: it requires the presence of other elements to form a meaningful proposition. As will be clear from (2) and (3) below, *devour* requires that it be specified who was engaged in the act of devouring something, and what it was that was being devoured:

(2) *Devoured a doughnut.

(3) *The crocodile devoured.

In (2) there is no Subject, whereas (3) lacks a Direct Object. Both situations lead to ungrammaticality. We will refer to elements that require the specification of the participants in the proposition expressed as *predicates* (e.g. *devour*), and we will refer to the participants themselves as *arguments* (*the crocodile, a doughnut*).

Below you will find some further examples of sentences containing argument-taking predicates. Each time the predicates are in bold and the arguments are in italics:

(4) *Henry* **smiled**.

(5) *The police* **investigated** *the allegation*.

(6) *Sara* **gave** [*Pete*] [*a parcel*].

(7) *Melany* **bet** [*Brian*] [*a pound*] [*that he would lose the game of squash*].

Sentence (4) has a predicate that takes only one argument. We will call such predicates *one-place predicates* (or *monadic predicates*). (5) is like (1) above: the predicate *investigate* requires the presence of two arguments. It is a *two-place predicate* (or *dyadic predicate*). In (6) the verb *give* takes three arguments, and is called a *three-place predicate* (or *triadic predicate*). Sentences like (7) are exceptional in English; a verb like *bet* can be said to take four arguments: three noun phrase arguments (*Melany, Brian, a pound*), and one clausal argument (*that he would lose the game of squash*). In each of the cases above we refer to the arguments inside the VP (i.e. following the verb) as ***internal arguments,*** and to the Subject argument as the ***external argument***. It is important to see that the *semantic notions* one-place predicate, two-place predicate and three-place predicate correspond to the *syntactic notions* intransitive verb, transitive verb and ditransitive verb.

In linguistics an alternative way of representing predicates and their arguments has been developed. Each predicate is associated with a unique *argument structure* which specifies the number of arguments a predicate takes and their categorial status. The predicates in (1) and (4)-(7) can be represented as follows:

(8)  *devour* (verb)

    [<u>1</u> <NP>, 2 <NP>]

(9)  *smile* (verb)

    [<u>1</u> <NP>]

(10)  *investigate* (verb)

    [<u>1</u> <NP>, 2 <NP>]

(11)  *give* (verb)

    [<u>1</u> <NP>, (2 <NP>), 3 <NP>]

(12)  *bet* (verb)

    [<u>1</u> <NP>, 2 <NP>, 3 <NP>, 4 <clause>]

These argument structures indicate not only the number of arguments each predicate takes, but also their categorial status. In addition, in each case the external argument is underlined. Notice that in (11) the second argument is in round brackets. This is because with the verb *give* it is possible to leave the Indirect Object argument implicit, as in B's response below to A's statement:

(13)  A: Ivan gave me a book for Christmas.

    B: Ivan is so boring: he always gives books!

The implicit Indirect Object can be interpreted here as 'his friends' or 'people'.

It is important to realise that not only verbs can be predicates. Nouns, adjectives and prepositions can too, as (14)-(16) make clear:

(14)  *Paul's* **study** *of art history.*

(15)  *Freddy is* **fond** *of his sister.*

(16)  *The bird is* **inside** *the house.*

In (14) the noun *study* requires the specification of a Subject expression, i.e. it requires the specification of a student, in this case *Paul*. It also requires the specification of an internal argument, i.e. what is being studied, namely *art history*. Compare (14) to the sentence *Paul studies art history*. In (15) and (16) the Subject expressions are *Freddy* and *the bird*, respectively, whereas *(of) his sister* and *the house* specify who Fred is fond of, and where the bird is located. The verb *be* in (15) and (16) is semantically empty; it only serves as a carrier of the present tense inflection.

## 2.2. Thematic Roles

Arguments are participants in what one linguist has called 'the little drama' that a proposition expresses. To be a participant in a drama you must be playing a role.

Apart from Agents and Patients, there are a number of other roles. Linguists don't agree exactly how many there are, nor do they agree exactly which roles we should recognise. However, the following thematic roles are widely accepted:

**Thematic roles (also known as theta roles, θ-roles and semantic roles) — Bas Aarts**

| | |
|---|---|
| Agent | The 'doer' or instigator of the action denoted by the predicate. |
| Patient | The 'undergoer' of the action or event denoted by the predicate. |
| Theme | The entity that is moved by the action or event denoted by the predicate. |
| Experiencer | The living entity that experiences the action or event denoted by the predicate. |
| Goal | The location or entity in the direction of which something moves. |
| Benefactive | The entity that benefits from the action or event denoted by the predicate. |
| Source | The location or entity from which something moves. |
| Instrument | The medium by which the action or event denoted by the predicate is carried out. |
| Locative | The specification of the place where the action or event denoted by the predicate is situated. |
| Proposition | The specification of a state of affairs. |

**EXERCISE** ...........................................................................................................................

Consider the sentences below and determine which thematic roles the bracketed phrases can be said to carry.

( i ) [His mother] sent [David] [a letter].

( ii ) [David] smelled [the freshly baked bread].

( iii ) [We] put [the cheese] [in the fridge].

( iv ) [Frank] threw [himself] [onto the sofa].

( v ) [Greg] comes [from Wales].

In (i) the Subject noun phrase carries the role of Agent, as do the Subjects in (iii) and (iv). The role of *David* in (ii) is that of Experiencer. Sentence (v) illustrates that it is by no means always easy to determine the thematic role of a particular phrase: which theta role do we assign to the NP *Greg?* None of the roles on our list is quite appropriate. We can adopt two possible solutions to this problem. Either we say that *Greg* carries one of the theta roles on our list, though marginally so, say Theme, or we invent a new role altogether, say Topic. The first solution has the advantage that we keep our list of thematic roles short; the second solution allows us to make finer distinctions. In this book we won't worry too much about such problems, and we will use the list as given above. What's important is to know which elements bear a thematic role in a particular sentence.

We have yet to discuss the roles of the non-Subject phrases in the exercise. In (i) *David* is the Goal of the act of sending. The NPs *a letter* in (i), *the cheese* in (iii) and *himself* in (iv) are Themes. They could also be said to be Patients, and it is for exactly this reason that you will often find the Theme and Patient theta roles lumped together in textbooks. *In the fridge* and *onto the sofa* are Goals (or perhaps locative in the case of *in the fridge),* while *from Wales* in (v) clearly carries the role of Source. There only remains one case, and that is the NP *the freshly baked bread* in (ii). Again, it is not entirely clear which thematic role we are dealing with here. Is it a Patient, or some other role? We won't rack our brains too much, and settle for Patient. Once again, the important thing is to be aware that this NP carries a thematic role.

We can add the thematic information about predicates, which we will refer to as their *thematic structure*, i.e. the number and types of thematic roles they assign, to their argument structures. If we do this for the predicates in (8)-(12), we derive the following results:

(17) *devour* (verb)

[1 <NP, Agent>, 2 <NP, Patient>]

(18) *smile* (verb)

[1 <NP, Agent>]

(19) *investigate* (verb)

[1 <NP, Agent>, 2 <NP, Patient>]

(20) *give* (verb)

[1 <NP, Agent>, (2 <NP, Benefactive>), 3 <NP, Theme>]

(21) *bet* (verb)

[1 <NP, Agent>, 2 <NP, Goal>, 3 <NP, Patient>, 4 <clause, Proposition>]

Frames like this can be hypothesised to be the kind of specifications that are attached to the lexical items that are part of our *mental lexicon*, i.e. the list of words (dictionary) stored in our brains.

Let us now turn to elements in sentences that do not receive thematic roles. What type of expression would qualify for non-participant status?

(22) **It** always rains in London.
(23) **There** were six policemen on the bus.

The grammatical Subjects in these sentences are *it* and *there*, respectively. We called *it* in (22) weather *it,* because it often occurs in sentences that tell you about the weather, and we called *there* in (23) existential *there,* because it is used in propositions about existence. Notice that unlike referential *it* and locative *there* in (24) and (25) below, the Subjects in (22) and (23) do not refer to entities in the outside world. **They are purely Subject slot fillers.**

(24) I hate the number 31 bus, *it* is always packed!

(25) I'll put your coffee over *there*.

Other non-arguments are expressions in sentences that furnish only circumstantial, non-participant, information. In English these are typically phrases or clauses that function as **Adjunct.** If we modified sentence (1) above as in (26), then the italicised phrases would not be arguments:

(26) *Last night,* the crocodile *greedily* devoured a doughnut.

Neither of the phrases *last night* and *greedily* can be said to participate in the mini-scene enacted by the crocodile and the doughnut. They merely tell us *when* it took place and *how*. **Adjuncts are never arguments,** and it follows that not all grammatical functions are linked to argument positions. The reverse, however, does hold true: each argument realises a grammatical function.

## 2.3. Grammatical Functions and Thematic Roles

Why do we need thematic roles? To answer this question, consider (1)-(4) below, all of which contain the verb *smash:*

(1) David smashed the window.

(2) The window was smashed by David.

(3) A brick smashed the window.

(4) David used a brick to smash the window.

Notice that although the grammatical functions of the argument expressions *David, the window* and *a brick* can be different in each of the sentences in which they appear, their thematic roles are the same. For example, the NP *David* carries the role of Agent in each case, despite the fact that it has two different syntactic functions, namely Subject in (1) and (4), and Complement of a preposition in (2). Similarly, in all sentences the NP *the window* is a Patient, regardless of the grammatical function it carries (Direct Object in (1), (3) and (4); Subject in (2)). Finally, the NP *the brick* carries the role of Instrument, and appears in two different functional slots: Subject (3) and Direct Object (4). What these examples clearly show, then, is that **there is no one-to-one relationship between grammatical functions and thematic roles**, and we therefore need to distinguish these notions. Remember that grammatical function is primarily a **syntactic** notion, whereas thematic roles are first and foremost **semantic** in nature.

## 2.4. Thematic Relations – Andrew Radford

In (1) below, we list some of the commonly assumed theta-roles, and for each such role provide an informal gloss, together with an illustrative example (in which the italicised Argument is assumed to have the thematic function specified):

(1) A. THEME (OR PATIENT) = Entity undergoing the effect of some action
   (*Mary* fell over)
   B. AGENT (OR ACTOR) = Instigator of some action
   (*John* killed Harry)
   C. EXPERIENCER = Entity experiencing some psychological state
   (*John* was happy)
   D. BENEFACTIVE = Entity benefitting from some action
   (John bought some flowers *for Mary*)
   E. INSTRUMENT = Means by which something comes about
   (John wounded Harry *with a knife*)
   F. LOCATIVE = Place in which something is situated or takes place
   (John hid the letter *under the bed*)
   G. GOAL = Entity towards which something moves
   (John passed the book *to Mary*)
   H. SOURCE = Entity from which something moves
   (John returned *from Paris*)

Thus, in a sentence such as:

(2) John gave Mary the book

*John* bears the theta-role agent to the verbal Predicate *gave, Mary* bears the role goal, and *the book* bears the role theme.

One such argument is that incorporating Thematic Functions into our model of Syntax allows us to capture the similarity between different (but related) uses of the same lexical item. For example, a Verb such as *roll* can be used both in *transitive* structures like (3a) below, and in so-called *ergative* structures such as (3b) (an ergative structure is one in which an expression which normally functions as the Object of a given transitive Verb is used intransitively as the Subject of the Verb):

(3) a. John rolled *the ball* down the hill

  b. *The ball* rolled down the hill

The italicised expression clearly has a different constituent structure status in the (a) and (b) sentences: more precisely, *the ball* is the Object of the Verb *rolled* in (3a), but its Subject in (3b). And yet, in another sense, the italicised expression seems intuitively to play the same role in the (a) sentence as in the corresponding (b) sentence: thus, *the ball* is the entity undergoing motion in both (3a) and (3b). We can capture this role-identity by saying that the italicised expression has the same *thematic role* in the (a) sentence as in the corresponding (b) sentence, in spite of the fact that it has a different constituent structure status in the two cases. To be precise, *the ball* has the theta-role **theme** in both (3a) and (3b), since in both cases it is the entity undergoing motion.

Thus far, we have argued that Thematic Functions enable us to reveal similarities and differences between related construction types which are not reflected in their constituent structure. However, a number of linguists have argued that the thematic structure of a sentence plays a much more pervasive role in Syntax. For example, it has been argued that the distribution of certain types of Adverbial and Prepositional Phrases is thematically determined: thus, Gruber (1976) argues that Adverbs like *deliberately* can co-occur only with agent phrases: cf.

(4) a. *John* (= AGENT) deliberately rolled the ball down the hill

  b. *The ball* (= THEME) deliberately rolled down the hill

Likewise, Fillmore (1972) argues that the Adverb *personally* can only co-occur with experiencer arguments: cf.

(5) a. Personally, *I* (= EXPERIENCER) don't like roses

    b. Personally, your proposal doesn't interest *me* (= EXPERIENCER)

    c. *Personally, *I* (= AGENT) hit you

    d. *Personally, you hit *me* (= THEME)

And in much the same vein, Anderson (1977) argues that only Verbs with agent subjects permit *by*-phrase nominal counterparts:

(6) a. *The mayor* (= AGENT) protested

    b. the protest *by the mayor*

(7) a. *The mayor* (= THEME) died

    b. *the death *by the mayor*

Many other areas of Syntax have also been argued to be subject to thematic constraints. For example, Fillmore (1968) argues that only constituents with the same Thematic Function can be conjoined. So, for example, since the two subject NPs *John* and *a hammer* play different thematic roles in the following sentences:

(8) a. *John* (= AGENT) broke the window

    b. *A hammer* (= INSTRUMENT) broke the window

the two subject NPs cannot be idiomatically conjoined—hence the oddity of:

(9) ??*John and a hammer* broke the window

## 2.5. Subcategorisation

There is a strong connection between Heads and Complements is to say that **Heads subcategorise for** (i.e. syntactically require the presence of) **their Complements.** Different Heads subcategorise for different Complements, and we can use so-called *subcategorisation frames* to specify exactly which Complements a Head takes. Here's the subcategorisation frame for the verb *destroy:*

*destroy* (verb)

[−, NP]

This frame contains two parts: on the top line we have the element that is subcategorised, with a word class label. On the bottom line, inside square brackets, we have a dash, indicating the position of the subcategorised element, followed by a comma and the category whose presence is required by the subcategorised element. *Destroy* is a verb that takes only one Complement. A ditransitive verb like *send* in the sentence *He sent her some details of the plan* takes the following frame:

*send* (verb)

[−, NP NP]

This frame indicates that *send* takes two Objects as its Complements: an Indirect Object (*her*) and a Direct Object (*some details of the plan*). However, *send* does not always require two Complements. For example, we can say the following: *Martin didn't come to the party, but he sent his sister,* where the verb *send* takes only one Complement. We revise the subcategorisation frame for *send* as follows:

*send* (verb)

[−, (NP) NP]

Here the first NP is placed inside round brackets to indicate its optionality.

Of course, some Heads do not take Complements at all, and this will be indicated in the subcategorisation frame by the zero symbol (Ø). The frame for *blush* looks like this:

*blush* (verb)

[−, Ø]

For some verbs there is a choice of Complements. As an example, consider the sentences below which contain the verb *believe:*

(1) I believed the allegations.
(2) I believed that the allegations were true.
(3) I believed the allegations to be true.

The subcategorisation frame for *believe* is as follows:

*believe* (verb)

$$[-, \left\{ \begin{array}{l} \text{NP} \\ \text{that-clause} \\ \text{to-infinitive clause} \end{array} \right\} ]$$

The curly brackets indicate that a choice should be made from one of the items inside them.

Verbs are not the only word classes that can be subcategorised. Nouns, adjectives, prepositions and adverbs also occur in subcategorisation frames. Here are some examples:

*fact* (noun)
[−, (*that*-clause)]
e.g. She hates the ***fact*** that he is a genius.

*appreciative* (adjective)
[−, *of*-NP]
e.g. She is ***appreciative*** of classical music.

*behind* (preposition)
[−, NP]
e.g. The bike is ***behind*** the shed.

*fortunately* (adverb)
[−, (*for*-NP)]
e.g. ***Fortunately*** for me the train departed late.

**EXERCISE** ...........................................................................................................................

Produce subcategorisation frames for *put* and *treat*. You will need to think of sentences or phrases containing these lexical items.

---

Your answers should look like this:

> *put* (verb)
>
> [−, NP PP]
>
> e.g. He *put* the glasses on the table.
>
> *treat* (verb)
>
> [−, NP AdvP]
>
> e.g. James *treat* his dog badly.

## 2.6. Selectional Restrictions

Consider the sentences below:

(1) The keyboard designed some clothes.
(2) The stapler took a break.
(3) My colleague broke his feelings.

You will agree that in the world we live in there is something odd about these sentences: keyboards are not in the habit of designing clothes, staplers don't take breaks, and feelings aren't entities that can be broken. We refer to the restrictions imposed by the predicates of the sentences above on their arguments as ***selectional restrictions***. Linguists have suggested that one way of dealing with selectional restrictions is to assign *features* to predicates and their arguments.

For example, we might say that the verb *design* carries a feature [+animate] and that its Subject must also carry this feature. If it doesn't, the resulting sentence is deviant. Clearly, in (1) the Subject expression *the keyboard* is not an animate entity and the sentence is odd as a result. (2) is strange for the same reason. (3) can also be handled in terms of features: we might say that the verb *break* carries the feature [+concrete] which must be matched by a Direct Object that carries the same feature. In (3) the DO is an abstract NP, and this accounts for its peculiarity.

# X-Bar Syntax: Cross-Categorial Generalisations

---

**KEY CONCEPT IN THIS CHAPTER**

• Head

• Complement

• Specifier

• Adjunct

## 3.1. Heads, Complements and Specifiers

The internal structure of English phrases is the topic of this chapter. All phrases have something in common, namely the fact that they must minimally contain a Head. In the bracketed phrases in the sentences below the Heads are shown in bold type:

(1) The defendants denied the charge: they claim that they did [$_{VP}$ not **destroy** the garden]

(2) She proposed [$_{NP}$ an **analysis** of the sentence]

(3) Jack is [$_{AP}$ so **fond** of coffee]

(4) They are [$_{PP}$ quite **in** agreement]

(5) My sister cycles [$_{AdvP}$ much **faster** than me]

Notice that apart from the obligatory presence of the Heads, there are further similarities between these phrases. First of all, there appears to be a **strong bond** between the Head and the constituent that follows it in each case. Thus, in (1) the verb *destroy* requires the presence of a noun phrase that refers to an entity that is destroyable. Similarly, in (2) the PP *of the sentence* complements the noun *analysis* in that it specifies what is being analysed. Notice that in this case the noun *analysis* with its associated Complement *of the sentence* can be contrasted with a verb + Complement sequence: *analyse the sentence*. Compare (2) with (6):

(6) She proposed to *analyse the sentence.*

In (3)-(5) something analogous to (1) and (2) is happening: in each case the constituent that follows **the Head is required to complete the sense of the Head.** *Complements* denote any constituent whose presence is required by another element. We now see that **all the major syntactic categories can take a Complement.**

How can we represent the close bond between a Head and its Complement in a tree diagram? One way of doing this is to assume that the two together share a node (i.e. they are sisters), as in (7) below:

(7)

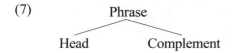

What about the elements that immediately precede the Heads, such as *not, an, so, quite* and *much* in (1)-(5)? Unlike Complements, **these seem to relate not so much to the Head, but to the Head and Complement taken together.** For example, in (1) we could say that *not* adds something to the sequence *destroy the garden:* it negates it. We can ask the question 'what did the defendants *not* do?', and the answer would be 'destroy the garden'. In (2) the determinative *an* relates to the sequence *analysis of the sentence*, not just to the Head. And in (3)-(5) the adverbs *so, quite* and *much* intensify the strings *fond of coffee, in agreement* and *faster than me,* respectively. We will say that the elements that precede the Head in (1)-(5) **specify the Head + Complement sequence** and we will accordingly refer to them as *Specifiers* (abbreviated as 'Spec'). We can now expand our partial tree in (7) as follows for each of the phrases in (1)-(5):

(8)

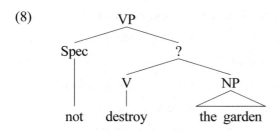

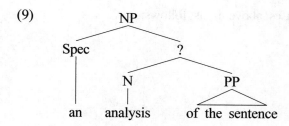

(9)

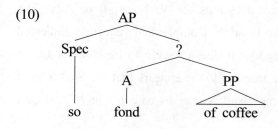

(10)

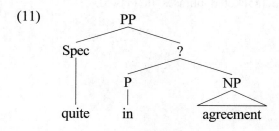

(11)

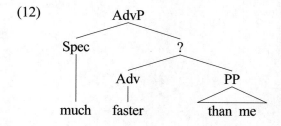

(12)

The generalised structure for each of the phrases above is as follows:

(13)

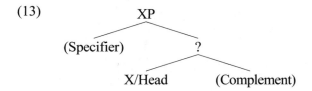

In this tree 'XP' is a phrase headed by X, where X stands for V, N, A, P or Adv. The Specifier is a sister of the node that dominates the Head + Complement sequence, indicated by '?'. What is the nature of this unlabelled category? It doesn't seem to have the status of something we have come across before. From the tree in (13) it appears that '?' is at a level that is **intermediate** between the phrase XP and the Head X. Let us call this level X′ (read: X-bar).

We can now present a full representation of the bracketed phrases in (1)-(5):

(14)

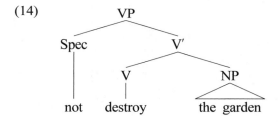

(15)

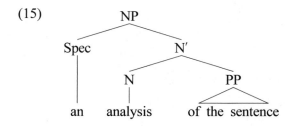

(16)

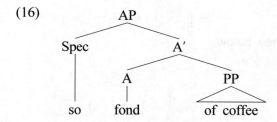

(17)

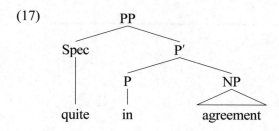

(18)

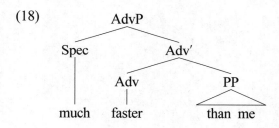

I have included Specifier nodes in the trees above. Strictly speaking this is inappropriate, because the notion Specifier is a functional one, and functional labels do not appear in trees. However, by including Specifiers in tree diagrams I follow common practice in linguistics.

In (13) we regard each of the levels XP, X′ and X as *projections* of the Head. To be more precise, XP is the *maximal projection* of the Head (also called a *double-bar projection*, sometimes written as X″), while the X′-level is a *single bar projection*. The Head itself is a *zero bar projection* (or *lexical projection*). **Every phrase, then, has three levels of structure: X″, X′ and X.**

**Assign tree structures to the bracketed phrases below:**

( i ) [the destruction of Carthage]

( ii ) He is [so envious of his sister]

(iii) We are [citizens of the world]

(iv) She [travelled to Rome]

( v ) He walked [straight through the door]

Your answers should look like this:

(19)

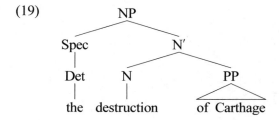

(20)

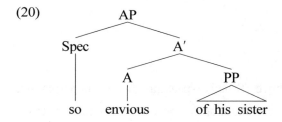

(21)

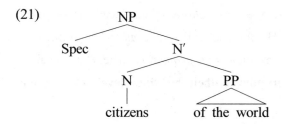

(22)

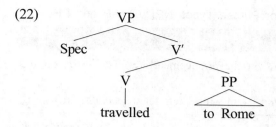

(23)

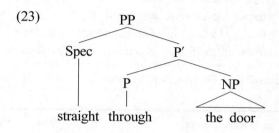

**Table 1.** Typical Specifiers for the Major Phrase Types NP, VP, AP and PP

| phrase | Specifier | example(s) |
|---|---|---|
| NP | determinatives | [*the* examination]<br>[*this* book]<br>[*those* bicycles]<br>[*many* answers] |
| VP | negative elements | He does [*not* like planes]<br>She [*never* eats meat] |
| AP | degree adverbs | [*how* nice]<br>They are [*so* eager to please]<br>He isn't [*that/this* fat]<br>[*too* bad]<br>That's [*rather/quite* disgusting]<br>She is [*as* rich as the Queen] |
| PP | adverbs | The supermarket is [*right* up your street]<br>The wedding ring went [*straight* down the drain]<br>The office is [*just* to your left] |

**Table 2.** Typical Complements for the Major Phrase Types NP, VP, AP and PP

| phrase | Head | Complement | example(s) |
|---|---|---|---|
| NP | N | PP | his *insistence* [PP on the arrangement] (cf. He *insists* on the arrangement.)<br>their *specialisation* [PP in wines] (cf. They *specialise* in wines.) |
| | | Clause | their *realisation* [that-clause that all is lost] (cf. They *realise* that all is lost.)<br>her *question* [whether-clause whether the expense was worth it] (cf. She *questioned* whether the expense was worth it.)<br>their *requirement* [for-clause for all candidates to comply with the rules] (cf. They *require* all candidates to comply with the rules.) |
| | | NP | a literature *teacher* (cf. He *teaches* literature/a teacher of literature) |
| VP | V | NP | She *placed* [NP an advertisement] |
| | | Clause | They *know* [that-clause that the sun will shine tomorrow] |
| | | PP | He *looked* [PP at the picture] |
| | | AP | He *is* [AP very healthy] |
| AP | A | PP | *glad* [PP about your decision]<br>*pleased* [PP with the result]<br>*dependent* [PP on his brother] |
| | | Clause | I am so *eager* [to-infinitive clause to work with you]<br>He's *engaged* [-ing clause teaching the students]<br>She's *unsure* [wh-clause what we should do next] |
| PP | P | NP | *in/under/behind* [NP the car] |
| | | PP | *out* [PP of love]<br>*from* [PP behind the bookcase]<br>*down* [PP by the sea] |
| | | Clause | He is uncertain *about* [wh-clause what you said to me] |

NOTE Complement-taking nominal heads often have a verbal counterpart.

## 3.2. Adjuncts

The phrases we have looked at so far contained only a Specifier, a Head and a Complement. Phrases can, however, be structurally more complicated. Consider first the bracketed VP below:

(1) The defendants denied the charge: they claim that they did [vp not destroy the garden deliberately]

In this sentence the AdvP *deliberately* modifies the sequence *destroy the garden*, and is positioned after the Head *destroy* and its Complement *the garden*. This AdvP functions as Adjunct. How can we now add the Adjunct? One way of doing this is simply to have a third branch coming from V′ for the AdvP, as in (2):

(2)

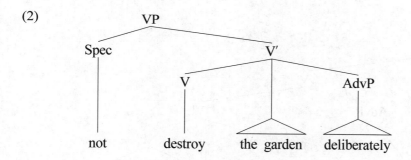

However, this representation cannot account for the fact that *deliberately* modifies *destroy* and *the garden* taken together: 'what did the defendants not do deliberately?' Answer: 'destroy the garden'.

Another way of positioning Adjuncts in VPs is to adjoin them to V′. This is done as follows:

(3)

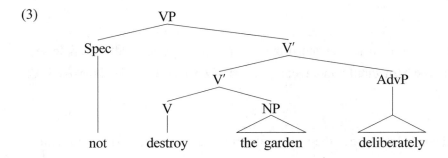

What we have done here is repeat the V'-node, and add the AdvP as its daughter. This process is called adjunction.

We can have adjunction to the right, as in (3), shown schematically in the definition above, but also adjunction to the left, as in (4) below, where *deliberately* is left-adjoined to the lower V':

(4)

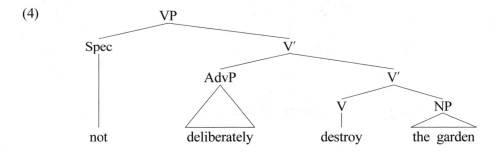

In this case the Adjunct is positioned between the Specifier and the Head. Notice that in both (3) and (4) the Complement *the garden* is **closer** to the Head *destroy* than the Adjunct *deliberately:* the Complement is a sister of V, whereas the Adjunct is a sister of the V' that immediately dominates V. This situation is exactly what we want: *deliberately* is not an argument of *destroy* and hence more peripheral to it than *the garden*, which is an argument of the verb.

Up to now we have used the term Adjunct in a somewhat restricted sense to refer to the grammatical function of a constituent that specifies the 'how', 'when', 'where' or 'why' of the situation expressed by a sentence. Under this definition the AdvP *deliberately* in (1) clearly qualifies as an Adjunct. We will now widen the notion of Adjunct, in such a way that not only VPs can contain them, but other phrase types as well. Consider the strings below:

(5) [NP an analysis of the sentence *with tree diagrams*]

(6) [AP so fond of coffee *after dinner*]

(7) [PP quite in agreement *about this*]

(8) [AdvP much faster than me *by far*]

The italicised strings in the bracketed phrases above, like *deliberately* in (3) and (4), have a modifying function, and we will therefore analyse them as Adjuncts. Like Adjuncts in VPs, they are adjoined to a bar-level category in tree structures, as follows:

(9)

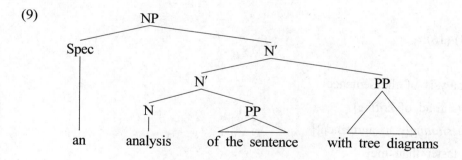

(10)

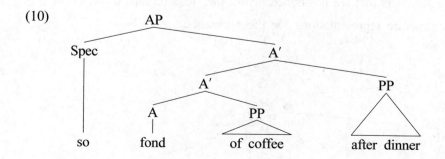

(11)

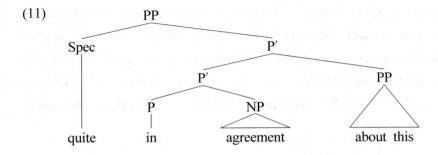

(12)

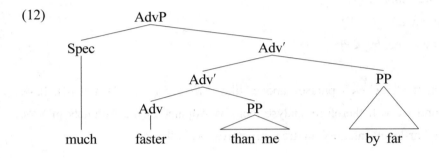

Consider next (13)-(16):

(13) [NP a *silly* analysis of the sentence]

(14) [AP so *terribly* fond of coffee]

(15) [PP quite *unhesitatingly* in agreement]

(16) [AdvP *clearly* faster than me]

In these cases we have Adjuncts that are positioned *before* the Head (compare the VP in (4)). (17)-(20) are the tree structure representations for these phrases:

(17)

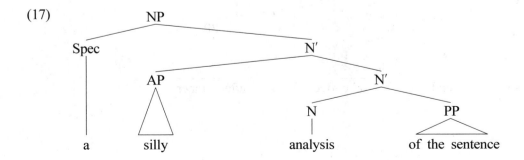

(18)

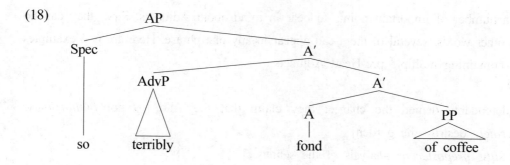

(19)

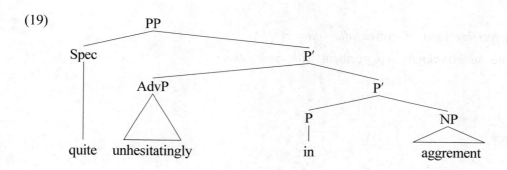

(20)

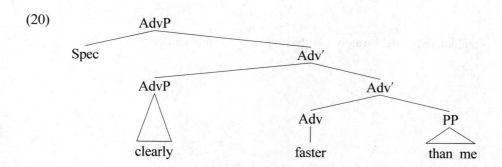

In all of these cases, just as in (4), the Adjuncts are left-adjoined to a bar-level category. Notice that Adjuncts are often adverb phrases, but can be of any category.

We can now make a generalisation and say that Adjuncts are always sisters of bar-level categories in phrases. They are adjoined either to the right or to the left of single-bar categories, and have a modifying function. **Complements**, as we have seen, **are always sisters of Heads**.

There are a number of important points to bear in mind about Adjuncts. First, they can be **stacked.** In other words, several of them can appear in any one phrase. Here are two examples of phrases containing multiple pre-Head Adjuncts:

(21) The defendants denied the charge: they claim that they did [vp not *unthinkingly, deliberately* destroy the garden]

(22) [np a *silly, preposterous* analysis of the sentence]

In (23) and (24) we have phrases that contain both a pre-Head and a post-Head Adjunct:

(23) [ap so *terribly* fond of coffee *after dinner*]

(24) [pp quite *unhesitatingly* in agreement *with each other*]

(25)

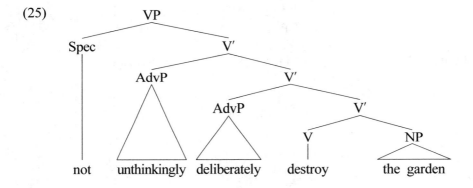

(26)

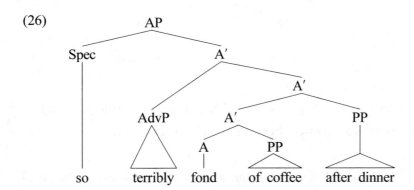

**EXERCISE** ..........................................................................................................

Draw the trees for (22) and (24). You may use triangles for the PPs.

Your answers should look like this:

(27)

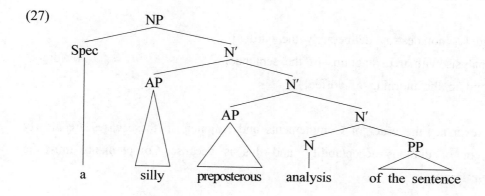

(28)

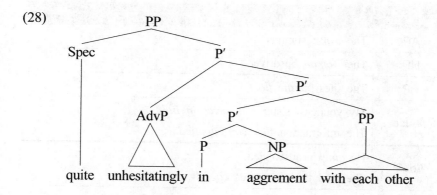

The property of being stackable differentiates Adjuncts on the one hand from Complements and Specifiers on the other: while phrases can in principle contain an unlimited number of Adjuncts (though they can become stylistically clumsy), lexical Heads, for example, verbs are restricted in the number of Complements they can take (rarely more than three), while Specifiers are generally not recursive (cf. *The my dog).

A second point to observe about Adjuncts, already mentioned in connection with verb phrases, is that the bond between them and their associated Heads is **less close** than the bond between Heads and their Complements. This fact is reflected in tree diagrams: as we have seen, Complements are sisters of Heads, whereas Adjuncts are sisters of a single-bar level above a Head. We can demonstrate the closer bond between Heads and their Complements by reversing the order of Complements and post-Head Adjuncts, as has been done below:

(29) *...they did [VP not destroy deliberately the garden]
(30) *[NP an analysis with tree diagrams of the sentence]
(31) *[AP so fond in the morning of coffee]

The results of reversing the order of Complements and Adjuncts in these cases are clearly ungrammatical, or of dubious acceptability, and this is because **Complements must be adjacent to their Heads**.

**Table 3.** Typical Adjuncts for the Major Phrase Types NP, VP, AP and PP

| phrase | Head | Adjunct | example(s) |
|--------|------|---------|------------|
| NP | N | AP | The *warm* summer |
| | | NP | The *woman* busdriver |
| | | PP | The tiles *on the floor* |
| | | clause | My youngest sister, *who lives in Italy*<br>The information *that you supplied* |
| VP | V | AdvP | He *quickly* absconded.<br>She read the prospectus *eagerly*. |
| | | PP | We came here *in the summer*. |
| | | clause | She phoned *because she likes you*. |
| AP | A | AdvP | We were *unconsolably* disappointed. |
| | | PP | He was abusive *to the extreme*. |
| PP | P | AdvP | I was *totally* over the moon. |
| | | PP | They designed the museum in tandem *with an Italian architect*. |

## 3.3. Cross-categorial Generalisations

Let us now return to our schematic tree in (13), modified as in (32) below:

(32)

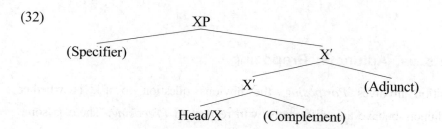

This tree embodies what has been called a cross-categorial generalisation which is part of X′-syntax (read: X-bar syntax), a theory of syntax which stipulates that all the major phrase types are structured in the same way, namely as in (32).

Notice that the labels Specifier, Adjunct, Head and Complement are functional notions, and that of these four **only the Head is always obligatory**. The existence of the single-bar level in phrases was posited largely on intuitive grounds, but we will obviously need to justify its existence on syntactic grounds as well. For now, we will simply assume that this intermediate category exists.

## 3.4. Complements vs. Adjuncts: Extraposition (Postposing)

It appears that PP Adjuncts can be extraposed from their Heads (i.e. separated from their Heads and moved to the end of their Clause) more freely than PP Complements: cf.

(1) a. a student came to see me yesterday [*with long hair*]
   b. *a student came to see me yesterday [*of Physics*]

It would seem that in some sense PP Complements are more 'inseparable' from their Heads than PP Adjuncts. Thus, we might posit that the more closely related a PP is to its Head, the less freely it can be extraposed. Complements are more resistant to being extraposed.

NOTE

(2) a. [A review <u>of my latest book</u>] has just appeared

   b. [A review _____ ] has just appeared <u>of my latest book</u>

## 3.5. Complements vs. Adjuncts: Preposing

Given that Extraposition involves *Postposing,* the obvious question to ask is whether Complements and Adjuncts behave any differently with respect to *Preposing.* There is some evidence that this is indeed the case. It would seem that an NP which is the Object of a Preposition heading a *Complement* PP can be preposed more freely than an NP which is the Object of a Preposition heading an *Adjunct* PP: cf. the contrast below:

(1) a. [*What branch of Physics*] are you a student of?

   b. *[*What kind of hair*] are you a student with?

Thus, in (1a), the preposed bracketed NP is the Object of the Preposition *of,* and *of* introduces a Complement phrase, so that (1a) involves preposing an NP which is part of a Complement PP. But by contrast, the bracketed preposed NP in (1b) is the Object of the Preposition *with,* and *with* introduces an Adjunct, so that the ungrammaticality of (1b) suggests that an NP which is part of an Adjunct PP cannot be preposed. Thus, there is an obvious contrast insofar as the Object of a Complement Preposition can be preposed, but not the Object of an Adjunct Preposition.

## 3.6. The Differences Between Complements and Adjuncts

We can illustrate the difference between these two types of postmodifier in terms of the contrast in (1) below:

(1) a. a student [*of Physics*] (= Complement)

   b. a student [*with long hair*] (= Adjunct)

## Rule 1 Semantic nature

In (1a), the PP seems to complete (or complement) the meaning of the noun. The bracketed PP [*of Physics*] specifies what the student is studying. In (1b), by contrast, the PP seems more optional and more loosely related to the NP. The bracketed PP [*a student with long hair*] doesn't tell us anything about what the student is studying; it merely serves to give us additional information about the student (i.e. that he happens to have long hair).

## Rule 2 Ordering of Adjuncts and Complements

Complements will always be 'closer' to their head Noun than Adjuncts. In other words, Complement phrase must precede the Adjunct phrase.

(2) a. the student [*of Physics*] [*with long hair*]
   b. *the student [*with long hair*] [*of Physics*]

## Rule 3 Stacking

Since the rule generating Adjuncts is recursive, it predicts that indefinitely many Adjunct PPs can be 'stacked' on top of each other. But because the rule introducing Complements is not recursive, it does not allow PP Complements to be stacked in this way.

(3) a. the student [*with long hair*] [*with short arms*]
   b. *the student [*of Physics*] [*of Chemistry*]

PP Adjuncts can be 'stacked' but PP Complements cannot.

## Rule 4 Ordinary Coordination

We can coordinate two PPs which are both Complements:

(4) a student [*of Physics*] and [*of Chemistry*]

And likewise we can coordinate two PPs which are both Adjuncts:

(5) a student [*with long hair*] and [*with short arms*]

But we cannot coordinate a Complement PP with an Adjunct PP:

(6) a. *a student [*of Physics*] and [*with long hair*]

    b. *a student [*with long hair*] and [*of Physics*]

Adjuncts and Complements are attached at different levels (Complements are sisters of N, and hence are attached at the N level; whereas Adjuncts are sisters of N-bar, and hence are attached at the N-bar level), and by positing that only constituents attached at the same level can be coordinated.

### Rule 5 Extraposition

It appears that PP Adjuncts can be extraposed from their Heads (i.e. separated from their Heads and moved to the end of their Clause) more freely than PP Complements:

(7) a. a student ___ came to see me yesterday [*with long hair*]

    b. *a student ___ came to see me yesterday [*of Physics*]

We might posit that the more closely related a PP is to its Head, the less freely it can be extraposed.

### Rule 6 Preposing

It would seem that an NP which is the Object of a Preposition heading a Complement PP can be preposed more freely than an NP which is the Object of a Preposition heading an Adjunct PP:

(8) a. [*What branch of Physics*] are you a student of?

    b. *[*What kind of hair*] are you a student with?

# Clauses & Movement

## 4.1. The I-node

In this chapter we will take a closer look at the internal structure of clauses and their tree structure representations. We analysed a simple sentence like (1) as in (2):

(1) My brother baked a cake.

(2)

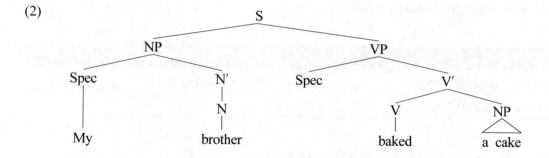

In this tree the S-node branches into NP and VP, and each of these phrases is structured in accordance with the principles of X′-syntax. Notice that, because (2) is not a negative sentence, the Spec-of-VP position remains empty.

How does the verb *bake* in (2) obtain its past tense *-ed* ending? In line with recent work in linguistics we will assume that sentences contain a node labelled '**I**' (short for 'inflection'), which is **immediately dominated by S**. This node is responsible for two things. One of them is making sure that **verbs acquire tense**, the other is taking care of **the agreement between Subjects and verbs** (e.g. the *-s* ending on *bakes* in *he bakes a cake*).

The I-node looks like this:

(3)

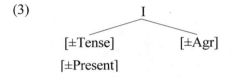

'I' contains a number of components, which we will refer to as *features*. One is the abstract feature [Tense], which can have either a positive or a negative value, i.e. it can be [+Tense] or [−Tense] (indicated by the symbol '±'). If it has a positive value, we have a further choice between [+present] or [−present], as follows: [+Tense, +present] or [+Tense, −present]. The other abstract feature in 'I' is [Agr], which is short for 'Agreement'. Again, this feature can have either a positive or a negative value: [+Agr] or [−Agr]. English makes use of only three combinations of features, namely:

| Finite clauses | Nonfinite clauses |
|---|---|
| [+Tense, +present] [+Agr] | [−Tense] [−Agr] |
| [+Tense, −present] [+Agr] | |

We can now revise the analysis of (2) as in (4) below:

(4)

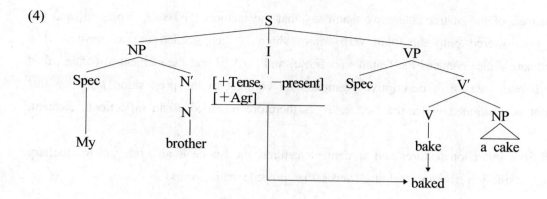

Let's assume that the tense and agreement features are lowered from the I-node onto the verb inside the VP (a process that is sometimes called *affix hopping*), and that they are spelled out as an inflectional ending on the verb.

What about nonfinite clauses? For them the I-node is marked [−Tense] and [−Agr]. In the following example the matrix clause is finite, but the bracketed subordinate clause, which functions as the Direct Object of the verb *want,* is nonfinite:

(5) She wanted [her brother to bake a cake].

(6)

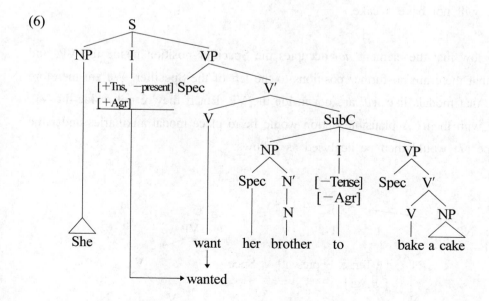

In the case of the matrix clause we again say that the features [+Tense, −present] and [+ Agr] are lowered onto the main verb *want,* which is then spelled out as *wanted.* If a subordinate clause contains the features [−Tense] and [−Agr] and the element *to* (often called an *infinitival marker* in descriptive grammars, in contrast to the preposition *to*), then this element is positioned under the I-node. *To* is therefore regarded as an inflectional element.

Apart from inflection features and agreement features, the I-node is also relevant to auxiliary verbs. Auxiliary verbs are 'helping' verbs that precede main verbs.

Consider the following sentence:

(7) My brother will bake a cake.

This sentence contains the modal auxiliary *will.* We might now ask where in a tree diagram this auxiliary is positioned. As *will* is a verb, it would be reasonable to assume that it is positioned inside the VP. It would then need to be placed in front of the main verb, i.e. before *bake.* It would also need to be placed in front of the negative element *not* when it is present, as the sentence below shows:

(8) My brother will not bake a cake.

However, we know that the element *not* occupies the Specifier position inside the VP, and we also know that there are no further positions to the left of the Specifier. We are therefore led to conclude that modals like *will* are not inside the VP. But if they're not inside the VP, what do we do with them? A plausible option would be to place modal auxiliaries under the I-node. Sentence (7) would then be analysed as follows:

(9)

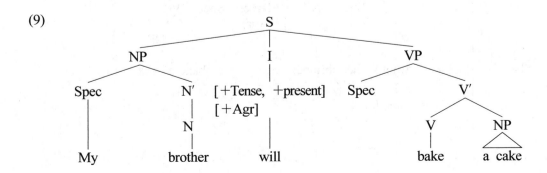

What motivation do we have for this analysis? Well, one reason is that modals are always tensed. This fact can be accounted for if we place them under 'I', the node that contains the tense feature. Another reason for placing the modals under 'I' is that this analysis is compatible with the behaviour of so-called *sentence adverbs*. Sentence adverbs, as their name implies, modify complete sentences. Examples are *however, frankly, perhaps, probably,* etc. These adverbs can occur in a variety of positions in sentences, as (10) below makes clear:

(10) a. *Perhaps* my brother will not bake a cake.
b. My brother *perhaps* will not bake a cake.
c. My brother will *perhaps* not bake a cake.
d. My brother will not bake a cake *perhaps*.

In a tree diagram *perhaps* can appear in the positions indicated by the symbol ▼:

(11)

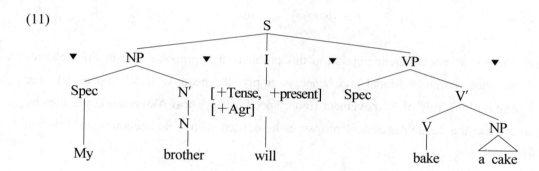

Now, given the fact that *perhaps* is a sentence adverb, i.e. immediately dominated by S in a tree diagram, and given also the fact that it can occur between a modal verb and the Specifier of a VP, a reasonable assumption would be to place the modal under I.

Summarising this section: we've seen that, apart from an NP and a VP, clauses also contain an I-node which accommodates tense and agreement features. Finite clauses contain the combination [+Tense, ±present] [+Agr], while nonfinite clauses contain [−Tense] [−Agr]. If a clause contains a modal verb or the infinitival marker *to,* these elements are positioned under 'I'. Notice that the modals and *to* cannot co-occur (e.g. *He will to sleep*), and this can be seen as further evidence that they fill the same slot in a tree diagram.

## 4.2. Affix Movement vs. V Movement

How can Tense/Agreement inflections associated with I end up on a Verb which originates as the head V of VP? Two rather different answers to this problem are suggested in the relevant literature. Consider the following sentence:

(1) John annoys me

First, the result of **affix movement** is that the V *annoy* acquires the relevant Tense/ Agreement features normally associated with I, and the resultant inflected verb-form *annoys* remains as the head V of VP.

(2) a. John     [$_I$ e]     [$_{VP}$     [$_V$ annoy]     me]

                └─AFFIX MOVEMENT ──┐
                                        ▼

     b. John            [$_{VP}$     [$_V$ *annoys*]     me]

However, there is a very different solution to this problem. It is proposed that in finite clauses where I does not contain a Modal and hence is empty, the head V of VP moves into the empty I position by a rule of **V movement** (more specifically, **V-to-I Movement**), and thereby comes to acquire the Tense/Agreement properties associated with I, so becoming an inflected verb-form.

(3) a. John     [$_I$ e]     [$_{VP}$     [$_V$ annoy]     me]

                   ┌─ V MOVEMENT ──┘
              ▼

     b. John    [$_I$ *annoys*]     [$_{VP}$         me]

The essential difference between the two analyses (2) and (3) is that under the affix movement analysis (2) the resultant inflected Verb *annoys* remains within VP, whereas under the V movement analysis (3) the inflected V *annoys* ends up as a constituent of I.

But which analysis is the right one? Well, as in any serious field of research, the consequences of making different assumptions about a particular phenomenon are often so complex and far-reaching that the full implications of the decision to adopt one analysis rather than another are not always immediately apparent.

### 4.2.1. V Movement analysis

It seems that there may be some evidence in support of such a rule in English, based on the behaviour of finite forms of the Verbs *have* and *be*. What the V movement analysis entails is that in a finite Clause with an empty I, the leftmost occurrence of *have* or *be* moves out of VP into the empty I constituent, thereby acquiring all the relevant Tense/Agreement inflections associated with I. Under this analysis, *have* and *be* would originate in VP in sentences such as the following:

(4) a. He has no money

   b. He has finished

   c. He is a fool

   d. He is working

   e. He was arrested

(5)

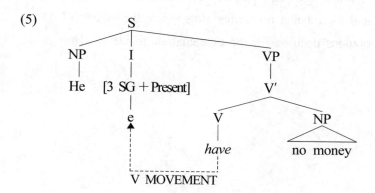

Thus, *have* would originate as the head V of VP, and would then be moved by the rule of V movement into the empty I, where it would acquire the relevant Tense/Agreement features, and so surface as the third person singular present tense form *has*.

I. Negation

   (6) a. He [I may] *not* [VP have finished]

     b. He [I may] *not* [VP be working]

We see that the negative particle *not* is positioned after the Modal *may* in I but before the Aspectual Auxiliaries *have* and *be* in VP. But in sentences such as (7) below:

(7) a. He <u>has</u> *not* finished

b. He <u>is</u> *not* working

we posit that *have* and *be* originate within VP, but that the leftmost occurrence of *have/be* gets moved out of VP into I by V movement, if I is finite and empty. The operation of the rule in a case such as (7a) above can be schematised as in (8) below:

(8) a. He       [I e]      not       [VP have finished]

                  ⌐——— V MOVEMENT ———⌐

b. He       [I has]    not       [VP — finished]

Consider the following examples:

(9) He has not broken the mirror.

Notice that the given sentence contains *not*. This element is positioned in the Specifier of the higher VP. This being so, and there being no further slots inside the higher VP to the left of the Specifier, the most obvious position for the aspectuals is inside 'I'. Here is the tree for (9):

(10)

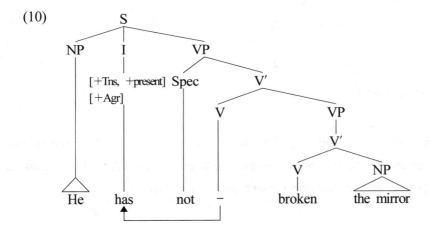

## II. Adverb distribution

English has a class of S-Adverbials (including *certainly, probably, definitely,* etc.), so called because they are restricted to occurring as immediate constituents of S. The assumption that *probably* is an S-Adverb accounts for contrasts such as the following:

(11) a. George will *probably* have been working

    b. *George will have *probably* been working

    c. *George will have been *probably* working

For, if we posit that *George will have been working* has the structure (12) below:

(12)

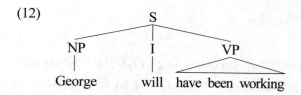

then it is apparent that the only internal positions which an S-Adverbial like *probably* can occupy are between NP and I, or between I and VP—but not any position internally within VP.

However, the distributional facts are rather different in sentences such as the following:

(13) a. George <u>has</u> *probably* been working

    b. *George <u>has been</u> *probably* working

Why should it be that the S-Adverb *probably* can be positioned after the Aspectual Auxiliary *have* in (13), but not in (11)?

The V movement analysis provides us with a very straightforward answer. We might suppose that although *have* originates as an Aspectual Auxiliary within VP in both (11) and (13), what happens in the case of (13) is that because the I constituent is finite and empty, the leftmost occurrence of *have/be* within VP moves into the empty I (so acquiring the relevant Tense/Agreement features, and surfacing in the form *has*) in the manner indicated schematically in (14) below:

(14) a. George        [ᵢ e]      not    [ᵥₚ have been working]

                            V MOVEMENT

    b. George        [ᵢ has]   not    [ᵥₚ — been working]

Thus, after the application of V movement, the resultant superficial structure will be as in (15) below:

(15)

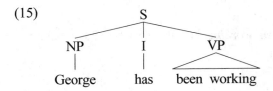

Why isn't V movement of *have* also possible in structures like (12)? The obvious answer is that V movement is only possible into an empty finite I, and so is blocked in (12) because I is already filled by the Modal *will*.

Further evidence that finite aspectual auxiliaries are in 'I' comes from the following pair of sentences, which contain the sentence adverb *probably*.

(16) He has probably broken the mirror.
(17) I am probably dreaming.

The reasoning here is as follows: because the sentence adverb *probably* is immediately dominated by S, and the aspectual auxiliaries *has* and *am* occur to the left of this adverb, we cannot assume that the latter are inside VPs. As they are in their finite forms (cf. *\*He have probably broken the window/\*I be probably dreaming*), it is reasonable to assume that they are in 'I'. But if they are, we will need to say that they moved from inside the verb phrase, because we have been assuming that aspectuals 'start out' in a VP. We can use the sentences in (18) and (19), which contain both sentence adverbs and negative elements, to make the same point.

(18) He has probably not broken the mirror.
(19) I am probably not dreaming.

(20)

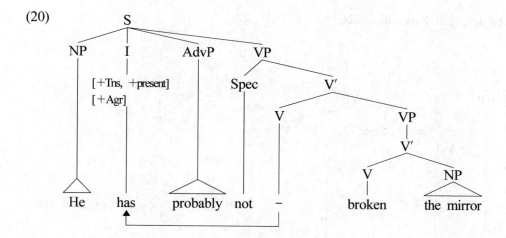

(21)

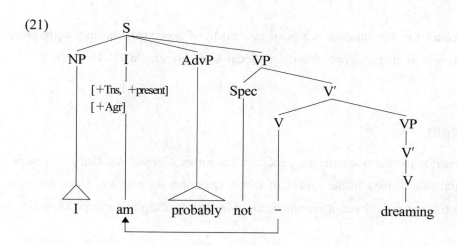

Why do we want to insist that aspectual auxiliaries originate inside a VP, and that they are different from modal auxiliaries, which I have claimed to be positioned in 'I', without being moved from inside a VP?

We can have combinations of modal auxiliaries with aspectual auxiliaries, as in (22):

(22) He will not have broken the mirror.

Here, as before, the modal *will* is positioned in 'I', where it originates, whereas the aspectual auxiliary turns up to the right of the negative element *not*. (Cf. also *He will probably not have broken the mirror*, where there is also a sentence adverb present.) In (22) the aspectual must therefore be inside the VP, to the right of the Specifier *not*.

The tree for (22) looks like this:

(23)

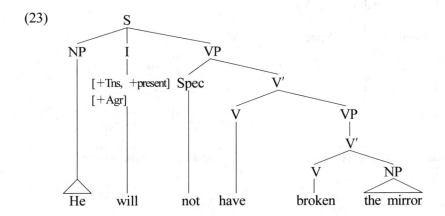

In order to account for this situation we posit movement of aspectual auxiliary verbs from VP to 'I', but *only* if there is not already a modal verb present in 'I' to block it.

## 4.3. I Movement

This rule is responsible for the phenomenon generally known as 'Subject-Auxiliary Inversion', which has a central role to play in the syntax of Direct Questions in English. Thus, the most obvious syntactic difference between a statement like (1a) below and the corresponding direct question (1b):

(1) a. [s He *will* tell the truth]
    b. *Will* [s he tell the truth]?

is that the Modal *will* is positioned within S after the Subject NP *he* in the declarative (1a), but is positioned outside S before the Subject NP *he* in the interrogative counterpart (1b). What we shall argue here is that in such cases, the italicised Modal originates in the I position within S, and is subsequently moved into an empty C position outside S by a rule which we might appropriately call **I movement** (or more precisely, **I-to-C Movement**). The operation of this rule in the case of (1) can be outlined schematically as in (2) below:

(2) a. [$_C$ e]    [$_S$ he   [$_I$ will]]    [$_{VP}$ tell the truth]]

     ⌐— I MOVEMENT —⌐
     ↓

 b. [$_C$ Will]  [$_S$ he   [$_I$ —]    [$_{VP}$ tell the truth]]?

In the terminology introduced at the end of the previous section, we might say that (2a) is the *Deep Structure* of the sentence, and (2b) is the corresponding *Surface Structure*. Obviously, the I movement analysis is based on two key assumptions: (i) inverted Modals like *will* originate in I, and (ii) they end up in C. Let's consider separately the motivation for each of these two assumptions.

### 4.3.1. I Movement analysis

I. Gap argument

 (3) a. *Will [$_S$ he [$_I$ can] tell the truth]?
  b. *Will [$_S$ he [$_I$ to] tell the truth]?

The I position was originally filled by the Modal *will*. When the rule of I movement applies to move *will* into C, a 'gap' is left behind in the original I position. What's wrong with (3) is that the I position was originally filled by the Modal *will;* and after *will* is moved into C by the rule of I movement, the original I position has subsequently been refilled by *can/to,* in violation of our 'no refilling' condition. (i.e. once a given position has been filled, it cannot be refilled.)

II. Subcategorisation

Modal Auxiliaries like *can* subcategorise an infinitival VP Complement (i.e. take a VP Complement headed by a Verb in the 'base' or 'infinitive' form).

(4) John can *go/*going/*gone/*goes/*went* to the party

Interestingly, precisely the same set of restrictions hold for 'inverted' Modals in direct questions; cf.

(5) Can [s John *go/\*going/\*gone/\*goes/\*went* to the party]?

(6)

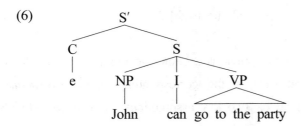

Thus, subcategorisation facts provide strong support for our assumption that inverted Modals which are positioned in C at Surface Structure originate in I.

## III. *Have* Contraction

Vocalic contraction of *have* down to /v/ is subject to two conditions. The first is that it takes place only after a Pronoun ending in a vowel or diphthong; and the second is that it is blocked by the presence of a 'gap' between the Pronoun and *have*. In the light of these two conditions, consider why vocalic contraction should be blocked in examples such as the following:

(7) a. Should *I have/\*I've* called the Police?

    b. Will we *have/\*we've* finished by 4 o'clock?

    c. Would *you have/\*you've* wanted to come with me?

    d. Could *they have/\*they've* done something to help?

Under I movement analysis, the initial Modals *should/will/would/could* originate at Deep Structure between the Pronoun *I/we/you/they* and the Auxiliary *have,* in the typical I position between NP and VP, as in the corresponding declaratives:

(8) a. I *should* have called the Police

    b. We *will* have finished by 4 o'clock

    c. You *would* have wanted to come with me

    d. They *could* have done something to help

They subsequently undergo 'inversion' (= I movement) in direct questions, and are moved out of their position between the Pronouns *I/we/you/they* and *have,* into pre-subject position in front of the Pronoun. If we symbolise this gap by Ø, we could say that after 'inversion' the sentences in (7) would have the respective structures:

(9) a. Should I Ø have called the Police?
 b. Will we Ø have finished by 4 o'clock?
 c. Would you Ø have wanted to come with me?
 d. Could they Ø have done something to help?

The presence of the 'gap' Ø here between the Pronoun and *have* would then suffice to block *have* contraction.

Having argued that 'inverted' Modals in direct questions originate within I, let's now turn to consider where exactly they get moved to when they are preposed (or, in more technical terms, what is the *landing-site* for inverted Modals). In (1) above, we assumed that Modals in I are moved into an empty C, in the manner indicated schematically in (10) below:

(10)

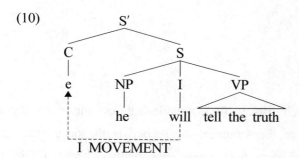

**EXERCISE** ......................................................................................................................

**Draw the tree for the following sentence.**

(11) Is Neil playing squash?

(12)

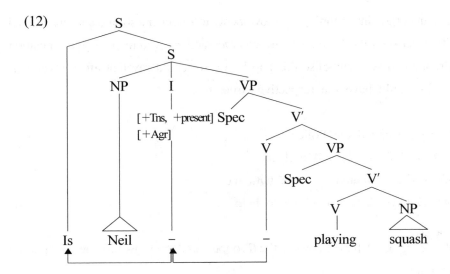

Remember that the aspectual auxiliary *be* moves twice: once to acquire Tense and Agreement, and a second time under Subject-Auxiliary Inversion!

## 4.4. Wh-Movement

Consider the following sentence:

(1) What will you buy?

This is a simple interrogative structure which displays three notable features: one is that there is a wh-element placed at the beginning of the sentence, the second is the occurrence of Subject-Auxiliary Inversion, and third, the verb *buy* appears apparently without a Direct Object.

Notice, however, that in (1) *buy* is not followed by an NP, but the sentence is nevertheless grammatical. Well, one way of doing so is to say that despite appearances, there is a Direct Object in (1), but that it is not in its normal place. Which element in (1) would qualify for DO status? Clearly, *what* is the most likely candidate. If this is correct, we need to account for the fact that it is not in its normal position.

We will assume that in (1) the *wh*-element is moved from the DO position following the main verb to the beginning of the sentence. This type of movement is called *Wh-Movement*, for obvious reasons. We can easily show that *what* in (1) is associated with the DO position by constructing a sentence in which it occurs in that location, for example (2):

(2) You will buy WHAT?

The important point about (2) is that the *wh*-element occurs after the verb. This shows that it functions as DO. It is now natural to say that in relating (2) to (1) we move the *wh*-element to the beginning of the sentence. In the process the Subject is inverted with the auxiliary.

The tree for (1) then looks like this:

(3)

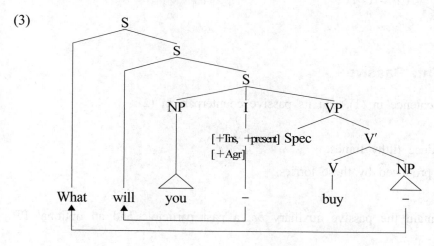

Consider the following sentence:

(4) What will he do?

(5)

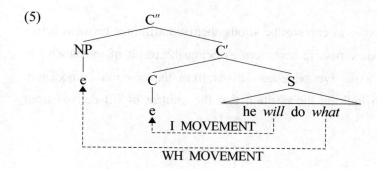

The Modal *will* in I will be moved into the empty C position by I movement, and the wh-NP *what* will be moved into the empty NP C-specifier position by WH movement. The resulting Surface Structure will thus be (6) below:

(6)

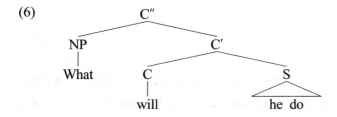

**NOTE** C-double-bar (= CP = Complementiser Phrase), corresponding to the traditional S-bar constituent (so that S' = CP = C")

## 4.5. NP-Movement: Passive

Consider the active sentence in (1), and its passive counterpart in (2):

(1) These lorries produce filthy fumes.
(2) Filthy fumes are produced by these lorries.

Passive sentences contain the passive auxiliary *be*, a past participle and an optional PP introduced by *by*.

If we consider (1) and (2) from the point of view of thematic roles, we observe that the NP *these lorries* carries an agentive role both in (1) and (2). The NP *filthy fumes* carries the role of Patient (or Theme if you prefer) in both sentences.

Linguists have suggested that in order to capture the strong thematic affinities between active and passive sentences we might view passive sentences as being the result of movement, in such a way that the Subject of a passive sentence derives from the position immediately following the main verb. We can indicate the position that the Subject of (2) derives from with a dash symbol: '—'

(3) <u>Filthy fumes</u> are produced − by these lorries

Such an account would explain how a phrase with a Patient thematic role ends up in Subject position, while its canonical position is after the main verb. Movement of this type in passive sentences is an instantiation of *NP-Movement*.

We might wonder where the passive auxiliary *be* should be located in a tree diagram. You may have noticed that auxiliaries share a property with transitive and ditransitive verbs. Transitive verbs subcategorise for an NP or clause, and ditransitive verbs subcategorise for two NPs. In the same way **auxiliary verbs subcategorise for VPs**.

Returning now to our passive sentence in (3), we can conclude that its tree looks like this:

(4)

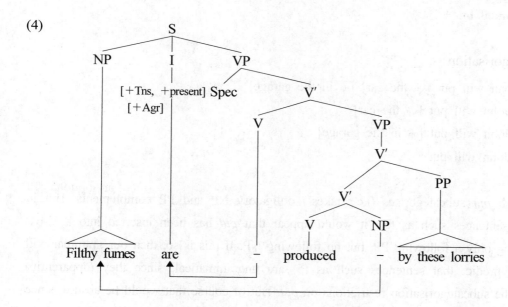

Notice that we have two movements here: the passive auxiliary *be* has moved to 'I' under Verb Movement, while the Direct Object has moved from a position following the main verb to the Subject position of the sentence under NP-Movement.

## 4.5.1. Evidence of NP movement in passive structures

Consider the following sentence:

(5) *The car* will be put — in the garage

Here, we shall argue that the italicised NP [*the car*] originates in the postverbal object NP position marked —, and is subsequently moved out of there into the italicised preverbal subject NP position, in the manner indicated schematically in (6) below:

(6) [s [NP  e] will be [v' put [NP the car] in the garage]]

       ┗━NP MOVEMENT ━┛

But what evidence is there that the preverbal NP italicised in (5) originates in the postverbal position marked by —?

I. Subcategorisation

(7) a. John will put [NP the car] [PP in the garage]

b. *John will put [NP the car]

c. *John will put [PP in the garage]

d. *John will put

The Verb *put* subcategorises (i.e. 'takes') obligatory NP and PP complements. But in passive sentences such as (5), it would appear that *put* has been inserted into a V-bar containing only a following PP, but no following NP. If this is so, then our grammar will wrongly predict that sentences such as (5) are ungrammatical, since they (apparently) violate the subcategorisation restrictions on *put*. But of course that would be absurd, since (5) is in fact perfectly well-formed. How can we account for this? One possible answer is to posit that the preverbal italicised Subject NP in passive sentences like (5) originates at Deep Structure in the postverbal Object NP position, as represented in (6) above.

## II. Gap argument

If there is indeed a rule of NP movement moving the Object of a passive Verb into Subject position, then we should expect that movement of the Object would leave behind a 'gap' in Object position which cannot be re-filled by another lexical NP.

(8) *[*The car*] will be put *the bike* in the garage

(8) shows us that the 'gap' left behind by the movement of the bracketed NP [*the car*] from Object into Subject position cannot be re-filled by another lexical NP such as [*the bike*]. Why should this be so? The answer is that if we assume the transformational analysis of passives proposed here, then [the car] in (8) will originate as a postverbal NP Complement of *put*, so that (8) will derive from the Deep Structure (9) below:

(9) — will be put [$_{NP}$ the car] [$_{NP}$ the bike] [$_{PP}$ in the garage]

But a Base Structure such as (9) will **fail to satisfy the subcategorisation frame for *put*,** since *put* in (9) has two NP Complements and a PP Complement, whereas we saw earlier in relation to (7) above that *put* subcategorises only a single NP and a PP Complement.

## III. Object Idiom Chunks

English has a class of Noun Phrases which are highly restricted in their distribution, in that (in their idiomatic use) they generally occur only in conjunction with some specific Verb: for example, each of the italicised expressions in (10) below generally occurs only immediately following the capitalised Verb in its idiomatic use:

(10) a. The government **keeps** *tabs* on his operations

　　 b. I want you to **pay** *heed* to what I say

　　 c. The Chief of Staff **pays** *lip service* to the President

　　 d. The Prime Minister **paid** *homage* to the dead

　　 e. You'll have to **grasp** *the nettle* and **bite** *the bullet*

　　 f. She **took** *note* of what I said

　　 g. Let's **take** *advantage* of the warm weather

For this reason, NPs like those italicised in (10) above are known as *idiom chunk NPs* (more particularly, as *Object idiom chunks*). They do not have the same syntactic freedom of distribution as other NPs—for example, they cannot occur in typical NP positions like those italicised in (11) below:

(11) a. *\*Tabs* won't affect me

    b. *Everyone needs *tabs*

    c. *I don't like talking about *tabs*

The relevant restrictions don't appear to be semantic in any obvious sense, since close synonyms of the items concerned are not subject to the same restrictions, as we can see by comparing *heed* with its close synonym *attention* (cf. *pay heed to = pay attention to*):

(12) a. You can't expect to have my *attention/*heed* all the time

    b. He's always trying to attract my *attention/*heed*

    c. He's a child who needs a lot of *attention/*heed*

    d. I try to give him all the *attention/*heed* he wants

It just happens to be an arbitrary syntactic fact about the distribution of the item *heed* that in contemporary English it is virtually never used in any position save immediately following the verb *pay* (and perhaps *take*).

In the light of the claim that Object idiom chunk NPs such as *advantage, tabs, heed, note* and *homage* have an extremely restricted distribution (i.e. are generally restricted to occurring immediately after specific verbs like *take, keep* and *pay*), consider how we are to account for the grammaticality of sentences like:

(13) a. *Little heed* was paid — to her proposal

    b. *Close tabs* were kept — on all Thatcherites

    c. *Little note* was taken — of what I said

    d. *Due homage* was paid — to the dead

    e. *Little advantage* was taken — of the situation

Idiom chunk NPs are restricted to occurring immediately after specific Verbs at *Deep Structure* (though of course they can subsequently be moved out of their underlying position by movement rules like NP movement).

## IV. Thematic Relations

It is interesting to note that *active Objects* (i.e. Objects of active sentences) play the same thematic role as the corresponding *passive Subjects*. For example, in the active sentence (14a) below the italicised Object NP fulfils the same thematic role (= THEME, or PATIENT) as its italicised Subject NP counterpart in the corresponding passive (14b):

(14) a. They rolled [*the ball*] down the hill

    b. [*The ball*] was rolled down the hill

Likewise, in the active sentence (15a) below, the italicised Primary Object NP *Mary* has the same θ-role (= GOAL) as its italicised Subject counterpart in the corresponding passive (15b):

(15) a. They will give [*Mary*] nothing

    b. [*Mary*] will be given nothing

Let's suppose that the *D-structure* of the passive (15b) *Mary will be given nothing* is along the lines indicated in (16) below:

(16) [$_{NP}$ e] will be [$_{V'}$ given *Mary* nothing]

If we further assume that the lexical entry for *give* specifies that the NP immediately following *give* in [V NP NP] structures is assigned the theta-role of GOAL, then it follows that the italicised NP *Mary* in (16) will be assigned the role of goal at *Deep Structure*; and we might assume that **theta-roles are 'preserved' under movement**, so that when NP movement applies to 'passivise' *Mary* (i.e. move *Mary* from Object to Subject NP position), ***Mary* retains the theta-role of GOAL.**

## 4.6. NP-Movement: Subject-to-Subject Raising

There is a further type of NP-Movement in English which we will discuss very briefly. Consider the sentences below:

(1) Danny seems to be working.
(2) Phil appears to be singing.

*Seem* and *appear* are linking verbs. In (1) and (2) they link the Subjects *Danny* and *Phil* to the strings *to be working* and *to be singing,* respectively.

If we now think about (1) and (2) from the point of view of meaning, observe that we can paraphrase them as follows:

(3) It seems that Danny is working.
(4) It appears that Phil is singing.

Notice the appearance of the dummy pronoun *it* in these sentences. This pronoun is never assigned a thematic role, and the very fact that it can appear as a Subject immediately before a linking verb suggests that **linking verbs do not assign thematic roles to their Subjects**. In fact, it would be hard to determine what kind of thematic role verbs like *seem* and *appear* would assign to their Subjects in (1) and (2). It is, however, less difficult to think of a thematic role that *(to be) working* and *(to be) singing* might assign. This would clearly be an Agent role. Linguists have suggested that sentences like (1) and (2) involve two clauses, and that *Danny* and *Phil* receive their thematic role from *(to be) working* and *(to be) singing* in a subordinate clause, before being moved to the matrix clause Subject position. We can now represent (1) and (2) as follows:

(5)  [$_{MC}$ Danny seems [$_{SubC}$ − to be working]]

(6)  [$_{MC}$ Phil appears [$_{SubC}$ − to be singing]]

This type of displacement, along with the movement discussed in the previous section, is an instance of **NP-Movement**. It is also sometimes referred to as *Subject-to-Subject Raising*. The reason for this is that the NP Subjects move from the Subject position of the subordinate clause to the Subject position of the matrix clause.

In a tree this movement can be represented as follows:

(7)

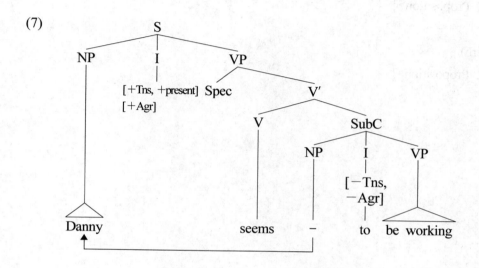

(8)

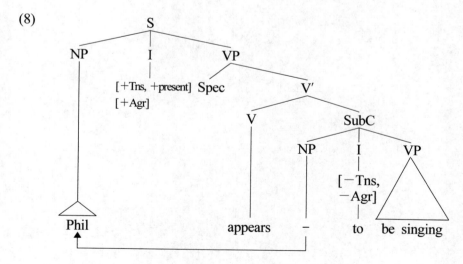

The upshot of all this is that **linking verbs are one-place predicates that take clausal arguments**. Thus, *seem* takes the clause *Danny to be working* as its argument, while *appear* takes *Phil to be singing* as its argument. The combined argument structure and thematic structure representations of *seem* and *appear* are as in (9) and (10):

(9)  *seem* (verb)

[1  <clause, Proposition>]

(10) *appear* (verb)

[1  <clause, Proposition>]

# Constituency

## KEY CONCEPT IN THIS CHAPTER

**Constituency Tests**

- **Movement Test**
  - Topicalisation
  - Heavy-NP-Shift
  - Extraposition of Subject clauses
  - Extraposition from NP
- **Substitution Test**
  - Proform Substitution
  - NP-Substitution and N′-Substitution
  - VP-Substitution and V′-Substitution/Deletion
- **Coordination Test**
  - Ordinary Coordination
  - Shared Constituent Coordination Test
- **Cleft and Pseudocleft Test**
- **Insertion Test**
- **Constituent Response Test**

**NOTE** The Coordination Test, the Cleft and Pseudocleft Test, the Insertion Test and the Constituent Response Test are not always as reliable as the Movement Test and Substitution Test. The order in which they are discussed roughly reflects their degree of reliability, the first test being the most reliable.

We very often have an **intuition** about which words make up units in particular sentences, but we really need a more reliable way of establishing how we can carve them up. **Constituents are strings of one or more words that syntactically and semantically behave as a unit.** We defined constituents formally in terms of the notion of dominance. Consider the tree diagram in (2) for the sentence in (1):

(1) My father admires my mother.

(2)

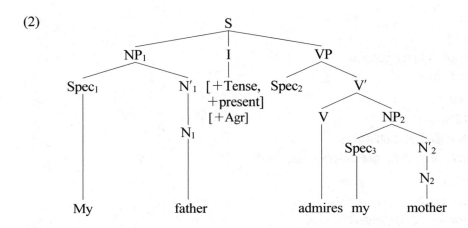

Y is a constituent of X if and only if X dominates Y.
Y is an immediate constituent of X if and only if X immediately dominates Y.

In the tree in (2) S dominates every single individual node, as well as the lexical items *my, father, admires, my* and *mother*. Thus, in (2) all the elements under S are constituents of S. Also, S immediately dominates NP$_1$, 'I' and VP, and so NP$_1$, 'I' and VP are immediate constituents of S. Furthermore, Spec$_1$ and N'$_1$ are immediate constituents of NP$_1$; Spec$_2$ and V' are immediate constituents of VP; V and NP$_2$ are immediate constituents of V', and so on.

## 5.1. The Movement Test

Linguists have argued that one way of finding out whether a particular sequence of words behaves like a unit is by trying to move it to another position in the sentence. The following principle can be established:

### Movement Test

If we can move a particular string of words in a sentence from one position to another, then it behaves as a constituent.

## 5.1.1. Topicalisation: movements to the left

Here's a fragment of an imaginary interchange between two people:

(1) Flora:      Do you like Belgian beer and Belgian wine?

    Ben:        [Belgian beer] I like —, but [Belgian wine] I hate —

Ben's response is somewhat out of the ordinary. He could simply have said (2):

(2) I like Belgian beer, but I hate Belgian wine.

Instead, he chose a different syntactic structure, which involves movement of the Direct Objects in (1) from the positions marked by '—' to a clause-initial position. This movement process is called *Topicalisation*. Ben answers the way he does because he wants the phrases *Belgian beer* and *Belgian wine* **to be more prominent** (more topic-like) than they would be if they occurred in their normal position following the verb, as in (2). In other words, his answer in (1) literally *brings to the fore* the topics *Belgian beer* and *Belgian wine*, as well as the **contrast** between what he thinks of these drinks.

Our principal concern here is that the strings *Belgian beer* and *Belgian wine* must be constituents because we can move them, as the contrast between (1) and (2) shows.

Now let us look at another example. One way of emphasising the sequence *your elder sister* in a sentence like:

(3) I can't stand [*your elder sister*]

is to prepose it—i.e. position it at the front of the rest of the sentence, as in:

(4) [*Your elder sister*], I can't stand (though your brother's OK)

But only a whole phrase (and not just part of a phrase) can be preposed in this way: thus, in a sentence such as (3) above *I can't stand your elder sister,* only the whole NP (Noun Phrase) [your elder sister] can be preposed for emphasis, not just part of the phrase: cf.

(5) a. Your elder sister, I can't stand

    b. *Your elder, I can't stand sister

    c. *Elder sister, I can't stand your

    d. *Sister, I can't stand your elder

    e. *Your, I can't stand elder sister

Topicalisation can involve complex phrases, as the following set of sentences shows:

(6) Nobody liked [NP the books about New York that she bought].

(7) [NP The books about New York that she bought] nobody liked —.

Notice that we cannot leave behind any of the component parts of the moved NP:

(8) *[NP The books about New York] nobody liked — that she bought.

Not only NPs can be topicalised, other phrases can too:

(9) Wendy:      Is Elly always so nervous?

   Al:         [Neurotic] I would say she is —, not nervous.

(10) Kate:      Does Greg really keep his pets in his attic?

    Len:       [In his attic] he keeps his plants —, not his pets.

(11) Nicky promised to write an essay, and [write an essay] he will —.

In (9) we've fronted an AP, in (10) a PP, and in (11) a VP. With regard to Topicalisation we can establish the following principle:

### Topicalisation

If we can topicalise a string of words whose Head is an X (where X stands for N, A, P or V), then that string is an XP-constituent.

## 5.1.2. VP-Preposing (VP-Topicalisation): movements to the left

Consider the sentence in (1):

(1) Ralph says that he will clean his room, and [clean his room] he will —.

A movement process has taken place here, such that the string *clean his room*, a verb with its Direct Object, has moved from a position at the end of the second clause to the beginning of that clause. Because the principal element of this string (i.e. its Head) is the verb *clean*, we conclude that we must be dealing with a verb phrase constituent. We refer to the movement process in (1) as *VP-Preposing* (a special type of Topicalisation). Here are some more examples:

(2) Sally says that she will return my book, and [return my book] she will —.

(3) Drew says that he will wash the dishes, and [wash the dishes] he will —.

We cannot leave the DOs behind:

(4) *Ralph says that he will clean his room, and [clean] he will — his room.
(5) *Sally says that she will return my book, and [return] she will — my book.
(6) *Drew says that he will wash the dishes, and [wash] he will — the dishes.

These data are a confirmation of the structure of verb phrases. Direct Objects are sisters of the main verb inside VP, as in the tree diagram below, which represents the VP of (1):

(7)

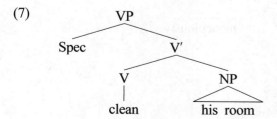

When VP-Preposing applies, the VP is moved to a clause-initial position. We will assume that **the entire VP is moved**, including the empty Spec-position. Notice that VP-Preposing can only apply if the sentence in question **contains an auxiliary verb**, such as *will* in the examples we have looked at, or did in (8):

(8) Sally said that she returned my book, and [return my book] she did —.

The following is impossible:

(9) *Sally said that she returned my book, and [returned my book] she —.

Another notable fact about (1)-(3) is that in each case *will* is left behind. This means that **modal auxiliary verbs are not part of the VP** of the sentence in which they occur. If they were, they would have been fronted along with the main verb and Direct Object. (10) shows that the auxiliary in (1) cannot also be preposed:

(10) *Ralph says that he will clean his room, and [will clean his room] he —.

Consider now the sentence below in which an adverb phrase functioning as an Adjunct has been added:

(11) Ralph says that he will clean his room meticulously.

(12)

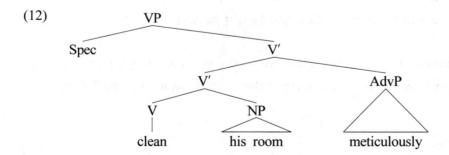

We now want to know whether we can show that the AdvP in (11) is indeed part of the VP or not. Let's apply VP-Preposing and see:

(13) Ralph says that he will clean his room meticulously, and [clean his room meticulously] he will −.

(14) *Ralph says that he will clean his room meticulously, and [clean his room] he will − meticulously.

The result of preposing the VP is that the AdvP must be moved along with the main verb and its Direct Object, and is therefore inside VP. Leaving the AdvP behind, as in (14), leads to an ungrammatical result.

### 5.1.3. Heavy-NP-Shift: movements to the right

Consider the following sentences:

(1) We brought − into the country *six boxes of excellent French wine*.
(2) She sold − at the market *the prints that she had made*.

Because Direct Objects as a rule occur immediately to the right of the verb that subcategorises for them, it is reasonable to assume that in (1) and (2) the italicised NPs have moved to the right from the position indicated by the dash. These movements are triggered by the relative 'heaviness' of the NPs in question caused by the PP *of excellent French wine* in (1) and by the relative clause *that she had made* in (2). For this reason this type of movement is called ***Heavy-NP-Shift*** (HNPS).

A restriction on HNPS is that we cannot move Indirect Objects or Objects of prepositions to the right:

(3) *I sent − a postcard *my cousin from London*.
(4) *I sent a postcard to − yesterday *my cousin from London*.

## 5.1.4. Extraposition of Subject clauses

Consider (1) and (2) below:

(1) That the film ended so soon was a shame.
(2) It was a shame that the film ended so soon.

In (1) the Subject of the sentence is the clause *that the film ended so soon*. We can move ('extrapose') it from a clause-initial to a clause-final position, as (2) shows. The pronoun *it* is inserted in the position vacated by the Subject clause. This movement establishes the constituent status of the Subject clause.

## 5.1.5. Extraposition from NP

Consider the following sentences:

(1) [Six women −] appeared with yellow hats.
(2) We employed [two people −] last week from European Union countries.
(3) [The dogs −] escaped that were chained to the house.

In (1) the PP *with yellow hats* has been extraposed out of the Subject NP, whereas in (2) the PP *from European Union countries* is moved out of the Direct Object NP. In (3) a relative clause has been displaced from the Subject NP. We call this kind of movement *extraposition from NP* (ENP). ENP seems to be more acceptable if the verb phrase is relatively light; for example, if it contains an intransitive verb or a raising verb (seem, appear, become, etc.). The following sentence, which contains a transitive verb, seems to be much less good:

(4) ?*[Three men −] noisily left the theatre who were drunk.

Just like HNPS, this type of movement can be used as a constituency test, as the example that follows will make clear. We might ask whether the string *with yellow hats on their heads* in (5) below is one PP constituent, or whether it should really be regarded as two separate PPs, namely *with yellow hats* and *on their heads*:

(5) Six women *with yellow hats on their heads* appeared.

If the former possibility is correct, we should be able to move the string *with yellow hats on their heads* by applying ENP; if the latter possibility is correct we should be able to move only the PP *with yellow hats*. The result of applying ENP to (5) is (6):

(6) [Six women −] appeared <u>*with yellow hats on their heads*</u>.

This sentence is fine, which means that *with yellow hats on their heads* is **one constituent**. By contrast, (7) is barred:

(7) *Six women − on their heads appeared <u>with yellow hats</u>.

This suggests that in (7) *with yellow hats* is not a constituent: we cannot move it without also moving *on their heads*. As you will have realised, the PP *on their heads* is an Adjunct of the Head *hats*. The tree for the italicised string in (6) looks like this:

(8)

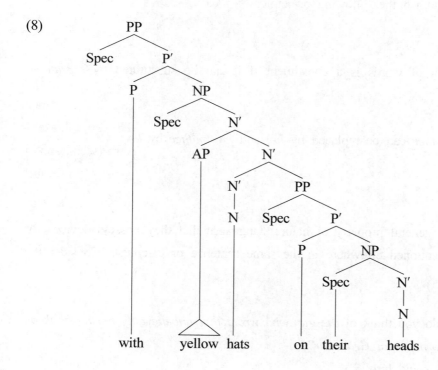

## 5.2. Substitution (Replacement)

A particular string of words must be a constituent if it can be replaced by something else: by a single word, by another string of words, or even by nothing at all. Like movement, substitution can affect full phrases, but we will see that it can affect clauses and bar-level constituents too.

### 5.2.1. Substitution of nominal projections: NP

Consider the following sentence:

(1) My father admires my mother.

We now want to be able to actually demonstrate that *my father* and *my mother* are constituents, other than by moving them. We can do so by means of the Substitution Test. We will say that a particular sequence of words is a constituent if it can be replaced by a so-called ***proform***, a word or word-sequence that 'stands in' for some other word or word-sequence. We establish the following principle:

> **Substitution Test**
> A particular string of words is a constituent if it can be substituted by a *suitable* ***proform***.

Notice now that *my father* can be replaced by *he*, and *my mother* by *her*:

(2) He admires her.

Pronominalisation is a general property of natural languages that they possess devices for referring to entities mentioned elsewhere in the same sentence or discourse. Consider the following discourse:

(3) Speaker A: What do you think of *the guy who wrote that unbelievably boring book on Transformational Grammar*?
    Speaker B: I can't stand **him**.

Using traditional terminology, we can say that [the guy who wrote that unbelievably boring book on Transformational Grammar] is the antecedent of the Pronoun *him*. However, the term Pronoun (although a traditional one) is peculiarly inappropriate here, simply because the antecedent of a Pronoun like *him* is not in fact a Noun, but rather a whole Noun Phrase: that is, *him* refers to the whole Noun Phrase [the guy who wrote that unbelievably boring book on Transformational Grammar], and not to any individual Noun within the Noun Phrase. Thus, words like *him*, it, etc. are more accurately described as **pro-NP (pro-Noun Phrase)** constituents, since they occur in NP positions in a sentence, and generally have NPs as their antecedents.

In more general terms, since Pronouns 'replace' or 'refer' back to other constituents, we might refer to them as *pro-constituents*, or ***proforms***. Not all pro-constituents are pro-NPs.

### 5.2.2. Other Phrase substitution

I. pro-PP: pro-Prepositional Phrase

(1) Speaker A: Have you ever been *to Paris*?
Speaker B: No, I have never been ***there***.

(2) Our neighbours will go on holiday on Sunday, and we will leave *then* too.

The word *there* is a **pro-PP**, in that it occupies the same sentence-position as the Prepositional Phrase *to Paris*.

II. pro-VP constituents

In much the same way, we might argue that in sentences such as the following, the italicised words function as pro-VP constituents, and hence refer back to the bracketed VP:

(3) a. John might [$_{VP}$ go home], and ***so*** might Bill
b. John might [$_{VP}$ resign his post], ***as*** might Bill

## III. pro-AP: pro-Adjectival Phrase

And in (4) below, we might argue that *so* functions as a pro-AP (pro-Adjectival Phrase) constituent:

(4) Many people consider John [AP extremely rude], but I've never found him *so*.

(5) They say that Wayne is <u>very unhappy</u> and *so* he is.

It is interesting to note that proforms generally **replace phrase-level constituents**, not word-level constituents.

### 5.2.3. Substitution of nominal projections: N′ (One-Substitution)

So far we have seen that proforms in the form of personal pronouns (*he, she, it,* etc.) can replace full NPs. English also possesses **a word that can replace less than a full NP**, and this is the **proform *one***. Consider (1):

(1) Mark is a dedicated teacher of language, but Paul is an indifferent one.

In this sentence, *one* replaces *teacher of language*. This proform cannot be a full NP, because it is preceded by the determinative *a* and the AP *indifferent*. We can show this more clearly in a tree diagram.

(2)

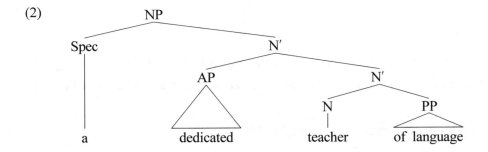

(3)

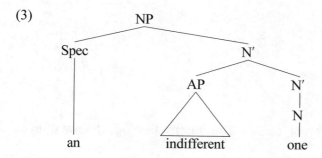

In these trees the APs *dedicated* and *indifferent* are analysed as pre-head Adjuncts, and the PP *of language* is regarded as a nominal Complement (cf. *he teaches language*). As *one* in (3) replaces *teacher of language* in (2) it must be replacing an **N′**. We thus reach the following conclusion:

### One-Substitution

The proform *one* replaces N′-constituents.

One-Substitution, apart from clearly establishing the existence of bar-level categories, also has a practical use in establishing constituency.

This operation replaces an N′ node with the word *one*. Look at the tree in (4):

(4)

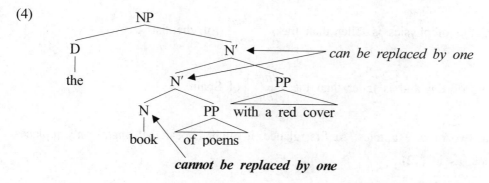

If you look closely at this tree you'll see that two possibilities for *one*-replacement exist. We can either target the highest N′, and get:

(5) the one

or we can target the lower N′ and get:

(6) the one with a red cover

But we cannot target the N head; it is not an N′. This means that *one* followed by a complement is ill-formed:

(7) *the one of poems with a red cover

Since complements are sisters to X and not X′, they cannot stand next to the word *one*. Adjuncts, by definition, can.

Consider some additional examples:

(8) This *student of chemistry* is more industrious than that $\begin{Bmatrix} student\ of\ chemistry \\ one \end{Bmatrix}$

(9) The [*student of physics* with long hair] is more intelligent than

the [$\begin{Bmatrix} student\ of\ physics \\ one \end{Bmatrix}$ with short hair].

In other examples, though, leaving something behind leads to unacceptability.

(10) *The *student* of physics is taller than the $\begin{Bmatrix} student \\ *one \end{Bmatrix}$ of chemistry.

(11) *The *king* of England is taller than the $\begin{Bmatrix} king \\ *one \end{Bmatrix}$ of Spain.

Let us look at two more examples. At first glance, it might appear that *one(s)* only replaces common nouns, as in (12).

(12) a. The big *dog* chased the small $\begin{Bmatrix} dog \\ one \end{Bmatrix}$

    b. This *town* is larger than that $\begin{Bmatrix} town \\ one \end{Bmatrix}$

**Summary**

We looked at proforms that can replace phrases or parts of phrases. When we looked at noun phrases we saw that **maximal projections** as well as **bar-projections** can be replaced by proforms: **pronouns replace full NPs** and *one* replaces N-bars.

NOTE A noun which has an overt Complement is simply an N, whereas a noun which lacks a complement has the status of N-bar (as well as N).

### 5.2.4. Substitution of verbal projections: VP

In this section we will take a closer look at the substitution of verbal projections. I will begin with a discussion of VP-Substitution, and then move on to V-bar Substitution.

Consider the following exchanges:

(1) Bill:　Will you please leave the room?
　　Dawn:　OK, I will ─ !

(2) Wayne: Can you play the piano?
　　Greg:　Yes, I can ─ !

(3) Henry:　You take a lot of risks.
　　Jake:　 I aim to ─ !

In (1) and (2) the strings *leave the room* and *play the piano* have been deleted after the modal verbs *will* and *can*, while in (3) *take a lot of risks* has been left out after the infinitival marker *to*. We can regard this deletion process as a special case of substitution, and say that *leave the room*, *play the piano* and *take a lot of risks* have been substituted by a ***null proform*** (i.e. by nothing), instead of by an overt proform (like, for example, *one* in the previous section). Now, we have seen that proforms can only replace constituents. It follows that, by virtue of being **a special form of substitution, deletion too applies only to constituents**. We will therefore refer to the deletion process in (1)-(3) as ***VP-Deletion***.

### 5.2.5. Substitution of verbal projections: V′ (*Do so*-Substitution)

The question now arises whether proforms can stand in for something *less* than a full VP. To answer this question, consider first the sentence below:

(1) Dawn cleaned the windows diligently.

In this sentence the NP *the windows* is a Direct Object, and the AdvP *diligently* is an Adjunct. The posited structure of its VP is as shown in (2):

(2)

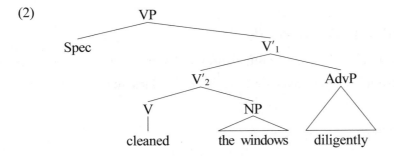

Consider now (3) and (4):

(3) Dawn cleaned the windows diligently, and Sean *did so* too.
(4) Dawn cleaned the windows diligently, but Sean *did so* lazily.

Here we have a new proform, namely *do so*, which replaces different lexical material in the two sentences above: in (3) it replaces *cleaned the windows diligently*, while in (4) it replaces *cleaned the windows*. We have seen that proforms can only replace constituents, so we conclude that these strings are constituents, thus confirming that V′₁ and V′₂ in (2) are **units**. This leads us to the following generalisation:

> **Do so-Substitution**
> *Do so* replaces V′-constituents.

Here are some more examples:

(5) Barry hired a big Jaguar, and Milly *did so* too.
(6) Lenny sent Will a postcard, and Gemma *did so* too.

What lexical material is replaced by *do so* here? In these cases what has been replaced are the strings *hired a big Jaguar* (V + DO) and *sent Will a postcard* (V + IO + DO). We have claimed that verbs and their Complements together form V′-constituents, so here again *do so* replaces V-bars. The structure of the VPs of the initial clauses in (5) and (6) is as in (7a) and (7b).

(7)

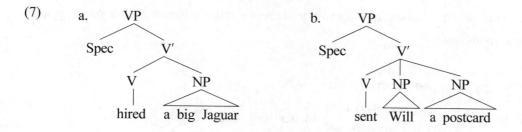

**Do so can never replace less than a V′.** The following sentence are ungrammatical:

(8) *Barry hired a big Jaguar, and Milly *did so* a Volkswagen.
(9) *Lenny sent Will a postcard, and Gemma *did so* a present.

In (8) the proform replaces only the main verb, but, as you can see in (7a), although this is a constituent, it is not a V′-constituent. In (9) *do so* replaces the verb and only one of its Complements, namely the Indirect Object. Again, this is not allowed, because these two nodes do not together form a V′-constituent.

Consider some additional examples:

(10) Martha *put some money in the bank on Friday*.

And Shirley $\begin{Bmatrix} \textit{put some money in the bank on Friday.} \\ \textit{did the same thing.} \end{Bmatrix}$

Here the whole verb phrase of the second sentence is identical with the whole verb phrase of the first sentence. As a result, it is possible to replace the second verb phrase in its entirety with *did the same thing*.

Now let us see what happens in a situation where the verb phrases are identical only up to the modifying time phrase, with the two time phrases being different.

(11) Martha *put some money in the bank* on Friday.

And Shirley $\left\{ \begin{array}{c} put\ some\ money\ in\ the\ bank \\ did\ the\ same\ thing \end{array} \right\}$ on Monday.

As (11) shows, it is completely acceptable to leave a modifier behind when we replace the second of two identical sequences with *did the same thing*. Now, what happens when we try to do this kind of replacement in a situation where we have different complements instead of different modifiers?

(12) Martha *put some money* in the bank.

And Shirley $\left\{ \begin{array}{c} put\ some\ money \\ *did\ the\ same\ thing \end{array} \right\}$ in her wall safe.

Here we have tried (unsuccessfully) to replace just the head verb and the noun-phrase complement, leaving behind the locative-phrase complement.

### 5.2.6. V′-Deletion

There exists another process that affects V-bars, called ***V′-Deletion***. Consider the following sentence:

(1) Dawn cleaned the windows diligently.

We saw above that *diligently* is inside the VP, and we analysed the VP of (1) as in (2):

(2)

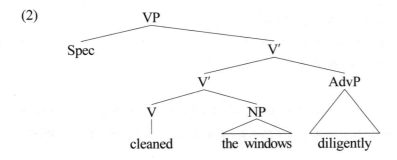

Consider now (3):

(3) Dawn **will** <u>clean the windows</u> *diligently*, but Sean **will** − *lazily*.

In (3) we deleted the string *clean the windows*. As we have seen, deletion is a special case of substitution, and we will say that *clean the windows* has been **substituted by a null proform**. Because proforms can only replace constituents, it follows that a sequence like *clean the windows* must be a constituent. In (2) we analysed this string as a V′-constituent, so that in (3) we are dealing with *V′-Deletion*.

## 5.3. The Coordination Test

Coordination involves the linking of two or more strings by a coordinating conjunction, typically *and, or* or *but*. Now we claim the following:

### Coordination Test
Only constituents can be coordinated.

### 5.3.1. Ordinary Coordination

Consider the following sentence:

(1) Frank washed his shirts yesterday.

For (1) we posited a structure like (2):

(2)

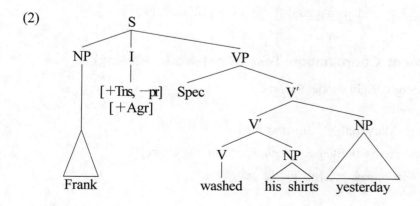

The constituent status of all of these strings is confirmed by the fact that they can be coordinated with other **similar units**:

(3) Frank *washed* and *ironed* his shirts yesterday. (coordinated main verbs)

(4) Frank *washed his shirts* and *polished his shoes* yesterday. (coordinated lower V-bars)

(5) Frank washed his shirts *yesterday* and *last week*. (coordinated Adjunct NPs)

(6) Frank *washed his shirts yesterday* and *polished his shoes last week*. (coordinated higher V-bars)

But can a constituent of one type (or category) be coordinated with a constituent of a different type? Consider the following paradigm:

(7) a. John wrote *to Mary* and *to Fred* (= PP and PP)

    b. John wrote *a letter* and *a postcard* (= NP and NP)

    c. *John wrote *a letter* and *to Fred* (= NP and PP)

    d. *John wrote *to Fred* and *a letter* (= PP and NP)

(8) Only **identical categories** can be conjoined.

We argued that only identical categories can be conjoined, idiomatically. However, apparent **exceptions** to this claim are not hard to find. For example, a variety of different phrase types can be coordinated when used ***predicatively***—e.g. as the complement of a Verb like *be:* cf.

(9) a. John is a banker and extremely rich (NP and AP)

    b. John is moody and under the weather (AP and PP)

    c. John is a superb athlete and in a class of his own (NP and PP)

### 5.3.2. Shared Constituent Coordination Test (Right Node Raising)

Only constituents can undergo Right Node Raising.

(1) a. John walked —, and Mary ran —, [*up the hill*]

    b. John denied —, but Fred admitted —, [*complicity in the crime*]

    c. John will —, and Mary may —, [*go to the party*]

(2) *John rang —, and Harry picked —, *up Mary's sister*

Why are sentences like (1) grammatical, but those like (2) ungrammatical?

(3) John walked <u>up the hill</u> and Mary ran <u>up the hill</u>
(4) John <u>rang up</u> Mary's sister and Harry <u>picked up</u> Mary's sister

In the first conjunct *up* 'goes with' the Verb *rang* to form the Phrasal Verb *rang up,* and in the second conjunct *up* 'goes with' the Verb *picked,* forming the Phrasal Verb *picked up.*

(5) ***Shared Constituent Coordination*** is only possible where the shared string is a possible constituent of each of the conjuncts.

NOTE **Right Node Raising**
(6) Frank washed —, and Dick ironed —, *the shirts.*

In (6) the main verbs *wash* and *iron* both take *the shirts* as Direct Object. Because Direct Objects are always on a right-hand branch inside V′ they are called 'right nodes'. In (6) *the shirts* has been raised from the positions indicated by the dashes, and one copy of this NP is placed at the end of the sentence, hence the term Right Node Raising. (Notice that unlike the kind of raising that was introduced, this type of raising is in a rightward direction.)

## 5.3.3. Coordination: Complementizer Phrases

We've observed that the TP rule and the CP rule stand out, since they don't fit X-bar theory. In X-bar theory, the head is always obligatory. This is not true of these two rules:

(1) a. CP → (C) TP
   b. TP → DP (T) VP

In fact, it is a fairly trivial matter to change these rules into X-bar-theoretic format. Let us deal with the CP rule first. If we take X-bar theory to extend to CPs, we can assimilate the rule in (1a) to get a tree like that in (2):

(2)

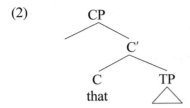

This CP structure has C as the head, a TP complement and an empty specifier position (this empty specifier position will become very important later for us when we do *wh*-movement).

We might ask how pervasive this rule is in our mental grammars. That is, do all clauses have CPs, or do only embedded clauses have CPs? On the surface, the answer to this question seems obvious: Only embedded clauses have CPs, since only embedded clauses appear to allow complementizers (3). However, there is evidence that all clauses, even root clauses like (3), require some kind of complementizer.

(3) a. John thinks that the asparagus is yummy.

    b. *That the asparagus is yummy. (cf. Asparagus is yummy.)

(4) Asparagus grows in California.

In particular, we'll claim that some sentences have null complementizers. Don't assume that I'm crazy. No matter how strange this proposal sounds, there is actually some good evidence that this is correct. The structure in (5) shows one of these null complementizers.

(5) [CP [C' Ø [TP Asparagus grows in California]]]

Of course, we haven't yet shown that non-question sentences have a root complementizer. For this, we need to add an extra step in the argument. You can only conjoin identical categories. If sentences showing subject-aux inversion use a null complementizer and if you can conjoin that question with a non-question (such as a statement), then that statement must also include a (null) complementizer and CP. It is indeed possible to conjoin a statement with a question:

(6) [You can lead a horse to water] but [will it drink]?

Since the second clause here shows subject-aux inversion, we know there is a $\emptyset_{[+Q]}$ question complementizer present. By extension, we know that the clause it is conjoined with must also have a complementizer – this time, a non-question $\emptyset_{[-Q]}$. A CP can only be conjoined with another CP.

(7)

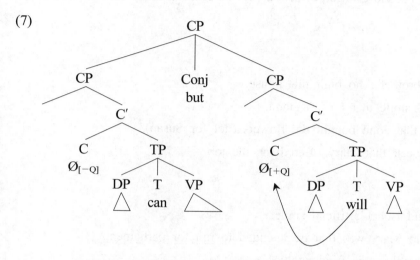

This is an argument for null complementizers attached to root clauses, even in simple statements. From this point forward, we will assume that there is a CP on top of every clause. For brevity's sake, I may occasionally leave this CP off my trees, but the underlying assumption is that it is always there.

## 5.4. The Cleft and Pseudocleft Test

Cleft and pseudocleft sentences are special constructions in English which enable language users to **highlight** a particular string of words in a sentence.

The skeletal structures of clefts and pseudoclefts are as follows:

- **Cleft sentence**

  *It* + form of *be*   focus   *who/that...*
  It +   was   Frank   who washed his shirts yesterday

- **Pseudocleft sentence**

| Wh-item | + | ⋯ | + | form of *be* | + | FOCUS |
|---------|---|---|---|--------------|---|-------|
| What | + | Frank did | + | was | + | WASH HIS SHIRTS YESTERDAY |

The two constructions illustrated in (1) and (2) are used to **focus**, or place **special emphasis** on, a constituent that conveys **new information**. In a cleft sentence (1) the focused constituent comes first, while in the Pseudo-Cleft construction (2), the focused constituent appears at the end of the sentence.

(1) **Cleft sentences:**

    a. It was <u>your big brother</u> who built this house.

    b. It is <u>her artificial smile</u> that I can't stand.

    c. It was <u>for Mary</u> that John bought the flowers (not for Susan).

    d. It was <u>just last week</u> that Mary offered me the job.

(2) **Pseudo-Clefts:**

    a. What I can't stand is <u>her artificial smile</u>.

    b. What John said to Mary was <u>that he intended to run for parliament</u>.

    c. What I like for breakfast is <u>fried noodles</u>.

In both constructions, the material that occurs in the focused position must be a **complete constituent**, and **only one constituent** may appear in this position at a time.

(3) **Cleft sentences:**

    a. *It was [a book] [to Mary] that John gave.

    b. *It was [last week] [your brother] that I arrested.

    c. *It was [your big] who built this house brother.

(4) **Pseudo-Clefts:**

    a. *What John gave was [a book] [to Mary].

    b. *?What Bill stole was [my diary] [from my desk drawer].

    c. *What I can't stand smile is [her artificial].

### Cleft and Pseudocleft Test

Only constituents can occur in the focus position of a cleft or pseudocleft sentence.

## 5.5. The Insertion Test

From a syntactic point of view, there are two different classes of Adverbials in English; one including Adverbs such as *certainly,* and the other including Adverbs such as *completely.* We find that these two classes of Adverbs can occupy rather different positions in the sentence, as (1) below illustrates:

(1) a. **Certainly / *completely**, the team can rely on my support

   b. *The **certainly / completely** team can rely on my support

   c. The team **certainly / *completely** can rely on my support

   d. The team can **certainly / completely** rely on my support

   e. The team can rely **completely / *certainly** on my support

   f. *The team can rely on **certainly / completely** my support

   g. *The team can rely on my **certainly / completely** support

   h. The team can rely on my support **completely / certainly**

(2) (i) Adverbs like *certainly* are **S-adverbs**, and hence can only be attached to an S-node

   (ii) Adverbs like *completely* are **VP-adverbs**, and so can only be attached to a VP-node

(3)

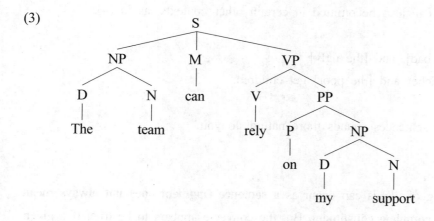

(4) Possible positions for S-adverbs like *certainly*

   [S ▼ The team ▼ can ▼ [VP rely on my support VP] ▼ S]

(5) Possible positions for VP-adverbs like *completely*

   [S The team can [VP ▼ rely ▼ [PP on my support] ▼ VP] S]

## 5.6. Sentence Fragment Test
## (The Constituent Response Test / Stand-alone Test)

When we are asked a question in the form of an open interrogative we often give a short response, rather than a lengthy one, as in the interchange below:

(1) A: What did you buy at the flea market?
    B: An old Swedish wineskin. / *An old Swedish.

(2) Dick: Where did you buy this bread?
    Frances: In the supermarket.

### Constituent Response Test
Only constituents can serve as responses to open interrogatives.

However, this test must be applied carefully, since there are various contexts in which an element which is normally obligatory can be omitted from a constituent. For example, in many languages adjectives can be used without any head noun to name classes of people, as in (3). Head nouns can also be omitted in certain other contexts, as in (4).

(3) a. [the good], [the bad], and [the ugly]
    b. [The rich] get richer and [the poor] get children.

(4) A: Which of these sentences sounds more natural to you?
    B: The second.

So the fact that a string of words can occur as **a sentence fragment does not always mean that the string forms a complete constituent.** But the converse appears to be true: if a given string cannot occur as a sentence fragment, that generally means that the string is not a constituent.

NOTE Consider for example the following dialogue:

(5) Speaker A: Who will clear up the mess?
Speaker B: The caretaker will.

We might suppose that Speaker B's reply in (5) is an S which has the simplified form (6) below:

(6)

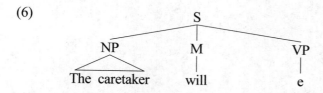

If this is so, then Speaker B's reply in (5) isn't in fact a *sentence fragment* at all, but rather a ***full sentence*** (S constituent) of the canonical form [NP M VP], in which the VP constituent was 'empty', as in (6) above. So, we have to be careful to differentiate between *sentence fragments* and ***elliptical sentences*** (= sentences containing empty categories).

# Verb Complements

## 6.1. Introduction

The notion of argumenthood is intimately related to constituency. Predicates are linguistic expressions that require arguments to satisfy them. Here are some examples:

(1) <u>Penny</u> **admires** <u>Judith</u>.

(2) <u>Imelda</u> **sent** <u>Darren</u> <u>presents</u>.

(3) <u>Pam</u> **thinks** <u>that she is clever</u>.

(4) <u>Being here</u> **annoys** <u>me</u>.

The elements in bold represent predicates, whereas the underlined units represent arguments. In English, predicates take minimally one, and usually no more than three, arguments. In most cases it is not difficult to decide how many arguments a particular predicate requires; however, some controversial cases do exist.

In deciding whether a particular element is an argument of some predicate we have recourse to a number of tests for argumenthood: meaning, dummy elements, idiom chunks and passivisation.

## 6.2. Believe Type: believe + NP + to-infinitive

### 6.2.1. Meaning

The number and type of arguments that a particular predicate needs is clearly determined to a large extent by the meaning of the predicate in question.

(5) Ed believes the story.

In (5) the meaning of *believe*, a two-place predicate, is such that it requires somebody who does the believing (a Subject) as well as a specification of what is being believed (a Direct Object).

(6) Ed believes that the story is false.

In (5) it takes two NP arguments, whereas in (6) it takes an NP Subject and a clausal DO. Notice that both the NP *the story* in (5) and the clause *that the story is false* in (6) are DOs which carry the thematic roles of Patient and Proposition, respectively. It is worth stressing again the fact that for some element to act as an argument of some predicate it must bear a thematic relation to that predicate.

(7) Ed believes the story to be false.

We might wonder how many further arguments *believe* has in this sentence. There are a number of possible analyses we can assign to (7). One common analysis involves taking the NP *the story* to be a DO, and the clause *to be false* to be a further Complement.

One reason for taking *the story* to be a DO is that when we passivise (7) it is this NP that is fronted:

(8) The story is believed __ to be false by Ed.

Furthermore, if we have a pronominal NP following *believe,* it must take accusative case:

(9) Ed believes him to be a traitor.

If something intervenes between the verb and the pronoun, for example a complementiser, as in (10), then the pronoun receives subjective case.

(10) Ed believes that he is a traitor.

Not only are the arguments in favour of an analysis of *the story* as a DO in (7) not wholly convincing, they lead to a serious problem: if *believe* indeed takes this NP as its DO, we would expect there to be a thematic relationship between *believe* and *the story,* such that *believe* assigns the thematic role of Patient to *the story,* exactly as in (5). With respect to its meaning, this entails that 'Ed believes the story'. Clearly, this is not what (7) means. Quite the contrary: (7) expresses Ed's incredulity with regard to the story in question. This suggests that the story is not a DO argument of *believe,* but the Subject of the string *the story to be false*. We conclude that **the string *the story to be false* is a clausal Object of *believe.***

### 6.2.2. Dummy elements and idiom chunks

Dummy elements are lexical elements without semantic content, i.e. they are meaningless. English has two such elements, namely nonreferential *it* and existential *there*.

(11) *It* is raining.
(12) *It* is cold.
(13) *There* are a number of solutions to this problem.
(14) *There* has been an increase in crime in America.

Because they are meaningless, there can be no thematic relationship between them and the associated predicate. Put differently, no thematic role is assigned to them, and for that reason they cannot act as arguments. Nonreferential *it* and existential *there* (also called *expletive* or *pleonastic* elements) **always occur in the Subject position** and should be distinguished from referential *it* and locative *there*.

(15) I don't like his pipe. *It* stinks.
(16) Los Angeles? I have no desire to go *there*.

We turn now to idioms and idiom chunks.

(17) The coast is clear.
(18) The fat is in the fire.

In these examples *the coast* and *the fat* are Subject idiom chunks. These NPs cannot be replaced by different NPs without the particular meanings associated with the full expressions being lost.

Dummy elements and Subject idiom chunks can be used to show that the NP in *believe* + NP + *to*-infinitive structures like (7) cannot be analysed as a DO.

(19) Ed believes *it* always to be raining in London.
(20) Ed believes *there* to be a traitor in the company.

Dummy elements must occur in the Subject position and they cannot be analysed as DOs, because an element must have a thematic relationship with a preceding main verb for it to occur in the DO slot. We therefore analyse them as Subjects of subordinate clauses.

We can pursue a similar line of reasoning for Subject idiom chunks.

(21) Ed believes [*the coast* to be clear].
(22) Ed believes [*the fat* to be in the fire].

We conclude that the idiom chunks *the coast* and *the fat* function as Subject in the subordinate clauses *the coast to be clear* and *the fat to be in the fire*.

### 6.2.3. Passivisation

There is an additional argument we can use to show that the NP in *believe* + NP + *to*-infinitive constructions is not a DO. Consider the following data:

(23) Ed believes the jury to have given the wrong verdict.
(24) Ed believes the wrong verdict to have been given by the jury.

Ed holds a belief in the content of a proposition, namely the proposition that the jury has given the wrong verdict. In other words, there exists no thematic relationship between *believe* and the NPs *the jury* in (23) and *the wrong verdict* in (24). These phrases cannot therefore function as the DO of *believe*.

With regard to (23) and (24) the generalisation we can now make is that if we can passivise the postverbal portion in any verb + NP + to-infinitive construction without a resulting change in meaning, then the postverbal NP is not a DO, but the Subject of a subordinate clause. (23) and (24) are bracketed as follows:

(25) Ed believes [the jury to have given the wrong verdict].
(26) Ed believes [the wrong verdict to have been given by the jury].

Incidentally, do not confuse the passive in (24) with an alternative passive version of (23), namely (27):

(27) The jury is believed to have given the wrong verdict by Ed.

Here the *main* clause, rather than the subordinate clause, has been passivised.

## 6.3. Persuade Type: persuade + NP + to-infinitive

### 6.3.1. Meaning

Take a look at the following sentence:

(28) Ed persuaded Brian to interview Melanie.

Unlike in the *believe* + NP + to-infinitive construction, notice that there is a thematic relationship between the verb *persuade* and the NP that follows it: in (28) the individual Brian undergoes Ed's act of persuasion, and the NP *Brian* can therefore be said to function as DO.

### 6.3.2. Dummy elements and idiom chunks

Now, if the postverbal NP in the *persuade* + NP + to-infinitive construction is indeed a DO, it should not be possible for this position to be occupied by dummy elements, because these can only occur in a Subject position.

(29) *Ed persuaded it to be hot in the room.
(30) *Ed persuaded there to be a party.

Idiom chunks also cannot occupy the position following *persuade:*

(31) *Ed persuaded the coast to be clear.
(32) *Ed persuaded the fat to be in the fire.

### 6.3.3. Passivisation

What about the passivisation test? Consider the following pair of sentences:

(33) Ed persuaded Brian to interview Melanie. (= (28))
(34) Ed persuaded Melanie to be interviewed by Brian.

Unlike in the case of the *believe* + NP + to-infinitive construction, we can establish a thematic relationship between the verb and the postverbal NPs here, i.e. between *persuade* and *Brian* in (33), and between *persuade* and *Melanie* in (34). Put differently, Ed persuaded an individual in both cases, not a proposition. We therefore conclude that the NP in the *persuade* + NP + to-infinitive construction functions as DO. In addition, we indicate the fact that the main clause DO and the Subject of the Complement clause are coreferential (i.e. share the same referent) by using a subscript letter 'i'. The representation for (28) is then as in (35):

(35) Ed persuaded Brian$_i$ [Ø$_i$ to interview Melanie]


## 6.4. Want Type: want + NP + to-infinitive

### 6.4.1. Meaning

Like *believe* and *persuade,* the verb *want* can also occur in the verb + NP + to-infinitive construction. Here is an example:

(36) Kate wants Ralph to get out of her life.

What is it that Kate wants? Clearly, what she wants is a situation, and situations are described by propositions, in this case 'that Ralph gets out of her life'. In other words, the thematic relationship in (36) holds between *want* and its Subject *Kate,* and between *want* and the string *Ralph to get out of her life.* The latter is a nonfinite clause which takes *Ralph* as its Subject, and functions as a Direct Object.


### 6.4.2. Dummy elements and idiom chunks

Consider (37) and (38):

(37) Kate wanted <u>it</u> to rain on Ralph's birthday.
(38) Ralph wanted <u>there</u> to be a ceasefire between him and Kate.

We must analyse *it* and *there* as the subjects of subordinate clauses. The same conclusion can be drawn from sentences that contain idiom chunks:

(39) Kate wants <u>the coast</u> to be clear, in order for her to escape from Ralph.

(40) Kate doesn't want <u>the fat</u> to be in the fire, because of some stupid action of Ralph's.

## 6.4.3. Passivisation

We find that if we passive the entire postverbal string of a *want* + NP + to-infinitive construction the meaning of the overall sentence remains constant:

(41) Kate wanted Janet to poison Ralph.

(42) Kate wanted Ralph to be poisoned by Janet.

We conclude that there is no thematic relationship between *want* and the NPs that follow it, namely *Janet* in (41) and *Ralph* in (42).

It seems, then, that our earlier supposition that *want* is like *believe* is warranted. However, this is only partially the case. The similarity between *believe* and *want* is that both verbs take a clausal postverbal argument in the verb + NP + to-infinitive pattern. The difference is that in the case of *believe,* but not in the case of *want,* the main clause can also be passivised:

(43) Ed believes the jury to have given the wrong verdict. (= (23))

(44) The jury is believed to have given the wrong verdict by Ed. (= (27))

(45) Kate wanted Janet to poison Ralph. (= (41))

(46) *Janet was wanted to poison Ralph by Kate.

This is a general difference between *believe* and *want,* which also shows up when these verbs take simple DOs in the form of a noun phrase:

(47) Ed believed the wild allegations.

(48) The wild allegations were believed by Ed.

(49) Ed wanted a new CD player.

(50) ?*A new CD player was wanted by Ed.

## 6.5. Summary

(51) Ed believes the story to be false.

(52) Ed persuaded Brian to interview Melanie.

(53) Kate wants Ralph to get out of her life.

**Believe class:** consider, expect, intend, know, suppose, understand

**Persuade class:** advise, convince, notify

**Want class:** demand, hate, hope, love, prefer, wish

NOTE This list is not exhaustive, and some of these verbs can also appear in other patterns.

# Raising and Control Constructions

- Subject Raising and Control
  - The semantic role of the subject
  - Expletive subjects
  - Subcategorization
  - Selectional Restrictions
  - Meaning preservation
- Object Raising and Control

## 7.1. Raising and Control Predicates

Certain verbs select an infinitival VP as their complement. Compare the following pairs of examples:

(1) a. John <u>tries</u> to fix the computer.

   b. John <u>seems</u> to fix the computer.

(2) a. Mary <u>persuaded</u> John to fix the computer.

   b. Mary <u>expected</u> John to fix the computer.

At first glance, these pairs are structurally isomorphic in terms of complements: both *try* and *seem* select an infinitival VP, and *expect* and *persuade* select an NP and an infinitival VP. However, there are several significant differences which motivate two classes, known as **control** and **raising** verbs:

(3) a. **Control verbs and adjectives**: try, hope, eager, <u>persuade</u>, <u>promise</u>, consider, etc.

    b. **Raising verbs and adjectives**: seem, appear, happen, likely, certain, <u>believe</u>, <u>expect</u>, etc.

Verbs like *try* are called '**control**' or '**equi**' verbs, where subject is understood to be 'equivalent' to the unexpressed subject of the infinitival VP. In linguistic terminology, the subject of the verb is said to 'control' the subject of the infinitival complement. Let us consider the 'deep structure' of (1a) representing unexpressed subject of the VP complement of *tries*.

(4) John tries [(for) John to fix the computer].

As show here, in this sentence it is John who does the action of fixing the computer. The second NP *John* would be deleted to produce the output sentence. This is why such verbs have the label of '**equi-verbs**'.

Meanwhile, verbs like *seem* are called '**raising**' verbs. Consider the deep structure of (1b):

(5) Δ **seems** [John to fix the computer].

In order to derive the 'surface structure' (1b), the subject *John* needs to be raised to the matrix subject position marked by Δ. This is why verbs like *seem* are called 'raising' verbs.

## 7.2. Differences Between Raising and Control Verbs

### 7.2.1. Subject Raising and Control

I. The semantic role of the subject

    **The semantic role of the subject:** One clear difference between raising and control verbs is the semantic role assigned to the subject. Let us compare the following examples:

(6) a. John tries to be honest.

    b. John seems to be honest.

These might have paraphrases as follows:

(7) a. John makes efforts for himself to be honest.

    b. It seems that John is honest.

As suggested by the paraphrase, the one who does the action of trying is *John* in (6a). How about (6b)? Is it John who is involved in the situation of 'seeming'? As represented in its paraphrase (7b), the situation that the verb *seem* describes is not about the individual John, but is rather about the proposition that John is honest. Due to this difference, we say that a control verb like *try* assigns a semantic role to its subject (the 'agent' role), whereas a raising verb *seem* does not assign any semantic role to its subject (this is what (5) is intended to represent).

## II. Expletive subjects

**Expletive subjects:** Since the raising verb does not assign a semantic role to its subject, certain expressions which do not have a semantic role or any meaning may appear in the subject position. Such items include the expletives *it* or *there:*

(8) a. It tends to be warm in September.

    b. It seems to bother Kim that they resigned.

The situation is markedly different with control verbs:

(9) a. *It/*There tries to be warm in September.

    b. *It/*There hopes to bother Kim that they resigned.

Since control verbs like *try* and *hope* require their subject to have an agent role, an expletive *it* or *there*, which takes no semantic role, cannot function as their subject.

We can observe the same contrast with respect to raising and control adjectives:

(10) a. It/*John is easy to please John.

    b. John/*It is eager to please Maja.

Since the raising adjective *easy* do not assign any semantic role to its subject, we can have *it* as its subject. On the other hand, the control adjective *eager* assigns a role and thus does not allow the expletive *it* as its subject.


## III. Subcategorization

**Subcategorization:** If we look into what determines the subject's properties, we can see that in raising constructions, it is not the raising verb or adjective, but the infinitival complement's predicate which determines the characteristic of the subject. In raising constructions, the subject of the raising predicate is selected as the subject of the complement VP. Observe the following contrast:

(11) a. Stephen seemed [to be intelligent].

　　b. It seems [to be easy to fool Ben].

　　c. There is likely [to be a letter in the mailbox].

　　d. Tabs are likely [to be kept on participants].

(12) a. *There seemed [to be intelligent].

　　b. *John seems [to be easy to fool Ben].

　　c. *John is likely [to be a letter in the mailbox].

　　d. *John is likely [to be kept on participants].

For example, the VP *to be intelligent* requires an animate subject, and this is why (11a) is fine but (12a) is not. Meanwhile, the VP *to be easy to fool Ben* requires the expletive *it* as its subject. This is why *John* cannot be the subject in (12b). The contrast in (c) and (d) is similar. The VP [to be a letter in the mailbox] allows its subject to be *there* (cf. *There is a letter in the mailbox*) but not *John*. The VP [to be kept on participants] requires a subject which must be the word *tabs* in order to induce an idiomatic meaning.

However, for control verbs, there is no direct selectional relation between the subject of the main verb and that of the infinitival VP. It is the control verb or adjective itself which fully determines the properties of the subject:

(13) a. Sandy tried [to eat oysters].

    b. *There tried [to be riots in Seoul].

    c. *It tried [to bother me that Chris lied].

    d. *Tabs try [to be kept on Bob by the FBI].

    e. *That he is clever is eager [to be obvious].

Regardless of what the infinitival VP would require as its subject, a control predicate requires its subject to be able to bear the semantic role of agent. For example, in (13b) and (13c), the subject of the infinitival VP can be *there* and *it*, but these cannot function as the matrix subject—because the matrix verb *tried* requires its own subject, a 'trier'.

## IV. Selectional Restrictions

**Selectional Restrictions:** Closely related to the difference in selection for the type of subject, we can observe a related similarity with regard to what are known as 'selectional restrictions'. The subcategorization frames, which we have represented in terms of VAL (valence) features, are themselves syntactic, but verbs also impose semantic selectional restrictions on their subjects or objects. For example, the verb *thank* requires a human subject and an object that is at least animate:

(14) a. The king thanked the man.

    b. #The king thanked the throne.

    c. (?)The king thanked the deer.

    d. #The castle thanked the deer.

And consider as well the following examples:

(15) a. The color red is his favorite color.

    b. #The color red understands the important issues of the day.

Unlike the verb *is*, *understands* requires its subject to be sentient. This selectional restriction then also explains the following contrast:

(16) a. The color red seems [to be his favorite color].

    b. #The color red tried [to be his favorite color].

The occurrence of the raising verb *seems* does not change the selectional restriction on the subject. However, *tried* is different: just like *understand,* the control verb *tried* requires its subject to be sentient, at least. What we can observe here is that the subject of a raising verb carries the selectional restrictions of the infinitival VP's subject. This in turn means that the subject of the infinitival VP is the subject of the raising verb.

## V. Meaning preservation

**Meaning preservation:** We have seen that the subject of a raising predicate is that of the infinitival VP complement, and it has no semantic role at all coming from the raising predicate. This implies that an idiom whose meaning is specially composed from its parts will still retain its meaning even if part of it appears as the subject of a raising verb.

(17) a. The cat seems to be out of the bag. (in the sense of: 'The secret is out')

    b. #The cat tries to be out of the bag.

In the raising example (17a), the meaning of the idiom *The cat is out of the bag* is retained. However, since the control verb *tries* assigns a semantic role to its subject *the cat*, 'the cat' must be the one doing the action of trying, and there is no idiomatic meaning. This preservation of meaning also holds for examples like the following:

(18) a. The dentist is likely to examine Pat.

    b. Pat is likely to be examined by the dentist.

(19) a. The dentist is eager to examine Pat.

    b. Pat is eager to be examined by the dentist.

Since the raising predicate *likely* does not assign a semantic role to its subject, (18a) and (18b) have more or less identical meanings—the proposition is about the dentist examining Pat, in active or passive grammatical forms: the active subject is raised in (18a), and the passive subject in (18b).

However, the control predicate *eager* assigns a semantic role to its subject, and this forces (19a) and (19b) to differ semantically: in (19a), it is the dentist who is eager to examine Pat, whereas in (19b), it is Pat who is eager to be examined by the dentist. Intuitively, if one of the examples in (18) is true, so is the other, but this inference cannot be made in (19).

## 7.2.2. Object Raising and Control

Similar contrasts are found between what are known as object raising and control predicates:

(20) a. Stephen believed Ben to be careful.
   b. Stephen persuaded Ben to be careful.

Once again, these two verbs look alike in terms of syntax: they both combine with an NP and an infinitival VP complement. However, the two are different with respect to the properties of the object NP in relation to the rest of the structure. Observe the differences between *believe* and *persuade* in (21):

(21) a. Stephen believed it to be easy to please Maja.
   b. *Stephen persuaded it to be easy to please Maja.

(22) a. Stephen believed there to be a fountain in the park.
   b. *Stephen persuaded there to be a fountain in the park.

One thing we can see here is that unlike *believe*, *persuade* does not license an expletive object (just like *try* does not license an expletive subject). And in this respect, the verb *believe* is similar to *seem* in that it does not assign a semantic role (to its object). The differences show up again in the preservation of idiomatic meaning:

(23) a. Stephen believed the cat to be out of the bag.
      (in the sense: 'Stephen believed that the secret was out'.)
   b. #Stephen persuaded the cat to be out of the bag.

While the idiomatic reading is retained with the raising verb *believed*, it is lost with the control verb *persuaded*.

Active-passive pairs show another contrast:

(24) a. The dentist was believed to have examined Pat.
   b. Pat was believed to have been examined by the dentist.

(25) a. The dentist was persuaded to examine Pat.

b. Pat was persuaded to be examined by the dentist.

With the raising verb *believe*, there is no strong semantic difference in the examples in (24). However, in (25), there is a clear difference in who is persuaded. In (25a), it is the dentist, but in (25b), it is Pat who is persuaded. This is one more piece of evidence that *believe* is a raising verb whereas *persuade* is a control verb, with respect to the object.

NOTE Subject Idiom chunks

(26) The fur flies. 큰 소동이 일어나다. / 난리가 나다.

The fur seems to fly every time they meet.

*The fur tries to fly every time they meet.

(27) The shit hits the fan. 궁지에 빠지다. / 문제가 생기다. / 재난이 닥치다.

The shit is certain ____ to hit the fan.

(28) The pot calls the kettle black. 냄비가 주전자 보고 검다고 한다. / 똥 묻은 개가 겨 묻은 개 탓한다.

John believes the pot to call the kettle black.

(29) The cat is out of the bag. 비밀이 누설되다.

The cat is likely to be out of the bag.

(30) The coast is clear. 들킬 위험이 없다.

Ed believes the coast to be clear.

(31) The fat is in the fire. 큰 실수를 저질렀다.

Ed believes the fat to be in the fire.

# Control Theory

- Obligatory Control
- Nonobligatory Control
- Arbitrary Control

## 8.1. Introduction

Consider the following examples:

(1) a. We expected to win.

    b. We expected [PRO to win].

A major question in analyzing an empty category is how it receives its interpretation. In (1), PRO's interpretation is CONTROLLED by the Subject of *expected*. For this reason, the phenomenon of the interpretation of PRO is called CONTROL. PRO does not form a chain with its controller. Instead, PRO and its controller each play an independent role in their own clause. In (1), **PRO and its controller each receive a theta-role from the predicate of their own clause**.

## 8.2. Obligatory and Nonobligatory Control

One important fact about PRO is that sometimes its interpretation is strictly delimited and sometimes it is not:

(2) a. John wants to leave.

    b. John wants [PRO to leave].

(3) a. To paint like Leonardo is the common fantasy.

    b. [PRO to paint like Leonardo] is the common fantasy.

PRO in sentences like (2) is said to be controlled. We understand PRO to have the same referent as *John,* so *John* is the controller. PRO in sentences like (3), on the other hand, is not controlled. We understand PRO to mean some underdetermined person, in this instance perhaps anybody or perhaps anybody relevant to the context (such as if (3) were said by someone running an art school). This is called **ARBITRARY PRO** (although its interpretation is not necessarily arbitrary), and it is often written as "$PRO_{arb}$" in the literature.

PRO occurs not only in infinitivals, but in other tenseless clause types, as well.

(4) John stopped [PRO crying].

(5) [PRO eating] is fun.

Example (4) is a controlled PRO. Example (5) is a $PRO_{arb}$.

There are two kinds of control of PRO. One is called OBLIGATORY CONTROL and the other is NONOBLIGATORY CONTROL. Obligatory control is control of a PRO that occurs in a position in which a lexical NP (phonetically realized) would be ungrammatical. For example, in (6) we must have a PRO as the Subject of the embedded clause:

(6) a. John tried [**PRO** to understand].

    b. *John tried [**Bill** to understand].

Nonobligatory control is control of a PRO that appears in a position that could easily be filled with a lexical NP.

(7) a. John wanted [**PRO** to understand].

    b. John wanted [**Bill** to understand].

Infinitivals introduced by *for* often alternate with infinitivals without *for* precisely when there is a lexical NP Subject of the infinitival. For example, consider:

(8) [PRO to leave without John] would be hard on me, not on you!

(9) [For me to leave without John] would be hard on me, not on you!

(10) *[Me to leave without John] would be hard on me, not on you!

**The NP *me* in (10) fails to receive Case, so this sentence is a violation of the Case Filter.** However, the presence of the *for* in (9) allows the infinitival to take a lexical Subject (here *me*), since the *for* will assign Case to the Subject of the following infinitival.

Example (8) might well be open to a PRO$_{arb}$ interpretation in your speech. But consider its control interpretation. On that interpretation, PRO is controlled by *me*. And on that interpretation, (8) is as close to synonymous with (9) as we can get. So if you are testing whether you have obligatory or nonobligatory control in an infinitival below, be sure to try PRO versus a lexical NP, and if the lexical NP is rejected, then try adding a *for* in front of the lexical NP. Obligatory control will never be saved by *for:*

(11) *I tried [for Bill to leave].

but nonobligatory control may (as in (9) versus (10)).

## 8.3. Restrictions on the Controller

We already saw above that both obligatory and nonobligatory control can have a Subject control the PRO. Can a DO be the controller in an obligatory control sentence? What about in a nonobligatory control sentence?

(12) I persuaded Bill [PRO to leave].

Here the DO is the controller. Is this obligatory or nonobligatory control? Your test of whether a lexical item can alternate with PRO here tells you that this is an instance of **obligatory control**:

(13) *I persuaded Bill (for) [Mary to leave].

What about in:

(14) [PRO to have been accused of cheating] humiliated Bill.

Here you might well allow a PRO$_{arb}$ reading. But on the controlled reading (where *Bill* is the controller), do we have obligatory or nonobligatory control? Again, your test of alternation with a lexical item tells you that (14) is an instance of **nonobligatory control**:

(15) [For Sally to have been accused of cheating] humiliated Bill.

So both kinds of control allow a DO controller (obligatory in (12) and nonobligatory in (14)). In sum, **obligatory and nonobligatory control can have Subject (6 and 7), DO (12 and 14), and OP (8) as controller.**

Looking back over the examples we have had thus far, we begin to see a pattern that will help us to find a major difference between the two types of control. Is the order of controller and PRO fixed above for either type of control? Yes; **for obligatory control the controller always precedes PRO, but for nonobligatory control, the controller may precede PRO (as in (7)) or follow PRO (as in (14)).** Is this just an accident of the examples we have looked at thus far? Try to devise a sentence in which the infinitival clause is in the Subject position of the matrix clause. Can the PRO here ever enter into obligatory control? Compare, for example:

(16) John tried {[PRO to leave] / [PRO leaving]}.
(17) a. That's been tried before.
     b. *[PRO to leave] was tried by John.
     c. *[PRO leaving] was tried by John.

*Try* is an obligatory control verb (as we saw in 6 and 11). We know from (17a) here that *try* is a verb which can occur in passive structures. Yet the passive sentences in (17b) are ungrammatical. If obligatory control requires the controller to linearly precede PRO, we can account for the ungrammaticality of (17b).

(18) *obligatory control requires that the controller linearly precede PRO*

There is another difference between obligatory and nonobligatory control that will come out upon examination of the sentences in (16) and (17). In every case of control, go back and delete the controller. What happens to the grammaticality of the sentence? Obviously, if the controller is in Subject position, the resulting sentence is ungrammatical because tensed clauses require overt Subjects in English. But if we line up all the examples with a DO controller or an OP controller, and if we delete the DO or the entire PP (note, we must delete the entire PP, not just the Object of the P, since we do not want to strand the P), we find the following results:

(19) [PRO to leave without John] would be hard.
   (cf. (8) [PRO to leave without John] would be hard on me, not on you!)

(20) *I persuaded [PRO to leave].
   (cf. (12) I persuaded Bill [PRO to leave].)

(21) *[PRO to have been accused of cheating] humiliated.
   (cf. (14) [PRO to have been accused of cheating] humiliated Bill.)

In (8), with nonobligatory control, the deletion of the controller results in the grammatical sentence (19) (with a PRO$_{arb}$ interpretation, of course). But in the other sentences, the deletion of the controller leads to an ungrammatical sentence. In (20)-(21) that is because the deleted element was required, regardless of the presence of the infinitival:

(22) a. *I persuaded.
   b. *That humiliated.

If you go through other examples in your head, you will find that in general, *if you omit the controller in an obligatory control situation, the resulting sentence is ungrammatical.* **But if you omit the controller in a nonobligatory control situation, the resulting sentence may or may not be ungrammatical** (depending on other factors, such as the subcategorization frame of the matrix verb and its interaction with varying time frames). That is the second additional difference between obligatory and nonobligatory control. And this difference accounts for the fact that obligatory control sentences are never ambiguous between a controlled reading and a PRO$_{arb}$ reading whereas nonobligatory control sentences often are.

# Section 09 — Binding Theory

**KEY CONCEPT IN THIS CHAPTER**

- Antecedent
- Anaphor
- Coindex
- Binding Domain

- Locality Conditions
- Binding Principle A
- Binding Principle B
- Binding Principle C

## 9.1. The Basic Concepts of Binding Theory

### 9.1.1. Dominance (Domination)

Node A dominates node B if and only if A is higher up in the tree than B and if you can trace a line from A to B going only downwards.

### 9.1.2. C-command

A node c-commands its sisters and all the daughters (and granddaughters and great-granddaughters, etc.) of its sisters.

## 9.1.3. Binding Principle

| | |
|---|---|
| *Binding Principle A* | (1) An anaphor must be bound in its binding domain.<br>(2) An anaphor must be locally bound.<br>(3) An anaphor must be bound within its governing category. |
| Anaphor | An **NP** that obligatorily gets its meaning from another NP in the sentence. ⇨ reflexives, reciprocals, etc. |
| *Binding Principle B* | (1) A pronoun must be free in its binding domain.<br>(2) A pronominal must be locally free.<br>(3) A pronominal must be free within its governing category. |
| pronoun (pronominal) | An **NP** that may (but need not) get its meaning from another NP in the sentence. ⇨ he, she, him, her, etc. |
| *Binding Principle C* | (1) An R-expression must be free (in all domains).<br>(2) An R-expression must be free everywhere. |
| R-expression<br>(Referential-expression) | An **NP** that gets its meaning by referring to an entity in the world. ⇨ Mary, Steve, Bill, etc |

## 9.2. The Notions Coindex and Antecedent

We're going to start with the distribution of anaphors. First, we need some terminology to set out the facts. An NP that gives its meaning to another noun in the sentence is called the *antecedent:*

(1) *Antecedent*: An NP that gives its meaning to another NP.

For example, in sentence (2), the NP *Heidi* is the source of the meaning for the anaphor *herself,* so *Heidi* is called the antecedent:

(2) <u>Heidi</u> bopped <u>herself</u> on the head with a zucchini.

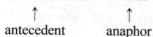

antecedent      anaphor

We use a special mechanism to indicate that two NPs refer to the same entity. After each NP we write a subscript letter. If the NPs refer to the same entity, then they get the same letter. If they refer to different entities they get different letters. Usually we start (as a matter of tradition) with the letter i and work our way down the alphabet. These subscript letters are called *indices* or *indexes* (singular: *index*).

(3) a. [Colin]$_i$ gave [Andrea]$_j$ [a basketball]$_k$.

    b. [Art]$_i$ said that [he]$_j$ played [basketball]$_k$ in [the dark]$_l$.

    c. [Art]$_i$ said that [he]$_i$ played [basketball]$_k$ in [the dark]$_l$.

    d. [Heidi]$_i$ bopped [herself]$_i$ on [the head]$_j$ with [a zucchini]$_k$.

In (3a), all the NPs refer to different entities in the world, so they all get different indexes. The same is true for (3b). Without the indices, this sentence is ambiguous; *he* can refer to Art or to someone else. But with indexing, we disambiguate this form. (3b) only has the meaning where is not Art, but someone else—the pronoun *he* and *Art* have different indexed. The indexing in sentence (3c), by contrast, has *he* and *Art* referring to the same person. In this sentence, *Art* is the antecedent of the pronoun *he*, so they have the same index. Finally in (3d), the anaphor *herself* refers back to *Heidi* so they get the same index. Two NPs that get the same index are said to be **coindexed.** NPs that are coindexed with each other are said to *corefer* (i.e., refer to the same entity in the world).

(4) *Coindexed*: Two NPs are said to be coindexed if they have the same index.

In (3c) *Art* and *he* are coindexed; in (3b) *Art* and *he* are not coindexed.

## 9.3. Binding

The notions of coindexation, coreference, and antecedence are actually quite general ones. They hold no matter what structural position an NP is the sentence. It turns out, however, that the relations between an antecedent and a pronoun or anaphor must bear particular structural relations. Contrast the three sentences in (5).

(5) a. Heidi<sub>i</sub> bopped herself<sub>i</sub> on the head with a zucchini.

   b. [Heidi<sub>i</sub>'s mother]<sub>j</sub> bopped herself<sub>j</sub> on the head with a zucchini.

   c. *[Heidi<sub>i</sub>'s mother]<sub>j</sub> bopped herself<sub>i</sub> on the head with a zucchini.

In particular notice the pattern of indexes on (5b) and (5c). These sentences show that, while the word *herself* can refer to the whole subject NP *Heidi's mother,* it can't refer to an NP embedded inside the subject NP, such as *Heidi.* Similar facts are seen in (6).

(6) a. [The mother of Heidi<sub>i</sub>]<sub>j</sub> bopped herself<sub>j</sub> on the head with a zucchini.

   b. *[The mother of Heidi<sub>i</sub>]<sub>j</sub> bopped herself<sub>i</sub> on the head with a zucchini.

Look at the trees for (5a and b), shown in (7a and b) below, and you will notice a significant difference in terms of the position where the NP immediately dominating ***Heidi*** is placed.

(7)   a.

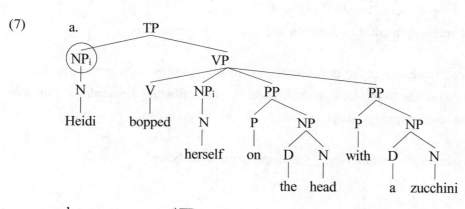

   b.

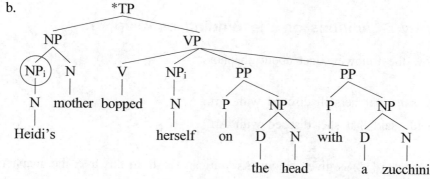

In (7a), the circled NP c-commands the NP dominating **herself**, but in (7b) it does not. It appears that the crucial relationship between an anaphor and its antecedent involves c-command. So in describing the relationship between an anaphor and an antecedent we need a more specific notion than simple coindexation. This is **binding:**

(8) *Binds*: A binds B if and only if A c-commands B and A and B are coindexed.

Binding is a special kind of coindexation. It is coindexation that happens when one of the two NPs c-commands the other. Notice that coindexation alone does not constitute binding. Binding requires both coindexation and c-command.

Now we can make the following generalization, which explains the ungrammaticality of sentences (9a) and (9b):

(9) a. *Herself$_i$ bopped Heidi$_i$ on the head with a zucchini.

    b. *[Heidi$_i$'s mother]$_j$ bopped herself$_i$ on the head with a zucchini.

In neither of these sentences is the anaphor bound. In other words, it is not c-commanded by the NP it is coindexed with. This generalization is called **Binding Principle A.** Principle A determines the distribution of anaphors:

(10) *Binding Principle A (preliminary):* An anaphor must be bound.

## 9.4. Locality Conditions on the Binding of Anaphors

Consider now the following fact about anaphors:

(11) *Heidi$_i$ said that herself$_i$ discoed with Art.

    (cf. Heidi$_i$ said that she$_i$ discoed with Art.)

A tree for sentence (11) is given below. As you can see from this tree, the anaphor is bound by its antecedent: [$_{NP}$ *Heidi*] c-commands [$_{NP}$ *Herself*] and is coindexed with it. This sentence is predicted to be grammatical by the version of Principle A presented in (10), since it meets the requirement that anaphors be bound. Surprisingly, however, the sentence is ungrammatical.

(12)

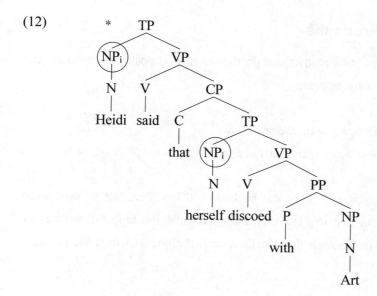

Notice that the difference between a sentence like (11) and a sentence like (5a) is that in the ungrammatical (11) the anaphor is in an embedded clause. The anaphor seems to need to find its antecedent in the same clause. This is called a ***locality constraint.*** The anaphor's antecedent must be near it or "local" in some way. The syntactic space in which an anaphor must find its antecedent is called a ***binding domain.*** For the moment let's just assume that the binding domain is the clause (TP).

(13) *Binding domain:* The clause containing the NP (anaphor, pronoun, or R-expression).

With this in mind, let's revise Principle A:

(14) *Binding Principle A (revised):* An anaphor must be bound in its binding domain.

## 9.5. The Distribution of Pronouns

Anaphors are not the only NP type with restrictions on their syntactic position. Pronouns can also be restricted in where they may appear:

(15) a. Heidi$_i$ bopped her$_j$ on the head with the zucchini.

    b. *Heidi$_i$ bopped her$_i$ on the head with the zucchini.

Pronouns like her in the sentences in (15) may not be bound. (They may not be coindexed by a c-commanding NP.) The sentence in (15) may only have the meaning where the *her* refers to someone other than *Heidi*. Contrast this situation with the one in which the pronoun is in an embedded clause:

(16) a. Heidi$_i$ said [$_{CP}$ that she$_i$ discoed with Art].

    b. Heidi$_i$ said [$_{CP}$ that she$_k$ discoed with Art].

In this situation, a pronoun may be bound by an antecedent, but it doesn't have to be. It can be bound, as in (16a), or not bound, as in (16b). Unlike the case of anaphors, which *must* be bound in a particular configuration, pronouns seem only to have a limitation on where they *cannot* be bound. That is, a pronoun cannot be bound by an antecedent that is a clause-mate (in the same immediate clause). You'll notice that this is exactly the opposite of where anaphors are allowed. This restriction is called ***Principle B*** of the binding theory. It makes use of the term free. ***Free*** is the opposite of bound.

(17) *Free:* Not bound.

(18) *Principle B:* A pronoun must be free in its binding domain.

Given that the binding domain is a clause, the ungrammaticality of (15b) is explained. Both *Heidi* and *her* are in the same clause, so they may not be bound to each other. The pronoun must be free. In (16) both indexings are allowed by Principle B. In (16b) the pronoun isn't bound at all (so is free within its binding domain). In (16a), the situation is little trickier: The pronoun is bound, but it isn't bound within its binding domain (the embedded clause). Its binder lies outside the binding domain, so the sentence is grammatical.

## 9.6. The Distribution of R-Expressions

R-expressions have yet another distribution. R-expressions don't seem to allow any instances of binding at all, not within the binding domain and not outside it either.

(19) a. *Heidi$_i$ kissed Miriam$_i$.

    b. *Art$_i$ kissed Geoff$_i$.

    c. *She$_i$ kissed Heidi$_i$.

    d. *She$_i$ said that Heidi$_i$ was a disco queen.

In none of these sentences can the second NP (all R-expressions) be bound by a c-commanding word. This in and of itself isn't terribly surprising, given the fact that R-expressions receive their meaning from outside the sentence (i.e., from the context). That they don't get their meaning from another word in the sentence (via binding) is entirely expected. We do have to rule out situations like (19), however. The constraint that describes the distribution of R-expressions is called ***Principle C.***

(20) *Principle C:* An R-expression must be free.

Notice that Principle C says nothing about a binding domain. Essentially R-expressions must be free everywhere. They cannot be bound at all.

# Case Theory

- Abstract Case
- Structural Case
- Inherent Case
- Adjacency Requirement

## 10.1. Morphological Case and Abstract Case

Case theory accounts for some of the formal properties of **overt NPs** and integrates the traditional notion of case into the grammar.

Consider the examples in (1):

(1) a. The butler attacked the robber.
    b. [That the butler attacked the robber] is surprising.
    c. [For the butler to attack the robber] would be surprising.

(1a) is a simple sentence, containing two NPs, *the butler* and *the robber*. In (1b), the simple sentence (1a) is used as the subject clause of an adjectival predicate (surprising). In (1c) we find the non-finite parallel of (1a) used as the subject of the adjectival predicate.

Let us replace the argument NPs in (1) by the corresponding pronouns:

(2) a. *He* attacked *him.*
    b. That *he* attacked *him* is surprising.
    c. For *him* to attack *him* would be surprising.

Depending on their positions in the sentences, the third person pronouns appear in different forms. When the pronoun is the internal argument of *attack*, it takes the form *him*. Adopting the terminology of traditional grammar, we call this form the **ACCUSATIVE case**. When the third person pronoun is the external argument of *attack*, it takes either the form *he* or the form *him*. The latter form is again the ACCUSATIVE case of the pronoun; the form *he* will be called the **NOMINATIVE case**. Pronouns thus can be seen to have different case forms: *he* is NOMINATIVE, *him* is ACCUSATIVE. A third case form found in English NPs is the **GENITIVE**, illustrated in (3a) and (3b).

(3) a. *The butler's* coat was too big.

   b. *His* coat was too big.

As can be seen in (2), the NOMINATIVE case (he) is reserved for the NP in the subject position of finite clauses. The ACCUSATIVE case (him) is used both for the object NP of a transitive verb [(2a), (2b) and (2c)] and for the subject NP of an infinitival subordinate clause (2c). We also find ACCUSATIVE case realized on the NP complement of a preposition.

(4) Jeeves moved towards him/*he.

Adopting the concepts of traditional grammar, we can say that subjects of finite clauses have NOMINATIVE case and that NPs that are complements of prepositions or verbs as well as NPs that are subjects of infinitival clauses appear in the ACCUSATIVE. But this informal system needs some discussion.

## 10.2. Complements: Accusative [V and P as Case Assigners]

Let us first look at the complements of transitive verbs and prepositions. Following traditional accounts of case we might say that transitive verbs and prepositions assign ACCUSATIVE case to the NP they govern. They case-mark an NP. Only transitive verbs and prepositions assign case. **Intransitive verbs** like *wander* or *overeat* **cannot assign case to a complement NP**:

(5) a. *He wandered them.

   b. *He overate them.

**Nouns and adjectives also do not assign ACCUSATIVE case.**

(6) a. *Poirot's attack him.

   b. *Poirot is envious him

We shall classify transitive verbs and prepositions as ACCUSATIVE case assigners. We propose that both **V and P are ACCUSATIVE case assigners**.

## 10.3. Subjects: Nominative and Accusative

Subjects of finite clauses have NOMINATIVE case (cf. (2a) *He* attacked *him*). In finite clauses, INFL is [+Tense, +AGR]; in non-finite clauses, INFL is [−Tense, −AGR]. This suggests that the assignment of NOMINATIVE case can be associated with finite INFL.

(7)

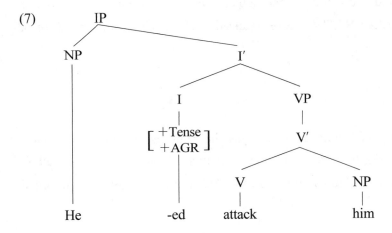

In order to ensure that **I can case-mark [Spec, IP]** under government we are forced to adopt the definition of government in terms of m-command. A definition in terms of c-command would not suffice: I does not c-command [Spec, IP].

It has been proposed (Sportiche 1988) that the subject NP in [Spec, IP] is assigned NOMINATIVE case not by virtue of government by I but rather by virtue of the specifier-head agreement between the subject NP and INFL. It could thus be argued that case-marking is achieved either via government or via specifier-head agreement.

How do we account for the ACCUSATIVE case of the subject NP of the infinitival clause? One possible answer would be to argue that it is the infinitival (to) that is responsible for case-marking the NP subject. This is unlikely in view of the following examples.

(8) a. *[Him to attack Bill] would be illegal.

　b. [That he should have attacked Bill] was surprising.

(8a) contains an infinitival subordinate clause. In this example the infinitive marker *to* is present but the sentence is not grammatical. In contrast, (8b) contains a finite subordinate clause; the head of the clause, I (INFL), assigns NOMINATIVE case to the subject NP. Potentially, there might be different ways of explaining the ungrammaticality of (8a), but a significant point to take into consideration is that the sentence is saved by the insertion of *for* as the complementizer of the non-finite clause:

(9) [**For** him to attack Bill] would be illegal.

Alternatively, the sentences are rescued by the omission of the overt subject of the infinitival clause.

(10) [__To attack Bill] would be illegal.

We call *for* in such examples a prepositional complementizer. *For* is a preposition, hence an ACCUSATIVE case assigner. We shall argue that the role of *for* is indeed to case-mark the subject *him*. The next question is why there should be any need for such a case on the NP.

Let us postulate that there is a universal requirement that all overt NPs must be assigned abstract case to satisfy the **case filter**.

(11) Case filter

　　Every overt NP must be assigned abstract case.

(8a) is ungrammatical, but can be saved either by insertion of the case assigner *for* or by omission of the overt subject. Our hypothesis will be that (8a) is ungrammatical because *to,* **the non-finite I of the infinitival clause, cannot assign case to the [Spec, IP]**. Finite I, which is [+Tense, +AGR], assigns NOMINATIVE case and contrasts with nonfinite I which is [−Tense, −AGR] and does not assign case. **(8a) is ungrammatical because it violates the case filter.** The case filter has nothing to say about the subject of the infinitives in (10) since these sentences lack an overt NP subject.

## 10.4. Exceptional Case-marking

Continuing the examination of subjects of infinitives in English, we turn to (12):

(12) John believes [him to be a liar].

In (12) *believe* takes an infinitival clause as its internal argument. The first question we may ask is which label to assign to the bracketed string: is the relevant constituent an IP or a CP? One argument in favour of the IP hypothesis is that it is not possible to insert the complementizer *for,* which is typical for infinitival clauses, in front of the subordinate clause:

(13) a. *John believes for him to be a liar.
     b. *John believes very much for him to be a liar.

(12) will have the syntactic representation (14):

> NOTE *Believe* may also take a finite CP as its complement:
>     (i) I believe [CP that [IP he is a liar]].

(14)

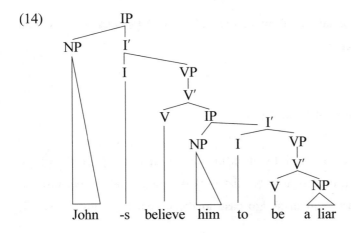

The question we address here is how *him* can satisfy the case filter, i.e. be assigned (ACCUSATIVE) case. Our hypothesis (see the discussion of 8) was that infinitival I is not a case assigner. The obvious candidate for case-marking *him* in (14) is the transitive verb *believe:*

(15) I believe this story.

In (15) *believe* case-marks the NP *this story*. On the basis of our previous discussion it is plausible that *believe* can assign case to *him,* the subject of the complement IP. *Believe* is separated from *him* by a maximal projection, infinitival IP. By assumption, infinitival IP will not constitute a barrier for outside government and hence **believe can assign case to the relevant NP**. The situation in which a verb like *believe* can govern into an IP and assign case to its subject NP is often referred to as **exceptional case-marking** abbreviated as **ECM.**

As a final illustration consider the following examples:

(16) a. I know [IP John to be the best candidate].
  b. I don't know [CP whether [IP —to go to the party]].
  c. *I don't know [CP whether [IP John to go to the party]].

(16a) is parallel to (14). *Know* takes an IP complement, governs into the maximal projection IP and case-marks *John*. In (16b), the presence of *whether* indicates that we have an infinitival clause of the type CP. In this example, there is no overt subject in the infinitival clause, thus the case filter (11) does not come into play with respect to the subject NP of the lower clause. In (16c) *know* again takes a clausal CP complement (witness the presence of *whether*). In this example the infinitival clause contains an overt NP subject *John*. **The sentence is ungrammatical because it violates the case filter. Infinitival *to* is assumed to be unable to assign case**. The potential case assigner *know* is separated from the relevant NP by the maximal projection CP, which is a barrier.

## 10.5. Adjectives and Nouns: *Of*-insertion

So far we have looked at case assignment by finite I—NOMINATIVE—and by verbs and prepositions (including *for*)—ACCUSATIVE. Nouns and adjectives are not case assigners in English:

(17) a. Poirot envies Miss Marple.

      b. *Poirot is envious Miss Marple.

      c. Poirot is envious of Miss Marple.

      d. *Poirot's envy Miss Marple

      e. Poirot's envy of Miss Marple

All the examples in (17) contain a main predicate morphologically and semantically related to the verb *envy*. In (17a) *envy*, the verb, is used; in (17b) and (17c) we find the related adjective *envious;* in (17d) and (17e) the noun *envy*.

Let us consider how the case filter (11) applies to these examples. In (17a) case assignment is straightforward: *Poirot* is assigned NOMINATIE by the finite inflection and *Miss Marple* is assigned ACCUSATIVE by the transitive verb *envy*.

(17b) is ungrammatical. If we compare it with the grammatical (17a) the only difference is that we have replaced the verb *envy* by the adjective *envious*. Apparently (17b) can be rescued by the insertion of the preposition *of* as seen in (17c). How can we account for these data?

We shall try to explain the ungrammaticality of (17b), without *of,* and the grammatically of (17c), with *of,* also in terms of the case filter. **If adjectives like *envious* cannot case-mark their complement then (17b) is ruled out by the case filter since the NP *Miss Marple* will not be assigned case**.

Let us turn to (17d) and (17e). First of all, we see that these NPs contain a GENITIVE NP, *Poirot's*, in front of their head N. We shall not discuss GENITIVE assignment in the pre-nominal position. Let us assume that there is an element **POSS in the specifier position** of NPs which is able to assign GENITIVE to the NP in that position.

We turn to the post-nominal complement of *envy,* the NP *Miss Marple.* Analogously to (17b) and (17c), we shall try to account for the ungrammaticality of (17d) and the grammaticality of (17e) in terms of case theory. **If nouns fail to assign case to their complements, (17d) violates the case filter.** *Of-*Insertion in (17e) enables the complement NP to receive case.

## 10.6. Adjacency and Case Assignment

Consider the following examples:

(18) a. Poirot speaks [$_{NP}$ English] fluently.
   b. *Poirot speaks fluently [$_{NP}$ English].
   c. Poirot sincerely believes [$_{IP}$ English to be important].
   d. *Poirot believes sincerely [$_{IP}$ English to be important].
   e. Poirot believes sincerely [$_{CP}$ that English is important].

In (18a) the verb *speak* takes an NP complement *English* and VP further includes an adjunct *fluently.* The NP *Poirot* is case-marked by the finite INFL; the NP *English* is case-marked by the transitive verb. In (18b) the constituents of the sentence are not altered and yet the sentence is ungrammatical. The only contrast with (18a) is that the V *speak* and the complement NP *English* are **no longer next to each other or adjacent.**

A similar pattern is found in (18c) and (18d). In both sentences *believe* takes an IP complement. In (18c) the verb *believe* case-marks the subject NP of the lower clause and the sentence is grammatical, while in (18d) the non-adjacency of the verb and the NP to which it should assign structural case leads to ungrammaticality.

The data in (18) have led linguists to propose that government is not a sufficient condition for case assignment in English and that a further structural requirement is that **the case assigner and the element to which case is assigned should be adjacent.** By the **adjacency requirement** case assigners must not be separated from the NPs which they case-mark by intervening material and hence (18b) and (18d) are ungrammmatical. In (18b) the verb *speak* would not be able to case-mark the NP *English* because there is intervening material; the NP *English* will violate the case filter (11). In (18d) the verb *believe* must case-mark the subject of the non-finite clause, hence ought not be separated from it; again the NP *English* violates the case filter.

The adjacency requirement has nothing to say about (18e). On the one hand, a finite clause does not need to be case-marked. **The case filter applies to NPs, not to clauses.** On the other hand, the subject of the finite clause, the NP *English,* will satisfy the case filter because it receives NOMINATIVE from the finite I.

(19) John really did go there.

In (19) we assume that the finite INFL on *did* will assign NOMINATIVE to the subject NP *John.* If there is an adjacency requirement on case assignment then it is surprising that *John* can be separated from *did* by the intervening adverb *really.* One strategy would be to assume that in (19), *John* in fact originates in the position to the immediate left of *did* and is moved across the adverb. Another possibility is to restrict the adjacency condition on case assignment to case assignment under government and to say that NOMINATIVE case assignment in (19) is not dependent on government but rather that it depends on the specifier-head relation between [Spec, IP] and INFL. We could then say that when case is assigned in a specifier-head agreement configuration the adjacency condition is not relevant.

## 10.7. Case and Passivization

Let us return to some of the earlier examples of case assignment.

(20) Italy beat Belgium in the semi-finals.

According to the case filter (11) all overt NPs in the sentence above must be assigned case. The reader can verify that the case filter is satisfied in (20). Now consider (21), the passive pendant of (20).

(21) Belgium were beaten in the semi-finals.

The effects of passivization will be familiar from the traditional literature. First, passivization affects the morphology of the verb: in (21) the verb *beat* turns up in its participial form and is accompanied by the auxiliary *be.* Furthermore, in the passive sentence the AGENT of the activity is not expressed by an NP. If we wish to refer to the AGENT of the action we need to use an adjunct PP headed by the preposition *by,* which itself carries the notion of AGENTIVITY.

(22) Belgium were beaten by Italy in the semi-finals.

(23) *It was beaten Belgium.

(24) *There was beaten Belgium.

Let us turn to (24). In our account NPs have one crucial property that distinguishes them from clauses: NPs need case. We capitalize on this difference and try to explain the ungrammaticality of (24) in terms of case theory. We shall assume that **a passivized verb loses the ability to assign structural ACCUSATIVE case to its complement**. Given the assumption that passive verbs absorb structural case. The object NP *Belgium* will not be able to receive ACCUSATIVE case from the verb *beaten*. Hence (24) violates the case filter: the object NP fails to be case-marked. Given this assumption, (23) will also be ruled out for case reasons: here too the NP *Belgium* cannot be assigned ACCUSATIVE case. Consider the examples in (25):

(25) a. I believe [Emsworth to have attacked Poirot].

> ACC          ACC

b. I believe [Poirot to have been attacked].

> ACC

c. *It was believed [Emsworth to have attacked Poirot].

> ACC

d. It was believed [that [Emsworth had attacked Poirot]].

> NOM

(25a) illustrates ECM. In the non-finite subordinate clause the external argument of *attack* is assigned ACCUSATIVE by *believe*, and the internal argument *Poirot* is assigned ACCUSATIVE by the active V *attacked*. In (25b) the verb *attacked* is passive. The external argument is not expressed. We have proposed that passive verbs cannot assign ACCUSATIVE. Hence, in order to pass the case filter the NP *Poirot* must be moved to the [Spec, IP] position of the non-finite clause where it can be assigned ACCUSATIVE case by the verb *believe*. The ungrammaticality of (25c) is due to the same reason as that in (24): the passive verb *believed* is unable to assign case, hence the NP *Emsworth,* subject of an infinitival clause, violates the case filter.

## 10.8. The Double Object Construction

If it is a property of inherent case that it survives passivization then it could be argued that GENITIVE is not the only inherent case in English. Consider (26).

(26) a. I gave John a book.

b. John was given a book.

We have not said anything about verbs like *give* in (26a) which appear to take two internal arguments. The question we address here is how both VP-internal NPs in (26a) are assigned case. One approach would be to say that in (26a) the direct object is inherently case-marked. Inherent case is not lost under passivization.

## 10.9. Movement and Chains

The visibility hypothesis raises further questions with respect to passive sentences.

Consider:

(27) [$_{IP}$ Poirot [$_{I'}$ will [$_{VP}$ be attacked −]]].

     ↑  NOM

Our hypothesis developed so far is that in (27) *Poirot* is assigned NOMINATIVE case by the finite INFL. We assume that it is theta-marked by the (passive) verb attacked, the head of VP. The question is how the verb *attacked* can theta-mark *Poirot*.

We seem to be in a dilemma. What we seem to want to say is that the NP *Poirot* must be present inside the VP headed by *attack,* in order to be assigned the internal theta role, and that it also must be moved out of the VP to the subject position where it can be assigned NOMINATIVE case. This looks like a desperate situation: we want *Poirot* to be in two positions simultaneously. However, the situation can be rescued.

*Poirot* starts out as the object of *attacked*. In a way, *Poirot* is the object of *attacked*. Then the NP *Poirot* is moved to the subject position. At this point *Poirot* is the subject of the sentence. There are two levels of syntactic representation for (27): one before the movement and one after. When *Poirot* has left the object position there remains an unfilled position or a gap inside the VP of (27).

We shall assume that the moved NP and the gap remain linked. *Poirot* is, as it were, chained to the VP-internal slot. The sequence of the two positions is referred to as a chain. We shall provisionally represent the vacant position by an *e,* for empty. We indicate that two positions are part of a chain by coindexation.

(28) [$_{IP}$ Poirot$_i$ [$_{I'}$ will [$_{VP}$ be attacked e$_i$]]]

We now propose that the internal theta role of *attacked* is not assigned to the NP *Poirot* as such, nor to the vacated position indicated by *e* in (30), but that it is the chain consisting of the vacant position *e* and the subject NP which will be assigned the theta role. The chain of two elements is represented as follows: <*NP$_i$, e$_i$*>

(29) [$_{IP}$ The robber [$_{I'}$ -ed [$_{VP}$ attack Poirot$_i$]]].

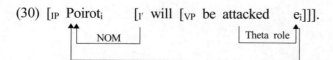

The NP is the internal argument of *attack,* but it has left the theta position in order to pick up NOMINATIVE case in the subject position. The moved NP forms a chain with the vacated position: <*Poirot$_i$, e$_i$*>. The chain is visible thanks to the NOMINATIVE case assigned to the highest position and is thus able to receive the internal theta role from *attacked.*

(30) [$_{IP}$ Poirot$_i$     [$_{I'}$ will [$_{VP}$ be attacked     e$_i$]]].

## 10.10. Summary

We came up with the Case Filter:

(31) Case filter

Every overt NP must be assigned abstract case.

Every NP with a phonetic matrix gets Case.

We also came up with some principles for Structural Case Assignment: The rule of Structural Case Assignment is from a Case-assigner onto an NP that it governs.

(32) The Case-Assigners for English are [+AGR], V, and P.

(33) The Case-Assigners V and P must be adjacent (linearly) to the phrase they give Case to.

In addition to Structural Case Assignment, there are three other rules of Case assignment in English:

(34) Genitive rule: An NP in the specifier position of NP gets genitive Case *(Bill's house)*.

(35) Double-Object Rule: The second NP in the Double-Object construction gets Objective Case *(gave Mary a ring)*.

(36) Exceptional Case-Marking: Certain verbs can assign Case to the Subject of an infinitival clause that is adjacent to them if that infinitival clause is the complement of the V.

# Prepositional Verbs and Phrasal Verbs

---

**KEY CONCEPT IN THIS CHAPTER**

- Differences between Prepositional Verb and Phrasal Verb
  - Movement Test
  - Sentence-fragment Test
  - The distribution of adverbial phrases
  - Coordination Test
  - Ellipsis Test
  - Pronominalisation

---

## 11.1. Structural Differences Between Prepositional Verb and Phrasal Verb

Having outlined our structural diagnostics, let's see how we might apply them to help us determine the constituent structure of the following pair of sentences:

(1) a. Drunks would get off the bus

    b. Drunks would put off the customers

Now at first sight, the two sentences in (1) might appear to be parallel in structure. And yet, what I'm going to suggest here is that the two sentences have very different constituent structures.

(2) a.

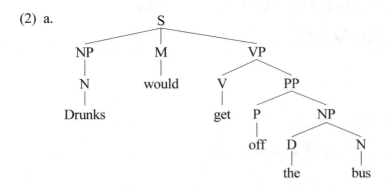

b.

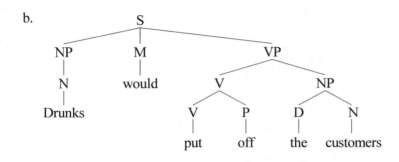

The essential difference between the two structures is that in (2a) the Preposition *off* 'goes with' the following Noun Phrase [*the bus*] to form the Prepositional Phrase [*off the bus*]; whereas in (2b), the Preposition *off* 'goes with' the Verb *put* to form the complex 'Phrasal Verb' [*put off*]. Thus, in traditional terms, we might say that *get* in (2a) is a ***Prepositional Verb*** (because it is a Verb which takes a Prepositional Phrase after it), whereas *put* in (2b) is a ***Phrasal Verb*** because the sequence [*put off*] seems to form some kind of 'compound verb'.

Let's now turn to further **syntactic evidence** in support of claiming that Prepositional and Phrasal Verbs have different structures.

### 11.1.1. Movement Test

**Only full phrases can undergo movement.** In this connection, it is interesting to note that in *get off* structures like (2a), the whole sequence [*off the bus*] can be preposed for emphasis: cf.

(3) Every afternoon, the big red bus would stop in front of the village clock, and [*off the bus*] would get Δ a dear old lady carrying a shopping bag.

Since only full phrases can undergo movement, it follows that the italicised sequence in (3) must be a full phrase; and since it contains the head Preposition *off,* it clearly must be a Prepositional Phrase. By contrast, note that the sequence *off the customers* can't be preposed in (2b): cf.

(4) *The manager suspects that drunks would put off the customers, and *off the customers* they certainly would put Δ

Why should this be? The answer suggested here is that only full phrases can be preposed in this way, and—as we see from the tree diagram in (2b) above—**the sequence *off the customers* isn't a phrase**: in fact, **it isn't even a constituent**.

## 11.1.2. Sentence-fragment Test

The sequence [*off the bus*] can serve as a sentence-fragment in (2a):

(5) Speaker A : Did he get off the train?
    Speaker B : No, *off the bus*

Since **only full phrases can serve as sentence-fragments**, this confirms the PP status of the italicised sequence. By contrast, the string *off the customers* in (2b) cannot function as a sentence-fragment, as (6) below illustrates:

(6) Speaker A : Would drunks [put off] the waitresses?
    Speaker B : *No, *off the customers*

Why can't *off the customers* function as a sentence-fragment? The answer suggested by analysis (2b) is that the italicised sequence in (6) is not even a constituent, let alone a Phrase (and recall that only full Phrases can function as sentence-fragments). So, our sentence-fragment test lends further support to analysis (2).

### 11.1.3. The distribution of adverbial phrases

Recall that we drew a distinction between **S-Adverbials** (which occur in positions where they are attached to an S node), and **VP-Adverbials** (which occur in positions where they are attached to a VP node). The class of VP-Adverbials includes expressions such as *quickly, slowly, completely,* etc. Now, since **VP-Adverbials can occur internally within VPs**, then we should expect that such an Adverbial could be positioned in between the Verb *get* and the Prepositional Phrase [*off the bus*] in (2a); and (7) below shows that this is indeed the case:

(7) Drunks would get *slowly* <u>off the bus</u>

By contrast, it is not possible to position a VP-Adverbial between *put* and *off* in (2b), as we see from the ungrammaticaly of (8) below:

(8) *Drunks would [put *completely* off] the customers

(9)  a.

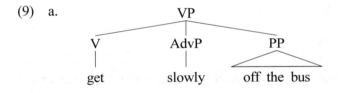

b.

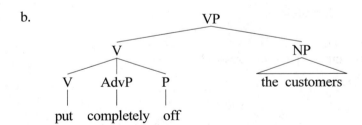

What's wrong with (9b) is that here we have a VP-Adverbial attached to a V node, not to a VP node.

## 11.1.4. Coordination Test

Given our assumption that [*off the bus*] is a PP constituent in (2a), we should expect that it can be coordinated with another PP of the same type: and as (10) below shows, this is indeed the case:

(10) Drunks would get [*off the bus*] and [*on the train*]

But given our assumption that the sequence *off the customers* is not a constituent of any type in (2b), we should expect that it cannot be coordinated with another similar sequence: and this is exactly the right prediction, as the ungrammaticality of (11) below illustrates:

(11) *Drunks would put *off the customers* and *off the waitresses*

Thus, **Ordinary Coordination** facts support the analysis we proposed in (2).

But what about the **Shared Constituent Coordination test**? Given our assumption that the sequence [*off the bus*] in (2a) is a PP constituent, we should expect that it can function as the 'shared constituent' in sentences involving Shared Constituent Coordination: and we see from (12) below that this is indeed the case:

(12) Drunks would get - and junkies would fall - *off the bus*

By contrast, the sequence *off the customers* cannot be used in the same way in (2b): cf.

(13) *Drunks would put - and junkies would also put - *off the customers*

## 11.1.5. Ellipsis Test (Gapping)

One such type is known as **gapping**, because it has the effect of leaving a 'gap' in the middle of some Phrase or Clause. For example, the second occurrence of the Verb *bought* can be gapped in this way in a sentence such as:

(14) John bought an apple, and Mary Δ a pear

When a Verb is gapped, any Modal preceding it can also be gapped along with the Verb, even if the two do not form a continuous sequence, as in (15) below:

(15) Could John close the window, and ~~could~~ Mary ~~close~~ the door?

The exact conditions determining what kind of constituent can and cannot undergo gapping in a given sentence are extremely complex, and need not be of concern to us here. What is of more immediate interest to us here is the fact that the Verb *get* can be gapped along with the Modal *would* in structures such as (2a), resulting in sentences such as:

(16) Drunks would get off the bus, and junkies ~~would get~~ off the train

However, what is even more interesting is that we cannot gap the Verb *put* along with the Modal *would* in structures like (2b), as illustrated by the ungrammaticality of:

(17) *Drunks would put off the customers, and junkies ~~would put~~ off the waitresses

By contrast, we can gap the whole expression *put off* along with *would:* cf.

(18) Drunks would put off the customers, and junkies ~~would put off~~ the waitresses

### 11.1.6. Pronominalisation

Simple Coordination facts tell us that they must be Noun Phrases, since they can be coordinated with other Noun Phrases: cf.

(19) a. Drunks would get off [*the bus*] and [*the train*]
　　 b. Drunks would put off [*the customers*] and [*the waitresses*]

Now, if they are Noun Phrases, we should obviously expect that they can be replaced by an appropriate pro-NP constituent such as *it* or *them.* And yet, while this is true of the object of a Prepositional Verb like *get off:* cf.

(20) The trouble with the bus was that drunks would want to get off _it_ every few miles, to exercise their natural bodily functions

it is not true of Phrasal Verbs such as _put off:_ cf.

(21) *What worries me about the customers is whether drunks would put off _them_

So, it would seem that Prepositional Verbs can take pronominal Objects, but Phrasal Verbs require non-pronominal Objects. Why this should be is not entirely clear.

In actual fact, our claim that Phrasal Verbs don't take pronominal objects is something of an oversimplification, as (22) below illustrates:

(22) a. *Drunks would put off _them_
　　 b. Drunks would put _them_ off

We see in (22) that a Phrasal Verb like _put off_ can indeed take a pronominal object, but only when the Preposition is positioned at the end of the sentence. Moreover, it isn't just a pronominal object which can appear between _put_ and _off:_ as (23) below indicates, an ordinary nominal NP can also appear in this position:

(23) Drunks would put [_the customers_] off

By contrast, a Prepositional Verb like _get off_ does not permit the Preposition to be moved to the end of the VP in this way: cf.

(24) *Drunks would get the bus _off_

Thus, whereas a Phrasal Verb allows its accompanying Preposition to be positioned either before or after a Noun Phrase Object (though when the Object is pronominal, the Preposition must be positioned after the Object), a Prepositional Verb only allows the Preposition to be positioned _before_ the NP Object.

The obvious question to ask at this point is what is the structure of a sentence such as (23), in which the Preposition is positioned at the end of the VP. We shall argue here that (23) has the structure (25) below:

(25)

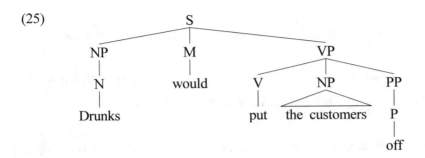

It seems clear that *off* must be a constituent of the VP here, since it can be preposed along with the other constituents of VP for emphasis: cf.

(26) The manager said that drunks would put the customers off, and [*put the customers off*] they certainly would

# Tough-Movement & Raising Sentences

KEY CONCEPT IN THIS CHAPTER

- Tough Movement Sentences
- Subject Raising Sentences

## 12.1. Tough Movement Sentences

The object of an infinitive clause in an extraposition pattern sentence like that shown in (1a) may be moved out of its clause into the position occupied by *it,* to produce a sentence that has an identical meaning as shown in (1b), The rule that does this is called ***tough movement***.

infinitive clause

(1) a. It is easy [to understand this lesson].

    b. This lesson is easy [to understand _____ ].

Although the infinitive clause in (1) has no overt subject, *tough* movement also operates on infinitive clauses with subjects, as illustrated in (2).

(2) a. It's easy for John to understand this lesson.

    b. This lesson is easy for John to understand.

Moreover, the object that is moved into main clause subject position can be the object of a preposition in the infinitive clause, as in (3).

(3) a. It's a real **pleasure** to work with John.

    b. John is a real **pleasure** to work with.

*Tough* movement cannot be applied to all extraposition pattern sentences with infinitive clauses. For *tough* movement to apply, the main clause must have *be,* or a similar verb, followed by either

- an ***ease/difficulty adjective*** such as *dangerous, difficult, easy, fun, hard, impossible, pleasant, simple, tough, or wonderful,* or
- an **NP** that has a similar "ease/difficulty" meaning, for example, *a chore, a cinch, a joy, a pain, a piece of cake, a pleasure, a snap.*

Applying *tough* movement to sentences in which *be* is followed by an adjective or NP that is not a member of the ease/difficulty set results in ungrammatical sentences, as illustrated in (4) and (5).

(4) a. It is <u>possible</u> to see the director.

    b. *The director is <u>possible</u> to see.

(5) a. It is a real <u>honor</u> to work with Professor Hobson.

    b. *Professor Hobson is a real <u>honor</u> to work with.

## 12.2. Subject Raising Sentences

(1) It $\left\{ \begin{array}{l} seems \\ happens \\ appears \end{array} \right\}$ [that Edith enjoys my company].

There is another possibility for these verbs: they can also occur in sentences with a following infinitive clause, the subject of which has been moved to subject position in the main clause. Thus, in addition to (1), we can have (2). Notice that (2) has the same meaning as (1).

(2) Edith $\left\{\begin{array}{l} seems \\ happens \\ appears \end{array}\right\}$ to enjoy my company.

To derive (2), we can start with a structure such as the one shown in (3) and apply a rule called **subject raising**, which moves the subject of the infinitive clause into subject position in the main clause.

(3) a. It seems [*Edith* to enjoy my company].

   b. *Edith* seems [ _____ to enjoy my company].

The subject raising rule also applies to sentences with *be* followed by an adjective that expresses a degree of probability, such as *certain, likely,* or *unlikely,* as shown in (4).

(4) The value of the dollar is $\left\{\begin{array}{l} likely \\ unlikely \\ certain \end{array}\right\}$ [to go up in January].

This sentence can be seen as the result of applying subject raising, as shown in (5).

(5) a. It is likely [*the value of the dollar* to go up in January].

   b. *The value of the dollar* is likely [ _____ to go up in January].

As with the verbs, with many of these adjectives, equivalent sentences with extraposed *that* clauses are possible. For example, along with (4), we can have *It is likely that the value of the dollar will go up in January.* However, with some probability adjectives, such as *sure* and *apt,* only the subject raising pattern with an infinitive is possible, as (6) illustrates.

(6) a. He is *sure/apt* to complain about something.

   b. *It is *sure/apt* that he will complain about something.

## 12.3. Sentences That Look Like Tough Movement or Subject Raising Structures

Both *tough* movement and subject raising structures have the grammatical pattern NP is + Adj [infinitive clause]. Not all sentences that have this pattern are one of these two sentence types.

Sentence (1) has the same pattern as (2a), a subject raising sentence, and (2b), a *tough* movement sentence.

(1) John is *eager* to please.

(2) a. John is *certain* to please.
    b. John is *easy* to please.

However, unlike (2a) and other subject raising sentences, (1) does not have a grammatical extraposed counterpart with a *that* clause, as (3) demonstrates. Thus, it cannot be a subject raising structure.

(3) *It is *eager* that John will please.
    (cf. It is *certain* that John will please.)

Unlike (2b) and other *tough* movement sentences, (1) does not have a grammatical extraposed version with an infinitive complement, as (4) shows. Moreover, whereas **in *tough* movement sentences, the subject was originally the infinitive clause object**, as in (1), *John* clearly is not understood as the object of *please*. Thus, (1) also cannot be a *tough* movement structure.

(4) *It is *eager* to please John.
    (cf. It is *easy* to please John.)

Sentence (1), in short, has a different structure, as illustrated in (5b). Unlike the other structures shown, this one does not relate to a structure with a subject noun clause; **the NP *John* originates in subject position.**

(5) a. John is *eager* to please.

    b. John is *eager* [(John) to please (someone)].

The structure in (5b) reflects our intuitions that the subject of the infinitive complement in square brackets is identical to the main clause subject. Sentences like (1) always have adjectives of willingness or ability (e.g., *able, eager, eligible, free, ready, welcome, willing*) between the main clause verb *be* and a following infinitive clause.

# Trace

## 13.1. WANNA Contraction

Let's now turn to look at a second argument to do with *wanna* contraction. In colloquial English, *want to* can contract to *wanna* in sentences like:

(1) a. I *want to* win

    b. I *wanna* win

In 'standard' varieties of English, *wanna* contraction can apply in sentences such as:

(2) a. Who do you *want to* beat  —?

    b. Who do you *wanna* beat?

but not in sentences like:

(3) a. Who do you *want*  —  to win?

    b. *Who do you *wanna* win?

How can we account for the fact that contraction is possible in (2), but not in (3)? Once again, the notion **underlying structure** seems to be central to any account of what is going on here. Let us assume that in underlying structure *who* originates in each case in the position marked —, and is subsequently moved into sentence-initial position by WH movement, **leaving a 'gap' behind**. And let's further suppose that **wanna contraction is blocked when there is a 'gap'** between *want* and *to*. Given these assumptions, then the fact that there is a 'gap' (marked by —) between *want* and *to* in (3a) but not in (2a) correctly predicts that *wanna* contraction will be blocked in (3), but will be possible in (2).

But of course for this account to be workable, we have to posit an abstract structure underlying sentences such as (2b) and (3b), and a rule of WH movement relating this underlying structure (i.e. Deep Structure) to the corresponding superficial syntactic structure (i.e. Surface Structure).

## 13.2. HAVE Contraction

Recall that we established that vocalic contraction of *have* down to /v/ is subject to two conditions. The first is that it takes place only after a Pronoun ending in a vowel or diphthong; and the second is that it is blocked by the presence of a 'gap' between the Pronoun and *have*. In the light of these two conditions, consider why vocalic contraction should be blocked in examples such as the following:

(1) a. Should *I have* / *\*I've* called the Police?

b. Will *we have* / *\*we've* finished by 4 o'clock?

c. Would *you have* / *\*you've* wanted to come with me?

d. Could *they have* / *\*they've* done something to help?

In each case, vocalic contraction of the sequences *I've/we've/you've/they've* is blocked. But why? The I movement analysis provides us with a ready answer. For, under this analysis, the initial Modals *should/will/would/could* originate at D-structure between the Pronoun *I/we/you/they* and the Auxiliary *have*, in the typical I position between NP and VP, as in the corresponding declaratives:

(2) a. I should have called the Police

    b. We will have finished by 4 o'clock

    c. You would have wanted to come with me

    d. They could have done something to help

They subsequently undergo 'inversion' (= I movement) in direct questions, and are moved out of their position between the Pronouns *I/we/you/they* and *have*, into pre-subject position in front of the Pronoun. This movement would have the effect of **leaving a 'gap' in the original position** out of which the Modal has been moved, between the Subject Pronoun and *have*. If we symbolise this gap by Ø, we could say that after 'inversion' the sentences in (1) would have the respective structures:

(3) a. Should *I* Ø have called the Police?

    b. Will *we* Ø have finished by 4 o'clock?

    c. Would *you* Ø have wanted to come with me?

    d. Could *they* Ø have done something to help?

The presence of **the 'gap' Ø** here between the Pronoun and *have* would then suffice to **block have contraction**. But note that this account of contraction rests heavily on the assumption that Modals originate in post-subject position, and get moved into pre-subject position by a rule of 'inversion' (= I movement), thereby **leaving a 'gap' in their original post-subject position which blocks have contraction**.

# Complementizers

---

**KEY CONCEPT IN THIS CHAPTER**

- **Complementisers**
  - that    = [−WH, +FINITE]
  - for     = [−WH, −FINITE]
  - whether = [+WH, ±FINITE]
  - if      = [+WH, +FINITE]

## 14.1. Complementisers

Complementisers can be classified into types on the basis of two different criteria: (i) syntactic (whether they are used in interrogative or noninterrogative Clauses), and (ii) morphological (whether they serve to introduce finite or nonfinite Clauses). So, for example, we might classify *that* as a noninterrogative finite Complementiser, since it only introduces finite Clauses, not Infinitives: cf.

(1) a. I am anxious [*that* you should arrive on time]

  b. *I am anxious [*that* you to arrive on time]

Conversely, we might classify *for* as a noninterrogative infinitive Complementiser, since it can introduce infinitive Clauses, but not finite Clauses—cf. e.g

(2) a. I am anxious [*for* you to arrive on time]

  b. *I am anxious [*for* you should arrive on time]

By contrast, *whether* is an interrogative Complementiser which can introduce finite and nonfinite Clauses alike; whereas *if* by is an interrogative Complementiser which can only introduce finite Complement Clauses: cf.

(3) a. I don't know [*whether/if*  I should agree]

b. I don't know [*whether/*if*  to agree]

If we were to use the feature [±WH] to indicate whether a Complementiser is interrogative or not, and the feature [±FINITE] to indicate whether a Complementiser can introduce a finite or nonfinite Clause (or both), then we could analyse each of the four Complementisers discussed above as having the feature structure (4) below:

(4) *that*　　= [−WH, +FINITE]

　　*for*　　= [−WH, −FINITE]

　　*whether* = [+WH, ±FINITE]

　　*if*　　　= [+WH, +FINITE]

We might further assume that the constituent C can be expanded into a feature complex by a feature rule such as (5) below:

(5) C → [±WH, ±FINITE]

and this rule would then generate the feature complexes specified in (6) below:

(6) [+WH, +FINITE] (can be filled by *whether/if*)

　　[+WH, −FINITE] (can be filled by *whether*)

　　[−WH, +FINITE] (can be filled by *that*)

　　[−WH, −FINITE] (can be filled by *for*)

# Ambiguity

---

**KEY CONCEPT IN THIS CHAPTER**

- Lexical Ambiguity
- Structural Ambiguity
  - Ambiguities of classification
  - Ambiguities of arrangement
- Differing Structures and Homonymy

## 15.1. Ambiguity

### 15.1.1. Introduction

Our syntactic knowledge crucially includes rules that tell us how words form groups in a sentence, or how they are *hierarchically* arranged with respect to one another. Consider the following sentence:

The captain ordered all old men and women off the sinking ship.

This phrase "old men and women" is ambiguous, referring either to old men and to women of any age or to old men and old women. The ambiguity arises because the words *old men and women* can be grouped in two ways. If the words are grouped as follows, *old* modifies only *men* and so the women can be any age.

[old men] and [women]

When we group them like this, the adjective *old* modifies both *men* and *women.*

[old [men and women]]

The rules of syntax allow both of these groupings, which is why the expression is ambiguous. The following hierarchical diagrams illustrate the same point:

In the first structure *old* and *men* are under the same node and hence *old* modifies *men*. In the second structure *old* shares a node with the entire conjunction *men and women,* and so modifies both. This is similar to what we find in morphology for ambiguous words such as *unlockable,* which have two structures, corresponding to two meanings.

### 15.1.2. Structural ambiguity

Many sentences exhibit such ambiguities, often leading to humorous results. Consider the following two sentences, which appeared in classified ads:

> For sale: an antique desk suitable for lady with thick legs and large drawers.
> We will oil your sewing machine and adjust tension in your home for $10.00.

In the first ad, the humorous reading comes from the grouping [a desk] [for lady with thick legs and large drawers] as opposed to the intended [a desk for lady] [with thick legs and large drawers], where the legs and drawers belong to the desk. The second case is similar.

Because these ambiguities are a result of different structures, they are instances of **structural ambiguity.**

### 15.1.3. Lexical or word-meaning ambiguities

Contrast these sentences with:

> This will make you smart.

The two interpretations of this sentence are due to the two meanings of smart—"clever" or "burning sensation."

### 15.1.4. Differing structures and homonymy

Often a combination of differing structure and double word-meaning creates ambiguity (and humor) as in the cartoon:

*Rhymes With Orange (105945) © Hilary B. Price. King Features Syndicate*

Syntactic rules reveal the grammatical relations among the words of a sentence as well as their order and hierarchical organization. They also explain how the grouping of words relates to its meaning, such as when a sentence or phrase is ambiguous. In addition, the rules of the syntax permit speakers to produce and understand a limitless number of sentences never produced or heard before—*the creative aspect of linguistic knowledge*. A major goal of linguistics is to show clearly and explicitly how syntactic rules account for this knowledge. A theory of grammar must provide a complete characterization of what speakers implicitly know about their language.

## 15.2. Lexical and Structural Ambiguity

### 15.2.1. Introduction

Ambiguity, as we all know, means double or multiple meaning, and it is customary to distinguish two kinds—**lexical** and **structural ambiguity**. Lexical ambiguity comes into being when two or more of the meanings of a word are applicable in a given situation. I heard a vivid example in a coffee-room exchange between two English professors. Professor A entered the room and said to B:

(1) I hear you had a good time with my wife.

Professor B looked startled and presumably did some high-speed thinking. But Professor A looked friendly, and in a few seconds B relaxed as he realized that A had used *with* to mean "in company with" and not "by means of." This was lexical ambiguity.

The second kind, structural ambiguity, stems from some aspect of English grammar, often from the **arrangement of words and structures** or from **the classification of words**. Let me offer one illustration of classification.

(2) We have mimeographed drafts of the guidelines.

Here *have mimeographed* can be classified as auxiliary + main verb, or as main verb (*have* = "possess") + adjectival participle. Each structure has its own meaning.

The grammatical situations which follow are a sampling of those which a composition teacher should know. But before listing them I must make two qualifications. First, we are dealing with ambiguity in the written language only, and some of the illustrations you will hear are clear in the spoken language. Secondly, each situation is potentially, not necessarily, ambiguous. Sometimes the ambiguity can occur only under specific grammatical restrictions. At other times the meanings of the words or the enclosing context will forestall ambiguity. Now let us look at a few situations.

## 15.2.2. Classificational Ambiguities

### Situation 1: *"-ing" verb* + *noun*
Here are a few examples:

(3) They are canning peas.

Here *canning peas* can be interpreted as a compound noun (i.e., peas for canning), or as a verb + noun object (i.e., They can peas).

(4) Mr. Carlson, is my son trying? Yes, madam, very.

Here we have still another conflict of structures. *Trying* can be an intransitive verb or an adjectival.

**Situation 2:** *Adverb of place or of direction*

(5) They stamped upstairs.

(6) The children ran outside.

**Situation 3:** *"Then"—adverb of time or of result*

(7) I'm not going home then.

**Situation 4:** *"Simply"—adverb or qualifier*

When *simply* is an adverb meaning "in a simple way," it may **appear before or after the -ed participle**, as in "The room was arranged simply," or "The room was simply arranged." But when it is a qualifier meaning "actually" or "really," it must **appear before the -ed participle**, as in "The room was simply destroyed beyond recognition." Thus because *simply* may have two meanings in the pre-participle position, an ambiguity is possible, as in

(8) The fort was simply demolished.

In a sentence like this, there is a strong analogical pull toward the qualifier reading because in similar sentences *simply* occurs only as a qualifier before adjectives, e.g., "The room was simply magnificent."

## 15.2.3. Ambiguities of arrangement

**Situation 5:** *Adjective + noun + noun head*

(9) new patient counselor

This can mean "a counselor of new patients" or "a new counselor of patients." Another instance is seen in the next sentence:

(10) Republicans in Congress want to set up a permanent crime commission.

**Situation 6:** *Predeterminer + noun + noun head*

(11) double job pay

Is this pay for a double job or double pay for a job?

**Situation 7:** *Noun head + participial phrase + prepositional phrase*

(12) The children watching the fireworks in the back yard were elated.

**Situation 8:** *Noun head + prepositional phrase + appositive*

(13) The married daughter of Sally, a slovenly woman, had untidy housekeeping habits.

**Situation 9:** *Noun head + infinitive phrase + prepositional phrase*

(14) attempt to break strike by Negroes

**Situation 10:** *Separable verb, or verb + prepositional phrase*

(15) Michael stood drinking in the moonlight.

In this sentence one reading gives us a separable verb *drinking in*, whose two parts can be separated by the object, thus: "Michael stood drinking the moonlight in"—that is, absorbing the moonlight. The second reading has *drinking* as the verb, followed by its modifier, *in the moonlight*. With this particular sentence, the latter reading has a much higher degree of probability.

MEMO

# Chapter 02

# Grammar

# The Semantics of the Verb Phrase

## 1.1. Stative and Dynamic Senses of Verbs

We draw a broad distinction between the stative and dynamic senses in which verbs are used to refer to situations. Verbs like *be, have,* and *know* have **stative senses** when they refer to a single unbroken state of affairs:

I *have known* the Penfolds all my life.

Verbs like *drive, speak,* and *attack* have **dynamic senses**, as can be seen when they are used with the present perfect to refer to a sequence of separate events:

I have driven sports cars for years.

NOTE

[a] A verb may shift in sense from one category to another. *Have,* for example, is usually **stative**: *She has two sisters*. But it has a **dynamic** sense in *We have dinner at Maxim's quite frequently*.

[b] Dynamic verb senses can regularly occur with the imperative and progressive, but stative verb senses cannot:

| | |
|---|---|
| *Learn* how to swim. | *\*Know* how to swim. |
| I *am learning* to swim. | *\*I *am knowing* how to swim. |

In general, only dynamic senses follow *do* in a pseudo-cleft sentence:

What she did was (to) *learn* Spanish.
\*What she did was (to) *know* Spanish.

## 1.2. Simple Past Tense for Past Time

The simple past is used to refer to a situation set at a **definite time** in the past.

(a) The event past is used with dynamic verb senses to refer to **a single definite event** in the past. The event may take place over an extended period (*The Normans invaded England in 1066*) or at a point of time (*The plane left at 9 a.m.*).

(b) The HABITUAL PAST is used with dynamic verb senses to refer to past events that repeatedly occur: *We spent our holidays in Spain when we were children.*

(c) The state past is used with stative verb senses to refer to a single unbroken state or affairs in the past: *I once liked reading novels.*

## 1.3. The Present Perfect

The present perfect is used to refer to a situation set at some **indefinite time** within a period beginning in the past and leading up to the present.

(a) The state present perfect is used with stative verb senses to refer to a state that began in the past and extends to the present, and will perhaps continue in the future:

> We *have lived* in Amsterdam for five years.
> She *has owned* the house since her father died.

(b) The EVENT PRESENT perfect is used with dynamic verb senses to refer to one or more events that have occurred at some time within a period leading up to the present. We distinguish two subtypes:

1. The event or events are reported as news; usually they have occurred shortly before the present time:

> The Republicans *have won* the election.
> I'*ve* just *got* a new job.
> There'*s been* a serious accident.

2. The event or events occurred at some more remote time in the past, but the implicit time period that frames the event or events leads up to the present:

> She *has given* an interview only once in her life (but she may yet give another interview).
> *Have you seen* the new production of King Lear at the National Theatre? (You still can do so.)

(c) The habitual present perfect is used with dynamic verb senses to refer to past events that repeatedly occur up to and including the present.

> The magazine *has been published* every month (since 1975).
> I*'ve been reading* only science fiction (till now).
> Socrates *has influenced* many philosophers (till now).

NOTE

Unlike the simple past, **the present perfect does not normally cooccur with adverbials that indicate a specific point or period of time** in the past. Contrast:

| | |
|---|---|
| I *saw* her <u>a week ago</u>. | [simple past] |
| *I *have seen* her <u>a week ago</u>. | [present perfect] |

Some adverbials cooccur with the present perfect and not with the simple past. They include the adverb ***since*** (*I haven't seen him since*); prepositional phrases and clauses introduced by *since* (*since Monday; since I met you*); the phrases ***till / up to now*** and ***so far***.

# Modal Auxiliaries

There are three main families of meanings that the modal auxiliaries express: **epistemic, deontic and dynamic.**

## 2.1. The Epistemic vs Deontic Contrast

**Epistemic** modality expresses meanings relating primarily to what is necessary or possible given what we know (or believe): the term derives from the Greek word for "knowledge". **Deontic** modality expresses meanings relating primarily to what's required or permitted: this term derives from the Greek word for "obligation". The two kinds of meaning are illustrated in the following pairs:

(1)  EPISTEMIC                                    DEONTIC

i.    a. He <u>must</u> have overslept.            b. He <u>must</u> apologise.

ii.   a. She <u>may</u> be ill.                    b. She <u>may</u> take as many as she needs.

iii.  a. The storm <u>should</u> be over soon.     b. We <u>should</u> call the police.

In the (a) examples the modals are interpreted **epistemically:** the varying degrees of non-factuality that they convey reflect limitations on the speaker's knowledge. In (ia), I may not know that he overslept, but I'm inferring that he did. In (iia), I don't know that she's ill, but I also don't know that she isn't, and I'm allowing it as a possibility. In (iiia), I don't know how long the storm will last, but the probability or expectation is that it will be over soon.

The (b) examples are interpreted **deontically:** the meanings have to do with **obligation or permission** of various kinds. More specifically, the operative notion in (ib) is obligation, in (iib) permission, and in (iiib) a milder kind of obligation where it is a matter of what is the right thing to do. These notions all have to do with authority and judgement rather than knowledge and belief. Very often declarative clauses with deontic meanings of modals are used to try and influence what happens rather than simply to make assertions.

The link between the two families of meanings is that the concepts of necessity and possibility—the key concepts in modal logic—apply to both. But with epistemic modality, necessity and possibility relate to whether or not something is the case, is true, whereas with deontic modality they relate to whether or not something happens, or is done. In (1i), for example, I'm saying in (a) that it is necessarily the case that he overslept, and in (b) that it is necessary for him to apologise: in neither do I countenance any other possibility.

Epistemic and deontic meanings are not in general associated with different expressions. Many examples are ambiguous, allowing either kind of interpretation for the modal:

(2)   You <u>must</u> be very tactful.          [epistemic or deontic]

There is an epistemic interpretation of this under which it means I have evidence that leads me to believe you're very tactful. And there is also a deontic one that I might use to tell you there is an obligation or need for you to be very tactful (and perhaps thus to tell you to behave with tact).


## 2.2. Dynamic Interpretations

Some of the modals have uses concerned with **properties** or **dispositions** of persons or other entities involved in the situation:

(3)   i.   She <u>can</u> speak five languages.

ii.   I've asked him to help us but he <u>won't</u>.

iii.   I <u>daren't</u> tell you any more.

These are called **dynamic** interpretations, and are somewhat peripheral to the concept of modality. In (i), *can* is used to describe an ability of hers; in (ii), the negative form of *will* talks about volition (his unwillingness to help us); in (iii), *dare* says something about whether my courage is sufficient for me to tell you any more. (*Dare* is unique among the modals in that it has only a dynamic use.)

With *can* we find clear cases of ambiguity between a dynamic and either an epistemic or a deontic interpretation:

(4)  i. You <u>can't</u> be serious.  [epistemic or dynamic]
    ii. She <u>can</u> drive.  [deontic or dynamic]

• The epistemic interpretation of (i) denies the possibility that you are being serious: it suggests a context where you have said something that I take to be absurd. The dynamic interpretation says something about your personality: you are incapable of being serious.

• In (ii) the deontic reading is that she has permission to drive, while the dynamic one attributes an ability to her—she knows to drive.

# Determiners

## 3.1. Order of Determiners in Noun Phrases

Quirk et al. maintain that there are three distinct subclasses of Determiner in English, with each class containing items such as those listed below:

| PREDETERMINER | CENTRAL DETERMINER | POSTDETERMINER |
|---|---|---|
| all/half | the | one, two, three... |
| double/treble | this/these | first, second... |
| once/twice... | each | much/few |
| | some/any | several |
| | either/neither | additional/further |
| | whose/which | next/last/past |
| | whatever/whichever/whosever | more/less |

*Transformational Grammar*

Their reasons for setting up these three different categories of Determiner are based on the distributional differences between them. More precisely, they maintain that items in one class can only be combined with items in another class in the order specified, so that we can have, for example:

predet + cendet + postdet: all the five boys
predet + cendet: double the quantity
predet + postdet: all three boys
cendet + postdet: the second occasion

Other orders, they maintain, are not possible: cf.

postdet + cendet + predet: *five the all boys
cendet + predet + postdet: *the all five boys

Moreover, items belonging to the same class generally cannot be combined with each other: cf.

cendet + cendet: *the this book

It is possible to identify a relative order of occurrence for these different types of determiners within a noun phrase by looking at them in terms of the general categories listed in the table below: *predeterminers, central determiners,* and *postdeterminers.*

| ORDER OF DETERMINERS IN NOUN PHRASES | | |
|---|---|---|
| Predeterminers | Central Determiners | Postdeterminers |
| quantifiers (*all, both, half*) multipliers (*double, twice, five times*) fractions (*three-fourths, two-fifths*) | quantifiers (*any, every, each, some*) articles (a/an, the) possessive determiners (*my, our, your*) nouns as possessive determiners (*John's, Anne's*) demonstrative determiners (*this/that*) | quantifiers (*many, much, few, little, less, least, more, most*) cardinal numbers (*one, two*) ordinal numbers (*first, second, another, next, last*) partitives (*glass/bottle/jar of*) |

*The Teacher's Grammar of English*

## 3.2. Genitive Meanings

The meanings expressed by the genitive can conveniently be shown through paraphrase; at the same time, we can compare the analogous use of the *of*-construction.

(a) Possessive genitive:

*Mrs Johnson's* coat.                    Mrs Johnson owns this coat.

*The ship's* funnel.                      The ship has a funnel.

(b) Genitive of attribute:

*The victim's* outstanding courage.      The victim was very courageous.

(c) Partitive genitive:

*The heart's* two ventricles.        The heart contains two ventricles.

(d) Subjective genitive:

*The parents'* consent.        The parents consented.

(e) Objective genitive:

*The prisoner's* release.        (⋯) released the prisoner.

(f) Genitive of origin:

*Mother's* letter.        The letter is from Mother.

*England's* cheeses.        The cheeses were produced in England.

(g) Descriptive genitive:

*Children's* shoes.        The shoes are designed for children.

*A doctor's* degree.        The degree is a doctorate.

## 3.3. The Grammatical Status of the Genitive

### 3.3.1. As determiner

For the most part, genitives function exactly like central definite determiners and thus preclude the cooccurrence of other determiners.

*A* new briefcase

*The* new briefcase        (*<u>A the</u> new briefcase)

*This* new briefcase        (*<u>The this</u> new briefcase)

*Joan's* new briefcase        (*<u>The Joan's</u> new briefcase)

This equally applies when the genitive is a phrase incorporating its own determiner.

*My cousin's* new briefcase    (≠ *My* new briefcase)

*My handsome cousin's* new briefcase

But an exception must be made where the preceding item is a predeterminer, since this may relate either to the genitive noun as in (1) or to the noun that follows as in (2).

(1) We attributed *both the girls'* success to their hard work.

　(*ie* the success of *both the girls*)

(2) Both *the girl's* parents were present.

　(*ie* both the parents *of the girl*)

### 3.3.2. As modifier

Where the genitive is used descriptively, however, it functions not as a determiner but as a modifier with a classifying role. Determiners in such noun phrase usually relate not to the genitive but to the noun following it, as can be plainly seen from the following, where the singular *a* could obviously not cooccur with the plural *women*:

　They attend a *women's* university in Kyoto.

## 3.4. Definite Articles in Discourse

The conditions that affect article choice are best phrased in terms of the use of definite articles. They require taking the discourse context into account.

I. First Versus Second Mention of a Noun

　Definite articles are used when we want to refer to something that has already been mentioned. This is sometimes referred to as the *anaphoric,* or *second-mention,* function of *the*. In (1), *a brother* and *a sister* are mentioned in the first sentence. When they are mentioned again in the second and third sentences, they are preceded by *the* to indicate that these are the same people referred to earlier.

　(1) She has *a brother* and *a sister*. *The brother* is a university student. *The sister* is still in high school.

In (2), the first sentence is the same as in (1), however, in the two following sentences, the nouns *brother* and *sister* are modified by the indefinite article *a*. It is immediately clear that the *brother* and *sister* do not refer back to these same nouns in the first sentence. The nouns are not anaphoric; rather, they denote brothers and sisters in general.

(2) She has *a brother* and *a sister*. *A brother* can either be a good friend to *a younger sister* or make her life miserable. The same can be said for *a sister*.

## II. Nouns Designating Objects in the Immediate Environment

When a speaker wants to refer to something specific that is present or visible in the immediate environment, a definite article is used. In (3), the object being referred to is visible to the speaker and the listener.

(3) Pass *the butter*, please.

We can use the even if we have not seen the thing we are referring to if we know that it is present in the immediate environment and can readily be identified by the hearer. For example, at a zoo, a sign might read *DO NOT FEED THE BEARS*. We may not see the bears referred to in the sign, but the use of *the* is appropriate since we know that bears are present.

## III. Nouns Designating Objects Present in a Larger Context

Definite articles are also used when the speaker assumes that because the listener belongs to the same community, he or she shares specific knowledge of their surroundings. For example, if two people who work in the same place are discussing where to meet for lunch, one of them might say something like the first sentence in (4).

(4) Rebecca: Let's meet at *the cafeteria* at 12:15.
   Paul: Okay, I'll see you then.

Here, the definite article is used because both speakers are part of the same work community; the cafeteria is part of their shared knowledge.

## IV. Knowledge of Relationships Between Things

Definite articles are used in situations where the speaker can assume that the listener knows about the relationships that exist between certain objects and things usually associated with them. This is referred to as the *associative anaphoric* use of definite articles. In (5), the speaker assumes that the listener knows that automobiles must have drivers and that they frequently have passengers. Thus, a definite article comes before both *driver* and *passengers*, even though this is the first time they are mentioned. Notice that the definite article in front of *freeway* is an example of the effect of assumptions related to larger context. The speaker assumes that the listener knows what specific freeway is intended.

(5) An SUV was involved in an accident on the freeway last night. *The driver* and *the passengers* were injured.

## V. Generic Reference

As discussed earlier, when a noun refers generally to members of a species or class (e.g., *cats, dogs, teachers*), this is called *generic reference*. Generic reference can be expressed three ways in English: by a plural noun preceded by zero article, as discussed earlier and as shown in (6a); by a singular noun preceded by an indefinite article, as in (6b); and by a singular noun preceded by a definite article, as in (6c).

(6) a. *Tigers* are dangerous animals.     *zero article*
    b. *A tiger* is a dangerous animal.     *indefinite article*
    c. *The tiger* is a dangerous animal.   *definite article*

The use of the definite article before a singular count noun for generic reference is very rare in conversation. It is more typical, however, in academic prose and seems to work better with complex NPs like *the howler monkey, the red-breasted merganser, the white-eyed vireo,* and so on.

# Negation

## 4.1. Negative/Positive Polarity Items

The affirmative sentence contains the noun phrase *some milk*, while the corresponding negative sentence reads *any milk*. This same shift from *some* to *any* is illustrated in (1),

|  | Affirmative | Negative |
|---|---|---|
| (1) | Ron brought *some* friends. | Ron didn't bring *any* friends. |

*Any* is one of a set of words that can appear in negative statements but normally do not appear in affirmative statements. This restriction on the use of *any* can be seen if we remove *not* from a negative sentence such as (2a). The resulting positive statement in (2b) is ungrammatical.

(2) a. She doesn't have *any* money.

   b. *She has *any* money.

Words such as ***any***, which normally occur only in negative statements but are themselves not negative, are called **negative polarity items**. Words such as ***some***, on the other hand, normally occur only in positive statements and are therefore referred to as **positive polarity items**. Examples are shown in (3).

(3) a. There are *some* crows roosting in that tree.

   b. *There aren't *some* crows roosting in that tree.

   c. There was *somebody* else in the car.

   d. *There wasn't *somebody* else in the car.

Clause negation is frequently followed (not necessarily directly) by one or more nonassertive items. The following examples illustrate the range of these items, which may be determiners, pronouns, or adverbs:

| Assertive | Nonassertive |
|---|---|
| We've had *some* lunch. | We haven't had *any* lunch. |
| I was speaking to *somebody*. | I wasn't speaking to *anybody*. |
| They will finish it *somehow*. | They won't finish it *at all*. |
| He *sometimes* visits us. | He doesn't *ever* visit us. |
| He's *still* at school. | He's not at school *any longer*. |
| Her mother's coming, *too*. | Her mother's not coming *either*. |
| I like her *a great deal*. | I don't like her *much*. |

## 4.2. Syntactic Features of Clause Negation

Negative clauses differ syntactically from positive clauses.

(1) They can typically be followed by positive tag questions:
They aren't ready, *are they*?
(cf: They are ready, *aren't they*?)

(2) They can be followed by negative tag clauses, with additive meaning:
They aren't ready, and *neither* are you.

(3) They can be followed by negative agreement responses:
A: He doesn't know Russian.　　　　B: No, he *doesn't*.

(4) They can be followed by nonassertive items:
He won't notice *any* change in you, *either*.

## 4.3. Tag Questions (Reversed Polarity Tag Questions)

Opposite polarity tag questions with positive stems always have contracted negative tags, as shown in the left-hand column in (1). Negating the stem of an opposite polarity tag question results in a positive tag, as shown in the right-hand column in (1).

(1)  **Affirmative**                                   **Negative**

    a. He likes football, doesn't he?     He doesn't like football, does he?

    b. She can come, can't she?       She can't come, can she?

    c. He is helping her, isn't he?     He isn't helping her, is he?

    d. She's a doctor, isn't she?       She isn't a doctor, is she?

## 4.4. The Types of Negation

Negation can occur at three levels.

(1) Lexical negation: *Harry is uncoordinated, isn't he?*

(2) Phrasal negation: *Marge has decided not to pay her taxes, hasn't she?*

(3) Sentential negation: *John is not at home, is he?*

We can demonstrate that only the third sentence has negation that is sentential in scope by adding a tag question to each. When tag questions in their unmarked form are negative, the sentence is affirmative; when they are affirmative, the sentence is negative.

The same question tag test can show that while *no* is only a determiner, its scope can be sentential.

    *No one came to fix the plumbing, did they?*

The same is true for the other negative forms associated with *no:*

    *Nothing is going right, is it?*

And with *not:*

    *They never answered, did they?*

## 4.5. Changes in the Relative Scope of Negation

In (1a), the scope of the negation is the entire sentence. This is because the *not* changes the meaning of its corresponding affirmative sentence in (1b).

(1) a. Tom did not destroy the evidence.
    b. Tom destroyed the evidence.

With adverbs like *deliberately, expressly, intentionally, knowingly, on purpose, purposely,* and *willfully,* the scope of negation is different, depending on whether the adverb is before *not,* as in (2), or after it, as in (3). The position or the adverb causes (2) and (3) to have different meanings.

(2) She expressly did not withhold information from the police.
(3) She didn't expressly withhold information from the police.

The meaning of (2) is "she didn't withhold information." The meaning of (3) is "she did withhold information, but this was not done on purpose."

## 4.6. Negative Constituents and C-command: Syntactic Restrictions

The word *ever* in English cannot normally occur in positive sentences: cf. the ungrammaticality of:

(1) *I will *ever* forgive you for that.

But it can occur in negative sentences: cf.

(2) Nobody will *ever* forgive you for that.
(3) I won't *ever* forgive you for that.

However, there are restrictions on the use of *ever* in negative sentences: for example, it can't occur in the following negative sentences:

(4) *I will *ever* forgive <u>nobody</u> for that.

(5) *Someone who di<u>dn</u>'t like you would *ever* forgive you for that.

Now, we might assume that the restrictions on the use of *ever* in negative sentences can be characterized in structural terms along the following lines:

(6) *Ever* is an Adverbial expression (ADVP) which occurs as an immediate constituent of S. **In negative sentences, *ever* must be preceded and c-commanded by a negative constituent** (e.g. by a negative Modal, or by a Noun Phrase containing the negative Determiner *no* as one of its immediate constituents).

# Nonreferential There

## 5.1. Thematic Roles and Dummy Elements

Nonreferential *there* and expletive *it* do not receive thematic roles. Consider the following examples:

(1) **It** always rains in London.
(2) **There** were six policemen on the bus.

**The grammatical Subjects** in these sentences are *it* and *there,* respectively. We called *it* in (1) weather *it,* because it often occurs in sentences that tell you about the weather, and we called *there* in (2) **existential *there,*** because it is used in propositions about existence. Notice that unlike referential *it* and locative *there* in (3) and (4) below, the Subjects in (1) and (2) do not refer to entities in the outside world. **They are purely Subject slot fillers.**

(3) I hate the number 31 bus, **it** is always packed!
(4) I'll put your coffee over **there**.

## 5.2. Nonreferential *There*

As we mentioned earlier, you have encountered *there* before as a pro-adverb. As a pro-adverb it can be used anaphorically (*Let's go to London. There we can see the crown jewels.*) and deictically—its meaning is understood within the context in which it occurs. One of the manifestations of this deictic meaning is that it is usually accompanied by some gesture, such as finger pointing. It is also stressed.

THERE is the little boy who looks after the sheep.

Deictic *there* calls attention to a location relative to the speaker. Contrast deictic *there* with the unstressed *there* in the next sentence.

> There is a little boy who looks after the sheep; his name is Little Boy Blue.

The *there* in this second sentence does not refer to any specific location. It is not accompanied by any typical gesture, and it does not bear stress; in fact, its vowel may well be reduced [ðər]. The *there* in the second sentence is called the nonreferential *there*.

In addition to its phonological and nonverbal differences, the nonreferential *there* has certain syntactic properties that the deictic *there* does not share. One is that the nonreferential *there* is the subject of the clause; the deictic *there* is not. To prove this, we can see that the deictic *there*, since it is an adverb, can be moved to another position in the sentence. This is not true of the nonreferential *there* because as the subject, it is always clause initial:

Deictic *there:* The little boy who looks after the sheep is THERE.
Nonreferential *there:* *A little boy who looks after the sheep is there. (Sequencing the words in this fashion forces a deictic interpretation to the *there;* that is, such an order is not possible with nonreferential *there.*)

Lakoff offers additional syntactic tests to distinguish the two forms of *there:*

### • Question tags test
Deictic *there:* *There's the little boy who looks after the sheep, isn't there?
Nonreferential *there:* There is a little boy who looks after the sheep, isn't there?

Recall that question tags are made with the subject of a sentence. Only the nonreferential *there* can be used in the question tag, demonstrating that it is indeed a subject.

### • Negation test
Deictic *there:* *There isn't the little boy who looks after the sheep.
Nonreferential *there:* There isn't a little boy who looks after the sheep.

Only sentences with nonreferential *there* can be negated.

· Deictic *here* test (substitute *here* for *there*)

Deictic *there:* Here's the little boy who looks after the sheep.

Nonreferential *there:* *Here's a little boy who looks after the sheep. (forces a deictic interpretation)

Deictic *here* can alternate syntactically with deictic *there,* but not with nonreferential *there.*

There are other tests that could be applied as well. The results of these should suffice to demonstrate that nonreferential *there* is a subject, therefore a noun phrase, not an adverb.

# Passive Sentences

## 6.1. Semantic Constraints on Using The Passive

The passive requires a transitive verb. This is not to say, however, that every passive sentence with a transitive verb is acceptable. Langacker (1987), for example, shows that the acceptability of passive sentences is influenced by several factors:

(1) The more definite the subject is, the more acceptable the sentence in passive form is:

This poem was written by Henry Wadsworth Longfellow.

?Poems were written by Henry Wadsworth Longfellow.

(2) With stative verbs, the more indefinite the object in the *by* phrase is, the more likely it is to be acceptable in its passive form.

Arthur Ashe was liked by everybody.

?Arthur Ashe was liked by me.

The movie has been seen by everyone in town.

?The movie has been seen by Jim.

(3) The more the verb denotes a physical action, as opposed to a state, the more acceptable its use in a passive sentence is:

The ball was kicked over the goalposts.

?The ball was wanted by the other team.

Notice, though, that if factors (1) and (2) are honored, then a stative verb like *want* can more easily be used in the passive voice.

This old jalopy of mine must be wanted by somebody!

Presumably the first two observations can be accounted for by recognizing that the information status of constituents appearing in initial position and in predicate position in English sentences is different. As you have already seen several times in this book, the subject NP is typically more definite than any predicate NP because it represents given information—what the predicate is about. We have more to say about this in the section on use.

The third observation stems from the fact that the subject of a passive sentence needs to be somehow affected by the action of the verb. Thus, certain transitive verbs, when used statively, are not likely to occur in the passive voice. This is true, for example, of the following verbs:

- **verbs of containing** (e.g., *contain, hold, comprise):*
  *Two gallons of water are held by the watering can.
- **verbs of measure** (e.g., *weigh, cost, contain, last):*
  *Five dollars is cost by the parking fine.
- **reciprocal verbs** (e.g., *resemble, look like, equal):*
  *Lori is resembled by her father.
- **verbs of fitting** (e.g., *fit, suit):*
  *He is suited by the plan.
- **verbs of possession** (e.g., *have, belong):*
  *A car is had by him.

## 6.2. Passive Look-Alikes: Pseudo-Passive/Stative Passive

Some sentences with *be* followed by a past participle may look like passives when they are in fact active sentences. In sentences like this, the past participle form is actually a participial adjective. For example, (1) looks like a short passive sentence, but it isn't.

(1) The library *is located* on the other side of the campus.

One way we know this is not a passive is that **it cannot be changed into a corresponding active sentence**. If we attempt to change (1) into an active sentence, we end up with something like (2), which does not have the same meaning.

(2) Someone locates the library on the other side of campus.

Sentences like (1) express the idea that the subject of the sentence is in a certain state, condition, or, in this case, place. For this reason, such sentences have sometimes been referred to as **stative passives**. This label is perhaps misleading since this is simply a case in which the past participle is a participial adjective in predicative position following *be*. We saw that these cases are common as there are many such participial adjectives (e.g., *he was frightened / amazed*). We also saw that another way of distinguishing them from passives is that adjectives often can be preceded by adverbs such as *very* or *too*. The presence of these or other degree adverbs (e.g., *a little, somewhat, quite*) is thus a good way of identifying passive look-alikes.

Sentence (1), with *located*, is unambiguously a sentence with a participial adjective; it has no sensible passive interpretation. However, some sentences are ambiguous: *The shop is closed at five o'clock* could mean either that at five o'clock the shop is not open (the adjective interpretation) or that someone closes it at 5:00 (the passive interpretation). In such cases, context will usually enable you to disambiguate the sentence. For example, context clarifies *the vase was smashed* as part of an active sentence with a predicative adjective in (3a) and as part of a passive sentence in (3b).

(3) a. When Mrs. Dalyrimple walked into the room, she saw that *the vase was smashed*. It lay in a thousand pieces on the floor next to the table.

    b. In the struggle between the thief and Mrs. Dalyrimple, *the vase was smashed* into a thousand pieces.

## 6.3. Get Passive Look-Alikes

As with *be* passives, sentences that look like *get* passives may actually be active sentences. In the main type of look-alike, *get* means "become" and is followed by a participial adjective.

### Get + Participial Adjective/Adjective

Sentence (1) looks like a short *get* passive, but it is in fact an active sentence in which the past participle form *complicated* is an adjective.

(1) His explanation is getting complicated.

Here the verb *get* expresses the idea or becoming or of coming into a state or condition. Sentence (1) may, for instance, be paraphrased as in (2).

(2) His explanation is becoming complicated.

As with *be* passives, there are several tests that help distinguish passive look-alikes from passive sentences:

• Sentences in which *get* means "become" do not have active counterparts; that is, they cannot be changed into active sentences while maintaining the same meaning. Thus, (3a) does not mean the same thing as (3b).

(3) a. He got stuck in the elevator.
    b. Someone stuck him in the elevator.

• In sentences in which *get* means "become" the participle can be preceded by words and expressions that relate to becoming—for example, *gradually (more/less), increasingly (more/less), less (and less),* and *more (and more)*. These are adverbs modifying the participial adjective. Insertion of these words and expressions is not possible with a passive sentence.

If, for example, we insert *more and more* between *getting* and the participle in (4), the resulting sentence remains grammatical, so (4) is not a passive.

(4) a. Education is getting specialized.

    b. Education is getting *more and more* specialized.

In contrast, if we do this with (5a), the resulting sentence in (5b) is ungrammatical, so (5a) is in fact a *get* passive.

(5) a. We're getting paid.

    b *We're getting *more and more* paid.

• Participial adjectives after *get* usually can be modified by adverbs indicating degree, such as *more* and *less,* mentioned earlier, and *very, a little, somewhat, moderately,* and so on. Notice that these adverbs can modify *specialized,* in (4). Moreover, some participial adjectives are especially common with *get*—including, for example, *alarmed, complicated, depressed, interested, lost, tired,* and *worried.* Thus, when we see *get* used with these past participles, as in (6a), we can suspect the sentence is not a passive, and we can confirm it by adding a relevant adverb, as in (6b).

(6) a. After waiting an hour she got *worried.*

    b. After waiting an hour she got *a little worried.*

Ambiguities are possible. Thus, *they got frightened,* which is likely to be *get* + an adjective, as in (7a), could be a passive sentence, as in (7b).

(7) a. They got very frightened.

    b. They got frightened out of their wits by a bunch of skinheads.

*Get* is also followed by a number of regular adjectives like *angry, anxious, busy, chilly, cold, hungry, old*, and so on. In all of these cases, *get* has the meaning "become." So *It suddenly got cold* means "It suddenly became cold."

## Section 07

# Relative Clauses

## 7.1. Restrictive Versus Nonrestrictive Relative Clauses

English relative clauses are classified as *restrictive* or *nonrestrictive* depending upon their function. A *restrictive relative clause* is one that serves to restrict the reference of the noun phrase modified. In (1), the restrictive relative clause *who lives in Canada* restricts *my sister* by specifying the sister in Canada. The sentence implies that the speaker has more than one sister, but only one sister in Canada is a biologist. It could be an answer to the question *Which of your sisters is a biologist?* The information added by the relative clause identifies the sister.

(1) My sister *who lives in Canada* is a biologist.

Sentence (2) contains a nonrestrictive relative clause, indicated as such by the commas around it. A *nonrestrictive relative clause* adds information about the noun modified. The noun's reference is already clear: the clause does not restrict it. Thus, in (2) the relative clause is just an added comment to the main clause content *my sister is a biologist*. The relative clause in essence says "Oh, by the way, she lives in Canada." There is no implication that the speaker has other sisters.

(2) My sister, *who lives in Canada*, is a biologist.

The commas around nonrestrictive relatives reflect the pauses in speech and a falling intonation pattern at the end of the clause, as shown in (3). There is no pause at the beginning or end of a restrictive relative clause, and falling intonation occurs only at the end of the sentence, as shown in (4).

(3)  nonrestrictive relative clause intonation

The students, *who had to take final exams today,* are tired.

(4)  restrictive relative clause intonation

The students who had to take final exams today are tired.

These two criteria—punctuation in written sentences and intonation in spoken sentences—are traditionally applied to distinguish restrictive from nonrestrictive relative clauses.


## 7.2. Form Criteria Distinguishing Nonrestrictive and Restrictive Relative Clauses

**I. Punctuation** Non restrictive relative clauses have commas around them, as in (1a). Restrictive relative clauses must not be separated by commas, as shown in (1b).

(1) a. My sister, who lives in Canada, is a biologist.
    b. My sister who lives in Canada is a biologist.

**II. Intonation** As mentioned earlier, non restrictive relative clauses are marked by pauses and by a falling intonation pattern at the end of the clause, as shown in (2a). Restrictive relative clauses, as in (2b), do not have this special intonation pattern.

(2) nonrestrictive relative clause intonation
    a. The students, *who had to take final exams today,* are tired.

    restrictive relative clause intonation
    b. The students who had to take final exams today are tired.

**III. Modification of proper nouns** Nonrestrictive relative clauses can modify proper nouns, as in (3a); restrictive relatives, as in (3b), cannot.

(3) a. John, who is a linguist, was not impressed by Professor Fish's arguments.
    b. *John who is a linguist was not impressed by Professor Fish's arguments.

**IV. Modification of any, every, no, etc.** Nonrestrictive relative clauses may not modify *any, every, or no* + noun or indefinite pronouns such as *anyone, everyone, or no one*, as shown by (4a); restrictive relatives may, as shown in (4b).

(4) a. *Any man, who goes back on his word, is no friend of mine.
    b. Any man who goes back on his word is no friend of mine.

**V. *That* as relative pronoun** Nonrestrictive relative clauses may not be introduced by *that*, as shown by (5a); restrictive relatives may, as in (5b).

(5) a. *The plan, that we discussed yesterday, will be adopted.
    b. The plan that we discussed yesterday will be adopted.

**VI. Stacking** Nonrestrictive relative clauses cannot be stacked. Stacking results in ungrammatical sentences like (6a). Restrictive relatives can be stacked, as in (6b).

(6) a. *They gave the job to Rob, **who** is very qualified, **who** starts next month.
    b. I really like that car **that** you have **that** your wife is always zipping around town in.

**VII. Sentence modification** Nonrestrictive relative clauses may modify an entire sentence, that is, a preceding independent clause, as in (7a). Restrictive relatives like (7b) may only modify noun phrases.

(7) a. Professor Fish gave everyone an A, which was just fine with Alice.
    b. *Professor Fish gave everyone an A which was just fine with Alice.

# Coordination

## 8.1. Combinatory and Segregatory Coordination of Noun Phrases

Phrases linked by *and* may express combinatory or segregatory meaning. The distinction is clearest with noun phrases. When the coordination is segregatory, we can paraphrase it by clause coordination:

> *John and Mary* know the answer.
> (= John knows the answer, and Mary knows the answer)

When it is combinatory we cannot do so, because the conjoins function in combination with respect to the rest of the clause:

> *John and Mary* make a pleasant couple.
> (≠ *John makes a pleasant couple, and Mary makes a pleasant couple)

Many conjoint noun phrases are in fact ambiguous between the two interpretations:

> *John and Mary* won a prize.

This may mean that they each won a prize or that the prize was awarded to them jointly.

Further examples of combinatory meaning:

> *John and Mary* played as partners in tennis against *Susan and Bill.*
> *Peter and Bob* separated (from each other).
> *Paula and her brother* look alike.
> *Mary and Paul* are just good friends.

*John and Peter* have different tastes (from each other).

*Mary and Susan* are colleagues (of each other).

*Law and order* is a primary concern of the new administration.

## 8.2. Indicators of Segregatory Meaning

Certain markers explicitly indicate that the coordination is segregatory:

| | | |
|---|---|---|
| both (...and) | neither... nor | respectively <formal> |
| each | respective <formal> | apiece (rather rare) |

While *John and Mary have won a prize* is ambiguous, we are left in no doubt that two prizes were won in:

John and Mary have *each* won a prize.

John and Mary have won a prize *each*.

*Both* John and Mary have won a prize.

John and Mary have *both* won a prize.

Similarly, whereas *John and Mary didn't win a prize* is ambiguous, *Neither John nor Mary won a prize* is unambiguously segregatory.

The adjective *respective* premodifies a plural noun phrase to indicate segregatory interpretation. For example, *Jill and Ben visited their respective uncles* can only mean that Jill visited her uncle or uncles and that Ben visited his uncle or uncles, whereas *Jill and Ben visited their uncles* is ambiguous between the *respective* reading and the reading that they visited persons who were uncles to both. The related nouns can be in different clauses or even in different sentences:

*Bob and his best friend* have had some serious trouble at school lately.

Their *respective* parents are going to see the principal about the complaints.

The adverb *respectively* indicates which constituents go with which in the two parallel sets of conjoint phrases:

John, Peter, *and* Robert play football, basketball, *and* baseball *respectively*.
(= John plays football, Peter plays basketball, and Robert plays baseball.)

Thomas Arnold *and* his son Matthew were *respectively* the greatest educator *and* the greatest critic of the Victorian age.
(= Thomas Arnold was the greatest educator of the Victorian age, and his son Matthew was the greatest critic of the Victorian age.)

## 8.3. Coordination Within Noun Phrases

### 8.3.1. Coordinated noun heads

When heads are coordinated, the usual interpretation is that the determiner, premodifier, and postmodifier apply to each of the conjoins:

*his* wife and child (= *his* wife and *his* child)

*old* men and women (= *old* men and *old* women)

*some* cows and pigs *from our farm*
(= *some* cows *from our farm* and *some* pigs *from our farm*)

*the* boys and girls *staying at the hostel*
(= *the* boys *staying at the hostel* and *the* girls *staying at the hostel*)

It is also possible to interpret some of these phrases as coordinated noun phrases:

old men and women (= women and old men)

some cows and pigs from our farm (= pigs from our farm and some cows)

## 8.3.2. Coordinated modifiers

Only the segregatory meaning is ordinarily possible when the coordinated modifiers denote mutually exclusive properties:

> old and new *furniture* (= old furniture and new furniture)
> *workers* from France and from Italy (= workers from France and workers from Italy)

Exceptions to this are colour adjectives (as in *red, white, and blue flags*), which allow the combinatory sense 'partly one colour, partly another'. On the other hand, only the combinatory meaning is possible if the head is a singular count noun:

> a dishonest and lazy *student* (= a student who is both dishonest and lazy)
> a *book* on reptiles and amphibians

The same meaning applies when the coordination is asyndetic: *a dishonest, lazy student*.

In other instances there may be ambiguity:

> old and valuable books
> (= books that are old and valuable or old books and valuable books)

> buses for the Houses of Parliament and for Victoria Station (either the same bus or buses go to both places or a different bus or buses go to each place)

[NOTE]

[a] The coordination of determiners (e.g. *these and those chairs*; *your and my problems*) is comparatively rare, and the synonymous construction with conjoint noun phrases (e.g. *these chairs and those*; *your problems and mine*) is preferred.

[b] Cardinal numbers are frequently coordinated with *or* in an idiomatic approximative function: *one or two guests* ('a small number'), *five or six letters* ('approximately in the range of five and six'), *ten or twenty students* ('a number from ten to twenty').

## 8.4. Coordination: Category vs. Function

In an acceptable coordination the coordinates are syntactically similar. The examples given so far contrast with the ungrammatical combinations shown in [1], where the underlined elements are manifestly quite different in kind:

[1] i *We invited [the Smiths and because they can speak Italian].

    ii *She argued [persuasively or that their offer should be rejected].

In a large majority of the coordinate structures found in texts, the coordinates belong to the same CATEGORY. But coordinates do not have to be of the same category. Other examples are given in [2]:

[2] i He won't reveal [the nature of the threat or where it came from].  [NP + clause]

    ii I'll be back [next week or at the end of the month].      [NP + PP]

    iii He acted [selfishly and with no thought for the consequences].  [AdvP + PP]

    iv They rejected the [United States and British] objections.    [Nom + Adj]

The coordinates here belong to the categories shown on the right; *where it came from* in [i] is, more specifically, a subordinate interrogative clause, while *United States* in [iv] is a nominal, the name we use for the unit intermediate between noun and noun phrase.

FUNCTION is more important than category in determining the permissibility of coordination. What makes the coordinations in [2] acceptable despite the differences of category is that each coordinate could occur alone with the same function.

[3] i  a. He won't reveal the nature of the threat. b. He won't reveal where it came from.

    ii  a. I'll be back next week.        b. I'll be back at the end of the month.

    iii  a. He acted selfishly.      b. He acted with no thought for the consequences.

    iv  a. They rejected the United States objections. b. They rejected the British objections.

In each pair here the underlined element in [b] has the same function as that in [a]: complement of the verb in [i], time adjunct in [ii], manner adjunct in [iii], attributive modifier in [iv]. Contrast these examples with those in [4]:

[4] i *We're leaving [Rome and next week].　　[NP + NP]

　ii *I ran [to the park and for health reasons].　　[PP + PP]

Here the coordinates belong to the same category, but don't satisfy the requirement of functional likeness. Each could appear in place of the whole coordination, but the functions would be different:

[5] i　a. We're leaving Rome.　　　　b. We're leaving next week.

　ii　a. I ran to the park.　　　　b. I ran for health reasons.

- Example [ia] has *Rome* as direct object, but *next week* in [ib] is an adjunct of time.
- In example [iia], *to the park* is a goal complement, but *for health reasons* in [iib] is an adjunct of reason.

In [6] we state the likeness requirement a bit more precisely in the light of these observations.

[6] A coordination of $X$ and $Y$ is admissible at a given place in sentence structure if and only if each of $X$ and $Y$ is individually admissible at that place with the same function.

To see how this works, consider the examples given in [7]:

[7] i　a. We invited [Kim and Pat].　　b. She is [very young but a quick learner].
　ii　a. We invited Kim.　　　　　　b. She is very young.
　iii　a. We invited Pat.　　　　　　b. She is a quick learner.

- In the [a] set, let $X$ be *Kim* and let $Y$ be *Pat*: we can replace *Kim* and *Pat* by *Kim,* and we can replace it by *Pat,* without change of function, so the coordination is admissible.
- The same holds in the [b] examples, where the coordinates are of different categories: *very young* and *a quick learner* can both stand in place of the coordination with the same function (predicative complement), so again this is an admissible coordination.

But [4i-ii] are not permitted by condition [6]. Although we can replace the coordination by each of the coordinates *Rome* and *next week* or *to the park* and *for health reasons*, the functions are not the same, as explained in the discussion of [5]. So condition [6] is not satisfied in these cases.

A number of qualifications and refinements to [6] are needed to cover various additional facts, but [6] does represent the basic generalisation. And of course, [6] does not have any application to the combination of *X* and *Y* in a head + dependent construction.

A special case of the syntactic likeness requirement applies in various constructions such as relative clauses. Compare the following examples:

[8]  i   <u>They attended the dinner</u> but <u>they are not members</u>.
    ii   The people [<u>who attended the dinner</u> but <u>who are not members</u>] owe $20.
    iii  *The people [<u>who attended the dinner</u> but <u>they are not members</u>] owe $20.

In [i] we have a coordination of main clauses. If we embed this to make it a modifier in NP structure, we have to relativise BOTH clauses, not just one.

- In [ii] both coordinates are relative clauses (marked by *who*): *who attended the dinner* is a relative clause and so is *who are not members*. That makes the coordination admissible.
- In [iii], by contrast, just the first embedded clause is relativised: *who attended the dinner* is a relative clause but *they are not members* isn't, so the coordination is ungrammatical.

Relativisation is thus said to work across the board, i.e. to all coordinates. Example [8iii] clearly doesn't satisfy condition [6]: the second underlined clause cannot occur alone in this context (*The people *<u>they are not members</u>* owe $20* is ungrammatical), so the coordination of the two underlined clauses is inadmissible.

We find a sharp contrast here with head + dependent constructions:

[9]  i   <u>They attended the dinner</u> although <u>they are not members</u>.
    ii   *The people [<u>who attended the dinner</u> although <u>who are not members</u>] owe $20.
    iii  The people [<u>who attended the dinner</u> although <u>they are not members</u>] owe $20.

But in [8] is a coordinator. Although in [9] is not: it's a preposition with a content clause complement. When we relativise here, then, it is just the *attend* clause that is affected, as in [9iii] (the clause *they are not members* is the complement of a preposition inside the *attend* clause). Version [9ii] is ungrammatical, because the relative clause *who are not members* is complement of a preposition. This is not a permitted function for relative clauses.

# Verb Complementation

## 9.1. Clause Types

(1) *SV*   The sun (S) is shining (V).

(2) *SVO*   The lecture (S) bored (V) me (O).

(3) *SVC*   Your dinner (S) seems (V) ready (C).

(4) *SVA*   My office (S) is (V) in the next building (A).

(5) *SVOO*   I (S) must send (V) my parents (O) an anniversary card (O).

(6) *SVOC*   Most students (S) have found (V) her (O) reasonably helpful (C).

(7) *SVOA*   You (S) can put (V) the dish (O) on the table (A).

[S: subject   V: verb   O: object   C: complement   A: adverb phrase]

## 9.2. Indirect Object and To-infinitive Clause Object

This pattern is used with verbs that introduce indirect directives. Only the indirect object can be made subject of the corresponding passive construction:

(1) I persuaded Mark to see a doctor.

(1) a. Mark was persuaded to see a doctor.

The subject of the superordinate clause ( *I* in (1)) refers to the speaker of a speech act, and the indirect object refers to the addressee (*Mark* in (1)). The implied subject of the infinitive clause is generally identified with the indirect object ('I persuaded Mark that he should see a doctor').

Here is a list of common verbs used in this pattern: *advise, ask, beg, command, entreat, forbid, implore, instruct, invite, order, persuade, remind, request, recommend, teach, tell, urge.*

NOTE

[a] With some superordinate verbs, the infinitive clause may be replaced in rather formal style by a *that*-clause containing a modal or a subjunctive:

(1) b. I persuade Mark that he should see a doctor.

[b] The verb *promise* is exceptional in that the implied subject of the infinitive clause is the superordinate subject: *I promised Howard to take two shirts for his father* ('I promised Howard that I would take two shirts for his father').

## 9.3. Infinitival Complementation:
## Monotransitive, Ditransitive, Complex-transitive

We can now distinguish three superficially identical structures that conform to the pattern N, V $N_2$ to V $N_3$, where N is a noun phrase and V is a verb phrase. The three structures display three types of complementation of the first verb phrase: monotransitive, ditransitive, and complex-transitive.

### MONOTRANSITIVE

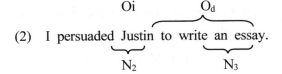

(1) The governors like all parents to visit the school.

### DITRANSITIVE

(2) I persuaded Justin to write an essay.

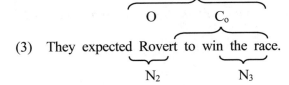

### COMPLEX-TRANSITIVE

(3) They expected Rovert to win the race.

**In monotransitive complementation,** N₂ is within the infinitive clause and functions as its subject. Accordingly, we find the following features associated with this type of complementation:

(a) The infinitive clause, including N₂, can be replaced by a pronoun:
The governors like *all parents to visit the school*, and the teachers like *that* too.

(b) When preceded by *for*, the infinitive clause, including N₂, can easily be made the focus of a pseudo-cleft construction:
What the governors like is *for all parents to visit the school*.

(c) The object of the infinitive clause can be made into its subject if the clause is turned into the passive:
The governors like *the school to be visited by all parents*.

(d) In a reduced construction, infinitival *to* is obligatorily retained:
The governors like them *to*.

(e) Existential *there* can function as subject of the infinitive clause:
We like *there to be a full attendance*.

**In ditransitive complementation,** none of the features (a)-(e) apply, since N₂ functions as indirect object within the superordinate clause and is not a constituent of the infinitive clause:

(2) a. *I persuaded *that*.
  b. *What I persuaded was *for Justin to write an essay*.
  c. *I persuaded *the essay to be written by Justin*.

The infinitive direct object clause can be omitted:

(2) d. I persuaded Justin.

On the other hand, the indirect object can be made passive subject of the superordinate clause:

(2) e. *Justin* was persuaded to write an essay.

Contrast, the unacceptability of:

*\**All parents* were liked to visit the school.

**A complex-transitive verb** such as *expect* in *They expected Robert to win the prize* displays the same features as a monotransitive verb such as *like,* except that (like ditransitive *persuade*) $N_2$ is an object and can become the passive subject of the superordinate clause:

(3) a. Robert *was expected* to win the prize.

With *expect,* though not with all complex-transitive verbs, there are two other possible passive constructions (the first applicable also to monotransitive complementation):

(3) b. They expected the prize *to be won* by Robert.
    c. The prize *was expected to be won* by Robert.

In (3c) there are passives in both the superordinate clause and the infinitive clause.

# Multiword Verbs

## 10.1. Introduction

The two main categories of multi-word verbs consist of a lexical verb plus a particle, a neutral designation for the overlapping categories of adverb and preposition that are used in such combinations. In **phrasal verbs** the particle is an adverb (e.g. *drink up, find out*) and in **prepositional verbs** it is a preposition (e.g. *dispose of, cope with*). In addition, there are **phrasal-prepositional verbs** with verbs with two particles, an adverb followed by a preposition (e.g. put up with).

## 10.2. Phrasal Verbs

Phrasal verbs consist of a verb and particle, which together have the meaning of a single verb. There are two types: intransitive and transitive.

### 10.2.1. Intransitive phrasal verbs

One common type of multi-word verb is the intransitive phrasal verb consisting of a verb plus an adverb particle, as exemplified in:

The plane has just *touched down*.
He is *playing around*.
I hope you'll *get by*.
How are you *getting on*?
The plane has now *taken off*.
Did he *catch on*?
The prisoner finally *broke down*.
She *turned up* unexpectedly.
When will they *give in*?

The tank *blew up*.

One of my papers has *gone astray*.

The two girls have *fallen out*. (='quarrelled')

In phrasal verbs like *give in* ('surrender') or *blow up* ('explode'), we cannot predict the meaning of the idiomatic combination from the meaning of verb and particle in isolation.

### 10.2.2. Transitive phrasal verbs

Transitive phrasal verbs may be separable, inseparable, or permanently separated.

I. Separable transitive phrasal verbs

Separable transitive phrasal verbs have parts that can be separated by the direct object of the phrasal verb through application of the particle movement rule.

We will *set up* a new unit.

Shall I *put away* the dishes?

She's *bringing up* two children.

Someone *turned on* the light.

They have *called off* the strike.

He can't *live down* his past.

I can't *make out* what he means.

I've *handed in* my resignation.

They may have *blown up* the bridge.

**Particle Movement**

The particle can generally either precede or follow the direct object:

They *turned on* the light. ~ They *turned* the light *on*.

But when the object is a personal pronoun (*him, her, it, them, etc.*) or a demonstrative pronoun (*this/that, these/those*), the particle movement rule must be applied:

*They *turned on* it. ~ They *turned* it *on*.

## II. Inseparable transitive phrasal verbs

Inseparable transitive phrasal verbs cannot take particle movement.

(1) a. He *ran across* a picture of his father in a photo album.
    b. *He *ran* a picture of his father *across* in a photo album.

(2) a. Don't *pick on* my brother.
    b. Don't *pick on* him.
    c. *Don't *pick* him *on*.

The meanings of inseparable transitive phrasal verbs usually cannot be deduced from the sum of their parts. For example, the meaning "annoy, pester" is not obvious from the verb + particle combination *pick on* in (2). This small group of verbs includes *come by* (= acquire), *get over* (= recover from), *look after* (= care for someone), *look into* (= investigate), *run into* (= encounter), and *stand by* (= support).

## III. Permanently separated transitive phrasal verbs

Permanently separated transitive phrasal verbs have parts that must be separated by the direct object.

(3) a. The coach's attitude is *getting* the team *down*.
    b. *The coach's attitude is *getting down* the team.

(4) a. The judge *let* the thief *off* with a light sentence.
    b. The judge *let* him *off* with a light sentence.
    c. *The judge *let off* the thief with a light sentence.

This group of verbs includes *ask [someone] out* (= invite), *do [something] over* (= redo), *get [someone] down* (= depress), *let [someone] off* (= excuse or reduce punishment), *narrow [something] down* (= reduce), *see [something] through* (= complete), and *string [someone] along* (= delude).

## 10.3. Prepositional Verbs

Prepositional verbs consist of a lexical verb followed by a preposition with which it is semantically and/or syntactically associated:

> *Look at* these pictures.
> I don't *care for* Jane's parties.
> We must *go into* the problem.
> Can you *cope with* the work?
> I *approve of* their action.
> His eyes *lighted upon* the jewel.

Like many phrasal verbs, prepositional verbs are transitive. However, their second element is a preposition and so their two parts cannot be separated by the object, in contrast to separable transitive phrasal verbs.

(1) a. He applied for the job.
    b. *He applied the job for.

Also, in contrast to phrasal verbs, with most prepositional verbs meaning can usually be deduced from the verb alone.

## 10.4. Phrasal Prepositional Verbs

Phrasal Prepositional Verbs have in addition to the lexical verb, both an adverb and a preposition as particles.

> We are all *looking forward to* your party on Saturday.
> He had to *put up with* a lot of teasing at school.
> Why don't you *look in on* Mrs Johnson on your way back?
> He thinks he can *get away with* everything.

The prepositional passive is possible, though liable to sound cumbersome. These examples, however, are normal and acceptable:

These tantrums could not be *put up with* any longer. ('tolerated')
The death penalty has been recently *done away with*. ('abolished')
Such problems must be squarely *faced up to*. ('confronted')
They were *looked down on* by their neighbours. ('despised')

NOTE

(1) I will have to [put up with] his bad behavior.
(2) Passivization → His bad behavior will have to be [put up with].
(3) Adverb Insertion → I haven't [**kept up** fully **with**] the work.

## 10.5. The Distinction Between Prepositional Verbs and Phrasal Verbs

Type I prepositional verbs resemble transitive phrasal verbs superficially, but the differences are both syntactic and phonological. The contrast is exemplified for the prepositional verb *call on* ('visit') and the phrasal verb *call up* ('summon').

(1) The particle of a prepositional verb must precede the prepositional object, but the particle of a phrasal verb can generally precede or follow the direct object:

She *called on* her friends.    She *called up* her friends.
~ *She *called* her friends *on*.    ~ She *called* her friends *up*.

(2) When the object is a personal pronoun, the pronoun follows the particle of a prepositional verb but precedes the particle of a phrasal verb:

She *called on* them.    She *called* them *up*.
~ *She *called* them *on*.    ~ *She *called up* them.

(3) An adverb (functioning as adjunct) can often be inserted between verb and particle in prepositional verbs, but not in phrasal verbs:

She *called* angrily *on* her friends.

~ \*She *called* angrily *up* her friends.

(4) The particle of a phrasal verb cannot precede a relative pronoun or wh-interrogative:

the friends *on* whom she *called.*     \*the friends *up* whom she *called.*

~ *On* which friends did she *call?*     ~ \**Up* which friends did she *call?*

(5) The particle of a phrasal verb is normally stressed, and in final position normally bears the nuclear tone, whereas the particle of a prepositional verb is normally unstressed and has the 'tail' of the nuclear tone that falls on the lexical verb:

Which friends did she CALL on?

~ Which friends did she call UP?

## 10.6. Type II Prepositional Verbs (Ditranstive): Passivization

Type II prepositional verbs are ditransitive verbs. They are followed by two noun phrases, normally separated by the preposition: the second noun phrase is the prepositional object:

He *deprived* the peasants *of* their land.

They *plied* the young man *with* food.

Please *confine* your remarks *to* the matter under discussion.

This clothing will *protect* you *from* the worst weather.

Jenny *thanked* us *for* the present.

May I *remind* you *of* our agreement?

They have *provided* the child *with* a good education.

The direct object becomes the subject in the corresponding passive clause:

The gang *robbed* her *of* her necklace.

~ She was *robbed of* her necklace (by the gang).

**NOTE**

There are two minor subtypes in which the direct object is part of the idiomatic combination:

(1) The first is exemplified by *make a mess of, make allowance for, take care of, pay attention to, take advantage of.* It allows a second less acceptable passive in which the prepositional object becomes subject:

> They have *made a (terrible) mess of* the house.
> → A (terrible) *mess* has been *made of* the house.
> ~ (?) The house has been *made a (terrible) mess of.*

(2) The second is exemplified by *catch sight of, keep pace with, give way to, lose touch with, cross swords with, keep tabs on, give rise to.* Only the prepositional object can become the passive subject, though it is considered somewhat clumsy:

> Suddenly they *caught sight of* the lifeboat.
> → The lifeboat was suddenly *caught sight of.*

# Adjectives

## 11.1. Ordering of Adjectives in Premodification

When two or more adjectives co-occur in attributive position, the order of the adjectives is to a large extent determined by their semantic properties. Here we will only mention the major positional ranges of adjectives in premodifying position. In the premodification structure of the noun phrase, adjectives are placed between the determiners and the head of the noun phrase.

We distinguish four zones:

### I. PRECENTRAL

Here, after the determiners, is where peripheral, nongradable adjectives are placed, in particular the intensifying adjectives; *e.g. certain, definite, sheer, complete, slight.*

### II. CENTRAL

This zone is the place of the central adjectives; *e.g. hungry, ugly, funny, stupid, silent, rich, empty.*

### III. POSTCENTRAL

This zone includes participles, *e.g. retired, sleeping,* and colour adjectives, *e.g. red, pink.*

### IV. PREHEAD

This zone includes the 'least adjectival and the most nominal' items, such as denominal adjectives denoting nationality, ethnic background, *e.g. Austrian, Midwestern,* and denominal adjectives with the meaning 'consisting of', 'involving', 'relating to', *e.g. experimental, statistical, political, statutory.* In the prehead zone we also find nouns in attributive position.

On the basis of this classification, we can expect the following order:

| | |
|---|---|
| I+II | *certain important* people |
| I+III | the *same restricted* income |
| I+IV | your *present annual* turnover |
| II+ III | a *funny red* hat |
| II+IV | an *enormous tidal* wave |
| I+II+IV | *certain rich American* producers |

## 11.2. Adjectives and Participles

Often the difference between the adjective and the participle is not clear cut. The verbal force of the participle is explicit for the *-ing* form when a direct object is present. Hence, the following *-ing* forms are participles that constitute a verb phrase with the preceding auxiliary:

Her views were *alarming* her audience.

You are *frightening* the children.

They are *insulting* us.

Similarly, the verbal force is explicit for the *-ed* form when a *by*-agent phrase with a personal agent is present, indicating the correspondence to the active form of the sentence:

The man was *offended* by the policeman.

He is *appreciated* by his students.

She was *misunderstood* by her parents.

For both participle forms, premodification by the intensifier *very* is an explicit indication that the forms have achieved adjective status:

Her views were very *alarming.*

You are very *frightening.*

The man was very *offended.*

We might therefore expect that the presence of *very* together with an explicit indicator of verbal force would produce an unacceptable sentence. This is certainly so for the -ing participle form:

*His views were very *alarming* his audience.

However, with the *-ed* participle, there appears to be divided usage, with increasing acceptance of the cooccurence of *very* with a *by*-agent phrase containing a personal agent:

?The man was very *offended* by the policeman.

Generally, *-ed* participle forms accepting *very* can retain *very* when they cooccur with a *by*-phrase containing a nonpersonal noun phrase that expresses the notion of cause or reason.

I'm *very disturbed* by your attitude.
We were *very pleased* by his behavior.

## 11.3. Semantic Subclassification of Adjectives

### 11.3.1. Stative/Dynamic

Adjectives are characteristically stative. Many adjectives, however, can be seen as dynamic. In particular, most adjectives that are susceptible to subjective measurement are capable of being dynamic. Stative and dynamic adjectives differ syntactically in a number of ways. For example, a stative adjective such as *tall* cannot be used with the progressive aspect or with the imperative:

*He's being *tall*.          *Be *tall*.

On the other hand, we can use *funny* as a dynamic adjective:

I didn't realize he was being *funny*.

Adjectives that can be used dynamically include *brave, calm, cheerful, conceited, cruel, foolish, friendly, funny, good, greedy, helpful, jealous, naughty, noisy, tidy.*

## 11.3.2. Gradable/nongradable

Most adjectives are gradable. Gradability is manifested through comparison:

| | | |
|---|---|---|
| tall | ~tall*er* | ~tall*est* |
| beautiful | ~*more* beautiful | ~*most* beautiful |

It is also manifested through modification by intensifiers:

| | | |
|---|---|---|
| *very* tall | *so* beautiful | *extremely* useful |

Gradability applies to adverbs as well as adjectives.

All dynamic and most stative adjectives (e.g. *tall, old*) are gradable; some stative adjectives are not, principally denominal adjectives like *atomic* (scientist) and *hydrochloric* (acid), and adjectives denoting provenance, e.g. *British*.

## 11.4. The Unmarked Term in Measure Expressions

We use the adjective *old* in measure expressions (x years old) when we refer to a person's age, regardless of the age:

> Mr Jespersen is 75 years *old*.
> His granddaughter is two years *old*.

In the scale of measurement, *old* indicates the upper range (*He is old*) but it is also the **unmarked term** for the whole range, so that *She is two years old* is equivalent to *Her age is two years*. The measure adjectives used in this way are the following, with the marked term in parentheses:

| | | | |
|---|---|---|---|
| *deep (shallow)* | *high (low)* | *long (short)* | |
| *old (young)* | *tall (short)* | *thick (thin)* | *wide (narrow)* |

These unmarked terms are also used in *how*-questions and, again, they do not assume the upper range. *How old is she?* is equivalent to *What is her age?* Other adjectives are also used in the same way in *how*-questions, e.g.

*big (small), bright (dim), fat (thin), heavy (light), large (little), strong (weak)*

*How heavy* is your computer?
*How accurate* is that clock?

Some adverbs are also used as an unmarked term in *how*-questions, e.g.

*How much* does it cost?
*How far* did you drive today?

**NOTE** If we use the marked term, as in *How young is John?*, we are asking a question that presupposes that the relevant norm is towards the lower end of the scale, *ie* that John is young, whereas the unmarked term in *How old is John?* does not presuppose that John is old. Notice that neither term is neutral in exclamations:

*How young* he is! ('He is extremely young!')
*How old* he is! ('He is extremely old!')

## 11.5. Attributive-Only Adjectives

A number of adjectives, including *drunken, erstwhile, eventual, future, mere, principal,* and *utter,* can appear only as modifiers of head nouns; that is, they can appear only in the attributive position, as shown in (1).

(1) a. At last night's party, he saw one of his *former* wives.

b. *At last night's party, he saw one of his wives who is *former*.

c. She thought that he was an *utter* fool.

d. *In terms of being a fool, he was *utter*.

Some major types of attributive-only adjectives can be established on the basis of meaning. Several of these types follow. In some cases, the adjectives are attributive-only just in contexts where they are not expressing a property that is inherent to the referent of the head noun. For example, with new, we can say *his new friend* but not *His friend is new*; and yet we can say both *his new jacket* and *His jacket is new*. The reason is that *new* expresses a property that is an inherent characteristic of the jacket but not of the person.

## Adjectives of Degree

Adjectives of degree describe the degree of the property expressed by the head noun. For instance, in the sentence *The show was an utter disaster*, the adjective utter describes the degree of the disaster. The degree expressed by such an adjective is usually absolute, as shown in (2).

(2) a. an *absolute* hero
    b. a *complete* ballplayer
    c. a *total* moron
    d. *sheer* nonsense

## Quantifying Adjectives

Quantifying adjectives indicate the amount, quantity, or frequency of the head noun, as illustrated in (3).

(3) a. the *only* way
    b. the *entire* crew
    c. an *occasional* cloud
    d. the *usual* suspects

## Adjectives of Time and Location

Adjectives of time and location place a head noun within a particular time frame or location, as shown in (4).

(4) a. a *future* appointment
    b. an *old* friend
    c. his *former* girlfriend
    d. a *previous* version
    e. her *left* arm
    f. the *northeastern* provinces

## Associative Adjectives

Associative adjectives do not express literal properties of a head noun but instead describe it in terms of some entity that is associated with it. For instance, the phrase *nuclear physicist* certainly does not imply that the physicist is somehow nuclear. Instead, the adjective describes the area of science in which the physicist works.

Similarly, in the phrase *criminal attorney,* the adjective does not express a property of the attorney but instead describes an entity with which the attorney is associated. More examples of associative adjectives are shown in (5).

(5) a. a *mathematical* journal
    b. *urban* planning
    c. a *gothic* novelist
    d. a *public* official
    e. a *moral* dilemma

## Adjective Compounds

English has a large number of adjective compounds, which function as adjectives. Many of these compounds combine an adjective and a word from any of various parts of speech, as exemplified in (6).

(6) a. grayish-blue     *adjective + adjective*
    b. big-name     *adjective + noun*
    c. street-smart     *noun + adjective*

Adjective compounds are also formed with past participles (*clean-shaven*) and present participles (*best-selling*). The process of compounding two nouns (*glass-bottom*) and a noun + participle (*world-renowned, community-planning*) is highly productive and is used particularly in fiction and in news reports.

All of these adjective compounds function as attributive adjectives, as illustrated in (7).

(7) a. He was driving a *grayish-blue* foreign sports car.

b. There were a number of *big-name* Hollywood producers at the party.

c. Mr. Stenson turned out to be a *clean-shaven* young man dressed in a white flannel suit.

d. He has just produced his fifth *best-selling* novel and is on tour promoting it.

e. They went for a short ride in a *glass-bottom* boat to a coral reef, where they saw differently colored coral and thousands of multicolored fish.

f. He is a *world-renowned* physicist.

Some of these adjective compounds are attributive-only adjectives, although others can also be used predicatively, in which case they are written as two words. The sentences in (8) exemplify the two types; only the compounds in (8a) and (8d) can be used predicatively.

(8) a. His foreign sports car is *grayish blue*.

b. *The Hollywood producers were *big name*.

c. *That boat is *glass bottom*.

d. The physicist is *world renowned*.

# Adverbials: The Grammatical Functions of Adverbials

## 12.1. Subjuncts

Subjuncts have a subordinate and parenthetic role in comparison with adjuncts. There are two main types. Those with ***narrow orientation*** are chiefly related to the predication or to a particular part of the predication. Those with ***wide orientation*** relate more to the sentence as a whole, but show their subjunct character in tending to achieve this through a particular relationship with one of the clause elements, especially the subject.

### 12.1.1. Wide orientation

I. Viewpoint subjuncts

The subjuncts which express a viewpoint are largely concerned with the semantic concept of respect, are predominantly expressed by nongradable adverb phrases, and are characteristically placed at *I(Initial)*. For example:

*Architecturally,* the plans represent a magnificent conception.

But there can be other forms of realization:

*From a personal viewpoint,* he is likely to do well in this post.
*Looked at politically,* the proposal seems dangerous.

Especially in AmE, we find adverbs in *-wise:*

*Weatherwise,* the outlook is dismal.

NOTE

*Scientifically,* the expeditions was planned. (I-position)    [subjunct]

The expeditions was planned *scientifically*. (E-position)    [adjunct]

The lawyer advised *legally*. (E-position)    [adjunct]

## II. Courtesy subjuncts

A small number of adverbs in *-ly,* along with *please,* serve to convey a formulaic tone of politeness to a sentence. They normally occur at **M** (medial):

You are *cordially* invited to take your places.

He asked if I would *please* read his manuscript.

Courtesy subjuncts obviously involve the semantic category manner but are quite distinct from manner adjuncts. Contrast:

She *kindly* [subjunct] offered me her seat.

('She was kind enough to offer ...')

She offered me her seat *kindly* [adjunct].

('She offered me her seat in *a kind manner*.')

## 12.1.2. Narrow orientation

## I. Item subjuncts

The commonest item to be associated with subjuncts is the *subject* of a clause, with the subjunct operating in the semantic area of *manner* but distinguished from the corresponding manner adjunct by being placed at **I** or **M**:

She has *consistently* opposed the lawyers's arguments.

This does not mean that her own arguments have been conducted consistently but that she has been consistent in always opposing the lawyer's. Many such subjuncts express volition, as in:

*Intentionally,* they said nothing to him about the fire.

*With great reluctance,* he rose to speak.


Paraphrase:


(1) *Bitterly,* he buried his child.

   → He was <u>bitter</u> when he buried his child.

(2) *With great pride,* he accepted the award.

   → He was <u>very proud</u> to accept the award.

(3) He *deliberately* misled us.

   → He was <u>being deliberate</u> when he misled us.

(4) *With great unease,* they elected him as their leader.

   → <u>They were very uneasy</u> when they elected him as their leader.


## 12.2. Disjuncts

Where adjuncts are seen as on a par with such sentence elements as S and O, while subjuncts are seen as having a lesser role, disjuncts have by contrast a superior role to sentence elements, being somewhat detached from and superordinate to the rest of the sentence. There are two broad types. First we have the relatively small class of (I) **STYLE disjuncts**, conveying the speaker's comment on the style and form of what is being said and defining in some way the conditions under which 'authority' is being assumed for the statement. Thus where (1) is stated as an unsupported fact, (2) is conditioned by a style disjunct:


(1) Mr Forster neglects his children.

(2) *From my personal observation,* Mr Forster neglects his children.


The second type is the much larger class of (II) **CONTENT disjuncts**, making an observation on the actual content of an utterance and on its truth conditions:


(3) *To the disgust of his neighbours,* Mr Forster neglects his children.


Although not restricted as to position (and while some, as we shall see are often at $M$), most disjuncts appear at $I$.

# I. Style disjuncts

Many style disjuncts can be seen as abbreviated clauses in which the adverbial would have the role of manner adjunct:

Frankly, I am tired. (cf: 'I tell you *frankly* that I am tired'.)

Sometimes the disjunct has full clausal form:

If I *may say so without giving you offence,* I think your writing is rather immature.

More often, a clausal disjunct is nonfinite, as in *to be frank, putting it bluntly, considered candidly.*

The semantic roles of disjuncts fall under two main heads:

(a) Manner and modality, thus involving items such as *crudely, frankly, honestly, truthfully; e.g.*
(To put it) *briefly,* there is nothing I can do to help.
You can, *in all honesty,* expect no further payments.

(b) Respect, thus involving items such as *generally, literally, personally, strictly; e.g.*
*Strictly (in terms of the rules),* she should have conceded the point to her opponent.
I would not, *(speaking) personally,* have taken offence at the remark.
*From what he said,* the other driver was in the wrong.


# II. Content disjuncts

Comment on the content of an utterance may be of two kinds:

(a) relating to certainty;
(b) relating to evaluation.

Both can be expressed by a wide range of adverb phrases, by prepositional phrases and—especially those in (a)—by clauses.

(a) *Certainty.* These disjuncts comment on the truth value of what is said, firmly endorsing it, expressing doubt, or posing contingencies such as conditions or reasons.

For example, beside the statement 'The play was written by Francis Beaumont', we may have:

The play was *undoubtedly (apparently/perhaps)* written by Francis Beaumont.

Compare also:

*In essence,* the judge called her evidence in question.
*Since she had no time to have the car fixed,* Rachel telephoned for a taxi.
The proposal would have been accepted *if the chairman had put it more forcibly.*

(b) ***Evaluation.*** These disjuncts express an attitude to an utterance by way of evaluation. Some express a judgment on the utterance as a whole, including its subject:

*Wisely,* Mrs Jensen consulted her lawyer.
('Mrs Jensen was wise in consulting her lawyer.')

So also *correctly, cunningly, foolishly, justly, rightly, stupidly,* etc. Other evaluation disjuncts carry no implication of comment on the subject:

*Naturally,* my husband expected me home by then.
('It was natural for my husband to expect me back by then'—not 'My husband was natural...')

So also *curiously, funnily (enough), strangely, unexpectedly, predictably, understandably, disturbingly, pleasingly, regrettably, fortunately, happily, luckily, sadly, amusingly, hopefully* <esp AmE>, *significantly.* Prepositional phrases and relative clauses (sentential and nominal) involving such lexical bases are also used:

*To my regret,* she did not seek nomination.
*What is especially fortunate,* the child was unhurt.
We were not, *which is surprising,* invited to meet the new members of staff.

NOTE

(1) The prisoner answered the questions *foolishly.*      [Adjunct]
(2) *Foolishly,* the prisoner answered the questions.      [Disjunct]
(3) *Wisely,* he answered the question *foolishly.*      [Disjunct / Adjunct]

# Aspect

## 13.1. Introduction

**ASPECT is a grammatical category that reflects the way in which the action of a verb is viewed with respect to time.** We recognize two aspects in English, the perfect and the progressive, which may combine in a complex verb phrase, and are marked for present or past tense.

## 13.2. Four Basic Aspectual Classes

This section will introduce four major aspectual classes. Intuitive descriptions and a few examples will be given here.

## I. STATES

The first aspectual class is the class of states. Examples of sentences that report states are given in (1).

(1) a. Roger had a rash.

   b. Karen felt happy.

   c. Jonah owned a horse.

   d. Fred's grandfather weighed two hundred pounds.

   e. This tree is dead.

   f. Thor has a tumor on his toe.

   g. Nora liked the book.

As noted above, states characteristically are interpreted as being more or less uniform throughout an interval; consequently, **they do not have natural endpoints**. In addition, they generally do not involve any action on the part of their subject.

## II. ACTIVITIES

The aspectual class consisting of activity sentences is one whose members, at first glance, look very much like states. Here are some examples:

(2) a. Karen talked to Martha.

    b. Jonah pestered the cat.

    c. Mavis snored.

    d. Martin wandered around.

As their name implies, activities are in general more "active" than states. However, they are similar to states in **not having any natural endpoints**. For instance, there is no point at which an episode of "talking to Martha" would necessarily come to a conclusion, as "eating a peach" would have to.

## III. ACCOMPLISHMENTS

The next aspectual class of verb phrases is generally referred to by the term *accomplishment*. In contrast with states and activities, **accomplishments have natural endpoints**. We have already seen two examples of accomplishment verb phrases: *write a sonnet* and *eat a peach*. Other accomplishment verb phrases occur in the following sentences:

(3) a. Ron peeled the carrot.

    b. Jody repaired the toaster.

    c. Dorothy built a house.

    d. Heifetz performed the Third Partita.

    e. Georgia wrote a sonnet.

    f. A man traveled from Jerusalem to Jericho.

The definable endpoints here are the point at which the carrot is completely peeled, the point at which the toaster works again, the point at which the house is finished, and so on.

## IV. ACHIEVEMENTS

The final aspectual class of verb phrases consists of achievements. Verb phrases of this class are like accomplishment verb phrases in **having a clear natural endpoint**. Yet, as we will see more clearly below, they differ from accomplishments in attaching much greater importance to the endpoint than to any earlier point. Several examples are given in (4).

(4) a. Linda finished her dissertation.
   b. Joel arrived at the meeting.
   c. Fred's goldfish died.
   d. Carol got to Boston.

## 13.3. Rules Concerning Aspectual Adverbial Phrases

Two kinds of adverbial phrases are commonly used to indicate the duration of a state or event. One kind is headed by *in,* the other by *for.*

As a preliminary matter, we need to observe that phrases such as *in four minutes* can be used in two distinct ways, only one of which is relevant in what follows. These phrases can indicate how long a certain event goes on, or they can indicate how long it is before a certain state or event begins. Both readings are possible in the following ambiguous sentence:

(1) Roger Bannister will run a mile in four minutes.

On one reading, the sentence means that the task of running a mile will require four minutes from start to finish. On the other reading, the sentence means that the running of the mile is scheduled to begin four minutes after utterance time. The former interpretation is aspectual in nature, having to do with the time internal to the event itself, whereas the latter interpretation is relational, having to do with the time of the event relative to another time.

In what follows, we will be interested exclusively in the aspectual interpretation.

We turn now to the matter of primary concern. *In* phrases are most acceptable in situations in which natural endpoints exist (accomplishments and achievements).

(2) a. Ron peeled the carrot *in three minutes (?for three minutes)*.  [accomplishment]

   b. Linda finished her thesis *in three months (?for three months)*. [achievement]

By contrast, *for* phrases are most natural in situations in which such endpoints do not exist (states and activities).

(3) a. Roger had a rash *for three days (?in three days)*.   [state]

   b. Karen talked to Martha *for thirty minutes (?in thirty minutes)*. [activity]

The above discussion affords a practical dividend that merits special attention: the differing hospitality to *for* phrases and *in* phrases provides an effective means for distinguishing between states and activities on one hand, and accomplishments and achievements on the other. For instance, suppose that we want to determine the class membership of the two sentences in (4).

(4) a. Simon treated Roger's rash.

   b. Simon healed Roger's rash.

When we add aspectual adverbials of these two kinds to the two sentences, we get a clear result.

(5) a. Simon *treated Roger's rash* for three weeks (*in three weeks).

   b. Simon *healed Roger's rash* in three weeks (*for three weeks).

We conclude from this experiment that treating Roger's rash is a state or an activity, whereas healing Roger's rash is an accomplishment or an achievement. (Tests described later will show that the former is an activity rather than a state, and that the latter is an accomplishment rather than an achievement.)

Applied to a variety of verb phrases, this test yields some surprises. In particular, we find many examples in which two nonstate verb phrases are headed by the same verb but nevertheless have to be placed in different classes. One group of examples is given in (6) and (7).

(6) a. Brenda *drove to San Francisco* in an hour (*for an hour).
   b. Brenda *drove toward San Francisco* for an hour (*in an hour).

(7) a. Gordon *rowed two miles* in an hour (*for an hour).
   b. Gordon *rowed* for an hour (*in an hour).

The contrast between (6a) and (6b) derives from the fact that in the former but not in the latter, a specific goal is attained. Similarly, (7a) asserts that a definite distance was covered, whereas (7b) does not. These examples, then, can be accounted for by the following rule:

(8) Motion verb phrases in which a definite goal is reached or a definite distance is covered count as accomplishments or achievements, whereas motion verb phrases in which neither of these conditions hold count as activities.

The examples in (9)-(12) illustrate another contrast between accomplishments and activities.

(9) a. Freddy *ate a pancake* in two minutes (*for two minutes).
   b. Freddy *ate pancakes* for two hours (*in two hours).

(10) a. Linda *drank a glass of beer* in thirty seconds (*for thirty seconds).
    b. Linda *drank beer* for thirty minutes (*in thirty minutes).

(11) a. Frances *read a story* in thirty minutes (*for thirty minutes).
    b. Frances *read stories* for three hours (*in three hours).

(12) a. Grant *wrote a poem* in three weeks (*for three weeks).
    b. Grant *wrote poetry* for three months (*in three months).

In each of these pairs of examples, the first sentence involves some definite unit or amount of something, whereas the second does not. These examples can be accounted for by the following rule:

(13) If a certain verb phrase has a direct object that denotes a definite number or amount, and the verb phrase is an accomplishment, then a corresponding verb phrase in which the object denotes an indefinite number or amount will count as an activity.

## 13.4. In Adverbials

The most frequently used test for telicity is modification of the event duration by an adverbial of the form *in ten minutes* or *for ten minutes*, in a sentence in the simple past tense. Telic predicates take *in* adverbials; atelic predicates take *for* adverbials.

With an accomplishment an *in* adverbial expresses the duration of the event, as shown in (1):

(1) **accomplishment**
   a. He can **eat** a meat pie **in** 60 seconds.
   b. They **built** the barn **in** two days.
   c. Jones **walked** to town **in** 45 minutes.

Recall that the main difference between accomplishments and achievements is that achievements have no duration. It follows that an adverbial of duration cannot generally express the duration of the event itself with an achievement predicate. Instead, the *in* adverbial is interpreted as stating the time which elapses before the event, and the event occurs at the end of the stated interval. This is illustrated in (2). Sentences like (2b, c) may sound more natural with *within five minutes* or *within three days*.

(2) a. He **recognized** her in a minute or so.
   b. Jones **noticed** the marks on the wallpaper **in** five minutes at most.
   c. Jones **lost** his keys **in** three days.

An atelic predicate is usually anomalous with an *in* adverbial, as illustrated in (3) and (4). For some examples, a possible 'repair' reading is that the stated time elapsed before the event began. For example, (3a) might be interpreted as 'After two years the couple began to be happy'. Even with this interpretation the sentence is usually awkward.

(3) **state**

    a. #The couple **were happy** in two years.

    b. #The room **was sunny** in an hour.

    c. #Jones **knew** him well in five years.

(4) **process**

    a. #They **walked** in the park in half an hour.

    b. #People waiting to buy tickets **chatted** in half an hour.

    c. #Jones **pushed** a supermarket trolley in 90 seconds.

It is essential with the *in* adverbial test to use simple past tense sentences, as *in* adverbials with future tense can modify any class of predicate, with the 'delay before event begins' reading. This is illustrated in (5)-(8). **With the accomplishment in (7) the adverbial is ambiguous between expressing the actual duration of the event and the time to pass before the event begins.**

(5) **state**

    a. They will **be happy** in a year.

    b. The room will **be sunny** in an hour.

    c. Jones will **know** him in five years.

(6) **process**

    a. We will **walk** in the park in an hour.

    b. They'll **chat** in a few minutes.

    c. Jones will **push** the supermarket trolley in 90 seconds.

(7) **accomplishment**

    a. He'll **eat** a meat pie in an hour.

    b. They'll **build** the barn in two weeks.

    c. Jones will **walk** to town in 45 minutes.

(8) **achievement**

    a. He will **recognize** her in a minute.

    b. Jones will **notice** the marks on the wallpaper in a few minutes.

    c. Jones will **lose** his keys in three days.

## 14.1. The Reflexives

The reflexive pronouns are always coreferential with a noun or another pronoun, agreeing with it in gender, number, and person:

(1) Veronica *herself* saw the accident.
(2) The dog was scratching *itself.*
(3) He and his wife poured *themselves* a drink.

The reflexives here are coreferential with *Veronica* (as appositive subject), *The dog* (as object), and *He and his wife* (as indirect object). By contrast, in

(4) He and his wife poured *them* a drink.

the indirect object *them* refers to people other than the subject.

The coreference must be within the clause; thus we have a contrast between

Penelope begged Jane to look after *her*. (= Penelope)
Penelope begged Jane to look after *herself*. (= Jane)

But the item determining the reflexive may be absent from the clause in question; for example, imperative clauses are understood to involve 2nd person, and nonfinite clauses may reveal the subject in a neighbouring main clause:

Look at *yourself* in the mirror!
Freeing *itself* from the trap, the rat limped away.

NOTE Appositive use of reflexives is associated with the need for emphasis.

A few transitive verbs require that subject and object are coreferential:

> They pride *themselves* on their well-kept garden.
> The witness was suspected of having perjured *himself.*

So also *absent oneself, ingratiate oneself, behave oneself,* though with this last the reflexive can be omitted. With some other verbs, there is a threefold choice:

(1) She dressed herself with care.
(2)=(1) She dressed with care.
(3) She dressed him with care.

So also *wash, shave, hide, prepare* etc.

Prepositional complements coreferential with an item in the same clause take reflexive form where the preposition has a close relationship with the verb (as in the prepositional verbs *look at, look after, listen to*). The same holds in sequences concerned with representation:

$$\text{Janet} \begin{Bmatrix} \text{took a photo of} \\ \text{told a story about} \end{Bmatrix} \begin{Bmatrix} herself \ (= \text{Janet}) \\ her \ (\neq \text{Janet}) \end{Bmatrix}$$

But where the prepositional phrase is adverbial (especially relating to space), coreference can be expressed without the reflexive:

> Fred closed the door behind *him.*
> Fred draped a blanket about *him.*

In such cases, context alone would show whether *him* referred to Fred or to someone else; replacement of *him* by *himself* would of course remove any doubt but this would be unusual unless emphasis were required.

## 14.2. Specific Reference

Central pronouns resemble noun phrases with *the* in normally having definite meaning, and they also usually have specific reference. In the case of 3rd person pronouns, the identity of the reference is typically supplied by the linguistic context, anaphorically as in (1) or cataphorically as in (2):

(1) There is *an excellent museum* here **and** everyone should visit *it*.
(2) **When** *she* had examined the patient, *the doctor* picked up the telephone.

In (1), *it* is understood as 'the museum'; in (2), *she* is understood as 'the doctor'. Cataphoric reference is conditional upon grammatical subordination; thus (2) could not be restated as:

*\*She* examined the patient **and** then *the doctor* picked up the telephone.

Anaphoric reference has no such constraint, and (2) could be replaced by:

**When** *the doctor* had examined the patient, *she* picked up the telephone.

# Focus

## 15.1. Dislocation

The prototypical **dislocation** construction has an extra NP located to the left or right of the main part of the clause, consisting of subject and predicate, which we call the nucleus. The extra NP serves as antecedent for a personal pronoun within the nucleus:

| (1)   | NON-DISLOCATED CLAUSE | DISLOCATED CLAUSE |
|-------|-------------------------|-------------------|
| i.   a. | <u>One of my cousins</u> has triplets. | b. <u>One of my cousins</u>, she has triplets. |
| ii.  a. | I think <u>the man next door's</u> car was stolen. | b. <u>The man next door</u>, I think his car was stolen. |
| iii. a. | <u>Her father</u> can be very judgemental. | b. He can be very judgemental, <u>her father</u>. |

Examples (ib/iib) illustrate **left dislocation** (the NP in question is positioned to the left of the clause nucleus), while (iiib) has **right dislocation**. Both are characteristic of relatively **informal style**, such as conversation, especially oral personal narrative.

The pronoun may be the subject within the nucleus, as in (ib) and (iiib). It can also be direct or indirect object, complement of a preposition, and so on. In (iib) it is subject-determiner within the subject of an embedded clause.

Dislocated constructions can be easier to understand than their basic counterpart.

• Left dislocation may put a complex NP early in the sentence, replacing it with a pronoun in the nucleus, so the nucleus is structurally simpler. (Note that in (1iib) the subject-determiner in the dislocated version is simply *his,* whereas in (1iia) it is the more complex genitive *the man next door's.*)

- Right dislocation often has an NP that clarifies the reference of the pronoun. (Imagine that (1iiib) was uttered following *Tom didn't dare tell her father:* the NP *her father* would make clear that *he* means her father, not Tom.)

## 15.2. Extraposition Is Not Right Dislocation

| (2) | BASIC VERSION | VERSION WITH EXTRAPOSITION |
|---|---|---|
| i.   a. | That he was acquitted disturbs her. | b. It disturbs her that he was acquitted. |
| ii.  a. | How she escaped remains a mystery. | b. It remains a mystery how she escaped. |
| iii. a. | To give up now would be a mistake. | b. It would be a mistake to give up now. |

### The difference between dislocation and extraposition

The extraposition construction looks superficially like a special case of right dislocation, but in fact it isn't. The differences are as follows:

- In dislocation the NP placed to the left or right of the nucleus is set apart prosodically from the rest of the clause, but extraposition clauses usually have unbroken intonation.

- The *it* of extraposition is a dummy, not a referential pronoun like the *he* of (1iiib). Thus the extraposed clause doesn't 'clarify the reference' of *it:* the *it* has no reference. If the extraposed clause were omitted, the speaker's intended meaning would normally be lost. The right dislocation (1iiib), by contrast, would make sense even without the final NP.

- Extraposition is stylistically quite neutral, whereas right dislocation, as noted above, belongs mainly to informal style.

## 15.3. Preposing and Postposing

### 15.3.1. Preposing

The contrast between basic order and preposing is seen in such pairs as the following:

| (3) | BASIC ORDER | PREPOSING |
|---|---|---|
| i. | a. I wasn't allowed to watch TV <u>when I was at school</u>. | b. <u>When I was at school</u> I wasn't allowed to watch TV. |
| ii. | a. I said he could have <u>the others</u>. | b. <u>The others</u> I said he could have. |
| iii. | a. They made <u>costume jewellery</u>. | b. <u>Costume jewellery(,)</u> they made. |
| iv. | a. Mr Brown is not <u>humble</u>. | b. <u>Humble(,)</u> Mr Brown is not. |

The preposed element in (ib) is an **adjunct**. Preposing of adjuncts occurs relatively freely. In the other examples it is a **complement** that is preposed. This is more constrained; a preposed complement serves as a link to the preceding discourse, and must be closely related to information previously introduced into the discourse. In (iib), for example, *the others* refers to a subset of some set of things already mentioned.

| The Difference between Dislocation and Fronting ||
|---|---|
| Left-dislocation | Fronting |
| leaves pronoun | does not leave pronoun |
| comma / pause (O) | comma / pause (X) |

### 15.3.2. Postposing

Further examples of postposing are given in (4), along with their default order counterparts:

| (4) | BASIC ORDER | POSTPOSING |
|---|---|---|
| i. | a. They brought <u>an extraordinarily lavish lunch</u> with them. | b. They brought with them <u>an extraordinarily lavish lunch</u>. |
| ii. | a. A man <u>whom I'd never seen before</u> came in. | b. A man came in <u>whom I'd never seen before</u>. |

Chapter

02

The postposed element is an object in (ib), and a dependent (modifier) within the subject NP in (iib).

The major factor leading to the choice of a postposing construction is relative **weight**. Weight of constituents is primarily a matter of length and complexity. In (4i) the object NP is quite heavy in comparison with the PP complement *with them,* and for this reason can readily be put at the end of the clause instead of in the default object position immediately after the verb. Note two things:

- If the object were simply *lunch* then the basic order would normally be required.
- If we lengthened it to something like *an extraordinarily lavish lunch that their daughter had helped them prepare,* then postposing would be more or less obligatory.

A postposed element occurs in a position that tends to receive greater phonological prominence and where complex material is easier to process. **Extraposition is syntactically distinct from postposing** in that it introduces the dummy pronoun *it* into the structure, but it shares with postposing the effect of positioning heavy material (a subordinate clause) at the end of the matrix clause.

# Chapter 03

# Phonetics and
# Phonology

# MEN
# TOR

Mentor Linguistics
전공영어
멘토영어학

# Phonetics (1) : Consonants

## KEY CONCEPT IN THIS CHAPTER

- Vocal Cords: Voiced and Voiceless Sounds
- Place of Articulation: Labials, Alveolars, Velars
- Manner of Articulation: Stops, Fricatives, Affricates, Approximants
- Active articulator vs. Passive articulator
- Consonants vs. Consonantal Sounds
- Classification of Consonants

## TIP

- Sonorants/Obstruents (2018)
- Alveopalatals/Velars (2017)
- Coronals/Alveolar Stops/Flap (2016)
- Alveolars/a Glottal Stop (2015)

**Phonetics** may be described as the study of the sounds of human language.

The understanding of phonological patterns cannot be done without the raw material, phonetics.

We will discuss speech sounds, how they are produced, and how they may be classified.

The sounds of all languages fall into two classes: **consonants** and **vowels**.

**Consonants** are produced with **some restriction or closure** in the vocal tract that impedes the flow of air from the lungs.

## 1.1. Voiced and Voiceless Sounds

The production of any sound involves the movement of air. Most speech sounds are produced by pushing lung air through the **vocal cords**, up the throat, into the mouth or nose and finally out of the body.

**Figure 1.** Open Vocal Cords          **Figure 2.** Closed Vocal Cords

The opening between the vocal cords is the **glottis** and is located in **the voice box** or **larynx**. The tubular part of the throat above the larynx is the **pharynx**. What sensible people call "the mouth," linguists call the **oral cavity** to distinguish it from the **nasal cavity**, which is the nose and the plumbing that connects it to the throat. Finally we have the **tongue** and the **lips**, both of which are capable of rapid movement and shape changing. All of these together make up the **vocal tract**.

Sounds are **voiceless** when **the vocal cords are apart** so that air flows freely through the glottis into the oral cavity.

If **the vocal cords are together**, the airstream forces its way through and causes them to vibrate. Such sounds are **voiced**.

## 1.2. Place of Articulation

We classify consonants according to <u>where in the vocal tract the airflow restriction occurs</u>, called the **place of articulation**. Movement of the tongue and lips creates the constriction, reshaping the oral cavity in various ways to produce the various sounds.

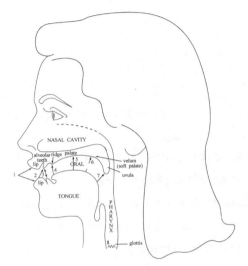

| | |
|---|---|
| 1 | bilabial |
| 2 | labiodental |
| 3 | (inter)dental |
| 4 | alveolar |
| 5 | (alveo)palatal |
| 6 | velar |
| 7 | uvular |
| 8 | glottal |

**Figure 3.** The Vocal Tract and Places of articulation

**Table 1.** Places of Articulation of English Pronunciation

| | | | | | | |
|---|---|---|---|---|---|---|
| **Bilabial** | p | b | m | | | |
| **Labiodental** | f | v | | | | |
| **(Inter)dental** | θ | ð | | | | |
| **Alveolar** | t | d | n | s | z | l | ɹ |
| **Alveopalatal** | ʃ | ʒ | ʧ | ʤ | | |
| **Velar** | k | g | ŋ | | | |
| **Glottal** | h | ʔ | | | | |

**Bilabials** [p] [b] [m] When we produce a [p], [b], or [m], we articulate by bringing both lips together.

**Labiodentals** [f] [v] We also use our lips to form [f] and [v]. We articulate these sounds by touching the bottom lip to the upper teeth.

**Interdentals** [θ] [ð] These sounds, both spelled *th*, are pronounced by inserting the tip of the tongue between the teeth. However, for some speakers the tongue merely touches behind the teeth, making a sound more correctly called **dental**. Watch yourself in a mirror and say *think* or *these* and see where your tongue tip goes.

**Alveolars** [t] [d] [n] [s] [z] [l] [r] All seven of these sounds are pronounced with the tongue raised in various ways to the alveolar ridge.

- For [t], [d], and [n] the tongue tip is raised and touches the ridge, or slightly in front of it.
- For [s] and [z] the sides of the front of the tongue are raised, but the tip is lowered so that air escapes over it.
- For [l] the tongue tip is raised while the rest of the tongue remains down, permitting air to escape over its *sides*. Hence, [l] is called a **lateral** sound. You can feel this in the "l's" of *Lolita*.
- For [r] (IPA [ɹ]), most English speakers either curl the tip of the tongue back behind the alveolar ridge, or bunch up the top of the tongue behind the ridge. As opposed to the articulation of [l], when [r] is articulated, air escapes through the central part of the mouth. It is a **central** liquid.

**Palatals** [ʃ] [ʒ] [ʧ] [ʤ] [j] For these sounds, which occur in *mission* [mɪʃən], *measure* [mɛʒər], *cheap* [ʧip], *judge* [ʤʌʤ], and *yoyo* [jojo], the constriction occurs by raising the front part of the tongue to the palate. (**Alveopalatals** [ʃ] [ʒ] [ʧ] [ʤ])

**Velars** [k] [g] [ŋ] Another class of sounds is produced by raising the back of the tongue to the soft palate or **velum**. The initial and final sounds of the words *kick* [kɪk] and *gig* [gɪg] and the final sounds of the words *back* [bæk], *bag* [bæg], and *bang* [bæŋ] are all velar sounds.

**Glottals** [h] [ʔ] The sound of [h] is from the flow of air through the open glottis and past the tongue and lips as they prepare to pronounce a vowel sound, which always follows [h]. If the air is stopped completely at the glottis by tightly closed vocal cords, the sound upon release of the cords is a **glottal stop** [ʔ]. The interjection *uh-oh*, which you hope never to hear your dentist utter, has two glottal stops and is spelled phonetically [ʔʌʔo]. The late singer Michael Jackson made free use of glottal stops in many of his most well-known songs.

We can summarize the places of articulation with the listings of active and passive articulators.

**Table 2.** Active and Passive Articulators

| Place of articulation | Active articulator | Passive articulator |
|---|---|---|
| Bilabial | upper and lower lips | none |
| Labiodental | lower lip | upper front teeth |
| Dental | tongue tip | upper front teeth |
| Alveolar | tongue blade | alveolar ridge |
| Alveopalatal | tongue blade | rear of alveolar ridge |
| Retroflex | tongue tip or blade | front of hard palate |
| Palatal | tongue front | hard palate |
| Velar | tongue back | soft palate (velum) |
| Glottal | vocal cords | none |

## 1.3. Manner of Articulation

We have described several classes of consonants according to their *places of articulation*, yet we are still unable to distinguish the sounds in each class from one another. What distinguishes [p] from [b] or [b] from [m]? All are bilabial sounds.

Speech sounds also vary in the way the airstream is affected as it flows from the lungs up and out of the mouth and nose. It may be **blocked** or **partially blocked**; the vocal cords may vibrate or not vibrate. We refer to this as the **manner of articulation**.

**Figure 4.** Apertures of Speech Sounds

**Table 3.** Manners of Articulation of English Pronunciation

| Stops | | p | b | t | d | k | g | ʔ | | |
|---|---|---|---|---|---|---|---|---|---|---|
| Affricates | | ʧ | ʤ | | | | | | | |
| Fricatives | | f | v | θ | ð | s | z | ʃ | ʒ | h |
| Nasals (or Nasal Stops) | | m | n | ŋ | | | | | | |
| Approximants | Liquids | l | ɹ | ɭ | | | | | | |
| | Glides | j | w | | | | | | | |
| Flaps | | ɾ | | | | | | | | |

**Stops** [p] [b] [m] [t] [d] [n] [k] [g] [ŋ] [ʧ] [ʤ] [ʔ] Both [t] and [s] are voiceless, alveolar, oral sounds. What distinguishes them? After all, *tack* and *sack* are different words. Stops are consonants in which the airstream is completely blocked in the oral cavity for a short period (tens of milliseconds). All other sounds are **continuants**. The sound [t] is a stop, but the sound [s] is not, and that is what makes them different speech sounds.

- [p], [b], and [m] are *bilabial stops*, with the airstream stopped at the mouth by the complete closure of the lips.
- [t], [d], and [n] are *alveolar stops*; the airstream is stopped by the tongue, making a complete closure at the alveolar ridge.
- [k], [g], and [ŋ] are *velar stops*, with the complete closure at the velum.
- [ʧ] and [ʤ] are *palatal affricates* with complete stop closures. They will be further classified later.
- [ʔ] is a *glottal stop*; the air is completely stopped at the glottis.

**Fricatives** [f] [v] [θ] [ð] [s] [z] [ʃ] [ʒ] [h] In the production of some continuants, the airflow is so severely obstructed that it causes friction, and the sounds are therefore called fricatives. The first of each the following pairs of fricatives is voiceless; the second voiced.

- [f] and [v] are *labiodental fricatives*; the friction is created at the lips and teeth, where a narrow passage permits the air to escape.
- [θ] and [ð] are *interdental fricatives*, represented by *th* in *thin* and *then*. The friction occurs at the opening between the tongue and teeth.

- [s] and [z] are *alveolar fricatives*, with the friction created at the alveolar ridge.
- [ʃ] and [ʒ] are *palatal fricatives*, and contrast in such pairs as *mission* [mɪʃən] and *measure* [mɛʒər]. They are produced with friction created as the air passes between the tongue and the part of the palate behind the alveolar ridge. In English, the voiced palatal fricative never begins words except for foreign words such as *genre*. The voiceless palatal fricative begins the words *shoe* [ʃu] and *sure* [ʃur] and ends the words *rush* [rʌʃ] and *push* [pʊʃ].
- [h] is a *glottal fricative*. Its relatively weak sound comes from air passing through the open glottis and pharynx.

All fricatives are continuants. Although the airstream is obstructed as it passes through the oral cavity, it is not completely stopped.

**Affricates** [ʧ] [ʤ] These sounds are produced by a stop closure followed immediately by a gradual release of the closure that produces an effect characteristic of a fricative. The palatal sounds that begin and end the words *church* and *judge* are voiceless and voiced affricates, respectively. Affricates are not continuants because of the initial stop closure.

**Liquids** [l] [r] In the production of the sounds [l] and [r], there is some obstruction of the airstream in the mouth, but not enough to cause any real constriction or friction. These sounds are liquids.

**Glides** [j] [w] The sounds [j] and [w], the initial sounds of *you* [ju] and *we* [wi], are produced with little obstruction of the airstream. They are always followed directly by a vowel and do not occur at the ends of words (don't be fooled by spelling; words ending in *y* or *w* like *say* and *saw* end in a vowel sound). After articulating [j] or [w], the tongue glides quickly into place for pronouncing the next vowel, hence the term **glide**. The glide [j] is a palatal sound; the blade of the tongue (the front part minus the tip) is raised toward the hard palate in a position almost identical to that in producing the vowel sound [i] in the word *beat* [bit]. The glide [w] is produced by both rounding the lips and simultaneously raising the back of the tongue toward the velum. It is thus a **labio-velar glide**. Where speakers of English have different pronunciations for the words *which* and *witch*, the labiovelar glide in the first word is voiceless, symbolized as [ʍ] (an upside-down *w*). The position of the tongue and the lips for [w] is similar to that for producing the vowel sound [u] in *suit* [sut].

**Approximants** The sounds [w], [j], [r], and [l] may also be called approximants because the articulators approximate a frictional closeness, but no actual friction occurs. The first three are central approximants, whereas [l] is a lateral approximant.

**Table 4.** Consonants of English

|  | Bilabial | Labio-dental | Inter-dental | Alveolar | Alveo-palatal | Retroflex | Palatal | Velar | Glottal |
|---|---|---|---|---|---|---|---|---|---|
| Stops | p  b |  |  | t  d |  |  |  | k  g |  |
| Affricates |  |  |  |  | tʃ  dʒ |  |  |  |  |
| Fricatives |  | f  v | θ  ð | s  z | ʃ  ʒ |  |  |  | h |
| Nasals | m |  |  | n |  |  |  | ŋ |  |
| Liquids |  |  |  | l |  | ɹ |  |  |  |
| Glides | (w) |  |  |  |  |  | j | w |  |

> **NOTE** Symbols between slashes / / are phonemic; those between square brackets [ ] are phonetic.

**Table 5.** Consonants (English and other languages)

|  | Bilabial | Labio-dental | Dental/Interdental | Alveolar | Alveo-palatal | Retro flex | Palatal | Velar | Uvular | Pharyn geal | Glottal |
|---|---|---|---|---|---|---|---|---|---|---|---|
| Stops | **p  b** |  | t̪  d̪ | **t  d** |  | ʈ(t̪)  ɖ(d̪) | c  ɟ | **k  g** | q  G |  | ʔ |
| Affricates | pᶠ |  | tˢ  dᶻ | **tʃ  dʒ** |  |  |  |  |  |  |  |
| Fricatives | ɸ  β | **f  v** | **θ  ð** | **s  z** | **ʃ  ʒ** | ʂ(ş)  ʐ(z) | ç  j | x  ɣ | X  ʁ | ħ  ʕ | **h  ɦ** |
| Nasals | **m** | ɱ | n̪ | **n** |  | ɳ(n̪) | ɲ | **ŋ** | N |  |  |
| Liquids |  |  |  | **l** r ɾ ɹ |  | ɭ(ɭ) | ʎ |  | R |  |  |
| Glides | **w** ɥ |  |  |  |  |  | **j** ɥ | **w** |  |  |  |

> **NOTE** Sounds given in bold type occur in English.

## 1.4. Phonetic Classes of Consonants

• **Noncontinuants and Continuants**

Stops and affricates belong to the class of **noncontinuants**. There is a total obstruction of the airstream in the oral cavity. Nasal stops are included, although air does flow continuously out the nose.

All other consonants, and all vowels, are **continuants**, in which **the stream of air** flows continuously out of the mouth.

(1)

| Noncontinuants | Stops, Affricates, **Nasal stops** |
|---|---|
| Continuants | Fricatives, Liquids, Glides, Vowels |

• **Obstruents and Sonorants**

The non-nasal stops, the fricatives, and the affricates form a major class of sounds called **obstruents**. The airstream may be **fully obstructed, as in nonnasal stops and affricates, or nearly fully obstructed, as in the production of fricatives.**

Sounds that are not obstruents are sonorants.

(2)

| Obstruents | Stops, Affricates, Fricatives |
|---|---|
| Sonorants | Nasals, Liquids, Glides, Vowels |

• **Consonantal Sounds**

**Obstruents, nasal stops, liquids,** and **glides** are all **consonants**. There is some degree of restriction to the airflow in articulating these sounds.

With **glides ([j], [w])**, however, the restriction is minimal, and they are the most vowel-like, and the least consonant-like, of the consonants. Glides may even be referred to as **"semi-vowels"** or **"semi-consonants."**

In recognition of this fact, linguists place the obstruents, nasal stops, and liquids in a subclass of consonants called **consonantal**, from which the glides are excluded.

(3)

| Consonantals | Stops, Affricates, Fricatives, Nasals, Liquids |
|---|---|
| Nonconsonantals | **Glides**, Vowels |

Here are some other terms used to form subclasses of **consonantal** sounds.

**Labials** [p] [b] [m] [f] [v] [w]

**Coronals** [θ] [ð] [t] [d] [n] [s] [z] [ʃ] [ʒ] [ʧ] [ʤ] [l] [ɹ] [ɾ] Coronal sounds are articulated by raising the tongue tip or blade. Coronals include the interdentals [θ] and [ð], the alveolars [t], [d], [n], [s], and [z], the alveopalatals [ʃ] and [ʒ], the affricates [ʧ] and [ʤ], and the liquids [l] and [ɹ].

**Anteriors** [p] [b] [m] [f] [v] [θ] [ð] [t] [d] [n] [s] [z] [l] [ɹ]

**Sibilants** [s] [z] [ʃ] [ʒ] [ʧ] [ʤ] This class of consonantal sounds is characterized by an **acoustic** rather than an **articulatory** property of its members. The friction created by sibilants produces a hissing sound, which is a mixture of high-frequency sounds.

(4)

| Labials | [p] [b] [m] [f] [v] [w] |
|---|---|
| Coronals | [t] [d] [n] [θ] [ð] [s] [z] [ʃ] [ʒ] [ʧ] [ʤ] [l] [ɹ] [ɾ] |
| Velars | [k] [g] [ŋ] [w] |

(5)

| Anteriors | [p] [b] [t] [d] [f] [v] [θ] [ð] [s] [z] [m] [n] [l] [ɹ] |
|---|---|
| Posteriors | [k] [g] [ʃ] [ʒ] [h] [ʧ] [ʤ] [ŋ] [ɹ] |

The three-term description for each of the phonetic symbols:

(6)  a.  [k]   →   voiceless velar stop
     b.  [θ]   →   voiceless (inter)dental fricative
     c.  [b]   →   voiced bilabial stop
     d.  [f]   →   voiceless labiodental fricative
     e.  [ʃ]   →   voiceless alveopalatal fricative
     f.  [j]   →   (voiced) palatal glide
     g.  [t]   →   voiceless alveolar stop

The phonetic symbol for each of the three-term descriptions:

(7)  a.  voiced alveopalatal fricative   →   [ʒ]
     b.  voiced alveolar stop            →   [d]
     c.  voiced velar stop               →   [g]
     d.  voiced dental fricative         →   [ð]
     e.  voiced labio-dental fricative   →   [v]

# Check Up the Points

## ① Glossary for this Section

**affricate**
폐찰음

A sound produced by a **stop** closure followed immediately by a slow release characteristic of a **fricative**; phonetically a sequence of stop + fricative: e.g., the *ch* in *chip*, which is [ʧ] and like [t] + [ʃ].

**alveolar**
치조음

A sound produced by raising the tongue to the **alveolar ridge**: e.g., [s], [t], [n].

**alveolar ridge**
치조, 치조돌기

The part of the hard palate directly behind the upper front teeth.

**alveopalatal**
치조−경구개음

The class of consonants articulated on the region immediately behind the alveolar ridge by raising the tip or blade of the tongue, e.g., [ʃ], [ʒ], [ʧ], [ʤ].

**anterior**
전방음

A phonetic feature of consonants whose place of articulation is in front of the alveo-palatal area, including labials, interdentals, and alveolars.

**approximants**
근접음

Sounds in which the articulators have a near frictional closeness, but no actual friction occurs: e.g., [w], [j], [r], and [l] in English, where the first three are central approximants, and [l] is a lateral approximant.

**continuant**
지속음

A speech sound in which the air stream flows continually through the mouth; all speech sounds except stops and affricates.

**coronals**
설정음

The class of consonants articulated by raising the tip or blade of the tongue, including dentals, alveolars and alveo-palatals: e.g., [θ], [t], [ʃ].

Chapter
03

**consonantal**
자음성

The phonetic feature that distinguishes the class of obstruents, liquids, and nasals, which are [+consonantal], from other sounds (vowels and glides), which are [−consonantal].

**dental**
치음

A place-of-articulation term for consonants articulated with the tongue against, or nearly against, the front teeth. See **interdental**.

**flap**
설탄음

A speech sound in which the tongue touches the alveolar ridge and withdraws. It is often an allophone of /t/ and /d/ in words such as *writer* and *rider*. Also called **tap**.

**fricative**
마찰음

A consonant sound produced with so narrow a constriction in the vocal tract as to create sound through friction: e.g., [s], [f].

**glide**
활음

A speech sound produced with little or no obstruction of the air stream that is always preceded or followed by a vowel: e.g., [w] in *we*, [j] in *you*.

**glottal/glottal stop**
성문음/성문폐쇄음

A speech sound produced with constriction at the glottis; when the air is stopped completely at the glottis by tightly closed vocal cords, a glottal stop is produced.

**glottis**
성문

The vocal cords themselves and/or the opening between the vocal cords.

**interdental**
치간음

A sound produced by inserting the tip of the tongue between the upper and lower teeth: e.g., the initial sounds of *thought* and *those*.

**International Phonetic Alphabet**
IPA, 국제음성기호

The phonetic alphabet designed by the International Phonetic Association to be used to represent the sounds found in all human languages.

**International Phonetic Association**
IPA, 국제음성협회

The organization founded in 1888 to further phonetic research and to develop the International Phonetic Alphabet.

**labial**
순음

A sound articulated at the lips: e.g., [b], [f].

**labiodental**
순치음

A sound produced by touching the bottom lip to the upper teeth: e.g., [v].

**labiovelar**
양순연구개음

A sound articulated by simultaneously raising the back of the tongue toward the velum and rounding the lips. The [w] of English is a labio-velar glide.

**lateral**
설측음

A sound produced with air flowing past one or both sides of the tongue: e.g., [l].

**liquids**
유음

A class of consonants including /l/ and /ɹ/ and their variants that share vowel-like acoustic properties and may function as syllabic nuclei.

**manner of articulation**
조음 방법

The way the air stream is obstructed as it travels through the vocal tract. Stop, nasal, affricate, and fricative are some manners of articulation. See **place of articulation**.

| | |
|---|---|
| **nasal (nasalized) sound**<br>비음 | Speech sound produced with an open nasal passage (lowered velum), permitting air to pass through the nose as well as the mouth: e.g., /m/. See **oral sound**. |
| **noncontinuant**<br>비지속음 | A sound in which air is blocked momentarily in the oral cavity as it passes through the vocal tract. See **stops**, **affricate**. |
| **obstruent**<br>장애음 | The class of sounds consisting of nonnasal stops, fricatives, and affricates. See **sonorants**. |
| **oral sounds**<br>구강음 | A non-nasal speech sound produced by raising the velum to close the nasal passage so that air can escape only through the mouth. See **nasal sound**. |
| **palatal**<br>경구개음 | A sound produced by raising the front part of the tongue to the palate. |
| **palate**<br>경구개 | The bony section of the roof of the mouth behind the alveolar ridge. |
| **place of articulation**<br>조음 위치 | The part of the vocal tract at which constriction occurs during the production of consonants. See **manner of articulation**. |
| **retroflex**<br>반전음 | A sound produced by curling the tip of the tongue back behind the alveolar ridge: e.g., the pronunciation of /ɹ/ by many speakers of English. |
| **secondary articulation**<br>이차 조음 | Any articulation that accompanies another (primary) articulation and that involves a less radical constriction than the primary articulation, such as **palatalization,** or **labialization**. |

| | |
|---|---|
| **sibilant**<br>치찰음 | The class of sounds that includes alveolar and palatal fricatives and affricates, characterized acoustically by an abundance of high frequencies perceived as "hissing," e.g., [s], [ʧ]. |
| **sonorant**<br>공명음 | The class of sounds that includes vowels, glides, liquids, and nasals; nonobstruents. See **obstruents**. |
| **stops**<br>폐쇄음 | [−continuant] sounds in which the airflow is briefly but completely stopped in the oral cavity: e.g., [p], [n], [g]. |
| **tap**<br>설탄음 | A speech sound in which the tongue quickly touches the alveolar ridge, as in some British pronunciations of /r/. Also called **flap**. |
| **velar**<br>연구개음 | A sound produced by raising the back of the tongue to the soft palate, or **velum**. |
| **velum**<br>연구개 | The soft palate; the part of the roof of the mouth behind the hard palate. |
| **voiced sound**<br>유성음 | A speech sound produced with vibrating vocal cords. |
| **voiceless sound**<br>무성음 | A speech sound produced ㅊh open, nonvibrating vocal cords. |

# Check Up the Points

## 2 Key-points in this Section

**Table 1.** Phonetic Sounds of English with Secondary Articulations

| | Bilabial | Labio-dental | (Inter)-dental | Alveolar | Alveo-palatal | Retroflex | Palatal | Velar | Glottal |
|---|---|---|---|---|---|---|---|---|---|
| Stops | p  b | | t̪  d̪ | t  d | | | c  ɟ | k  g | ʔ |
| Labialized Stops | pʷ  bʷ | | | tʷ  dʷ | | | | kʷ  gʷ | |
| Palatalized Stops | pʲ  bʲ | | | tʲ  dʲ | | | | kʲ  gʲ | |
| Aspirated Stops | pʰ | | | tʰ | | | | kʰ | |
| Affricates | | | | | ʧ  ʤ | | | | |
| Fricatives | | f  v | θ  ð | s  z | ʃ  ʒ | | | x  ɣ | h |
| Nasals | m | ɱ | n̪ | n | | ɳ(ŋ) | ɲ | n  ŋ | |
| Devoiced Nasals | m̥ | | | n̥ | | | | n  ŋ̊ | |
| Syllabic Nasals | m̩ | | | n̩ | | | | n  n̩ | |
| Liquids | | | | l  ɹ | | ɻ | | ɫ | |
| Syllabic Liquids | | | | l̩  ɹ̩ | | | | ɫ | |
| Glides | (w) | | | | | | j | w | |

# Phonetics (2) : Vowels

---

## KEY CONCEPT IN THIS CHAPTER

- Tongue Height
- Tongue Position
- Lip Roundness
- Tense vs. Lax
- Monophthongs and Diphthongs
- Oral Vowels vs. Nasalized Vowels

---

(TIP)

- Diphthongs /aɪ/, /ɔɪ/, /aʊ/, /oʊ/ (2018)
- Schwa, Reduced Vowels [ə], [ɪ] (2017)
- Diphthong /aʊ/ (2016)

---

**Vowels** are <u>sounds which are produced without any constriction of the vocal tract</u>. They are nearly always voiced and are usually produced with airflow solely through the oral cavity. (cf. Nasalized Vowels)

**Vowels** are produced with **little restriction** <u>of the airflow from the lungs out through the mouth and/or the nose.</u>

The **quality of a vowel** depends on <u>the shape of the vocal tract</u> as the air passes through. <u>Different parts of the tongue may be high or low in the mouth; the lips may be spread or pursed; the velum may be raised or lowered.</u>

## 2.1. Tongue Height, Tongue Position, and Lip Roundness

We classify vowels according to three questions:

(1) a. How high or low in the mouth is the tongue?

b. How forward or backward in the mouth is the tongue?

c. Are the lips rounded (pursed) or spread?

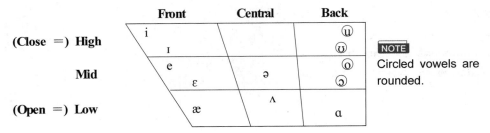

**Figure 1.** English Vowels (from AEP)

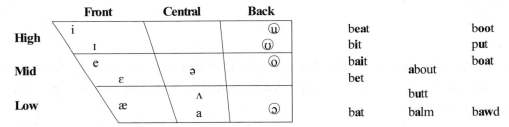

**Figure 2.** Classification of American English Vowels
(from *An Introduction to Language*)

## 2.2. Tense and Lax Vowels

Figure 2 shows that the vowel **[i]** has a slightly higher tongue position than **[ɪ]**. This is also true for **[e]** and **[ɛ]**; and **[u]** and **[ʊ]**. The first vowel in each pair is generally produced with greater tension of the tongue muscles than its counterpart, and it is often a little longer in duration. These vowels can be distinguished by the features tense and lax, as shown in the first three rows of the following:

(2)

| | Tense | | Lax | |
|---|---|---|---|---|
| i | beat | ɪ | bit |
| e | bait | ɛ | bet |
| u | boot | ʊ | put |
| o | boat | ʌ | hut |
| ɔ | saw | æ | hat |
| a | pa | ə | about |
| aɪ | high | | |
| aʊ | how | | |
| ɔɪ | boy | | |

**Tense vowels** may occur at the ends of words: [si], [se], [su], [so], [sɔ], [pa], [saɪ], [haʊ], and [sɔɪ] represent the English words *see, say, sue, sew, saw, pa, sigh, how,* and *soy*.

**Lax vowels** do not ordinarily occur at the ends of words: *[sɪ], *[sɛ], *[sʊ], *[sʌ], *[sæ], and *[sə] are not possible words in English.

A lax vowel is a vowel produced with relatively less tension in the vocal cords and little tendency to diphthongize: e.g., [ʊ] in *put*, [pʊt]. Most lax vowels do not occur at the ends of syllables, that is, [bʊ] is not a possible English word.

Tense vowels are somewhat longer in duration and higher in tongue position and pitch than the corresponding lax vowels: e.g., in English [i] is a high front tense vowel whereas [ɪ] is a high front lax vowel.

## 2.3. Schwa

It is the first vowel sound which occurs in most speakers' pronunciation of the word *about*. This vowel is referred to as **schwa**; it is produced without lip rounding, and with the body of the tongue lying in the most central part of the vowel space, between high-mid and low-mid, and between back and front. Schwa is transcribed as [ə].

This vowel is typically even shorter than the short vowels we have just described, and it differs from those in that it may never occur in a stressed syllable (in *about*, it occurs in the unstressed first syllable; in *elephant*, it occurs in the unstressed second syllable; in *Belinda*, it occurs in the unstressed initial and final syllables).

This vowel occurs in the speech of almost every speaker of English; in later sections, we will consider its relation to English stressed vowels in more detail.

## 2.4. Monophthongs and Diphthongs

A **diphthong** is a sequence of two vowel sounds "squashed" together. Diphthongs are present in the phonetic inventory of many languages, including English. The vowels we have studied so far are simple vowels, called **monophthongs**.

A diphthong is a sequence of two vowels run together as a single phonological unit: e.g., [aɪ], [aʊ], [ɔɪ] as in *bite, bout, boy.*

## 2.5. Oral Vowels and Nasalized Vowels

Vowels, like consonants, can be produced <u>with a raised velum</u> that prevents the air from escaping through the nose, or <u>with a lowered velum</u> that permits air to pass through the nasal passage. When the nasal passage is blocked, **oral vowels** result; when the nasal passage is open, **nasal** (or **nasalized**) **vowels** result. In English, **nasal vowels** occur for the most part <u>before nasal consonants in the same syllable</u>, and **oral vowels** occur <u>in all other places</u>.

The words *bean, bone, bingo, boom, bam,* and *bang* are examples of words that contain nasalized vowels. To show the nasalization of a vowel in a narrow phonetic transcription, an extra mark called a **diacritic**—the symbol ~ (tilde) in this case—is placed over the vowel, as in *bean* [bĩn] and *bone* [bõn].

## 2.6. Syllable

The syllable is a phonological unit consisting of segments around the pivotal vowel or vowel-like (diphthong) sound, which is known as the *nucleus*. The nucleus is the element that every syllable contains, and the other elements are defined in relation to it; the consonant(s) before the nucleus are called the *onset*, and the consonant(s) after it the *coda*. Thus, in the following three words we have syllables with different elements: in <u>a</u> [e], we have only the nucleus with no onset and no coda; in <u>at</u> [æt], the syllable consists of the nucleus and the coda and there is no onset; finally, in <u>cat</u> [kæt], we have all three elements present.

Nucleus and coda together (the elements after the onset) are known as the *rhyme* (or *rime*), thus giving us the following hierarchical structure:

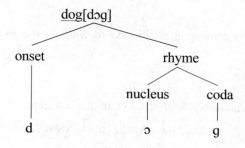

Depending on the structure of the rhyme, syllables are classified as *closed* (with coda(s)) and *open* (lacking coda(s)). Thus, in the word <u>beacon</u> [bi.kən] we have an open first syllable followed by a closed second syllable.

### 1 Glossary for this Section

**diacritic**
첨가부호

Any one of various written or printed marks which, in some particular system of orthography or transcription, may conventionally be added to a letter, phonetic symbol or other character in order to represent some distinction not otherwise representable in the system being used.

**diphthong**
이중모음

A sequence of two vowels run together as a single phonological unit: e.g., [aɪ], [aʊ], [ɔɪ] as in *bite, bout, boy*. See monophthong.

**front vowels**
전설 모음

Vowel sounds in which the tongue is positioned forward in the mouth: e.g., [i], [æ].

**lax vowel**
이완 모음

A vowel produced with relatively less tension in the vocal cords and little tendency to diphthongize: e.g., [ʊ] in *put*, [pʊt]. Most lax vowels do not occur at the ends of syllables, that is, [bʊ] is not a possible English word. See **tense**.

**length**
장단

The duration of a syllable, or the vowel or diphthong it contains, regarded as a phonological characteristic; the phonological correlate of duration. In the IPA, a greater value of length is marked by a following ː .

**monophthong**
단모음

Simple vowel: e.g., [ɛ] in [bɛd]. See diphthong.

**nasal vowel**
비강 모음

A vowel articulated with the velum lowered and hence accompanied by nasal resonance; strictly, a **nasalized vowels**.

**rounded vowel**

원순 모음

A vowel sound produced with pursed lips: e.g., [o].

**schwa**

애매 모음

The unrounded mid central vowel [ə], the neutral vowel produced with the tongue and lips in their rest positions. Schwa is the most frequent vowel in English, occurring for example in the first syllable of *about* and in the second syllable of *carrot*.

**tense**

긴장음, 긴장성

A phonetic feature that distinguishes similar pairs of vowels. Vowels that are [+tense] are somewhat longer in duration and higher in tongue position and pitch than the corresponding [−tense] (lax) vowel: e.g., in English [i] is a high front tense vowel whereas [ɪ] is a high front lax vowel. See **lax vowel**.

**vowel**

모음

A sound produced without significant constriction of the air flowing through the oral cavity.

**vowel quality**

모음의 질

The totality of those distinguishing characteristics of a particular vowel which result from the positions of the tongue and the lips during its articulation, but excluding such features as pitch, loudness, duration and usually also phonation type.

## 2 Key-points in this Section

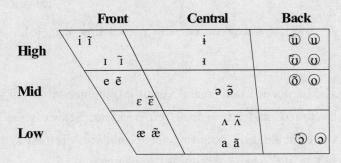

**Figure 1.** Phones of English Vowels

# Phonemes and Their Allophones

## KEY CONCEPT IN THIS CHAPTER

- Phonemes
- Allophones
- Distribution
  - Complementary Distribution
  - Overlapping Distribution
- Minimal Pairs
- Contrastive vs. Non-contrastive
- Phonetic Similarity
- Free Variation

**TIP**

- Minimal Pairs (2017)
- Phonemes /t/, /d/ and their Allophone [ɾ] (2016)
- Phoneme /t/ and its Allophone [ʔ] (2015)

The study of how speech sounds form patterns is **phonology**.

These patterns may be as simple as the fact that the velar nasal cannot begin a syllable in English, or as complex as why *g* is silent in *sign* but is pronounced in the related word *signature*.

To see that this is a pattern and not a one-time exception, just consider the slippery *n* in *autumn* and *autumnal*, or the illusive *b* in *bomb* and *bombard*.

## 3.1. Phonemic Analysis: Sounds That Are the Same but Different

Consider the t-sounds in 'tea', 'steam' and 'sit': the 't' in 'tea' is likely to be aspirated, the 't' in 'steam' unaspirated and the 't' in 'sit' may be unreleased (indicated by ').

> t-sounds: tea [tʰiː] steam [stiːm] sit [sɪt']

It is not difficult to find other groupings of sounds that are both the same and different in just the same way. In parallel with the t-sounds we find that English also has a set of p-sounds—those in 'pea', 'spin' and 'sip'—and a set of k-sounds—those in 'key', 'skin' and 'sick'.

> p-sounds: pea [pʰiː] spin [spɪn] sip [sɪp']
>
> k-sounds: key [kʰiː] skin [skɪn] sick [sɪk']

These groupings like English [t], [tʰ] and [t'], with respect to their simultaneous unity and diversity, have traditionally been dealt with in terms of two levels of representation. That is to say that at a concrete physical level the members of these groups of sounds are different phonetically—they have different phonetic properties—but that abstractly it is useful to group them together as being related. In fact, grouping them together this way reflects the intuition of the native speaker that these sounds are 'the same' in some sense. Taking this view we can say that abstractly English has a 't' and that concretely the pronunciation of this 't' depends on the context in which it occurs. That is, if the 't' of English appears at the beginning of a word it is pronounced as [tʰ], if it appears as part of a consonant cluster following [s] it is pronounced as [t], if it appears at the end of a word it may be pronounced as [t'] (or indeed as [ʔ] or [t]). In the same way, we can say that English 'p' has several concrete representatives: [p], [pʰ] and [p'].

In order to make it clear which level of representation we are dealing with, abstract or concrete, the convention is to use square brackets—[ ]—to enclose the symbol(s) for concrete speech sounds as they are pronounced—phonetic material—and to use slashes—/ /—to enclose the symbols representing the abstract elements—underlying material. Taking again the p-sounds of English, we can say that the group is represented abstractly by /p/, which is pronounced concretely as [p], [pʰ] or [p'], depending on where it occurs in a word. In this same way, the k-sounds consist of /k/, representing the group which is pronounced [k], [kʰ] or [k'].

By using this approach we can distinguish between the surface sounds of a language—those that are spoken—and the underlying organising system. If we know, for instance, that we're talking about underlying /p/, we can predict for English which member of the group of phonetic p-sounds—[p], [pʰ] or [p']—will occur in a particular position. The abstract underlying units are known as **phonemes** while the predictable surface elements are known as **allophones**. In these terms we can say that the phoneme /p/ is realised as the allophone [pʰ] word-initially, as the allophone [p] in an initial cluster following [s] and as the allophone [p'] at the end of a word. The relationship can be shown graphically as follows.

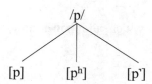

It is important to recognise that this kind of abstraction from the concrete to the underlying is not unique to linguistics and is, in fact, a familiar concept from the natural sciences. Consider water. We all know certain facts about water. First of all, we know that, abstractly, it is composed of two hydrogen molecules and an oxygen molecule, which we represent formally as $H_2O$. We also know that at a temperature below 0°C $H_2O$ appears as ice; between 0°C and 100°C $H_2O$ appears as liquid water and above 100°C $H_2O$ appears as water vapour. Just as the p-sounds [p], [pʰ] and [p'] are underlyingly /p/, water, ice and water vapour are underlyingly $H_2O$.

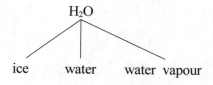

What this means is that in both cases, the phonological and the physical, we have a single entity—i.e. /p/ and $H_2O$—that occurs in various forms in specific environments.

## 3.2. Phonemes: The Phonological Units of Language

**Phonemes** are <u>the basic form of a sound as sensed mentally rather than spoken or heard</u>. Each phoneme—a mental abstraction in itself—is manifested aurally by one or more sounds, called **allophones**, which are <u>the perceivable sounds corresponding to the phoneme in various environments</u>.

For example, the phoneme /p/ is pronounced with the aspiration allophone [pʰ] in *pit* but without aspiration [p] in *spit*.

**Phonological rules** operate on **phonemes** to make explicit <u>which **allophones** are pronounced in which environments</u>.

Consider the voiceless alveolar stop /t/ along with the following examples:

(1)

| Spelling | Phonemic representation | Phonetic representation |
|----------|-------------------------|-------------------------|
| tick | /tɪk/ | [tʰɪk] |
| stick | /stɪk/ | [stɪk] |
| blitz | /blɪts/ | [blɪts] |
| bitter | /bɪtər/ | [bɪɾər] |

In *tick* we normally find an **aspirated** [tʰ], whereas in *stick* and *blitz* we find an **unaspirated** [t], and in *bitter* we find the **flap** [ɾ].

(2)

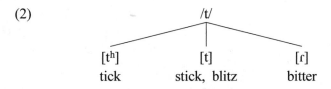

Swapping these sounds around will not change word meaning. If we pronounce *bitter* with a [tʰ], it will not change the word; it will simply sound unnatural (to most Americans). (cf. Allophonic Free Variation)

We account for this knowledge of how t is pronounced by positing a **phoneme** /t/ with three **allophones** [tʰ], [t], and [ɾ].

We also note **phonological rules** to the effect that the **aspirated voiceless stop** [tʰ] occurs <u>initially in a stressed syllable</u>, the **unaspirated** [t] occurs <u>directly before or after /s/</u>, and the **flap** [ɾ] occurs <u>between a stressed vowel and an unstressed vowel</u>.

## 3.3. Phonemes and How to Find Them

**Phonemes** are not physical sounds and directly observable. They are abstract mental representations of the phonological units of a language, the units used to represent words in our mental lexicon.

### 3.3.1. Minimal Pairs

The process of substituting one sound for another in a word to see if it makes a difference is a good way to identify the phonemes of a language. Here are twelve words differing only in their vowels:

(3)

| | | | | | |
|---|---|---|---|---|---|
| beat | [bit] | [i] | boot | [but] | [u] |
| bit | [bɪt] | [ɪ] | but | [bʌt] | [ʌ] |
| bait | [bet] | [e] | boat | [bot] | [o] |
| bet | [bɛt] | [ɛ] | bought | [bɔt] | [ɔ] |
| bat | [bæt] | [æ] | bot | [bat] | [a] |
| bite | [baɪt] | [aɪ] | bout | [baʊt] | [aʊ] |

Any two of these words form a **minimal pair:** <u>two different words that differ in one sound in the same position</u>. The two sounds that cause the word difference belong to <u>different phonemes</u>.

<u>When two sounds are capable of occurring in the same environment, we say that these sounds are in overlapping distribution.</u>

When two sounds are found in an overlapping distribution and the substitution of one sound for the other changes the meaning of the word ([lek] vs. [ɹek], [kɪn] vs. [kɪŋ]), we say that they are in ***contrast***, and they are the manifestations of different phonemes.

The pair [bid] and [bĩd] are not different words; they are variants of the same word. Therefore, [i] and [ĩ] do not belong to different phonemes. They are two actualizations of the same phoneme.

To that total we can add a phoneme corresponding to [ʊ] resulting from **minimal pairs** such as *book* [bʊk] and *beak* [bik]; and we can add one for [ɔɪ] resulting from **minimal pairs** such as *boy* [bɔɪ] and *buy* [baɪ].

(4)      book     [bʊk]     [ʊ]          boy     [bɔɪ]     [ɔɪ]
         beak     [bik]     [i]          buy     [baɪ]     [aɪ]

Our minimal pair analysis has revealed eleven monophthongal and three diphthongal vowel phonemes, namely, /i/, /ɪ/, /e/, /ɛ/, /æ/, /u/, /ʊ/, /o/, /ɔ/, /a/, /ʌ/, and /aɪ/, /aʊ/, and /ɔɪ/. (This set may differ somewhat in other variants of English.)

A particular realization (pronunciation) of a phoneme is called a **phone**. The aggregate of phones that are the realizations of the same phoneme are called the *allophones* of that phoneme.

In English, each vowel phoneme has both an oral and a nasalized allophone. The choice of the allophone is not random or haphazard; it is **rule-governed**.

To distinguish graphically between a phoneme and its allophones, we use slashes / / to enclose **phonemes** and continue to use square brackets [ ] for **allophones** or **phones**. For example, [i] and [ĩ] are allophones of the phoneme /i/.

## 3.3.2. Complementary Distribution

**Minimal pairs** illustrate that some speech sounds in a language are **contrastive** and can be used to make different words such as *big* and *dig*. These contrastive sounds group themselves into the phonemes of that language.

Some sounds are **non-contrastive** and cannot be used to make different words. The sounds [tʰ] and [ɾ] were cited as examples that do not contrast in English, so [ɹaɪtʰəɹ] and [ɹaɪɾəɹ] are not a minimal pair, but rather alternate ways in which *writer* may be pronounced.

Oral and nasal vowels in English are also non-contrastive sounds. What's more, the oral and nasal allophones of each vowel phoneme never occur in the same phonological context, as Table 1 illustrates.

**Table 1.** Distribution of Oral and Nasal Vowels in English Syllables

|  | In Final Position | Before Nasal Consonants | Before Oral Consonants |
|---|---|---|---|
| Oral vowels | Yes | No | Yes |
| Nasal vowels | No | Yes | No |

Where oral vowels occur, nasal vowels do not occur, and vice versa. In this sense the phones are said to complement each other or to be in **complementary distribution**.

Table 2 also shows that aspirated and unaspirated voiceless stop consonants are in **complementary distribution**. In general, then, the allophones of a phoneme are in complementary distribution—never occurring in identical environments.

**Table 2.** Distribution of Aspirated Voiceless Stops

| Syllable-Initial before a Stressed Vowel | | | After a Syllable-Initial /s/ | | | Nonword* | | |
|---|---|---|---|---|---|---|---|---|
| [pʰ] | [tʰ] | [kʰ] | [p] | [t] | [k] | | | |
| *pill* | *till* | *kill* | *spill* | *still* | *skill* | [pɪl]* | [tɪl]* | [kɪl]* |
| [pʰɪl] | [tʰɪl] | [kʰɪl] | [spɪl] | [stɪl] | [skɪl] | [spʰɪl]* | [stʰɪl]* | [skʰɪl]* |
| *par* | *tar* | *car* | *spar* | *star* | *scar* | [paɹ]* | [taɹ]* | [kaɹ]* |
| [pʰaɹ] | [tʰaɹ] | [kʰaɹ] | [spaɹ] | [staɹ] | [skaɹ] | [spʰaɹ]* | [stʰaɹ]* | [skʰaɹ]* |

**Two sounds are in complementary distribution if /X/ never appears in any of the phonetic environments in which /Y/ occurs.**

If two sounds are in complementary distribution, then they are the **allophones of the same phoneme**.

**Complementary distribution** is a fundamental concept of phonology, and interestingly enough, it shows up in everyday life.

### 3.3.3. Phonetic Similarity

Complementary distribution alone is insufficient for determining the allophones when there is more than one allophone in the set. The phones must also be **phonetically similar**, that is, share most phonetic features.

In English, the velar nasal [ŋ] and the glottal fricative [h] are in complementary distribution; [ŋ] does not occur word-initially and [h] does not occur word-finally.

But they share very few phonetic features; [ŋ] is a voiced velar nasal stop; [h] is a voiceless glottal fricative.

Therefore, they are not allophones of the same phoneme; [ŋ] and [h] are allophones of different phonemes.

Two or more sounds are **allophones** (positional variants) **of the same phoneme**, if (a) they are in complementary distribution, and (b) they are phonetically similar.

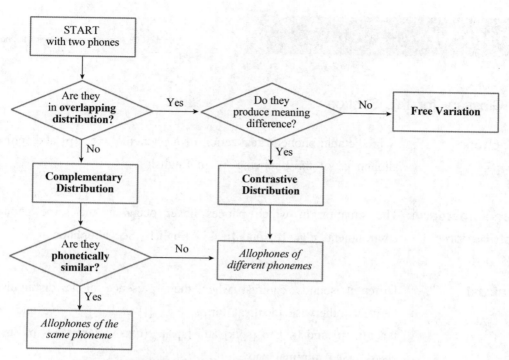

**Figure 1.** Flowchart for Finding Phonemes From Two Sounds

### 3.3.4. Free Variation

**Free variation** is, most commonly, the phenomenon in which any of two or more **phones** can appear in the same position without any effect upon meaning. For example, a single speaker of English may at various times pronounce the word *eat* with two or more of aspirated [tʰ], unaspirated [t], glottalized [ʔt], or unreleased [t̚].

Less commonly, the phenomenon in which either of two or more **phonemes** may be used in the same position in the same word without affecting meaning, as when *economics* or *evolution* may be pronounced either with initial /i/ or initial /ɛ/.

The first type of free variation is related to the allophones of the same phoneme (***allophonic free variation***, as in [k] and [k̚] of *back*). The second type of free variation is related to the realizations of separate phonemes (***phonemic free variation***, as in [i] and [aɪ] of *either*).

# Check Up the Points

## 1 Glossary for this Section

**allophone**
변이음

A predictable phonetic realization of a phoneme: e.g., [p] and [ph] are allophones of the phoneme /p/ in English.

**complementary distribution**
상보적 분포

The situation in which phones never occur in the same phonetic environment: e.g., [p] and [pʰ] in English. See **allophone**.

**contrast**
대립하다

Different sounds contrast when their presence alone distinguishes between otherwise identical forms: e.g., [f] and [v] in *fine* and *vine*, but not [p] and [pʰ] in [spik] and [spʰik] (two variant ways of saying *speak*). See **minimal pair**.

**contrastive distribution**
대립적 분포

The relation between two (or more) phones in which either can occur in the same position in identical surroundings to produce different meanings. See the examples under **contrast**.

**free variation**
자유변이

Alternative pronunciations of a word in which one sound is substituted for another without changing the word's meaning: e.g., pronunciation of *bottle* as [batəl] or [baʔəl].

**minimal pair**
최소대립쌍

Two (or more) words that are identical except for one phoneme that occurs in the same position in each word: e.g., *pain* /pen/, *bane* /ben/, *main* /men/.

**overlapping distribution**
중복적 분포

The relation between two (or more) phonemes occur in some, but not all, of the same positions in words—as, for example, the three English nasals.

**phonetic similarity**
음성적 유사성

Refers to sounds that share most phonetic features.

**phoneme**
음소

A contrastive phonological segment whose phonetic realizations are predictable by rule.

## 2 Key-points in this Section

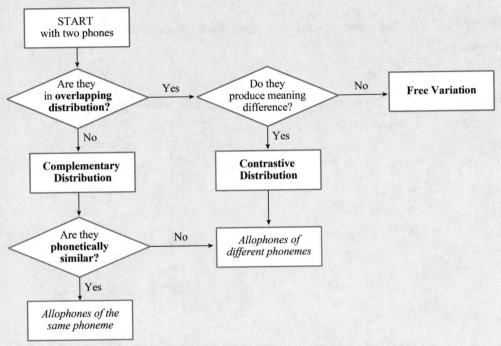

**Figure 1.** Flowchart for Finding Phonemes From Two Sounds

# Distinctive and Nondistinctive Features

## KEY CONCEPT IN THIS CHAPTER

- Distinctive Features or Phonemic Features
- Nondistinctive Features or Allophonic Features
- Redundant Features
- Feature Matrix
- Place of Articulation Features vs. Manner of Articulation Features

## TIP

- [labial], [coronal], [dorsal] (2016)
- Some Distinctive Features for Consonants (2014)
  - [sonorant], [continuant]
  - [anterior], [coronal]

## • Phonemic Consonants and Vowels in English

**Table 1.** Phonemes of English Consonants

|  | Bilabial | Labio-dental | Inter-dental | Alveolar | Alveo-palatal | Retroflex | Palatal | Velar | Glottal |
|---|---|---|---|---|---|---|---|---|---|
| Stops | p  b |  |  | t  d |  |  |  | k  g |  |
| Affricates |  |  |  |  | ʧ  ʤ |  |  |  |  |
| Fricatives |  | f  v | θ  ð | s  z | ʃ  ʒ |  |  |  | h |
| Nasals | m |  |  | n |  |  |  | ŋ |  |
| Liquids |  |  |  | l |  | ɻ |  |  |  |
| Glides | (w) |  |  |  |  |  | j | w |  |

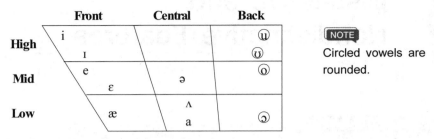

**Figure 1.** Phonemes of English Vowels (from *An Introduction to Language*)

• **Distinctive Features of Phonemes**

**Phonetics** provides the means to describe the phones (sounds) of language, showing how they are produced and how they vary. **Phonology** tells us how various sounds form patterns to create phonemes and their allophones.

When a feature distinguishes one phoneme from another, hence one word from another, it is a **distinctive feature** or, equivalently, a **phonemic feature**.

We consider the phonetic and phonemic symbols to be cover symbols for sets of distinctive features. They are a shorthand method of specifying the phonetic properties of segments. Phones and phonemes are not indissoluble units; they are composed of **phonetic features**, similar to the way that molecules are composed of atoms.

## 4.1. Major Phonetic Classes

Biologists divide life forms into larger and smaller classes. They may distinguish between animals and plants; within animals, between vertebrates and invertebrates; and within vertebrates, between mammals and reptiles; and so on.

Linguists describe speech sounds similarly. All sounds are consonant sounds or vowel sounds, though some play dual roles. Within consonants, all are voiced or unvoiced, and so on. All the classes of sounds described so far in this chapter combine to form larger, more general classes that are important in the patterning of sounds in the world's languages.

Chapter

03

## 4.1.1. Noncontinuants and Continuants

Stops and affricates belong to the class of **noncontinuants**. There is a total obstruction of the airstream in the *oral cavity*. Nasal stops are included, although air does flow continuously out the nose. All other consonants, and all vowels, are continuants, in which the stream of air flows continuously out of the mouth.

## 4.1.2. Obstruents and Sonorants

The non-nasal stops, the fricatives, and the affricates form a major class of sounds called **obstruents**. The airstream may be fully obstructed, as in non-nasal stops and affricates, or nearly fully obstructed, as in the production of fricatives.

Sounds that are not obstruents are **sonorants**. Vowels, nasal stops [m], [n], and [ŋ], liquids [l] and [r], and glides [j] and [w] are all sonorants. They are produced with much less obstruction to the flow of air than the obstruents, which permits the air to resonate. Nasal stops are sonorants because, although the air is blocked in the mouth, it continues to resonate in the nasal cavity.

## 4.1.3. Consonantal Sounds

Obstruents, nasal stops, liquids, and glides are all consonants. There is some degree of restriction to the airflow in articulating these sounds. With glides ([j], [w]), however, the restriction is minimal, and they are the most vowel-like, and the least consonant-like, of the consonants. Glides may even be referred to as "semivowels" or "semi-consonants." In recognition of this fact, linguists place the obstruents, nasal stops, and liquids in a subclass of consonants called **consonantal**, from which **the glides are excluded**.

Here are some other terms used to form subclasses of consonantal sounds. These are not exhaustive, nor are they mutually exclusive (e.g., the interdentals belong to two subclasses). A full course in phonetics would note further classes that we omit.

**Labials** [p] [b] [m] [f] [v] [w] Labial sounds are those articulated with the involvement of the lips. They include the class of *bilabial* sounds [p], [b], and [m], the *labiodentals* [f] and [v], and the *labiovelars* [w].

**Coronals** [θ] [ð] [t] [d] [n] [s] [z] [ʃ] [ʒ] [ʧ] [ʤ] [l] [r] [y] Coronal sounds are articulated by raising the tongue blade. Coronals include the *interdentals* [θ] and [ð], the *alveolars* [t], [d], [n], [s], and [z], the *palatals* [ʃ] and [ʒ], the *affricates* [ʧ] and [ʤ], and the *liquids* [l] and [r].

**Anteriors** [p] [b] [m] [f] [v] [θ] [ð] [t] [d] [n] [s] [z] [l] [r] Anterior sounds are consonants produced in the front part of the mouth, that is, from the alveolar area forward. They include the labials, the interdentals, and the alveolars.

**Sibilants** [s] [z] [ʃ] [ʒ] [ʧ] [ʤ] This class of consonantal sounds is characterized by an acoustic rather than an articulatory property of its members. The friction created by sibilants produces a hissing sound, which is a mixture of high-frequency sounds.

### 4.1.4. Syllabic Sounds

Sounds that may function as the core of a syllable possess the feature **syllabic**. Clearly vowels are syllabic, but they are not the only sound class that anchors syllables.

Liquids and nasals may also be syllabic, as shown by the words *dazzle* [dæzl̩], *faker* [fekr̩], *rhythm* [rɪðm̩], and *wagon* [wægn̩]. (The diacritic mark under the [l̩], [r̩], [m̩], and [n̩] is the notation for syllabic.) Placing a schwa [ə] before the syllabic liquid or nasal also shows that these are separate syllables. The four words could be written as [dæzəl], [fekər], [rɪðəm], and [wægən]. We will use this transcription. Similarly, the vowel sound in words like *bird* and *verb* are sometimes written as a syllabic r: [br̩d] and [vr̩b]. For consistency we shall transcribe these words using the schwa: [bərd] and [vərb].

**Obstruents and glides are never syllabic sounds because an obstruent or glide is always accompanied by a vowel, and that vowel functions as the syllabic core.**

## 4.2. Phonemic Classes of English Phonemes

**Table 2.** Basic Classification of English Phonemes

| Segments | True Consonants | Obstruents | Stops | Voiceless |
|---|---|---|---|---|
| | | | | Voiced |
| | | | Affricates | Voiceless |
| | | | | Voiced |
| | | | Fricatives | Voiceless |
| | | | | Voiced |
| | | Sonorants | Nasals | |
| | | | Liquids | Lateral |
| | | | | Retroflex |
| | Glides | Palatal/Velar | | |
| | Vowels | High/Mid/Low | | |
| | | Front/Central/Back | | |
| | | Rounded/Unrounded | | |
| | | Tense/Lax | | |

**Table 3.** More Specific Classification of English Phonemes

| Segmentals | Consonantals | Obstruents | Noncontinuants | Stops | Voiceless |
|---|---|---|---|---|---|
| | | | | | Voiced |
| | | | | Affricates | Voiceless |
| | | | | | Voiced |
| | | | Continuants | Fricatives | Voiceless |
| | | | | | Voiced |
| | | Sonorants | Noncontinuants | Nasals | |
| | | | Continuants | Liquids | Lateral |
| | | | | | Retroflex |
| | Nonconsonantals | Glides | Palatal/Velar | | |
| | | Vowels | High/Mid/Low | | |
| | | | Front/Central/Back | | |
| | | | Rounded/Unrounded | | |
| | | | Tense/Lax | | |

## 4.3. Distinctive Features of English Consonants

A more explicit description of the phonemes /p/, /b/, and /m/ may thus be given in a **feature matrix** of the following sort.

(1)

|        | p | b | m |
|--------|---|---|---|
| **labial** | + | + | + |
| **voiced** | − | + | + |
| **nasal**  | − | − | + |

Because the phonemes /b/, /d/, and /g/ contrast in English by virtue of **the place of articulation features**—*labial, alveolar,* and *velar*—these place features are also distinctive in English.

(2)

|          | b | m | d | n | g | ŋ |
|----------|---|---|---|---|---|---|
| **voiced**   | + | + | + | + | + | + |
| **labial**   | + | + | − | − | − | − |
| **alveolar** | − | − | + | + | − | − |
| **velar**    | − | − | − | − | + | + |
| **nasal**    | − | + | − | + | − | + |

**Table 4.** Feature Specification of Major Natural Classes of Sounds

| Features | Obstruents | Nasals | Approximants | | Vowels |
|----------|------------|--------|--------------|--------|--------|
|          |            |        | Liquids | Glides |        |
| consonantal | + | + | + | − | − |
| syllabic    | − | − | − | − | + |
| sonorant    | − | + | + | + | + |
| nasal       | − | + | − | − | − |

**Table 5.** Classification of English Segments by Features

| [+ segmental] | $\begin{bmatrix} + & \text{consonantal} \\ - & \text{syllabic} \end{bmatrix}$ | [−sonorant] | $\begin{bmatrix} - & \text{continuant} \\ - & \text{del. rel.} \end{bmatrix}$ | [−voiced] |
|---|---|---|---|---|
| | | | | [+voiced] |
| | | | $\begin{bmatrix} - & \text{continuant} \\ + & \text{del. rel.} \end{bmatrix}$ | [−voiced] |
| | | | | [+voiced] |
| | | | $\begin{bmatrix} + & \text{continuant} \\ - & \text{del. rel.} \end{bmatrix}$ | [−voiced] |
| | | | | [+voiced] |
| | | [+sonorant] | [+nasal] | |
| | | | [−nasal] | [+lateral] |
| | | | | [−lateral] |
| | $\begin{bmatrix} - & \text{consonantal} \\ - & \text{syllabic} \end{bmatrix}$ | [−back]/[+back] | | |
| | $\begin{bmatrix} - & \text{consonantal} \\ + & \text{syllabic} \end{bmatrix}$ | $\begin{bmatrix} + & \text{high} \\ - & \text{low} \end{bmatrix} / \begin{bmatrix} - & \text{high} \\ - & \text{low} \end{bmatrix} / \begin{bmatrix} - & \text{high} \\ + & \text{low} \end{bmatrix}$ | | |
| | | $\begin{bmatrix} - & \text{back} \\ - & \text{central} \end{bmatrix} / \begin{bmatrix} - & \text{back} \\ + & \text{central} \end{bmatrix} / \begin{bmatrix} + & \text{back} \\ - & \text{central} \end{bmatrix}$ | | |
| | | [+rounded]/[−rounded] | | |
| | | [+tense]/[−tense] | | |

**Table 6.** Feature Classification of English Phonemic Consonants (1)

| | [+ anterior] | | [− anterior] | | |
|---|---|---|---|---|---|
| [− continuant] | m | n | | ŋ | [+ sonorant] |
| | p b | t d | tʃ dʒ | k g | [− sonorant] |
| [+ continuant] | f v | θ ð s z | ʃ ʒ | ʍ    h | |
| | | l ɹ | (ɹ) | j w | [+ sonorant] |
| | [− coronal] | [+ coronal] | | [− coronal] | |

**Table 7.** Feature Classification of English Phonemic Consonants (2)

| [+ labial] | | | [− labial] | | | | |
|---|---|---|---|---|---|---|---|
| [− coronal] | | | [+ coronal] | | | [− coronal] | |
| [− velar] | | | | | | [+ velar] | [− velar] |
| p b | | | t d | | | k g | |
| | | | | tʃ dʒ | | | |
| ʍ | f v | θ ð | s z | ʃ ʒ | | ʍ | h |
| m | | | n | | | ŋ | |
| | | | l | | | | |
| | | | ɹ | (ɹ) | | | |
| w | | | | | j | w | |
| [− alveolar ] | | | [+ alveolar] | | | [− alveolar ] | |
| [− palatal] | | | | [+ palatal] | | [− palatal] | |
| [+ anterior] | | | | [− anterior] | | | |

**Table 8.** Feature Specifications for American English Consonants

| Features | p | b | m | t | d | n | k | g | ŋ | f | v | θ | ð | s | z | ʃ | ʒ | tʃ | dʒ | l | ɹ | j | w | h |
|---|---|---|---|---|---|---|---|---|---|---|---|---|---|---|---|---|---|---|---|---|---|---|---|---|
| consonantal | + | + | + | + | + | + | + | + | + | + | + | + | + | + | + | + | + | + | + | + | + | − | − | + |
| syllabic | − | − | − | − | − | − | − | − | − | − | − | − | − | − | − | − | − | − | − | − | − | − | − | − |
| sonorant | − | − | + | − | − | + | − | − | + | − | − | − | − | − | − | − | − | − | − | + | + | + | + | − |
| continuant | − | − | − | − | − | − | − | − | − | + | + | + | + | + | + | + | + | − | − | + | + | + | + | + |
| delayed release | − | − | − | − | − | − | − | − | − | − | − | − | − | − | − | − | − | + | + | − | − | − | − | − |
| nasal | − | − | + | − | − | + | − | − | + | − | − | − | − | − | − | − | − | − | − | − | − | − | − | − |
| voiced | − | + | + | − | + | + | − | + | + | − | + | − | + | − | + | − | + | − | + | + | + | + | + | − |
| labial | + | + | + | − | − | − | − | − | − | + | + | − | − | − | − | − | − | − | − | − | − | − | + | − |
| alveolar | − | − | − | + | + | + | − | − | − | − | − | − | − | + | + | − | − | − | − | + | − | − | − | − |
| palatal | − | − | − | − | − | − | − | − | − | − | − | − | − | − | − | + | + | + | + | − | + | + | − | − |
| velar | − | − | − | − | − | − | + | + | + | − | − | − | − | − | − | − | − | − | − | − | − | − | + | − |
| anterior | + | + | + | + | + | + | − | − | − | + | + | + | + | + | + | − | − | − | − | + | − | − | − | − |
| coronal | − | − | − | + | + | + | − | − | − | − | − | + | + | + | + | + | + | + | + | + | + | − | − | − |
| sibilant | − | − | − | − | − | − | − | − | − | − | − | − | − | + | + | + | + | + | + | − | − | − | − | − |

NOTE  The phonemes /ɹ/ and /l/ are distinguished by the feature [lateral], not shown here.
/l/ is the only phoneme that would be [+lateral].

## 4.4. Distinctive Features of English Vowels

Vowels, too, have distinctive features. For example, the feature [±back] distinguishes the vowel in *look* [lʊk] ([+back]) from the vowel in *lick* [lɪk] ([−back]) and is therefore distinctive in English. Similarly, [±tense] distinguishes [i] from [ɪ] (*beat* versus *bit*)—[u] from [ʊ] (*pool* versus *pull*)—and is also a distinctive feature of the English vowel system.

(3)

|  | u | ʊ | ɪ | i |
|------|---|---|---|---|
| **high** | + | + | + | + |
| **back** | + | + | − | − |
| **tense** | + | − | − | + |

**Table 9.** Feature Classification of English Phonemic Vowels

| | | [−back] | | [+back] | |
|---|---|---|---|---|---|
| | | [−central] | [+central] | [−central] | |
| [+high] | [−low] | i | | u | [+tense] |
| | | ɪ | | ʊ | [−tense] |
| [−high] | | e | | o | [+tense] |
| | | ɛ | ə | | [−tense] |
| | [+low] | æ | ʌ | | |
| | | a | | ɔ | [+tense] |
| | | [−round] | | [+round] | |

**Table 10.** Feature Specifications for American English Vowels

| Features | i | ɪ | e | ɛ | æ | u | ʊ | o | ɔ | a | ʌ | ə |
|----------|---|---|---|---|---|---|---|---|---|---|---|---|
| high | + | + | − | − | − | + | + | − | − | − | − | − |
| low | − | − | − | − | + | − | − | − | + | + | + | − |
| back | − | − | − | − | + | + | + | + | − | − | − | − |
| central | − | − | − | − | − | − | − | − | − | + | + | + |
| round | − | − | − | − | + | + | + | + | − | − | − | − |
| tense | + | − | + | − | − | + | − | + | + | + | − | − |

## 4.5. Nondistinctive Features

As we saw, **aspiration** is not a distinctive feature of English consonants. It is a **nondistinctive** or **redundant** or **predictable** feature (all equivalent terms).

Some features may be distinctive for one class of sounds but nondistinctive for another. For example, **nasality** is a distinctive feature of English consonants but not a distinctive feature for English vowels. Thus the feature **nasal** is **nondistinctive** for *vowels*.

Another nondistinctive feature in English is aspiration for voiceless stops. The voiceless aspirated stops [pʰ], [tʰ], and [kʰ] and the voiceless unaspirated stops [p], [t], and [k] are in complementary distribution. The presence of this feature is predicted by rule and need not be learned by speakers when acquiring words.

## 4.6. Natural Classes of Speech Sounds

Many languages have rules that refer to [+voiced] and [−voiced] sounds. For example, the aspiration rule in English applies to the class of [−voiced] noncontinuant sounds in word-initial position. The rule automatically applies to initial /p/, /t/, /k/, and /ʧ/.

**Phonological rules** often apply to **natural classes** of sounds. A **natural class** is a group of sounds described by a small number of distinctive features such as [−voiced], [−continuant], which describe /p/, /t/, /k/, and /ʧ/. Any individual member of a natural class would require more features in its description than the class itself, so /p/ is not only [−voiced], [−continuant], but also [+labial].

The relationships among **phonological rules** and **natural classes** illustrate why segments are to be regarded as bundles of features. If segments were not specified as feature matrices, the similarities among /p/, /t/, and /k/ or /m/, /n/, and /ŋ/ would be lost. It would be just as likely for a language to have a rule such as

(4) Rule 1 : Nasalize vowels before p, i, or z.

as to have a rule such as

(5) Rule 2 : Nasalize vowels before m, n, or ŋ.

Rule 1 has no phonetic explanation, whereas Rule 2 does: the lowering of the velum in anticipation of a following nasal consonant causes the vowel to be nasalized. In Rule 1, the environment is a motley collection of unrelated sounds that cannot be described with a few features. Rule 2 applies to the natural class of nasal consonants, namely sounds that are [+ consonantal, +nasal].

The various classes of sounds also define **natural classes** to which the phonological rules of all languages may refer. They also can be specified by + and − feature values.

Formally, any class which can be characterized using less information than is required to characterize any part of it. Thus, the class of voiceless segments in English is a **natural class**, since it is picked out by the single specification [−voiced], whereas any subclass of voiceless segments can only be specified by adding further information. Informally, any class of linguistic objects which pattern in the same way and which therefore need to be referred to in a linguistic description as a single unitary class. One of the chief functions of **distinctive features** is to allow us to represent **natural classes** in the second sense as **natural classes** in the first sense.

# Check Up the Points

## 1 Glossary for this Section

**aspirated**
기식음, 기식성

Describes a voiceless stop produced with a puff of air that results when the vocal cords remain open for a brief period after the release of the stop: e.g., the [pʰ] in *pit*. See *unaspirated*.

**consonantal**
자음성

The phonetic feature that distinguishes the class of obstruents, liquids, and nasals, which are [+consonantal], from other sounds (vowels and glides), which are [−consonantal].

**delayed release**
지연개방성

A distinctive feature defined as 'released with turbulence ... in the vocal tract', and designed to distinguish affricates [+del. rel.] from stops [−del. rel.]. Ant. **instantaneous release**.

**distinctive**
변별적

Describes linguistic elements that contrast, e.g., [f] and [v] are distinctive segments. Voice is a distinctive phonetic feature of consonants.

**distinctive features**
변별 자질

Phonetic properties of phonemes that account for their ability to contrast meanings of words, e.g., *voice*, *tense*. Also called **phonemic features**.

**feature matrix**
자질 묶음

A representation of phonological segments in which the columns represent segments and the rows represent features, each cell being marked with a + or − to designate the presence or absence of the feature for that segment.

**natural class**
자연 부류

A class of sounds characterized by a phonetic property or feature that pertains to all members of the set: e.g., the class of stops. A natural class may be defined with a smaller feature set than that of any individual member of the class.

| | |
|---|---|
| **nonredundant**<br>비잉여적 | A phonetic feature that is distinctive: e.g., stop, voice, but not aspiration in English. |
| **phone**<br>음성 | A phonetic realization of a phoneme. phoneme A contrastive phonological segment whose phonetic realizations are predictable by rule. |
| **phonemic feature**<br>음소 자질 | Phonetic properties of phonemes that account for their ability to contrast meanings of words, e.g., *voice*, *tense*. Also called **distinctive features**. |
| **phonemic representation**<br>음소 표기 | The phonological representation of words and sentences prior to the application of phonological rules. |
| **phonetic alphabet**<br>음성 기호 | Alphabetic symbols used to represent the phonetic segments of speech in which there is a one-to-one relationship between each symbol and each speech sound. |
| **phonetic features**<br>음성 자질 | Phonetic properties of segments (e.g., voice, nasal, alveolar) that distinguish one segment from another. |
| **phonetic representation**<br>음성 표기 | The representation of words and sentences after the application of phonological rules; symbolic transcription of the pronunciation of words and sentences. |
| **phonetic similarity**<br>음성적 유사성 | Refers to sounds that share most phonetic features. |

| | |
|---|---|
| **phonological rules**<br>음운 규칙 | Rules that apply to phonemic representations to derive phonetic representations or pronunciation. |
| **phonology**<br>음운론 | The sound system of a language; the component of a grammar that includes the inventory of sounds (phonetic and phonemic units) and rules for their combination and pronunciation; the study of the sound systems of all languages. |
| **predictable feature**<br>예측가능 자질 | A nondistinctive, noncontrastive, redundant phonetic feature: e.g., aspiration in English voiceless stops, or nasalization in English vowels. |
| **redundant**<br>잉여적 | Describes a nondistinctive, nonphonemic feature that is predictable from other feature values of the segment, e.g., [+voice] is redundant for any [+nasal] phoneme in English because all nasals are voiced. |
| **sonorant**<br>공명성 | A distinctive feature defined as 'produced with a configuration of the vocal tract cavity in which spontaneous vocal cord vibration is possible'. Obstruents are [−sonorant]; all other segments are [+sonorant]. |
| **syllabic**<br>음절핵성 | A phonetic feature of those sounds that may constitute the nucleus of syllables; all vowels are syllabic, and liquids and nasals may be syllabic in such words as *towel*, *button*, *bottom*. |
| **unaspirated**<br>무기음 | Phonetically voiceless stops in which the vocal cords begin vibrating immediately upon release of the closure: e.g., [p] in *spot*. See **aspirated**. |

## 2 Key-points in this Section

**Table 1.** Feature Specifications for American English Consonants

| Features | p | b | m | t | d | n | k | g | ŋ | f | v | θ | ð | s | z | ʃ | ʒ | tʃ | dʒ | l | ɹ | j | w | h |
|---|---|---|---|---|---|---|---|---|---|---|---|---|---|---|---|---|---|---|---|---|---|---|---|---|
| consonantal | + | + | + | + | + | + | + | + | + | + | + | + | + | + | + | + | + | + | + | + | + | − | − | + |
| syllabic | (−) | (−) | (−) | (−) | (−) | (−) | (−) | (−) | (−) | (−) | (−) | (−) | (−) | (−) | (−) | (−) | (−) | (−) | (−) | (−) | (−) | − | − | (−) |
| sonorant | − | − | (+) | − | − | (+) | − | − | (+) | − | − | − | − | − | − | − | − | − | − | + | + | + | + | − |
| continuant | − | − | (−) | − | − | (−) | − | − | (−) | + | + | + | + | + | + | + | + | − | − | (+) | (+) | (+) | (+) | + |
| delayed release | − | − | (−) | − | − | (−) | − | − | (−) | (−) | (−) | (−) | (−) | (−) | (−) | (−) | (−) | + | + | (−) | (−) | (−) | (−) | (−) |
| nasal | − | − | + | − | − | + | − | − | + | − | − | − | − | − | − | − | − | − | − | − | − | − | − | − |
| voiced | − | + | (+) | − | + | (+) | − | + | (+) | − | + | − | + | − | + | − | + | − | + | (+) | (+) | (+) | (+) | − |
| labial | + | + | + | − | − | − | − | − | − | + | + | − | − | − | − | − | − | (−) | (−) | (−) | (−) | − | + | − |
| alveolar | − | − | − | + | + | + | − | − | − | − | − | − | − | + | + | − | − | − | − | + | + | − | − | − |
| palatal | − | − | − | − | − | − | − | − | − | − | − | − | − | − | − | + | + | + | + | − | − | + | − | − |
| velar | − | − | − | − | − | − | + | + | + | − | − | − | − | − | − | − | − | − | − | − | − | − | + | − |
| anterior | + | + | + | + | + | + | − | − | − | + | + | + | + | + | + | − | − | − | − | + | + | − | + | − |
| coronal | − | − | − | + | + | + | − | − | − | − | − | − | − | + | + | + | + | + | + | + | + | + | − | − |
| sibilant | − | − | − | − | − | − | − | − | − | − | − | − | − | + | + | + | + | + | + | − | − | − | − | − |

**NOTE** The parenthesized feature values in the above table are generally predictable.

**Table 2.** Feature Specifications for American English Vowels

| Feature | i | ɪ | e | ɛ | æ | u | ʊ | o | ɔ | ɑ | ʌ | ə |
|---|---|---|---|---|---|---|---|---|---|---|---|---|
| consonantal | (−) | (−) | (−) | (−) | (−) | (−) | (−) | (−) | (−) | (−) | (−) | (−) |
| syllabic | + | + | + | + | + | + | + | + | + | + | + | + |
| high | + | + | − | − | (−) | + | + | − | (−) | (−) | (−) | − |
| low | (−) | (−) | − | − | + | (−) | (−) | − | + | + | + | − |
| back | − | − | − | − | − | + | + | + | + | − | − | − |
| central | − | − | − | − | − | − | − | − | − | + | + | + |
| round | − | − | − | − | − | + | + | + | + | − | − | − |
| tense | + | − | + | − | − | + | − | + | + | + | − | − |

**NOTE** The parenthesized feature values in the above table are generally predictable.

# Syllables and Syllabification

(TIP)

- The Word-Internal Consonant Sequence -*st*- and Syllabification (2018)
- Stressd Syllables and Reduced Syllables (2017)
- Codas following the diphthong /aʊ/ (2016)
- /t/-Glottalization in a Coda Position of a Syllable (2015)
- /l/-Velarization in a Rhyme Position (2014)

By far the most widely discussed phonological suprasegmental is the syllable.

## 5.1. Syllable Structure

Words are composed of one or more syllables. A syllable is a phonological unit composed of one or more phonemes. Every syllable has a nucleus, which is usually a vowel (but can be a syllabic liquid or nasal). The nucleus may be preceded and/or followed by one or more phonemes called the syllable onset and coda.

From a very early age English-speaking children learn that certain words rhyme. In rhyming words, the nucleus and the coda of the final syllable of both words are identical, as in the following jingle:

(1)　Jack and **Jill**　　　　　Jack fell **down**
　　　Went up the **hill**　　　And broke his **crown**
　　　To fetch a pail of water.　And Jill came tumbling after.

For this reason, the nucleus + coda constitute the subsyllabic unit called a rime.

A syllable thus has a hierarchical structure. Using the IPA symbol σ (lowercase Greek letter 'sigma') for the phonological syllable, the hierarchical structure of the monosyllabic word *splints* can be shown:

(2)

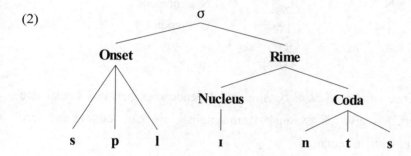

Beyond its relevance for the phonological rules, syllable has an important role with respect to the phonotactic constraints in languages. This refers to the system of arrangement of sounds and sound sequences.

It is on this basis that a speaker of English can judge some new form as possible or impossible word.

For example, both [blɪt] and [bmɪt] are non-existent as English words. If asked to choose between the two, a native speaker of English, without a moment's hesitation, would go for [blɪt].

The reason for this is that [bl] is a possible onset cluster in English, whereas [bm] is not.

This is not to say that no English word can have a [bm] sequence. Words such as submarine [sʌbməɹin] and submission [sʌbmɪʃən] are clear demonstrations of the fact that we can have /m/ after /b/ in English.

This, however, is possible only if these two sounds are in different syllables.

So the rejection of a word such as [bmɪt] is strictly based on a syllable-related generalization but not on a segment-related generalization.

(3)

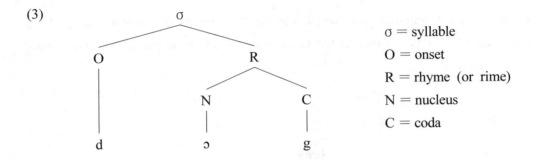

σ = syllable
O = onset
R = rhyme (or rime)
N = nucleus
C = coda

Further attesting the existence of rhyme as a constituent, dependencies between nuclei and codas are commonly found. To give an example from English, we can look at the /aʊ/ nucleus and its relationship with its coda:

(4)    brown    [bɹaʊn]        But    *[bɹaʊŋ] / [bɹaʊm]
       spouse   [spaʊs]               *[spaʊf]
       trout    [tɹaʊt]               *[tɹaʊp] / [tɹaʊk]
       rouse    [ɹaʊz]                *[ɹaʊv]
       crowd    [kɹaʊd]               *[kɹaʊg] / [kɹaʊb]

What these examples demonstrate is that the coda that follows /aʊ/ has to be alveolar or interdental (e.g. *mouth, south*); this nucleus cannot be followed by labial or velar consonants.

        cf. mouth [maʊθ], south [saʊθ]        cf, [labial], [coronal], [velar]

Let us look at the words *blue, side, wind,* and *ground.*

(5)

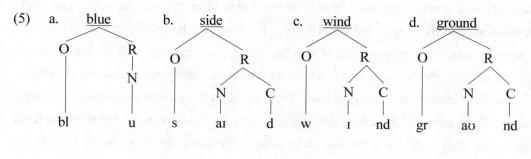

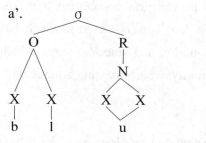

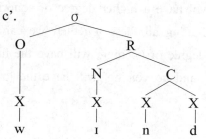

And let us look at the words *dog, chart* and *drench.*

(6)

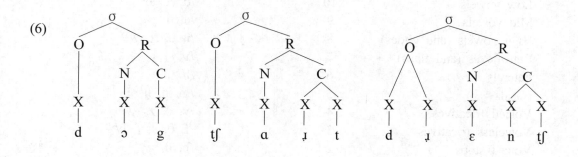

## 5.2. Sonority

The sonority of a sound is primarily related to the degree of opening of the vocal tract during its articulation. The more open the vocal tract is for a sound, the higher its sonority will be. Thus vowels, which are produced with a greater degree of opening, will be higher on the sonority scale than fricatives or stops, which are produced either with a narrow opening or with a complete closure of the articulators. The second, and relatively secondary (ancillary), dimension is the sound's propensity for voicing. This becomes relevant when the stricture (degree of opening) is the same for two given sounds; the sound that has voicing (e.g. voiced fricative) will have a higher degree of sonority than its voiceless counterpart (e.g. voiceless fricative). Putting all these together, we can say that low vowels (/æ, ɑ/), which have the maximum degree of opening, will have the highest sonority; and voiceless stops, which have no opening and no voicing, will have the lowest sonority. The remaining sounds will be in between.

In this book, we adopt the following 10-point scale suggested by Hogg and McCully (1987):

| (7) | **Sounds** | **Sonority values** | **Examples** |
|---|---|---|---|
| | Low vowels | 10 | /ɑ, ʌ, æ/ |
| | Mid vowels | 9 | /e, o/ |
| | High vowels (and glides) | 8 | /i, u, (j, w)/ |
| | Retroflexes (and flaps) | 7 | /ɹ/ |
| | Laterals | 6 | /l/ |
| | Nasals | 5 | /m, n, ŋ/ |
| | Voiced fricatives | 4 | /v, ð, z, ʒ/ |
| | Voiceless fricatives | 3 | /f, θ, s, ʃ, h/ |
| | Voiced stops | 2 | /b, d, g/ |
| | Voiceless stops | 1 | /p, t, k/ |

(8)

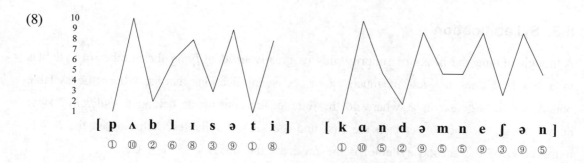

As we saw earlier, in English we can have syllables that do not contain a vowel. In these cases, the most sonorant consonant will be the syllable peak (i.e. syllabic consonant):

(9)

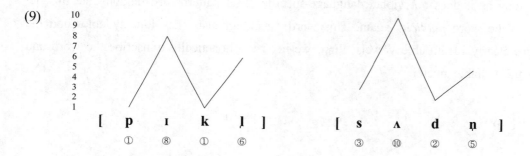

Although the principle of equating the sonority peaks to the number of syllables would hold for thousands of English words, it does not mean that it is without exceptions. We must acknowledge the fact that some English onset clusters with /s/ as the first consonant (e.g. stop [stɑp]), and coda clusters with /s/ as the last consonant (e.g. box [bɑks]), do violate this principle.

(10)

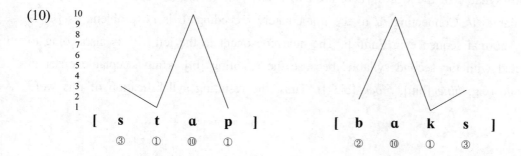

## 5.3. Syllabification

Although finding the peaks of sonority aids us greatly in identifying the number of syllables in a word, it does not tell us much about the syllabification, that is, where the syllable boundaries lie. For example, where do the intervocalic consonants belong in *publicity*? How do we assign /b/ and /l/ between the first and the second syllables? What about the /s/? Is it the coda of the second syllable or the onset of the third?

The principle on which we make the decision in these cases, which is known as the "**maximal onset principle**," simply assigns any series of intervocalic consonants to the syllable on the right as long as it does not violate language-specific onset patterns. To demonstrate this, let us look at the word *publicity* again. This word, unambiguously, has four syllables and the nuclei are clearly identifiable vowels. First, we need to phonetically transcribe the word and identify the syllable nuclei.

(11)     [ p   ʌ   b   l   ɪ   s   ə   t   i   ]

The next step is to go to the end of the word and start connecting the nucleus of each syllable with the surrounding consonants. The last syllable has no coda, and the nucleus will be attached to the preceding /t/, because [ti] is an acceptable sequence in English. After this, we move to the nucleus of the preceding (third) syllable, which is an [ə]; the lack of any coda in this syllable and the acceptability of a [sə] sequence in English tell us that this will be the third syllable of the word. There are two consonants to the left of the nucleus of the second syllable /ɪ/. Connecting /l/ to the immediately preceding /l/ is no problem, as [lɪ] is a perfectly normal sequence in English. The next consonant to the left, /b/, is also going to be connected with the second syllable, because the resulting [bl] is an acceptable onset in the language (e.g. *blue* [blu], *block* [blɔk]). Thus, the resulting syllabification of this word will be:

(12)     [ p   ʌ   .   b   l   ɪ   .   s   ə   .   t   i   ]

Sometimes, we see the same sequences of sounds syllabified differently in different words. We will illustrate this phenomenon in the following two words, *complain* and *temptation*. The syllabifications of these two words are given in the following:

(13)　　a.　　[ k　　ə　　m　　.　　p　　l　　e　　n　　]

　　　　 b.　　[ t　　ɛ　　m　　p　　.　　t　　e　　.　　ʃ　　ə　　n　　]

Our focus will be the [mp] sequence the two words share. As the syllabifications above make clear, the same sequence behaves differently in the two words. While in *temptation* [tɛmp.te.ʃən] the [mp] sequence is the double coda of the first syllable, in *complain* [kəm.plen] the two sounds fall into separate syllables; [m] belongs to the coda of the first syllable, and [p] is part of the double onset of the second syllable. The reason for this difference is what is allowed as a maximal onset in English. Since [pt] is not a possible onset, [p] has to stay in the first syllable of *temptation*. In *complain,* however, [p] is part of the onset of the second syllable because [pl] is a permissible onset in English.

Dividing the word *complain* as [kəmp.len] would not have resulted in any violation of English onsets or codas, because both [kəmp] and [len] are permissible in the language. However, doing this would have meant maximizing the coda. The observed syllabification [kəm.plen], on the other hand, follows the maximization of allowed onsets in English. Assigning intervocalic consonants as onsets of the following syllable rather than coda of the preceding syllable forms the basis of the maximal onset principle, and this is derived from the fact that onsets are more basic than codas in languages. All languages, without a single exception, have CV (open) syllables, whereas many languages lack VC (closed) syllables.

## 5.4. Syllable Weight and Ambisyllabicity

A consonant that is (part of) a permissible onset (cluster) is **ambisyllabic** if it occurs immediately after a short vowel /ɪ, ɛ, æ, ʌ, ʊ, ɔ/ɑ/ (i.e., lax vowels plus [ɔ/ɑ]) that forms the nucleus of a stressed syllable.

If we ask for the spoken syllabification of the following words

(14) medicine      federal

     origin      positive

     happen      Canada

     finish      river

     funny      punish

we may receive different reactions from native speakers of English.

While several speakers go along with the syllabifications based on the maximum onset principle and give [mɛ/də/sən], [hæ/pən], [pɑ/zə/təv], etc., some others may not feel very comfortable with such divisions and may suggest the inclusion of the consonants after the vowel in the first syllable as the coda of that syllable. There are some obvious similarities between these words and the ones we discussed in relation to written syllabification above. This is related to the kind of vowel sounds that are represented by the orthographic letters a, e, i, o, u. In all these words, the vowel sounds /ɛ, ɔ, æ, I, ʌ/ (from top to bottom of the list of examples) represented by the orthographic letters in question are in the stressed syllables, and the problem is related to what happens to the consonant following that vowel. This issue is directly related to stress and syllable weight.

Syllable weight is an important factor in stress assignment in languages. The weight of a syllable is determined by its rhyme structure. In English, a syllable is light if it has a non-branching rhyme (a short vowel and no coda in its rhyme, as in the first syllable of around); it is heavy if it has a branching rhyme (a short vowel followed by a coda (simple or complex), or a long vowel or a diphthong with or without a following coda). This can be shown as follows:

**Rhyme of a light syllable**

short V: **a**.mong

**Rhyme of a heavy syllable**

short V + coda: **net, nest**

long V/diph. + (coda): **seed, sea, side**

(15)

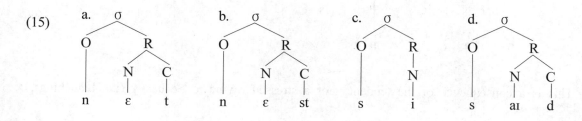

In (a), (b), and (d), the branching rhymes are obvious; in (c), the syllable is heavy because it has a branching nucleus.

Having made this digression to explain syllable weight, we can conclude that heavy syllables attract stress, and essentially, in English, no stressed syllable may be light. With this information, we are now ready to go back to the problematic cases we considered above. In *medicine, happen, finish*, etc., we have a conflict between the maximal onset principle and stress. While the maximal onset principle dictates that the first syllables of each of these words be light, the stress that falls on this very syllable contradicts the principle that light syllables cannot receive stress. This is the reason why some speakers are not comfortable with the syllabic divisions in these words. In such cases, linguists invoke the concept of **ambisyllabicity**, whereby the consonant in question is treated as behaving both as the coda of the preceding syllable and as the onset of the following syllable at the same time. To put it succinctly, we can say that a consonant that is (part of) a permissible onset (cluster) is ambisyllabic if it occurs immediately after a short vowel / I, ɛ, æ, ʌ, ʊ, ɔ/ɑ / (i.e. lax vowels plus [ɔ/ɑ]) that forms the nucleus of a stressed syllable. We can represent this as follows:

(16)

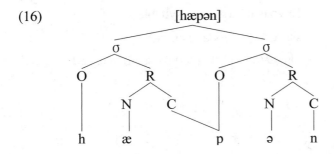

This is a consequence of the tendency for a stressed rhyme to be heavy (i.e. branching).

**EXERCISE** ....................................................................................................

**Which of the following would qualify for ambisyllabicity? Circle the word(s), state your rationale, and give the tree diagram(s).**[1]

metric,   regime,   anecdote,   integrity,   panic,   majesty,   Africa,   rival,   pity,   study,
radical,   legal,   action,   many,   liquid,   penalty,   garbage,   picnic,   spinach

---

[1] Answer: metric, anecdote, integrity, panic, majesty, Africa, pity, study, radical, many, liquid, penalty, spinach
A consonant that is part of a permissible onset is ambisyllabic if it occurs immediately after a short stressed vowel.

# Check Up the Points

## 1 Glossary for this Section

**ambisyllabic**
양음절성의

(of a consonant) Simultaneously forming part of two consecutive syllables, such as the /k/ of *ticker* or the /t/ of *petrol*. In *petrol*, for example, the presence of /t/ in the first syllable is shown by the occurrence in the coda position of that syllable (and in some dialects by the glottalization of the /t/), while its presence in the second syllable is shown by devoicing of the /ɹ/. Abstr. **ambisyllabicity**.

**coda**
종성

One or more phonological segments that follow the nucleus of a syllable: e.g., the /st/ in /prist/ *priest*.

**Maximal Onset Principle**
최대초성원리

A putative universal principle of Syllablification. It says: a consonant which may in principle occupy either rhyme or onset position will occupy onset position.

**nucleus**
음절핵

(also syllabic nucleus, peak) The most prominent (sonorous) part of a syllable, most often a vowel or a diphthong.

**onset**
초성

One or more phonemes that precede the syllable nucleus: e.g., /pr/ in /prist/ *priest*.

**phonotactic constraints**
음소배열제약

Rules stating permissible strings of phonemes within a syllable: e.g., a word-initial nasal consonant may be followed only by a vowel (in English). See **possible word, nonsense word, accidental gap**.

**rime/rhyme**
운모

The **nucleus + coda** of a syllable: e.g., the /en/ of /ren/ *rain*.

**sonority**
공명도

A particular sort of prominence associated with segment by virtue of the way in which that segment is intrinsically articulated. Sonority is an elusive notion. One approach holds that it is a measure of the output of acoustic energy associated with the production of a particular segment, and hence of its intrinsic loudness: the greater such output, the greater the sonority of the sound. Others would associate sonority chiefly with the degree of aperture of the vocal tract.

**sonority hierarchy**
공명도 위계

A particular ranking of segment types in order of their intrinsic sonority. Views differ, but a common ranking is (from least to most sonorous) oral stops > fricatives > nasals > liquids > glides > vowels. Some would add further elaborations, such as voiceless plosives > voiced plosives and high vowels > mid vowels > low vowels.

**syllable**
음절

A phonological unit composed of an onset, nucleus, and coda: e.g., elevator has four syllables: el e va tor; man has one syllable.

**syllabification**
음절화

Any analytical procedure for dividing a phonological representation into a well-defined sequence of syllables.

## ② Key-points in this Section

→ Syllable Structure

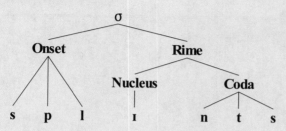

→ The "**maximal onset principle**" simply assigns any series of intervocalic consonants to the syllable on the right as long as it does not violate language-specific onset patterns.

→ Sonority

| Sounds | Sonority values | Examples |
|---|---|---|
| Low vowels | 10 | /ɑ, ʌ, æ/ |
| Mid vowels | 9 | /e, o/ |
| High vowels (and glides) | 8 | /i, u, (j, w)/ |
| Retroflexes (and flaps) | 7 | /ɹ/ |
| Laterals | 6 | /l/ |
| Nasals | 5 | /m, n, ŋ/ |
| Voiced fricatives | 4 | /v, ð, z, ʒ/ |
| Voiceless fricatives | 3 | /f, θ, s, ʃ, h/ |
| Voiced stops | 2 | /b, d, g/ |
| Voiceless stops | 1 | /p, t, k/ |

→ **Ambisyllabicity**

A consonant that is (part of) a permissible onset (cluster) is **ambisyllabic** if it occurs immediately after a short vowel /ɪ, ɛ, æ, ʌ, ʊ, ɔ/ɑ/ (i.e., lax vowels plus [ɔ/ɑ]) that forms the nucleus of a stresse syllable.

# Phonological Rules

---

**KEY CONCEPT IN THIS CHAPTER**

- Allophonic Rules
- Morphophonemic Rules
- Feature Changing Rules
  - Feature Addition Rules
  - Feature-Value Changing Rules
- Assimilation and Dissimilation
- Segment Deletion and Segment Insertion

---

**TIP**

- Velarization (2019)
- Glide Insertion, [ɹ]-Insertion (2018)
- Schwa Deletion, Trisyllabic Laxing (2017)
- Flapping (2016)
- /j/-Deletion, Glottalization (2015)
- /l/-Velarization (2014)

---

The relationship between the phonemic representation of a word and its phonetic representation, or how it is pronounced, is **rule-governed**. Phonological rules are part of a speaker's knowledge of the language.

Many rules change features from one value to its opposite or even add features not present in the phonemic representation.

In English, the /z/ plural morpheme has its voicing value changed from plus ($+$) to minus ($-$) when it follows a voiceless sound. Similarly, the /n/ in the phonemic negative prefix morpheme /ɪn/ undergoes a change in its place of articulation feature when preceding bilabials or velars.

The rule in English that aspirates voiceless stops at the beginning of a syllable simply **adds a nondistinctive feature**.


## 6.1. The Function of Phonological Rules

The function of the phonological rules in a grammar is to provide the phonetic information necessary for the pronunciation of utterances. We may illustrate this point in the following way:

(1)  input  *Phonemic Representation of Words in a Sentence*

↓

*Phonological Rules* (P-rules)

↓

output  *Phonetic Representation of Words in a Sentence*

The input to the P-rules is the phonemic representation. The P-rules apply to the phonemic strings and produce as output the phonetic representation.

The application of rules in this way is called a **derivation**. We have given examples of derivations that show how plurals are derived, how phonemically oral vowels become nasalized, and how /t/ and /d/ become flaps in certain environments. A derivation is thus an explicit way of showing both the effects and the function of phonological rules in a grammar.

For example, the word *tempest* is phonemically /tɛmpɛst/ (as shown by the pronunciation of *tempestuous* [tʰɛ̃mpʰɛstʃuəs]) but phonetically [tʰɛ̃mpəst]. Three rules apply to it: the aspiration rule, the vowel nasalization rule, and the schwa rule. We can **derive** the phonetic form **from the phonemic representation** as follows:

| (2) | Underlying phonemic representation | / | t | ε | m | p | ε | s | t | / |
|---|---|---|---|---|---|---|---|---|---|---|
| | Aspiration rule | | t$^h$ | | | | | | | |
| | Nasalization rule | | | $\tilde{\varepsilon}$ | | | | | | |
| | Schwa rule | | | | | | ə | | | |
| | Surface phonetic representation | [ | t$^h$ | $\tilde{\varepsilon}$ | m | p | ə | s | t | ] |

## 6.2. Allophonic Rules (1) : Assimilation

A particular kind of feature-changing rule is **assimilation**. Assimilation rules in languages reflect **coarticulation**—the spreading of phonetic features either in the anticipation or in the perseveration (the "hanging on") of articulatory processes. The auditory effect is that words sound smoother.

### 6.2.1. Aspiration

The rule in English that aspirates voiceless stops at the beginning of a syllable simply **adds a nondistinctive feature**. Generally, **aspiration** occurs only if the following vowel is stressed. The /p/ in *pit* and *repeat* is an **aspirated** [p$^h$], but the /p/ in *inspect* or *compass* is an **unaspirated** [p]. We also note that even with an intervening consonant, the aspiration takes place so that words such as *crib, clip,* and *quip* ([k$^h$hɹɪb], [k$^h$lɪp], and [k$^h$wɪp]) all begin with an aspirated [k$^h$]. And finally, the affricate /ʧ/ is subject to the rule, so *chip* is phonetically [ʧ$^h$hɪp].

We can now state **the aspiration rule**:

(3) A voiceless noncontinuant has [+aspirated] added to its feature matrix at the beginning of a syllable when followed by a stressed vowel with an optional intervening consonant.

Aspiration is not specified in any phonemic feature matrix of English. The aspiration rule adds this feature for reasons having to do with the timing of the closure release.

## 6.2.2. Vowel Nasalization

We have seen that nasalization of vowels in English is **nonphonemic** because it is predictable by rule. The vowel nasalization rule is an **assimilation rule** that makes neighboring segments more similar by adding the feature [+nasal] **to** the vowel.

We now wish to look more closely at the phonological rules we have been discussing. Previously, we stated **the vowel nasalization rule**:

(4) Vowels are nasalized before a nasal consonant within the same syllable.

This rule specifies the **class of sounds** affected by the rule:

(5) a. *Vowels*

It states what **phonetic change** will occur by applying the rule:

(5) b. *Change phonemic oral vowels to phonetic nasal vowels.*

And it specifies the **context** or **phonological environment**.

(5) c. *Before a nasal consonant within the same syllable.*

A shorthand notation to write rules, similar to the way scientists and mathematicians use symbols, makes the rule statements more concise. We can use notations to state the nasalization rule as:

(6) V → [+nasal] / _____ [+nasal] $

Let's look at the rule piece by piece.

(7) V → [+nasal] / \_\_\_\_ [+nasal] $
Vowels become nasalized in the before nasal within a
environment segments syllable

(8)

|  | "bob" | | | "boom" | | |
|---|---|---|---|---|---|---|
| Phonemic representation | /b | ə | b/ | /b | u | m/ |
| Nasality: phonemic feature value | – | 0* | – | – | 0* | + |
| Apply nasal rule | | NA | | | ↓ | |
| Nasality: phonetic feature value | – | – | – | – | + | + |
| Phonetic representation | [b | ə | b] | [b | ũ | m] |

*The 0 means not present on the phonemic level.

A word such as *den$tal* /dɛn$təl/ will be pronounced [dɛ̃n$təl]: we have showed the syllable boundary explicitly. However, the first vowel in *de$note*, /dɪ$not/, will not be nasalized, because the nasal segment does not precede the syllable boundary, so the "within a syllable" condition is not met.

### 6.2.3. Glottalization and Preglottalization

Finally, mention should be made of **the glottal stop** or **the preglottalized /t/** and the contexts in which it manifests itself. A glottal stop is the sound that occurs when the vocal cords are held tightly together. In most speakers of American and British English (AmE, BE), **glottal stops** or **the preglottalized /t/** are commonly found as allophones of /t/ in words such as:

(9)　Batman　[bæʔmæn]　Hitler　[hɪʔlɚ]　atlas　[æʔləs]
　　　Atlanta　[əʔlæntə]　he hit me　[hihɪʔmi]　eat well　[iʔwɛl]
　　　hot water　[hɑʔwɑɾɚ]

While the glottal stop can replace the /t/ in these words, it is not allowed in *atrocious* [ətɹoʃəs] (not *[əʔɹoʃəs]), *attraction* [ətɹækʃən] (not *[əʔɹækʃən]; the asterisk here means "wrong" or "unattested"). The reason for this is that the **glottal stop replacement** requires the target /t/ to be **in a syllable-final position** ([bæʔ.mæn], [əʔ.læn.tə]). The words that do not allow the replacement have their /t/ in the onset position ([ə.tɹo.ʃəs], [ə.tɹæk.ʃən]), as /tɹ/ is a permissible onset in English. We should point out, however, that /tɹ/ being permissible is not carried over across words, as the compound *court-room* illustrates. The expected production of this sequence is with a glottal replacement [kɔɹʔ ɹum], because the syllabification is not [kɔɹ.tɹum].

The glottal stop replacement of syllable-final /t/ is also observable **before the syllabic nasal** (e.g. *beaten* [biʔn̩], *kitten* [kɪʔn̩]). The process under discussion is most easily perceived after short vowels (e.g. *put*, *hit*), and least obvious after consonants (e.g. *belt, sent*).

As pointed out above, in absolute final position, some speakers do not replace the /t/ with a glottal stop entirely, but insert a glottal stop before /t/, as in *hit* [hɪʔt] ("**preglottalization**" or "**glottal reinforcement**").

The only difference between **a glottal stop [ʔ]** and **a glottally reinforced [ʔt]** is that the tip of the tongue makes contact with the alveolar ridge in the latter case but not in the former. It is also worth pointing out that this **glottal reinforcement** may be applicable to **other voiceless stops** for many speakers, as shown in *tap* [tæʔp], *sack* [sæʔk].

### 6.2.4. Vowel Lengthening

Length of vowels (and diphthongs) varies predictably according to the context they appear in. More specifically:

(a) Vowels are longer **before voiced consonants** than before their **voiceless** counterparts. Thus, the phonetic realization of the vowel /æ/ in bag [bæg] is longer than its realization in back [bæk].

(b) Vowels are longer **before sonorant consonants** than before **obstruents**. Thus, the phonetic realization of the vowel /o/ in *goal* [gol] is longer than its realization in *goad* [god].

(c) Vowels are longer **in open syllable** than in **closed syllables**. Thus, the phonetic realization of the vowel /e/ in *bay* [be] is longer than its realization in *bait* [bet].

We can combine the three rules above and say that we find a vowel longest in an open syllable (e.g. /i/ in *knee* [ni]); next longest in a syllable closed by a sonorant consonant (e.g. /i/ in *kneel* [nil]); next longest in a syllable closed by a voiced consonant (e.g. /i/ in *need* [nid]); shortest in a syllable closed by a voiceless consonant (e.g. /i/ in *neat* [nit]).

(10) *neat* [nit] < *need* [nid] < *kneel* [nil] < *knee* [ni]

(d) <u>Vowels are longer **in stressed syllables** than in **unstressed syllables**</u>. Thus, the phonetic realization of the vowel /i/ in stressed syllable of the word *appreciate* [ə.pɹi.ʃɪ.et] is longer than its realization in the following unstressed syllable.

## 6.2.5. /l/-Velarization

Let us turn to a phoneme /l/. /l/ has only two main allophones in English, depending on its position in the word. If you say *lull*, or *lilt*, you will notice that the first *l* in each case is pronounced with the tip of your tongue up behind your top front teeth, while the second additionally has the tongue raised further back.

In the case of /l/, what matters (roughly speaking) is whether the /l/ precedes or follows the vowel in the word. If /l/ comes first, it is pronounced as 'clear', fronter [l], as also in *clear*; and if the vowel comes first, /l/ is realized as 'dark', more back [ɫ], as in *dull*. The two are obviously **in complementary distribution**, and hence can both straightforwardly be assigned to the same phoneme, /l/, in Modern English.

The rule for velarization of /l/ was informally stated as:

(11) The liquid /l/ is velarized when it follows a vowel in a word.

This rule specification gives the correct results for *clear* versus *hill*, for instance. This works well enough when we are only dealing with word-initial versus word-final clusters, but it leaves a grey area in word-medial position, where we find dark [ɫ] in *falter, hilltop*, but clear [l] in *holy, hilly*.

This is resolvable <u>if we state the rule in terms of the **syllable**</u>:

(12) Clear [l] appears in onset position, and dark [ɫ] in the coda.
    (or The liquid /l/ is velarized when it appears in coda position.)

In fact, this process does not only provide evidence for the contrast between onset and coda position, but for the superordinate rhyme constituent, which consists of the nucleus plus the optional coda. In cases of **consonant syllabification**, where /l/ (or another sonorant consonant) comes to play the role of a vowel and therefore occupies the nuclear position, as in *bottle, little*, we find the dark allophone. **/l/-velarization**, then, takes place in syllable rhymes.

## 6.2.6. Palatalization

Another pair, alveolar fricatives /s, z/, echoing the alveolar stops, may undergo **palatalization** and turn into [ʃ, ʒ] respectively, when they occur before the palatal glide /j/. Commonly heard forms such as

(13)　　[aɪmɪʃju]　　(I miss you)　　　[aɪpliʒju]　　(I please you)

　　　　[ðɪʃjɪɹ]　　(this year)　　　[huʒʊɹ bɑs]　　(who's your boss?)

demonstrate this clearly. Thus, we can put together the behavior of /t, d, s, z/ and state that

(14) The **alveolar obstruents** of English become palatoalveolar when followed by a word that starts with the palatal glide /j/

(since there are no palatoalveolar stops in English, the replacements are affricates for /t, d/).

## 6.2.7. Palatalization and Labialization of Velar Stops

The velar stops of English, /k, g/, have appreciably **different contact points** in the beginnings of the following two-word sequence: *car key* [kaɹ ci]. The initial stop of the first word is made at a significantly more back point in **the velum area** than that of the initial sound of the second word, which is almost making the stop closure at **the hard palate**. The reason for such a difference is the back/front nature of the following vowel. Thus, velars are more front when before a front vowel than when before a back vowel.

The other assimilatory process velar stops undergo relates to **the different lip position** in *geese* and *goose*. While in the latter example the lips are rounded during the stop articulation, they are not so in the former. Again, the culprit is the rounded/unrounded nature of the following vowel. The stop is produced with lip rounding if it is followed by a rounded vowel.

Putting together the two assimilatory processes we have just discussed, we can see why the velar stops in the sequence *keep cool* are produced differently. Predictably, the /k/ of the first word, followed by /i/, is unrounded and **more front** (or **palatalized**), while that of the second word, followed by /u/, is back and **rounded** (or **labialized**).

## 6.2.8. Dentalization of Nasals

The alveolar nasal, /n/, is articulated in a more forward fashion (dental) when it is followed by an interdental (/θ, ð/): *tenth* [tɛn̪θ], *ban the film* [bæn̪ðəfilm], *when they* [wɛn̪ðe].

## 6.2.9. Nasal Devoicing

Finally, /m/ and /n/ are also subject to progressive assimilation in cases of partial devoicing after the voiceless obstruent /s/, as in *snail* [sn̥el], *small* [sm̥ɔl].

## 6.3. Allophonic Rules (2) : Dissimilation

It is understandable that so many languages have **assimilation rules**; they permit greater **ease of articulation**. It might seem strange, then, to learn that languages also have feature-changing rules called **dissimilation rules**, in which certain segments becomes less similar to other segments. Ironically, such rules have the same explanation: it is sometimes **easier to articulate** dissimilar sounds.

## 6.3.1. Fricative Dissimilation

An example of easing pronunciation through dissimilation is found in some varieties of English, in which there is a fricative dissimilation rule. This rule applies to sequences /fθ/ and /sθ/, changing them to [ft] and [st]. Here the fricative /θ/ becomes dissimilar to the preceding fricative by becoming a stop. For example, the words *fifth* and *sixth* come to be pronounced as if they were spelled *fift* and *sikst*.

## 6.3.2. Liquid Dissimilation

A classic example of the same kind of **dissimilation** occurred in Latin, and the results of this process show up in the derivational morpheme /-aɹ/ in English. In Latin a derivational suffix -*alis* was added to nouns to form adjectives. When the suffix was added to a noun that contained the liquid /l/, the suffix was changed to -*aris;* that is, the liquid /l/ was changed to the dissimilar liquid /ɹ/. These words came into English as adjectives ending in -*al* or in its dissimilated form -*ar,* as shown in the following examples:

(15)

| -al | -ar |
|---|---|
| anecdot-al | angul-ar |
| annu-al | annul-ar |
| ment-al | column-ar |
| pen-al | perpendicul-ar |
| spiritu-al | simil-ar |
| ven-al | vel-ar |

All of the -*ar* adjectives contain /l/, and as *columnar* illustrates, the /l/ need not be the consonant directly preceding the dissimilated segment.

## 6.4. Allophonic Rules (3) : Segment Deletion

Phonological rules may **add** or **delete** entire segments. These are **different from** the feature-changing rules, which affect only parts of segments.

### 6.4.1. Schwa Deletion (1)

**Segment deletion rules** are commonly found in many languages and are far more prevalent than **segment insertion rules**. One such rule occurs in **casual** or **rapid speech**.

We often **delete** the unstressed vowels in words like the following:

(16) mystery    general    memory    funeral    vigorous    Barbara

These words in casual speech can sound as if they were written:

(17) mystry    genral    memry    funral    vigrous    Barbra

## 6.4.2. Schwa Deletion (2)

The schwa vowel /ə/, which is a reduced or weak vowel in English, can be deleted in fast speech, as exemplified in (18).

(18) Schwa Deletion

|  | **Careful Speech** | **Fast Speech** |
|---|---|---|
| camera | [ˈkæməɹə] | [ˈkæmɹə] |
| veteran | [ˈvɛtəɹən] | [ˈvɛtɹən] |

However, schwa deletion is not observed in fast speech for the following words.

(19) No Schwa Deletion

|  | **Careful Speech** | **Fast Speech** |  |
|---|---|---|---|
| facilitate | [fəˈsɪləteɪt] | [fəˈsɪləteɪt] | *[fəˈsɪlteɪt] |
| famous | [ˈfeɪməs] | [ˈfeɪməs] | *[ˈfeɪms] |

In the following examples of morphologically related words, schwa deletion may or may not be observed.

(20)

|  |  | **Careful Speech** | **Fast Speech** |  |
|---|---|---|---|---|
| a. | principal | [ˈpɹɪnsəpəl] | [ˈpɹɪnspəl] |  |
|  | principality | [pɹɪnsəˈpæləti] | [pɹɪnsəˈpæləti] | *[pɹɪnˈspæləti] |
| b. | imaginative | [ɪˈmædʒənətɪv] | [ɪˈmædʒnətɪv] |  |
|  | imagination | [ɪmædʒəˈneɪʃən] | [ɪmædʒəˈneɪʃən] | *[ɪmædʒˈneɪʃən] |

Schwa deletion occurs in fast speech when a preceding vowel is stressed and a following vowel is another schwa vowel.

### 6.4.3. /g/-Deletion

The silent *g* that torments spellers in such words as *sign* and *design* is actually the result of a segment deletion rule. Consider the following examples:

(21)

| **A** | | **B** | |
|---|---|---|---|
| sign | [sãɪn] | signature | [sɪgnəʧər] |
| design | [dəzãɪn] | designation | [dɛzɪgneʃə̃n] |
| paradigm | [pʰærədãɪm] | paradigmatic | [pʰærədɪgmærək] |

In none of the words in column A is there a phonetic [g], but in each corresponding word in column B a [g] occurs. Our knowledge of English phonology accounts for these phonetic differences.

The "[g] ~ no [g]" alternation is regular and is also seen in pairs like *gnostic* [nastɪk] and *agnostic* [ægnastɪk].

This rule may be stated as:

(22) Delete a /g/ word-initially before a nasal consonant or before a syllable-final nasal consonant.

Given this rule, the phonemic representations of the stems in *sign/signature, design/designation, malign/malignant, phlegm/phlegmatic, paradigm/paradigmatic, gnostic/agnostic,* and so on will include a /g/ that will be deleted by the regular rule if a prefix or suffix is not added. By stating the class of sounds that follow the /g/ (nasal consonants) rather than any specific nasal consonant, the rule deletes the /g/ before both /m/ and /n/.

### 6.4.4. /t/-Deletion

Another characteristic of **American English** in **informal conversational speech** is the creation of homophonous productions for pairs such as *planner ─ planter* [plænɚ], *canner ─ canter* [kænɚ], *winner ─ winter* [wɪnɚ], *tenor ─ tenter* [tɛnɚ]. **The loss of /t/** in the second member of these pairs is also in many other words, as in *rental, dental, renter, dented, twenty, gigantic, Toronto.* In all these examples we see that the /t/ that is lost is following an /n/.

However, that such as *contain, interred, entwined*, in which /t/ following an /n/ can**not** be deleted. The difference between these words and the earlier ones is that **/t/ is deleted only in an unstressed syllable**.

### 6.4.5. Interdental Fricative Deletion

Interdental fricatives /θ, ð/ may undergo **the elision process** (i.e. they may be left out) when they occur before the alveolar fricatives /s, z/, as exemplified by *clothes* [kloz], *months* [mʌns].

(23)   clothes     /kloð+z/                          kloðz       —ð-Deletion→     [kloz]
       months      /mʌnθ+z/   —Devoicing→   mʌnθs     —θ-Deletion→     [mʌns]

### 6.4.6. /j/-Deletion

Words such as *music* [mjuzɪk] and *cube* [kjub] are pronounced in the same way in both American English and British English. However, words such as *tuition, endure*, and *annuity* vary, as shown in (24a) and (24b).

(24) a. British English

   tuition [tjuɪʃən]              duration [djʊɹeɪʃən]
   endure [ɪndjʊə]              annuity [ənjuəti]
   perpetuity [pɜːpətjuəti]      voluminous [vəljumənəs]

   b. American English

   tuition [tuɪʃən]              duration [dʊɹeɪʃən]
   endure [ɪndʊɹ]               annuity [ənuəti]
   perpetuity [pɜːpətuəti]      voluminous [vəlumənəs]

While in British English we see a /j/ after the underlined consonants /t/, /d/, /n/, and /l/ in the words given in (24a), the expected American English pronunciations are without a /j/ after the same underlined consonants, as shown in (24b). The same difference is observed after the underlined consonants /s/ and /z/ for the words in (25a) and (25b).

(25) a. British English

　　　　assume [əsjum]　　　　　　　superb [sjupɜːb]

　　　　exude [ɪgzjud]　　　　　　　résumé [ɹɛzjʊmeɪ]


　　b. American English

　　　　assume [əsum]　　　　　　　superb [supɜˑb]

　　　　exude [ɪgzud]　　　　　　　résumé [ɹɛzʊmeɪ]


However, the words given in (26) show that the underlined alveolars /n/ and /l/ are followed by a /j/ in American English as well as in British English.

(26) British English and American English

　　　　continue [kəntɪnju]　　　　　biannual [baɪænjuəl]

　　　　voluble [vɑljʊbəl]　　　　　valuation [væljueɪʃən]


These examples may suggest that /j/ may **not** follow an **alveolar** in the same morpheme in AmE (across morphemes this is possible, as in *would you*, *bet you*).

This generalization, however, has to be amended, because words such as *onion* [ɑnjən], *tenure* [tɛnjɚ], *annual* [ænjuəl], *value* [vælju], *failure* [feljɚ], *million* [mɪljən] have alveolars /n/ or /l/ followed by a /j/ in AmE as well as in BE. Thus, the correct characterization of the **AmE** restriction on alveolar should read as "**/j/ cannot follow an alveolar obstruent; it can follow an alveolar sonorant when in an unstressed syllable**."

In AAVE, /j/ can be deleted in a [CjV] sequence (e.g. *computer* [kəmpjutɚ] or [kəmputɚ]). cf. AAVE: African American Vernacular English

## 6.5. Allophonic Rules (4) : Segment Insertion

The process of inserting a consonant or vowel is called **epenthesis**.

If you say *hamster* slowly and carefully, it will sound like [hæmstə] (or [hæmstəɹ]). If you say the word quickly several times, you will produce something closer to your normal, casual speech pronunciation, and it is highly likely that there will be an extra consonant in there, giving [hæmpstə] (or [hæmpstəɹ]) instead.

As the rate of speech increases, adjacent sounds influence one another even more than usual, because the same complex articulations are taking place in even less time. Here, the articulators are moving from a **voiced nasal stop** [m], to a **voiceless alveolar fricative** [s], so that almost every possible property has to change all at once.

In fast speech, not all these transitions may be perfectly coordinated: the **extraneous [p]** appears when the speaker has succeeded in switching off voicing, and raising the velum to cut off airflow through the nose, but has not yet shifted from stop to fricative, or from labial to alveolar.

A very similar process arises in words like *mince* and *prince*, which can become homophonous (that is, identical in sound) to *mints* and *prints* in fast speech. Here, the transition is from [n], a voiced alveolar nasal stop, to [s], a voiceless alveolar oral fricative, and the half-way house is [t], which this time shares its place of articulation with both neighbours, but differs from [n] in voicing and nasality, and from [s] in manner of articulation.

In both *hamster* and *mince/prince*, however, the casual speech process creating the **extra medial plosive** is an **optional** one.

## 6.6. Morphophonemic Rules

Up to this point we have looked at allophonic variations (contextual variation of the sounds belonging to the same phoneme), which take place within a single morpheme ("**the smallest unit of linguistic meaning function**"). We should also point out that several of the processes that are shown to be crucial in accounting for the allophonic variations in languages can also be found active **across morpheme boundaries**.

When morphemes are combined to form bimorphemic (with two morphemes) or polymorphemic words many of the assimilatory phenomena discussed can be present there too. Such things can also manifest themselves when two words are spoken consecutively. What we see in these instances, then, is **the contextually determined alternations (different phonetic forms) of a morpheme**.

The same/similar phonetically motivated **nasal assimilation** is found **across morpheme boundaries** in several other languages.

### 6.6.1. Nasal Place Assimilation

In English the **negative morpheme prefix** spelled *in-* or *im-* agrees in place of articulation with the word to which it is prefixed, so we have *impossible* [ĩmpʰasəbəl], *intolerant* [ĩntʰalərə̃nt], and *incongruous* [ĩŋkʰãngruəs]. In this case the place of articulation—bilabial, alveolar, velar—of the nasal assimilates to the place of articulation of the following consonant. In effect, the rule makes two consonants that appear next to each other more similar.

Observe the following:

(27)   impersonal [ɪmpɚsənəl]     independent [ɪndəpɛndənt]     incomplete [ɪŋkəmplɪt]
        improbable [ɪmpɹabəbəl]     intolerant [ɪntaləɹənt]      inconclusive [ɪŋkənklusɪv]
        impossible [ɪmpasəbəl]      inadvisable [ɪnædvaɪzəbəl]     incapable [ɪŋkepəbəl]

The pronunciation of the negative prefix is different only with respect to the nasal consonant, which is <u>bilabial, [m], before adjectives that start with a bilabial sound (left column)</u>, and <u>velar, [ŋ], before ones that start with a velar sound (right column)</u>. <u>In other instances, the nasal is alveolar, [n], in the prefix (middle column)</u>. This predictable alternation of the nasal is the result of the place of articulation assimilation.

*The case of the English negative prefixes* does **not** deal with allophones of the same phoneme, **but** rather shows contextually predictable alternations among separate phonemes.

*What is revealed in the case of English negative prefixes* is that there is **an alternation of different phonemes for the same morpheme** (indicators of the same meaning unit). Such cases are traditionally called **morphophonemic alternations**, and <u>the different phonetic manifestations of the same morpheme</u> (**morpheme alternants**) are called the **allomorphs**.

## 6.6.2. Devoicing and Schwa Insertion

Another possibility is to find <u>**some feature-changing assimilatory processes that are restricted only across morpheme boundaries**</u> (i.e. acting only as morphophonemic processes), and with no parallels in allophonic processes of monomorphemic words.

Recall that the voiced /z/ of the **English regular plural suffix** is changed to [s] after a voiceless sound, and that similarly the voiced /d/ of the **English regular past-tense suffix** is changed to [t] after a voiceless sound. These are instances of voicing assimilation. In these cases the value of the voicing feature goes from [+voice] to [−voice] because of assimilation to the [−voice] feature of the final consonant of the stem, as in the derivation of *cats*:

(28) /kæt + z/ → [kæts]

To illustrate this, examine the following **past tense endings in English**:

(29)  attempted [ətɛmtəd]    walked [wɔkt]    robbed [ɹabd]

blended [blɛndəd]    pushed [pʊʃt]    seemed [simd]

tested [tɛstəd]    sipped [sɪpt]    swayed [swed]

The above examples show that **the regular past tense ending in English** has three predictable phonetic manifestations. We have [-əd] if the last sound of the verb is an alveolar stop, /t, d/ (schwa insertion before another alveolar stop). If the verb-final sound is not an alveolar stop, however, then the shape of the past tense ending is an alveolar stop, [-t] or [-d], which is determined by the voicing of the verb-final sound.

We have voiceless [t] if the verb-final sound is voiceless (middle column); however, the form is the voiced [d] if the verb-final sound is voiced (right column). This is a clear case of voicing assimilation.

**However,** this does **not** mean that this sequencing restriction occurs throughout. While the past tense of the verb *ban* [bæn] is necessarily [bænd] and cannot be [bænt], this does not mean that we cannot have a final consonant cluster with different voicing in its members ([-nt] sequence) in English. Words such as *bent*, *tent*, etc. reveal that there is no such restriction **within a single morpheme**.

The rules for forming regular plurals, possessive forms, and third-person singular verb agreement in English all require an epenthesis rule. Here is the first part of that rule that we gave earlier for plural formation:

(30) Insert a [ə] before the plural morpheme /z/ when a regular noun ends in a sibilant, giving [əz].

Letting the symbol Ø stand for 'null,' we can write this morphophonemic epenthesis rule more formally as "null becomes schwa between two sibilants," or like this:

(31) Ø → ə / [+sibilant] + _____ [+sibilant]

There is a plausible explanation for insertion of a [ə]. If we merely added a [z] to *squeeze* to form its plural, we would get [skwizː], which would be hard for English speakers to distinguish from [skwiz] because in English we do not contrast long and short consonants.

### 6.6.3. Glide Insertion and [ɹ]-Insertion

In a number of dialects of British English, a glide is inserted in certain environments, as shown in (32) and (33).

(32) /j/ insertion

| | | |
|---|---|---|
| being | /biːŋ/ | [bijɪŋ] |
| my other (car) | /maɪʌðə/ | [maɪjʌðə] |
| free a (prisoner) | /friə/ | [frijə] |
| enjoy ice cream | /ɛndʒɔɪaɪskɹim/ | [ɛndʒɔɪjaɪskɹim] |

(33) /w/ insertion

| | | |
|---|---|---|
| sewer | /suə/ | [suwə] |
| few arrests | /fjuəɹɛsts/ | [fjuwəɹɛsts] |
| now or never | /naʊɔnɛvə/ | [naʊwɔnɛvə] |
| go away | /goʊəweɪ/ | [goʊwəweɪ] |

However, in such dialects, glide insertion is not attested in the examples in (34). Instead, /ɹ/ is inserted.

(34) No glide insertion

| | | | |
|---|---|---|---|
| drawing | [dɹɔɹɪŋ] | *[dɹɔjɪŋ] | *[dɹɔwɪŋ] |
| ma and pa | [maɹənpa] | *[majənpa] | *[mawənpa] |
| law and order | [lɔɹənɔdə] | *[lɔjənɔdə] | *[lɔwənɔdə] |
| media event | [midɪəɹɪvɛnt] | *[midɪəjɪvɛnt] | *[midɪəwɪvɛnt] |

A glide is inserted between two vowels when the first is a high vowel (or a diphthong). The palatal glide /j/ is inserted between the two vowels when the preceding vowel is a high front vowel (or a diphthong with a final high front vowel, /aɪ/, /ɔɪ/). The velar glide /w/ is inserted when the preceding vowel is a high back vowel (or a diphthong with a final high back vowel, /aʊ/ or /oʊ/).

A non-lateral liquid /ɹ/ is inserted between two vowels when the first is a non-high vowel.

### 6.6.4. Trisyllabic Laxing

**Trisyllabic laxing** is <u>a rule which changes a tense vowel into a lax vowel. This rule applies</u> <u>when the target vowel is pushed into the ante-penultimate syllable (i.e., the third syllable from</u> <u>the end) due to the attachment of a suffix</u>, as exemplified below.

(35)  supreme     —  supremacy
      apply       —  application
      sane        —  sanity
      divine      —  divinity
      opaque      —  opacity

The tense vowels in words like 'nightingale' and 'ivory' do not undergo trisyllabic laxing although these words contain the minimum of three syllables required by the trisyllabic laxing rule. The explanation is that these forms are exempt from trisyllabic laxing since they do not have any suffix.

## 6.7. Neutralization

### 6.7.1. Consonant Neutralization

Sometimes the sounds that belong to two separate phonemes may lose their contrast in certain environment(s).

For example, the two alveolar stops of English are in contrast at the beginning and the end positions of the word, as exemplified in the following pairs of <u>tip</u> vs. <u>dip</u>, and <u>bet</u> and <u>bed</u>. However, <u>when we have them in intervocalic position in unstressed syllables</u>, the contrast between /t/ and /d/ disappears and they are both realized identically as, what is called the "**flap**," as shown in *writer — rider* [ɹaɪɾɚ].

Such an event is termed "**neutralization**," which simply means that <u>a contrast which is very</u> <u>much alive in several contexts ceases to exist in a given environment</u>.

To give another example, we can look at the contrast between the voiceless and voiced stops, /p, t, k/ and /b, d, g/ respectively. While /p/ and /b/ contrast in <u>pin</u> vs. <u>bin</u> and /k/ and /g/ contrast in <u>could</u> vs. <u>good</u>, the contrasts **are neutralized** <u>following /s/ in word-initial position</u>. Although we generally see the transcriptions of <u>spit</u> and <u>skin</u> as [spɪt] and [skɪn] respectively, they are not in any way different from [sb..] and [sg..].

Finally, a vocalic example is in order. The two front vowels /ɪ/ and /ɛ/ can easily be shown in contrast, as in <u>bit</u> [bɪt] vs. <u>bet</u> [bɛt], or <u>pit</u> [pɪt] vs. <u>pet</u> [pɛt]. However, <u>if the consonant after the vowel is nasal</u>, then, for several speakers of American English, the contrast **is neutralized** in favor of [ɪ], as in <u>pin</u> [pɪn] vs. <u>pen</u> [pɛn].

### 6.7.2. Vowel Neutralization

In most forms of American English some form of r-sound after a vowel is permitted. When the following /ɹ/ is **in the same syllable** (as in *ear, cure, work, party*), <u>the vowel takes on some retroflex quality, which is commonly known as "**r-coloring**."</u> When this happens, **several otherwise well-established vowel contrasts of English are neutralized (i.e. lost)** with many speakers of American English. For example, **the contrast between the two high front vowels /i/ and /ɪ/** seems to disappear in words such as *ear, fear, beard, pier,* etc. <u>The r-colored production resembles neither /i/ nor /ɪ/; it is somewhere in between</u> (traditionally transcribed as [iɹ]).

A similar situation can be observed **between the two high back vowels /u/ and /ʊ/** in words such as *tour, mature, endure,* and *poor*. The r-colored vowel is not identical to either /u/ or /ʊ/.

<u>This phenomenon of **neutralizations of contrasts**</u> continues with full force in the front and back mid vowel series.

For many speakers of American English, the r-colored vowel in *Mary, merry,* and *marry* is the same, thus revealing a **neutralization** of **the contrasts between /e/, /ɛ/, and /æ/**.

As for the back vowels, words such as *pork, bore, horn,* and *fork* do not seem to reveal **any distinction between /o/ and /ɔ/**, as the /ɹ/ has <u>the effect of **raising the /ɔ/ toward /o/**</u> (cf. *morning* vs. *mourning*). Similarly, with respect to the high back vowels, **the contrast between /u/ and /ʊ/** may be **neutralized** in words such as *poor* and *cure*.

<u>Some speakers even go further and neutralize the four back vowels /o, ɔ, u, ʊ/ before /ɹ/ in conversational speech</u> (e.g. *pour, pore, poor*).

**R-coloring** is present in th following two diphthongs: /aɪɹ/ (e.g. *fire, entire, inspire*) and /aʊɹ/ (e.g. *sour, devour*).

Finally, <u>**the central vowel schwa** has two r-colored manifestations</u>: [ɝ] in stressed syllables and [ɚ] in unstressed syllables (e.g. *herder* [hɝdɚ]).

We summarize the r-colored vowels with the tautosyllabic /ɹ/ in Figure 1.

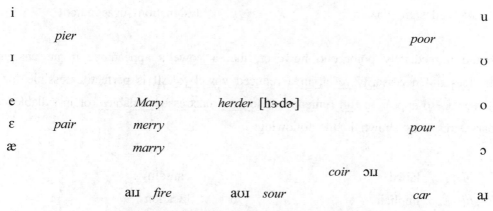

**Figure 1.** Vowels Before the Tautosyllabic /ɹ/

## 6.7.3. Vowel Reduction

While all vowels of English (except [ə]) can occur in stressed syllables, many of these vowels reveal alternations with an [ə] in unstressed syllables in a morphologically related word.

(36)

| | | **Stressed syllable with a full vowel** | **Reduced syllable with [ə]** |
|---|---|---|---|
| /i/ | | homogeneous [homodʒiniəs] | homogenize [homɑdʒənaɪz] |
| /ɪ/ | | implicit [ɪmplɪsət] | implication [ɪmpləkeʃən] |
| /e/ | | rotate [ˌɹotet] | rotary [ˌɹotəˌɹi] |
| /ɛ/ | | perpetuate [pəˈpɛtʃuet] | perpetuity [pəˈpɛtʃuəti] |
| /æ/ | | enigmatic [ənɪgmætɪk] | enigma [ənɪgmə] |
| /ɑ/ | | stigmata [stɪgmɑtə] | stigma [stɪgmə] |
| /ɔ/ | | author [ɔθɚ] | authoritarian [əθɔˌɹətɛˌɹiən] |
| /o/ | | photograph [fotəgɹæf] | photography [fətɑgɹəfi] |
| /ʌ/ | | confront [kənfɹʌnt] | confrontation [kɑnfɹənteʃən] |
| /u/ | | compute [kəmpjut] | computation [kɑmpjəteʃən] |
| /aɪ/ | | design [dəzaɪn] | designation [dɛzəgneʃən] |

We should immediately point out, however, that a vowel's appearance in an unstressed syllable does **not necessarily** result in a reduced vowel [ə]. It is perfectly possible for the English vowels to appear **in full (unreduced) form** in unstressed syllables (or in syllables with secondary stress), as shown in the following:

(37)

| | | | | |
|---|---|---|---|---|
| /i/ | lábial | /ɔ/ | causálity |
| /ɪ/ | implícit | /o/ | locátion |
| /e/ | rótate | /ʊ/ | bóyhood |
| /ɛ/ | centénnial | /u/ | acoustician [æ̀kustíʃən]] |
| /æ/ | sárcasm | /aɪ/ | titrátion |
| /ɑ/ | Octóber | /aʊ/ | outsíde |
| | | /ɔɪ/ | èxploitátion |

Thus, **the unidirectional generalization** to be made is the following: while a reduced vowel is **necessarily** in an unstressed syllable, a vowel in an unstressed syllable is **not necessarily** reduced.

## 6.8. Consonant Cluster Simplification

Some modifications are commonly observed with respect to **deletions in final clusters**. When the word ending in a cluster is followed by a word that begins with a consonant, the final member of the cluster is deleted, as shown below:

(38)  /nd/       hand made        [hæn med]          (cf. hand out)

        spend money      [spɛn mʌni]        (cf. spend it)

        grand bargain    [gɹæn bɑɹgən]      (cf. grand illusion)

  /st/    next class       [nɛks klæs]        (cf. next hour)

        just now         [dʒʌs naʊ]         (cf. just as)

        best thing       [bɛs θɪŋ]          (cf. best option)

  /ft/    left street      [lɛf stɹit]        (cf. left arm)

This pattern repeats itself in words with suffixes and in compounds, as in the following:

(39)  /nd/    handsome      [hænsəm]

  /st/    textless      [tɛksləs]

  /ft/    softness      [sɔfnəs]

However, the deletion is **not** observed if the consonant after the final cluster is /**h**/.

(40)  wild horse    [waɪld hɔɹs]    NOT    *[waɪl hɔɹs]

  guest house   [gɛst haʊs]    NOT    *[gɛs haʊs]

Also, if the consonant after the cluster is a **liquid**, the deletion is **optional**.

(41)  hand luggage    [hæn(d) lʌgədʒ]

  guest list      [gɛs(t) lɪst]

Finally, if clusters are created by the addition of **grammatical endings**, this simplification is much less likely, if at all, to occur. Thus, we can normally get the following **non-reduced forms**:

(42)    /nd/    planned  trip         [plænd t̠ɹɪp]

        /st/    fixed  game           [fɪkst gem]

        /ft/    autographed  book     [ɔtəgɹæft bʊk]

## 6.9. Vowel Deletion and Normally Impermissible Clusters

**Normally impermissible clusters are created because of reduced vowel deletions in connected speech**. This process is not restricted to any combination of a consonants, as shown below:

(43)                    **Slow speech**    **Fast speech**

        Topeka          [təpikə]           [**tp**ikə]        (voiceless stop + voiceless stop)

        tobacco         [təbæko]           [**tb**æko]        (voiceless stop + voiced stop)

        because         [bəkɑz]            [**bk**ɑz]         (voiced stop + voiceless stop)

        debate          [dəbet]            [**db**et]         (voiced stop + voiced stop)

        cassette        [kəsɛt]            [**ks**ɛt]         (stop + fricative)

        photography     [fətɑgɹəfi]        [**ft**ɑgɹəfi]     (fricative + stop)

        façade          [fəsɑd]            [**fs**ɑd]         (fricative + fricative)

        Canadian        [kənediən]         [**kn**ediən]      (obstruent + nasal)

        marina          [məɹinə]           [**mɹ**inə]        (nasal + liquid)

        metallic        [mətælɪk]          [**mt**ælɪk]       (nasal + obstruent)

        fanatics        [fənætɪk]          [**fn**ætɪk]       (fricative + nasal)

## 6.10. Metathesis

Metathesis is an exchange in the positions of two segments in a word, either as a historical change or as a synchronic rule. The phonological process reorders segments, often by transposing two sequential sounds: e.g., the pronunciation of *ask* /æsk/ in some English dialects as [æks].

## 6.11. Stem-Bounded Rule

Bounding effects can also be found in the interior of words. For studying such effects, it is useful to set up a linguistic unit which I will refer to as the stem. Although the word stem has multiple meanings in linguistics, for purposes of this discussion I will assume that it is the minimal constituent within a word that can stand as an independent word. Thus, in *jumping* [[dʒʌmp]ᵥ ɪŋ]ₙ, the stem is [dʒʌmp]ᵥ. In *identifier* [[[aɪdɛnt] ɪfaɪ]ᵥ ɚ]ₙ, the stem is [aɪdɛntɪfaɪ]ᵥ. Although we can recognize a smaller root morpheme [aɪdɛnt] within this word (compare *identity, identical*), we will not consider it to be the stem, since it cannot occur as an independent word. This definition of stem is only an approximation, but will serve for present purposes.

Consider now an example of a stem-bounded rule. The following rule occurs in some version in a number of English dialects:

**Pre-/l/ Monophthongization**

oʊ → o / _____ l

We can see the effects of the rule in the following data:

| **/oʊ/ before /l/: [o]** | | | | **/oʊ/ in other environments: [oʊ]** | | | |
|---|---|---|---|---|---|---|---|
| *pole* | [pol] | *Coltrane* | [kolʧɹeɪn] | *Poe* | [poʊ] | *propane* | [pɹoʊpeɪn] |
| *hole* | [hol] | *told* | [told] | *hope* | [hoʊp] | *toad* | [toʊd] |
| *mole* | [mol] | *fold* | [fold] | *moat* | [moʊt] | *phone* | [foʊn] |
| *poultry* | [polʧɹi] | *mold* | [mold] | *Oakley* | [oʊkli] | *most* | [moʊst] |

The above are all simple, monomorphemic forms. The more subtle effects occur when we add suffixes to stems that end in /oʊ/ or in /oʊ/ plus /l/.

First, if we add a suffix or compound member starting with /l/ to a stem that ends in /oʊ/, we get [oʊ], contrary to what we might have expected:

| | |
|---|---|
| *lowly* | [loʊli] |
| *slowly* | [sloʊli] |
| *lowlands* | [loʊləndz] |
| *toeless* | [toʊləs] |

There is nothing about suffixation per se that produces this result. Thus, if we add a vowel-initial suffix to a stem that ends in /oʊ/ plus /l/, then the monophthongal allophone appears:

*goalie* [goli]
*hole-y* [holi]
*rolling* [ɹolɪŋ]
*Pol-ess* [poləs] 'a female Pole'

These facts can be accounted for if we assume that Pre-/l/ Monophthongization is a stem-bounded rule. Below, I have labeled the stem morphemes within the full words.

| *lowly* | *goalie* | |
|---|---|---|
| [[loʊ]stem li]word | [[goʊl]stem i]word | underlying forms |
| BLOCKED | o | Pre-/l/ Monophthongization |
| loʊli | goli | surface forms |

It can be seen that underlying /oʊ/ gets monophthongized only if it is in the same stem as the immediately following /l/.

Another rule that seems to be stem-bounded in English is Vowel Nasalization, which converts underlying oral vowels to their nasal counterparts before a nasal consonant. I find that many English speakers have near-minimal pairs for nasality of the following type:

| | | |
|---|---|---|
| *Venus* [vĩnəs] | *freeness* [fɹinəs] | |
| *bonus* [bõʊnəs] | *slowness* [sloʊnəs] | |
| *Uranus* [jʊɹêĩnəs] | *greyness* [gɹeɪnəs] | |
| *Linus* [lãĩnəs] | *dryness* [dɹaɪnəs] | |

These distinctions can be derived under the assumption that the rule that derives nasalization is stem-bounded:

**Vowel Nasalization** (refined)
[+syllabic] → [+nasal] / ____ [+nasal]     Domain: Stem

A stem-bounded rule will match up to an underlying representation like /[[vinəs]stem]word/ but not to /[[fɹi]stem nəs]word/.

# Check Up the Points

## 1 Glossary for this Section

**assimilation rules/ assimilation**
동화 규칙

A phonological process that changes feature values of segments to make them more similar: e.g., a vowel becomes [+nasal] when followed by [+nasal] consonant. Also called **feature-spreading rules**.

**aspiration**
기식음화

The phonetic phenomenon in which a segment (normally an obstruent) is followed by a period of voiceless breathing, a 'puff of breath'.

**devoicing**
무성음화

Any phonological process in which a segment which is historically or underlyingly voiced loses its voicing. See partial devoicing, full devoicing, initial devoicing, final devoicing.

**dissimilation rules**
이화 규칙

Phonological rules that change feature values of segments to make them less similar, e.g., a fricative dissimilation rule: /θ/ is pronounced [t] following another fricative. In English dialects with this rule, *sixth* /sɪks + θ/ is pronounced [sɪkst].

**feature-changing rules**
자질값 변환 규칙

Phonological rules that change feature values of segments, either to make them more similar (see **assimilation rules**) or less similar (see **dissimilation rules**).

**feature-spreading rules**
자질 확산 규칙

See **assimilation rules**.

**glottalization**
성문음화

A broad term applied loosely to a wide range of phenomena involving some kind of activity in the glottis, including at least glottalling, glottal reinforcement, the use of creaky voice, and the use of glottal airstream mechanism.

Chapter

03

## Check Up the Points

**glottalling**
성문음화

The replacement of an oral plosive by a glottal stop, as in the pronunciation of *butter* as [ˈbʌʔə]

**glottal reinforcement**
성문음 강화

The articulation of an oral plosive with a simultaneous glottal stop, as in the pronunciation of *quite good* [kwaɪʔt gʊd] or *stop talking* as [stɒʔp tɔːkɪŋ].

**hiatus**
모음연접

The occurrence of two consecutive vowles forming separate syllables, as in Leo, skiing, lower, or playoff. The vowels in question are said to be **in hiatus**. There is considerable evidence that hiatus is unstable: vowels in hiatus frequently undergo phonological changes which remove the hiatus. Latin *hiatus* 'gap'.

**homorganic consonants**
동일위치 자음

Two sounds produced at the same place of articulation: e.g., [m] and [p]; [t], [d], [n]. See **assimilation rules**.

**labialization**
순음화

The presence in an articulation of some degree of lip-rounding as a scecondary articulation. In the IPA, labialization is represented by a superscript w: hence [sʷ] represents a labialized vloceless alveolar fricative, such as often occurs in English *soon* or *swim*.

**lengthening**
장음화

Any process which, phonetically or phonologically, increases the duration of a segment, most often a vowel.

**metathesis**
전위

The phonological process that reorders segments, often by transposing two sequential sounds: e.g., the pronunciation of *ask* /æsk/ in some English dialects as [æks].

| | |
|---|---|
| **morphophonemic rules**<br>형태음소 규칙 | Rules that specify the pronunciation of morphemes; a morpheme may have more than one pronunciation determined by such rules: e.g., the plural morpheme /z/ in English is regularly pronounced [s], [z], or [əz]. |
| **neutralization**<br>중화 | Phonological processes or rules that obliterate the contrast between two phonemes in certain environments: e.g., in some dialects of English /t/ and /d/ are both pronounced as voiced flaps between vowels, as in writer and rider, thus neutralizing the voicing distinction so that the two words sound alike. |
| **palatalization**<br>구개음화 | 1. The phenomenon in which a segment whose primary articulation is at some other location is articulated with a secondary articulation involving the raising of the front of the tongue towards the palate or (with the back consonants) the moving of the constriction forward towards the palate. (p → pʲ, t → tʲ,k → kʲ) 2. Any phonological process in which a non-palatal segment is converted to a palatal or palato-alveolar segment. (s → ʃ, t → ʧ) |
| **reduced vowel**<br>약화 모음 | A vowel that is unstressed and generally pronounced as schwa [ə] in English. |
| **transcription, phonemic**<br>음소 전사 | The phonemic representation of speech sounds using phonetic symbols, ignoring phonetic details that are predictable by rule, usually given between slashes: e.g., /pæn/, /spæn/ for *pan*, span as opposed to the phonetic representation [pʰæn], [spæn]. |
| **transcription, phonetic**<br>음성 전사 | The representation of speech sounds using phonetic symbols between square brackets. It may reflect nondistinctive predictable features such as aspiration and nasality: e.g., [pʰat] for *pot* or [mæn] for *man*. |

Chapter

03

**trisyllabic laxing**

3음절 이완모음화

(also **trisyllabic shortening**) 1. The historical process in English by which tense (long) vowels underwent laxing (shortening) whenever followed by two or more further syllables in the word. This process is responsible for such modern alternations as *sane/sanity, devine/divinity, and profound/profundity*. 2. In some descriptions of English, a synchronic rule posited to account for these alternations.

**velarization**

연구개음화

The presence during the articulation of a segment of the raising of the back of the tongue towards the velum as a second articulation. Velarization is represented in the IPA by a following superscript [ɣ], as in [lˠ]; it was formerly represented by an overprinted tilde, as in [ɫ].

**vowel reduction**

모음 약화

Any phonological process in connected speech which makes a vowel shorter, less loud, lower in pitch or more central in quality, or which neutralizes some vowel contrasts in unstressed syllables.

## ❷ Key-points in this Section

### Table 1. Types of Phonological Rules in English

| | | | | |
|---|---|---|---|---|
| **Allophonic Rules** | Assimilation | Feature Addition | Aspiration | § 6.2.1 |
| | | | Vowel Nasalization | § 6.2.2 |
| | | | Glottalization/Glottal Reinforcement | § 6.2.3 |
| | | | Vowel Lengthening | § 6.2.4 |
| | | Feature-Value Changing | /l/-Velarization | § 6.2.5 |
| | | | Palatalization | § 6.2.6 |
| | | | Palatalization of Velar Stops | § 6.2.7 |
| | | | Labialization | § 6.2.7 |
| | | | Nasal Dentalization | § 6.2.8 |
| | | | Nasal Devoicing | § 6.2.9 |
| | Dissimilation | | Fricative Dissimilation | § 6.3.1 |
| | | | Liquid Dissimilation | § 6.3.2 |
| | Segment Deletion | | Schwa Deletion | § 6.4.1, § 6.4.2 |
| | | | /g/-Deletion | § 6.4.3 |
| | | | /t/-Deletion | § 6.4.4 |
| | | | Interdental Fricative Deletion | § 6.4.5 |
| | | | /j/-Deletion | § 6.4.6 |
| | Segment Insertion | | Voiceless Stop Insertion | § 6.5 |
| **Morpho-phonemic Rules** | Assimilation | | Nasal /n/ Place Assimilation | § 6.6.1 |
| | | | Morpheme /z/ Devoicing | § 6.6.2 |
| | | | Morpheme /d/ Devoicing | § 6.6.2 |
| | Segment Insertion | | Schwa Insertion | § 6.6.2 |
| | | | Glide Insertion for Hiatus Resolution | § 6.6.3 |
| | | | [ɹ]-Insertion for Hiatus Resolution | § 6.6.3 |
| | | | Trisyllabic Laxing | § 6.6.4 |
| **Neutralization** | Consonant Neutralization | | Flapping | § 6.7.1 |
| | Vowel Neutralization | | Prenasal ɪ/ɛ-Neutralization | § 6.7.2 |
| | | | Vowel Neutralization before /ɹ/ | § 6.7.3 |
| | | | Vowel Reduction | § 6.7.4 |
| **Cluster Simplification** | | | | § 6.8 |
| **Metathesis** | | | | § 6.10 |

# Suprasegmental Phonology: Introduction

**TIP**

- Stress in Nouns of at least three syllables (2018)
- Stress and Kinds of Suffixes (2016)

Much of the current research in phonology has focused on units larger than the segment. **Stress**, **tone**, and **duration** (vowel and consonant length) are often claimed to be properties of <u>suprasegmental units such as the syllable or word</u>, while vowel harmony and nasalization are also sometimes included under this heading (Firth, 1948; Robins, 1957b). That is, prosodic features such as those just mentioned are best seen as extending over <u>units which can encompass more than one segment</u>. (from Hyman *Phonology: Theory and Analysis*)

## 7.1. Prosody

Prosody is a term to refer to properties of language such as **pitch**, **loudness**, **tempo** and **rhythm**. Importantly, prosody also covers the phenomenon of **stress** which is found in most languages. This means that, in words of more than one syllable, there is one which is more acoustically **prominent** than the others. This **prominence** can be realized on the phonetic level by one of the following three features or a combination of them.

(1) a. greater relative length of the stressed syllable

    b. relatively high pitch

    c. greater relative loudness

(1a) is nearly always a characteristic of stressed syllables. However, languages usually have either (1b) or (1c) as well. (1c) is most common for so-called lexical stress, that is the normal stress on a word said without particular emphasis, e.g. the second syllable in *polite* or the first in *constant*. There is also the phenomenon of contrastive stress which refers to a situation where the speaker wishes to highlight a whole word and does this by altering the prosody of the syllable carrying lexical stress. In English, syllables given contrastive stress tend to have a higher pitch so that in a phrase like *He struck the ʹteacher!* there is a recognizable rise on the first syllable of *teacher*.

## 7.2. Prosodic Features

*Length*, *pitch*, and *stress* (or "*accent*") are **prosodic** or **suprasegmental** features. They are features *over and above* the segmental values such as place or manner of articulation, thus the *supra-* in *suprasegmental*. The term *prosodic* comes from poetry, where it refers to the metrical structure of verse.

Speech sounds that are identical in their place or manner features may differ in **length** (duration). Tense vowels are slightly longer than lax vowels, but only by a few milliseconds.

The colon-like ꞉ is the IPA symbol for **segment length or doubling**.

When we speak, we also change the **pitch** of our voices. The pitch depends on how fast the vocal cords vibrate: the faster they vibrate, the higher the pitch.

In many languages, certain syllables in a word are louder, slightly higher in pitch, and somewhat longer in duration than other syllables in the word. They are **stressed** syllables.

English is a "**stress-timed**" language. In general, at least one syllable is stressed in an English word. French is not a stress-timed language. The syllables have approximately the same loudness, length, and pitch. It is a "**syllable-timed**" language.

## 7.3. Stress: Introduction

**Stress** is a cover term for **the prosodic features of** *duration, intensity,* **and** *pitch*; thus, the prominence of stressed syllables is generally manifested by their characteristics of being longer, louder, and higher in pitch than unstressed syllables. From the speaker's point of view, this corresponds to **the amount of effort expanded**, while from the hearer's point of view, it is **the perceptual prominence**.

English has **variable** stress. For example, in the following trisyllabic nouns, *article*, *tomato*, and *kangaroo*, the stress moves from the first to the second and then to the third syllable, respectively ([ɑ́ˌtɪkl̩], [təméɾo], [kæŋəˌɹú]).

In addition to **variability**, English stress is said to be **mobile**. This can be shown **in morphologically related words** in which the stress shifts on to different syllables:

(2)

| democrat | [dɛ́məkˌɹæt] | democracy | [dəmɑ́kˌɹəsi] | democratic | [dɛməkˌɹǽtɪk] |
|---|---|---|---|---|---|
| origin | [ɔ́ˌɹədʒən] | original | [ɔˌɹídʒənəl] | originality | [ɔˌɹədʒənǽləri] |
| constitute | [kɑ́nstətut] | constitutional | [kɑnstətúʃən̩l] | constitutionality | [kɑnstətuʃənǽləri] |
| photograph | [fótəgˌɹæf] | photography | [fətɑ́gˌɹəfi] | photographic | [fotəgˌɹǽfɪk] |
| diplomat | [dípləmæt] | diplomacy | [dɪplóməsi] | diplomatic | [dɪpləmǽtɪk] |

Although the above discussion may suggest a highly **variable** and **unpredictable** situation, this does not mean that there are no rules or principles underlying the stress patterns of English. It should be noted, however, that these regularities are **tendencies** rather than **airtight rules**. It is a characteristic of English that the grammatical category or morphological structure of words frequently affects the stress patterns.

**Syllable weight** is an important factor in stress assignment in that heavy syllables attract stress. The weight of a syllable is determined by its rhyme structure. If the rhyme is non-branching (a short vowel, and no coda), **the syllable is light**. If, on the other hand, the rhyme is branching (has a short vowel, **except [ə], which is weightless and cannot carry stress**, followed by a coda (simple or complex), or has a long vowel or a diphthong with or without a following coda), **the syllable is heavy**.

It is also useful to define the terms *ult* (the last syllable), *penult* (the syllable before the ult), and *antepenult* (the syllable before the penult), which will be used for the location of the syllables in a word. These can be shown in the following word, _probability_:

(3)  　　　　　[ p ɹ ə . b ə . b ɪ .　　　l ə .　　　t i ]
　　　　　　　　　　*ante-penult*　　　　*penult*　　*ult*

## 7.4. Word Stress

In many languages, including English, one or more of the syllables in every content word are stressed. A stressed syllable, which can be marked by an **acute accent** (´), is perceived as more prominent than an unstressed syllable, as shown in the following examples:

(4)　pérvert　　(noun)　　as in　"My neighbor is a pervert."
　　　pervért　　(verb)　　 as in　"Don't pervert the idea."
　　　súbject　　(noun)　　as in　"Let's change the subject."
　　　subjéct　　(verb)　　 as in　"He'll subject us to criticism."

These pairs show that stress can be **contrastive** in English. In these cases it distinguishes between nouns and verbs. It may also distinguish between words of other categories, such as the adjective *inválid* (not valid) and the noun *ínvalid* (a sickly person).

Some words may contain more than one stressed vowel, but exactly one of the stressed vowels is more prominent than the others. The vowel that receives primary stress is marked by an **acute accent** (´). The other stressed vowels are indicated by **grave accents** (`) over the vowels (these vowels receive secondary stress).

The stress pattern of a word may differ among English-speaking people. For example, in most varieties of **American English** the word *láboratòry* [lǽbərətʰɔ̀ri] has two stressed syllables, but in most varieties of **British English** it receives only one stress [ləbɔ́rətri]. Because English vowels generally **reduce to schwa** or **delete** when they are not stressed, the British and American vowels differ in this word. In fact, in the British version the fourth vowel is deleted because it is not stressed.

Stress is a property of the syllable rather than a segment; it is a prosodic or suprasegmental feature. To produce a stressed syllable, one may change the pitch (usually by raising it), make the syllable louder, or make it longer. We often use all three of these phonetic means to stress a syllable.

## 7.5. Sentence and Phrase Stress

When words are combined into phrases and sentences, one syllable receives greater stress than all others. Just as there is only one primary stress in a word spoken in isolation, only one of the vowels in a phrase (or sentence) receives primary stress or accent. All of the other stressed vowels are demoted to secondary stress.

In English we place primary stress on the adjectival part of a compound noun (which may be written as one word, two words separated by a hyphen, or two separate words), but we place the stress on the noun when the words are a noun phrase consisting of an adjective followed by a noun. The differences between the following pairs are therefore predictable:

| (5) | **Compound Noun** | **Adjective + Noun** |
|---|---|---|
| | tíghtrope ('a rope for acrobatics') | tight rópe ('a rope drawn taut') |
| | Rédcoat ('a British soldier') | red cóat ('a coat that is red') |
| | hótdog ('a frankfurter') | hot dóg ('an overheated dog') |
| | Whíte House ('the President's house') | white hóuse ('a house painted white') |

These pairs show that stress may be predictable from the morphology and syntax. The phonology interacts with the other components of the grammar. The stress differences between the noun and verb pairs (*subject* as noun or verb) are also predictable from the syntactic word category.

## 7.6. The Rhythm of English

Human beings speak *rhythmically*: they engage in the act of speaking by putting regular beats in the speech signal. You can hear those beats in an English utterance such as *The man went to the bar*. Here, the beats are on *man*, *went* and *bar*. In most varieties of English, we do not necessarily place a beat on every single syllable. In this utterance, no beat falls on the preposition *to*, or on the two occurrences of *the*. This is because English, unlike certain other languages, is *stress-timed*: the rhythmic beats fall only on *stressed* syllables. In our example, only *man*, *went* and *bar* are stressed, so the beats fall only on those. English is unlike many other languages in this respect.

Take the phrase *Chicken MacNuggets*, the name for a product sold by a well-known fast-food company. This is pronounced [ˌtʃɪkənmək'nʌɡəts]. There are two stressed syllables in this sequence. (The second is more prominent than the first.) The sequences ['tʃɪkənmək] and ['nʌɡəts] form rhythmic units in the utterance. Those units are called **metrical feet**. A metrical foot in English consists of a stressed syllable followed by zero or more unstressed syllables. In our example, the first metrical foot contains a stressed syllable and two unstressed syllables: [ˌtʃɪkənmək]. The second metrical foot contains a stressed syllable and one unstressed syllable: ['nʌɡəts].

Notice that divisions between the metrical feet need not coincide with word boundaries: the word boundary falls between the words *Chicken* and the word *MacNuggets*. But the rhythmic boundary falls between [ˌtʃɪkənmək] and ['nʌɡəts]. We call these metrical feet **trochaic**. This is an adjective derived from the noun *trochee*. A trochee is essentially a stressed−unstressed sequence, such as ['nʌɡəts].

# Check Up the Points

## ① Glossary for this Section

**accent**
액센트

1. Prominence. See **stressed syllable**; 2. the phonology or pronunciation of a specific regional dialect: e.g., Southern accent; 3. the pronunciation of a language by a nonnative speaker: e.g., French accent.

**acute accent**
고음조성 액센트

The diacritic ´, conventionally used in various orthographies and transcription systems for a variety of purposes. It was first used in Ancient Greek orthography to mark one of the distinctive pitch accents of that language. Latin *acutus* stands for 'sharpened'.

**antepenultimate syllable**
끝에서 세 번째 음절

The syllable before the penultimate syllable.

**contour tones**
굴곡성조

In tone language, tones in which the pitch glides from one level to another: e.g., from low to high as in a rising tone.

**contrastive stress**
대립 강세

Additional stress placed on a word to highlight it or to clarify the referent of a pronoun: e.g., in Joe hired Bill and he hired Sam, with contrastive stress on he, it is usually understood that Bill rather than Joe hired Sam.

**foot**
음보

1. The basic unit of rhythm in poetry, generally consisting of a group of two or more syllables in which one syllable bears the main stress. Among the commonest types of foot are the **iamb**, the **trochee**, and the **dactyl**. 2. The fundamental unit of rhythm in phonology, most typically consisting of a sequence of syllables one of which bears a stress or other prosodic element.

| | |
|---|---|
| **grave accent**<br>저음조성 액센트 | The diacritic `, conventionally used in various orthographies and transcription systems for a variety of purposes. It was first used in Ancient Greek orthography to mark one of the distinctive pitch accents of that language. Latin *gravis* stands for 'heavy'. |
| **heavy syllable**<br>중음절 | (rarely also **strong syllable**) A syllable which ends in any of long vowel, a diphthong, or one or more consonants. |
| **length**<br>장단 | A prosodic feature referring to the duration of a segment. Two sounds may contrast in length: e.g., in Japanese the first vowel is [+long] in /bi : ru/ 'beer' but [−long], therefore short, in /biru/ 'building.' |
| **level tones**<br>수평 성조 | Relatively stable (nongliding) pitch on syllables of tone languages. Also called **register tones**. |
| **light syllable**<br>경음절 | A syllable which is not heavy syllable. |
| **penultimate syllable**<br>끝에서 두 번째 음절 | The syllable before the ultimate syllable. |
| **pitch**<br>음정 | The fundamental frequency of sound perceived by the listener. |
| **pitch contour**<br>음정 굴곡 | The intonation of a sentence. |
| **prosodic feature**<br>운율 자질 | The duration (length), pitch, or loudness of speech sounds. |

| | |
|---|---|
| **prominence**<br>탁립 | The property of a syllable which stands out from adjoining syllables by virtue of any of several phonetic characteristics, such as greater loudness, greater duration, higher or lower pitch, greater syllable weight. |
| **sentence stress**<br>문장 강세 | (also **tonic stress**) Prominence attached to a single syllable in a single word of a complete sentence in an unmarked style of pronunciation—in English, normally to the last lexical item: *Janet lóves it* vs. *Janet loves her fóod.* |
| **stress, stressed syllable**<br>강세, 강세음절 | A syllable with relatively greater length, loudness, and/or higher pitch than other syllables in a word, and therefore perceived as prominent. Also called **accent**. |
| **stress-timed language**<br>강세−시간결정 언어 | A language in which at least one syllable of a word receives primary stress. English is such a language. |
| **syllable-timed language**<br>음절−시간결정 언어 | A language in which the syllables have approximately the same loudness, length, and pitch, as opposed to a stress-timed language. French, for example, is such a language. |
| **ultimate syllable**<br>끝 음절 | The last syllable. |
| **vowel reduction**<br>모음 약화 | Any phonological process in connected speech which makes a vowel shorter, less loud, lower in pitch or more central in quality, or which neutralizes some vowel contrasts in unstressed syllables. |

## ② Key-points in this Section

➡ **Stress**, **tone**, and **duration** are often claimed to be properties of suprasegmental units such as the syllable or word.

➡ English is a "**stress-timed**" language, not a "**syllable-timed**" language.

➡ **Stress** is a cover term for **the prosodic features of** *duration*, *intensity*, **and** *pitch*; thus, the prominence of stressed syllables is generally manifested by their characteristics of being longer, louder, and higher in pitch than unstressed syllables.

➡ It is a characteristic of English that the **grammatical category** or **morphological structure** of words frequently affects the stress patterns.

➡ Syllable Weight
The weight of a syllable is determined by its rhyme structure. If **the rhyme is non-branching** (a short vowel, and no coda), the syllable is **light**. If, on the other hand, **the rhyme is branching** (has a short vowel, except [ə], which is weightless and cannot carry stress, followed by a coda, or has a long vowel or a diphthong with or without a following coda), the syllable is **heavy**.

➡ A metrical foot in English consists of a stressed syllable followed by zero or more unstressed syllables.

# Phonotactics

## KEY CONCEPT IN THIS CHAPTER

- Phonotactics
- English Syllable Phonotactics
- Sonority Sequencing Principle (SSP)
- Homorganic
- Suffixed Forms and Non-Suffixed Forms

### TIP

- A Permissible Sequence of the Double Onset, *st-* (2018)
- Phonotactics of Syllable Structure, Coronals or [coronal] (2016)

The area which is concerned with the possible sequences of sounds in a language is **phonotactics**.

The general formula of English syllable structure can be stated as:

(1)         (C) (C) (C) V (C) (C) (C) {C}

What this characterization says is that a V (vowel or diphthong), which is the nucleus, is the only obligatory element in an English syllable (e.g. a [e]).

**Table 1.** Possible Syllable Structures in English

| V<br>a [e] | VC<br>at [æt] | VCC<br>act [ækt] | VCCC<br>angst [æŋst] | VCCCC<br>**angsts** [æŋsts] |
|---|---|---|---|---|
| CV<br>say [se] | CVC<br>beat [bit] | CVCC<br>binge [bɪndʒ] | CVCCC<br>text [tɛkst]<br>next [nɛkst] | CVCCCC<br>**worlds** [wɝldz]<br>**bursts** [bɝsts] |
| CCV<br>pray [pɹe] | CCVC<br>break [bɹek] | CCVCC<br>print [pɹɪnt] | CCVCCC<br>sphinx [sfɪŋks] | CCVCCCC<br>**twelfths** [twɛlfθs] |
| CCCV<br>spray [spɹe] | CCCVC<br>strike [stɹaɪk] | CCCVCC<br>sprint [spɹɪnt] | CCCVCCC<br>**sprints** [spɹɪnts] | CCCVCCCC<br>? |

CCCVCCCC is a logically possibility with no commonly found vocabulary.


## 8.1. Single Onsets

The only consonant that is not allowed to take the onset position in English is /ŋ/.

Another sound, /ʒ/, does not start an English word (save for items such as genre [ʒɑnɹə], as well as some foreign names such as Zhivago [ʒɪvəgo]) but is capable of occurring in non-word-initial onsets, as in vision [vɪ.ʒən] and measure [mɛ.ʒɚ].

Finally, /ð/ deserves a mention for its restricted occurrence in word-initial position; this sound is found only in grammatical (function) words (e.g. *the, then, there,* etc.) word-initially. (cf. mother [ma.ðɚ], *brother* [bɹa.ðɚ])


## 8.2. Single Codas

The only sound that cannot occur in English codas is /h/.

Also, /ʒ/ is somewhat less solid than other consonants; although it is firm for several speakers, we can still hear the [dʒ] realizations in *garage* [gəɹɑdʒ] and *massage* [məsɑdʒ] from some speakers.

(2)     /ʒ/ → [dʒ]       cf. fricative → affricate   (affrication)

Two other sounds, /j, w/, are also frequently included in the list of consonants that cannot occur in codas. While this is true, the existence of diphthongs /aɪ, ɔɪ/ and /aʊ/ weakens the case, as the endings of these diphthongs are very similar, if not identical, to /j/ and /w/ respectively. (This can be attested in alternative phonetic symbols used in some systems, (/aj, aw, ɔj/).)

## 8.3. Double Onsets

Table 2 shows the occurring double onsets of English.

**Table 2. English Double Onsets**

| C₁＼C₂ | p | t | k | f | m | n | l | ɹ | w | j |
|---|---|---|---|---|---|---|---|---|---|---|
| p | ■ | | | | | | ✓ | ✓ | | ✓ |
| b | | | | | | | ✓ | ✓ | | ✓ |
| t | | ■ | | | | | | ✓ | ✓ | (✓) |
| d | | | | | | | | ✓ | ✓ | (✓) |
| k | | | ■ | | | | ✓ | ✓ | ✓ | ✓ |
| g | | | | | | | ✓ | ✓ | ✓ | |
| f | | | | ■ | | | ✓ | ✓ | | ✓ |
| v | | | | | | | | | | ✓ |
| θ | | | | | | | | ✓ | | ✓ |
| s | ✓ | ✓ | ✓ | ✓ | ✓ | ✓ | ✓ | | ✓ | (✓) |
| ʃ | | | | | | | | ✓ | | |
| h | | | | | | | | | | ✓ |
| m | | | | | | ■ | | | | ✓ |
| n | | | | | | | ■ | | | (✓) |
| l | | | | | | | | ■ | | (✓) |

g ← cf. régular
θ ← cf. thew

> **NOTE**
> ✓ Double onsets that are allowed in English
> (✓) Double onsets that are **not** found for **most speakers of American English**
> ■ Impossible combination

**Table 3.** English Double Onsets With Possible Phonemic Sequences

| C₁＼C₂ | p | t | k | f | m | n | l | ɹ | w | j | |
|---|---|---|---|---|---|---|---|---|---|---|---|
| p | ■ | | | | | | pl | pɹ | | pj | |
| b | | | | | | | bl | bɹ | | bj | |
| t | | ■ | | | | | | tɹ | tw | **(tj)** | |
| d | | | | | | | | dɹ | dw | **(dj)** | |
| k | | | ■ | | | | kl | kɹ | kw | kj | |
| g | | | | | | | gl | gɹ | gw | | ← cf. régular |
| f | | | | ■ | | | fl | fɹ | | fj | |
| v | | | | | | | | | | vj | |
| θ | | | | | | | | θɹ | θw | | ← cf. thew |
| s | sp | st | sk | sf | sm | sn | sl | | sw | **(sj)** | |
| ʃ | | | | | | | | ʃɹ | | | |
| h | | | | | | | | | | hj | |
| m | | | | | ■ | | | | | mj | |
| n | | | | | | ■ | | | | **(nj)** | |
| l | | | | | | | ■ | | | **(lj)** | |

**Table 4.** English Double Onsets With Actual Words

| C1 \ C2 | p | t | k | f | m | n | l | ɹ | w | j | |
|---|---|---|---|---|---|---|---|---|---|---|---|
| p | ■ | | | | | | play | pray | | pew | |
| b | | | | | | | blue | bring | | beauty | |
| t | | ■ | | | | | | try | twin | **(tune)** | |
| d | | | | | | | | dry | dwarf | **(dune)** | |
| k | | | ■ | | | | clue | cry | queen | cute | |
| g | | | | | | | glue | grow | gweep | | ← cf. régular |
| f | | | | ■ | | | fly | free | | few | [ɹɛgjulɚ] |
| v | | | | | | | | | | view | |
| θ | | | | | | | | three | thwart | | ← cf. thew |
| s | spy | still | skill | sphere | smile | snail | slide | | swing | **(assume)** | [θju] |
| ʃ | | | | | | | | shrimp | | | |
| h | | | | | | | | | | hue | |
| m | | | | | ■ | | | | | music | |
| n | | | | | | ■ | | | | **(news)** | |
| l | | | | | | | ■ | | | **(lute)** | |

We can make the following observations. Affricates are the only class of consonants that do not appear in onset clusters. Besides this general statement, there are several other restrictions for two-member onset clusters:

(3)  a. No voiced fricatives can serve as $C_2$. Only /v/ can be a $C_1$, and it can combine only with /j/ (e.g. *view* [vju]).

b. No non-lateral approximant (/ɹ, w, j/) can serve as $C_1$; the lateral can only precede /j/ (only for some speakers).

c. No voiced stop can serve as $C_2$.

d. No fricative other than /f/ can serve as $C_2$, and this can only be preceded by a /s/ in rarely found vocabulary (e.g. *sphere* [sfiə]).

e. No stops and nasals are allowed as $C_2$, except after /s/ (e.g. *speak, small*).

f. /s/ and /ʃ/ are complementary: /s/ does not occur before /ɹ/, and /ʃ/ occurs only before /ɹ/ (e.g. *shrimp* [ʃɹɪmp]).

g. /h/ and /m/ can only occur before /j/ (e.g. *huge* [hjudʒ], *music* [mjuzɪk]).

h. /θ/ can precede only /ɹ/ and /w/ (e.g. *three* [θɹi], *thwart* [θwɔɹt]).

i. Labials ($C_1$) do not cluster with a labial approximant (*\$pwV, *\$bwV, *\$mwV, *\$fwV, *\$vwV).

j. No geminates (i.e. doubled consonant sounds) are allowed.

k. Alveolar stops ($C_1$) do not cluster with /l/ (*\$tlV, *\$dlV).

We can summarize the situation in the following manners. In general, English double onsets are

(4)  a. /s/ + C (where C = any consonant that can assume the position of $C_2$, except /ɹ/; /ʃ/ appears before /ɹ/), and

b. obstruent + approximant, with the limitations cited above.

## 8.4. Sonority Sequencing Principle (SSP)

While the pattern of $C_1$ as an obstruent and $C_2$ as a sonorant is very common, we do not have any double onset in which the reverse ($C_1$ = sonorant and $C_2$ = obstruent) is true. This pattern that we observe for English is also commonly found in many other languages, and can be accounted for by the principle known as "sonority sequencing." We referred to sonority earlier for syllable peaks, and now make reference to it for the sequencing of sounds with respect to a syllable peak by the **Sonority Sequencing Principle** (**SSP**). As given by Selkirk (1984: 116), SSP states that:

(5) In any syllable, there is a segment constituting a sonority peak that is preceded and/or followed by a sequence of segments with progressively decreasing sonority values.

Thus, the expected pattern is that, going from $C_1$ to $C_2$, the sonority level will rise. Such is the case in the overwhelming majority of English double onsets (e.g. *play* [ple], *cry* [kɹaɪ], *quick* [kwɪk]).

The violations of this principle are /s/ + stop clusters (/sp. st. sk/), in which the sonority level drops, instead rises, going from $C_1$ to $C_2$.

As we will see with triple onsets as well as with double and triple codas. /s/ behaves exceptionally. To account for such cases, several scholars have suggested a special "adjunct" status for /s/ clusters.

## 8.5. Triple Onsets

Triple onsets can be described as an addition of /s/ as $C_1$ to voiceless stop + approximant double onsets. Thus, we have:

(6)    $C_1$ = /s/,    $C_2$ = voiceless stop,    $C_3$ = approximant.

Although the combinations can give us 12 logical possibilities, only seven of these occur:

(7) a.

| | | | ɹ | e.g. <u>spring</u> |
| | | | l | e.g. <u>splash</u> |
| s | p | | j | e.g. <u>spew</u> |
| | | | w | e.g. * (excluded because /w/ cannot occur after labials: |

  *$pwV, *$bwV, *$mwV, *$fwV, *$vwV)

b.

| | | ɹ | e.g. <u>string</u> |
| | | l | e.g. * (excluded because no lateral after an alveolar stop: |

  *$tlV, *$dlV)

| s | t | | |
| | | j | e.g. * (/tj/ non-existent for most speakers) ← cf. **stew** [stʲu] |
| | | w | e.g. * |

c.

| | | | ɹ | e.g. <u>scrape</u> |
| | | | l | e.g. * (very rare, <u>sclerosis</u> [sklɪəɹosɪs]) |
| s | k | | j | e.g. <u>skewer</u> ([skjuɚ]) |
| | | | w | e.g. <u>squeeze</u> |

## 8.6. Double Codas

Double non-suffixed English codas can be generalized in the following fashion:

(8) a. $C_1$ is a nasal and $C_2$ is an obstruent (no voiced obstruent permitted except /d, z, dʒ/). Nasals ($C_1$) combining with stops ($C_2$) are invariably **homorganic**.

b. If $C_1$ is /s/, then $C_2$ is a voiceless stop.

c. $C_1$ is a liquid (/l, ɹ/), then $C_2$ is any consonant except for /z, ʒ, ð/. <u>Also non-existent is the /lg/ cluster.</u>

d. If $C_1$ is a voiceless non-alveolar stop (/p, k/), then $C_2$ is a voiceless alveolar obstruent (/t, s/). Also permitted is the /ft/ cluster.

Possibilities increase considerably if we add to these the clusters created by the suffixes with /t, d, s, z, θ/ (past tense, plural, possessive, ordinals, etc.) Table 5 gives the actually occurring double codas.

Table 5. English Double Codas

| C1 \ C2 | p | b | t | d | k | g | tʃ | dʒ | f | v | θ | s | z | ʃ | m | n | l |
|---|---|---|---|---|---|---|---|---|---|---|---|---|---|---|---|---|---|
| p | ■ |  | ✓ |  |  |  |  |  |  |  | ✗ | ✓ |  |  |  |  |  |
| b |  | ■ |  | ✗ |  |  |  |  |  |  |  |  | ✗ |  |  |  |  |
| t |  |  | ■ |  |  |  |  |  |  |  | ✗ | ✗ |  |  |  |  |  |
| d |  |  |  | ■ |  |  |  |  |  |  | ✗ |  | ✗ |  |  |  |  |
| k |  |  | ✓ |  | ■ |  |  |  |  |  |  | ✓ |  |  |  |  |  |
| g |  |  |  | ✗ |  | ■ |  |  |  |  |  |  | ✗ |  |  |  |  |
| tʃ |  |  | ✗ |  |  |  | ■ |  |  |  |  |  |  |  |  |  |  |
| dʒ |  |  |  | ✗ |  |  |  | ■ |  |  |  |  |  |  |  |  |  |
| f |  |  | ✓ |  |  |  |  |  | ■ |  | ✗ | ✗ |  |  |  |  |  |
| v |  |  |  | ✗ |  |  |  |  |  | ■ |  |  | ✗ |  |  |  |  |
| θ |  |  | ✗ |  |  |  |  |  |  |  | ■ | ✗ |  |  |  |  |  |
| ð |  |  |  | ✗ |  |  |  |  |  |  |  |  | ✗ |  |  |  |  |
| s | ✓ |  | ✓ |  | ✓ |  |  |  |  |  |  | ■ |  |  |  |  |  |
| z |  |  |  | ✗ |  |  |  |  |  |  |  |  | ■ |  |  |  |  |
| ʃ |  |  | ✗ |  |  |  |  |  |  |  |  |  |  | ■ |  |  |  |
| ʒ |  |  |  | ✗ |  |  |  |  |  |  |  |  |  |  |  |  |  |
| m | ✓ |  | ✗ | ✗ |  |  |  |  | ✓ |  |  |  | ✗ |  | ■ |  |  |
| n |  |  | ✓ | ✓ |  |  | ✓ | ✓ |  |  | ✓ | ✓ | ✓ |  |  | ■ |  |
| ŋ |  |  | ✗ | ✓ |  |  |  |  |  |  | ✗ |  | ✗ |  |  |  |  |
| l | ✓ | ✓ | ✓ | ✓ | ✓ |  | ✓ | ✓ | ✓ | ✓ | ✓ | ✓ | ✗ | ✓ | ✓ | ✓ | ■ |
| ɹ | ✓ | ✓ | ✓ | ✓ | ✓ | ✓ | ✓ | ✓ | ✓ | ✓ | ✓ | ✓ | ✗ | ✓ | ✓ | ✓ | ✓ |

NOTE
✓ Non-suffixed double codas
✗ Suffixed double codas
■ Impossible combination

**Table 6.** English Double Codas With Possible Phonemic Sequences

| C₁\C₂ | p | b | t | d | k | g | tʃ | dʒ | f | v | θ | s | z | ʃ | m | n | l |
|---|---|---|---|---|---|---|---|---|---|---|---|---|---|---|---|---|---|
| p | ■ | | pt | | | | | | | | p+θ | ps | | | | | |
| b | | ■ | | b+d | | | | | | | | | b+z | | | | |
| t | | | ■ | | | | | | | | t+θ | t+s | | | | | |
| d | | | | ■ | | | | | | | d+θ | | d+z | | | | |
| k | | | kt | | ■ | | | | | | | ks | | | | | |
| g | | | | g+d | | ■ | | | | | | | g+z | | | | |
| tʃ | | | tʃ+t | | | | ■ | | | | | | | | | | |
| dʒ | | | | dʒ+d | | | | ■ | | | | | | | | | |
| f | | | ft | | | | | | ■ | | f+θ | f+s | | | | | |
| v | | | | v+d | | | | | | ■ | | | v+z | | | | |
| θ | | | θ+t | | | | | | | | ■ | θ+s | | | | | |
| ð | | | | ð+d | | | | | | | | | ð+z | | | | |
| s | sp | | st | | sk | | | | | | | ■ | | | | | |
| z | | | | z+d | | | | | | | | | ■ | | | | |
| ʃ | | | ʃ+t | | | | | | | | | | | ■ | | | |
| ʒ | | | | ʒ+d | | | | | | | | | | | | | |
| m | mp | | m+t | m+d | | | | | mf | | | | m+z | | ■ | | |
| n | | | nt | nd | | | ntʃ | ndʒ | | | nθ | ns | nz | | | ■ | |
| ŋ | | | | ŋ+d | ŋk | | | | | | ŋ+θ | | ŋ+z | | | | |
| l | lp | lb | lt | ld | lk | | ltʃ | ldʒ | lf | lv | lθ | ls | l+z | lʃ | lm | ln | ■ |
| ɹ | ɹp | ɹb | ɹt | ɹd | ɹk | ɹg | ɹtʃ | ɹdʒ | ɹf | ɹv | ɹθ | ɹs | ɹ+z | ɹʃ | ɹm | ɹn | ɹl |

**Table 7.** English Double Codas With Actual Words

| | p | b | t | d | k | g | tʃ | dʒ | f | v | θ | s | z | ʃ | m | n | l |
|---|---|---|---|---|---|---|---|---|---|---|---|---|---|---|---|---|---|
| p | ■ | | apt | | | | | | | | **p+θ** | lapse | | | | | |
| b | | ■ | | **b+d** | | | | | | | | | **b+z** | | | | |
| t | | | ■ | | | | | | | | **t+θ** | **t+s** | | | | | |
| d | | | | ■ | | | | | | | **d+θ** | | **d+z** | | | | |
| k | | | act | | ■ | | | | | | | | tax | | | | |
| g | | | | **g+d** | | ■ | | | | | | | **g+z** | | | | |
| tʃ | | | **tʃ+t** | | | | ■ | | | | | | | | | | |
| dʒ | | | | **dʒ+d** | | | | ■ | | | | | | | | | |
| f | | | left | | | | | | ■ | | **f+θ** | **f+s** | | | | | |
| v | | | | **v+d** | | | | | | ■ | | | **v+z** | | | | |
| θ | | | **θ+t** | | | | | | | | ■ | **θ+s** | | | | | |
| ð | | | | **ð+d** | | | | | | | | | **ð+z** | | | | |
| s | grasp | | east | | ask | | | | | | | ■ | | | | | |
| z | | | | **z+d** | | | | | | | | | ■ | | | | |
| ʃ | | | **ʃ+t** | | | | | | | | | | | ■ | | | |
| ʒ | | | | **ʒ+d** | | | | | | | | | | | | | |
| m | camp | | **m+t** | **m+d** | | | | | humph | | | | **m+z** | | ■ | | |
| n | | | pint | sand | | | ranch | hinge | | | month | dance | lens | | | ■ | |
| ŋ | | | | **ŋ+d** | sink | | | | | | **ŋ+θ** | | **ŋ+z** | | | | |
| l | help | bulb | belt | mild | bulk | | milch | indulge | golf | solve | health | else | **l+z** | welsh | film | (kiln) | ■ |
| ɹ | sharp | curb | sort | card | dark | berg | arch | large | scarf | curve | birth | horse | **ɹ+z** | marsh | arm | barn | perle |

As stated earlier, the sonority sequencing principle (SSP) dictates the opposite of onset sequencing for codas. This means that optimal codas should have the sonority level dropping as we move from $C_1$ to $C_2$. Indeed, as Table 5 shows, this is the case for the double codas we find in non-suffixed (monomorphemic) forms in English (e.g. *arm* [ɑɹm], *sharp* [ʃɑɹp], *belt* [bɛlt]).

Exceptions are

(9)   a. two-stop sequences, which are never homorganic (e.g. apt [æpt], act [ækt]), and
      b. stop + /s/, which always agree in voicing (e.g. lapse [læps], tax [tæks]).

## 8.7. Triple Codas

The triple codas of English do not lend themselves to the rather simple formula we gave for triple onsets. We can say, in more general terms, that with the exception of (10-1), below, which has three obstruents, all the other combinations consist of a liquid or a nasal (sonorant) followed by two obstruents. The following combinations are found in non-suffixed forms:

| (10) | | $C_1$ | $C_2$ | $C_3$ | Examples |
|---|---|---|---|---|---|
| 1 | | stop | fricative | stop | /dst/ **midst**, /kst/ next |
| 2 | (a) | nasal | stop | stop | /mpt/ exempt, /ŋkt/ sacrosanct |
| | (b) | nasal | stop | fricative | /mps/ mumps, /ŋks/ jinx |
| | (c) | nasal | fricative | stop | /nst/ **against**, /ŋst/ amongst |
| 3 | (a) | l | stop | stop | /lpt/ sculpt |
| | (b) | l | stop | fricative | /lts/ waltz |
| | (c) | l | fricative | stop | /lst/ **whilst** |
| 4 | (a) | ɹ | stop | stop | /ɹkt/ infarct, /ɹpt/ excerpt |
| | (b) | ɹ | stop | fricative | /ɹps/ corpse, /ɹts/ quartz |
| | (c) | ɹ | fricative | stop | /ɹst/ first |
| | (d) | ɹ | l | stop | /ɹld/ world |
| | (e) | ɹ | l | fricative | /ɹlz/ Charles |

We have to acknowledge the fact that *midst* in (10-1), *against* in (10-2c), and *whilst* in (10-3c) are controversial and may be included in the suffixed category, as we encounter in some publications.

In addition to theses, a multiplicity of other triple codas is created via suffixation, the great majority of which are provided by /t, d/ of the simple past tense and by /s, z/ of the plural, the possessive, and the third person singular of the simple present. Also noteworthy are the possibilities created by /θ/, the "ordinal number morpheme" (e.g. *sixth* [sɪksθ]) and the ending deriving nouns from adjectives (deadjectival nominal morpheme) (e.g. *warmth* [wɔɹmθ]).

The following list gives the possibilities of triple codas via suffixation in terms of general classes; thus, actually occurring clusters have many more combinations than the examples cited here:

| (11) | | C$_1$ | C$_2$ | C$_3$ | Examples |
|---|---|---|---|---|---|
| 1 | | nasal | obstruent | /t, d, s, z/ | lame**nts** |
| 2 | | /s/ | stop | /t, d, s, z/ | lis**ped** |
| 3 | (a) | /l/ | obstruent | /t, d, s, z/ | gul**ped** |
| | (b) | /l/ | nasal | /d, z/ | fil**med** |
| 4 | (a) | /ɹ/ | obstruent | /t, d, s, z/ | whar**fs** |
| | (b) | /ɹ/ | /l/ | /d, z/ | cur**ls** |
| | (c) | /ɹ/ | nasal | /d, z/ | tur**ned** |
| 5 | | obstruent | obstruent | obstruent (only /pts, kts, fts, pst, kst/) | li**fts** |

While nasals and liquids serve frequently as C$_1$ in triple codas, and the sequences of /lk, mp, sk/ freely occur as double codas in English, triple codas combining these elements are very restricted. Thus, <u>it is a noteworthy fact that English lacks /ɹlk, ɹmp, ɹsk, lmp, nsk/ as triple codas. Like double codas, clusters of obstruents in triple codas always agree in voicing (e.g. /spt/ lisped).</u>

# Check Up the Points

## 1 Glossary for this Section

**accidental gap**
우연공백

Phonological or morphological form that constitutes possible but nonoccurring lexical items: e.g., *blick*, *unsad*.

**geminate**
중복음

A sequence of two identical sounds; a long vowel or long consonant denoted either by writing the phonetic symbol twice as in [biiru], [sakki] or by use of a colon-like symbol [bi : ru], [sak : i].

**homorganic**
동일위치의

Having the same place of articulation, such as the /nd/ in *candy* or the /mp/ in *lamp*. Ant. **heterorganic**.

**phonotactics/**
**phonotactic**
**constraints**
음소배열제약

Rules stating permissible strings of phonemes within a syllable: e.g., a word-initial nasal consonant may be followed only by a vowel (in English). See **possible word, nonsense word, accidental gap**.

**nonsense word**
무의미어

A permissible phonological form without meaning: e.g., *slithy*.

**possible word**
가능어

A string of sounds that obeys the phonotactic constraints of the language but has no meaning: e.g., *gimble*. Also called a **nonsense word**.

**Sonority**
**Sequencing**
**Principle**
공명도 연속 원리

A widely accepted constraint on syllable structure. It says: that sonority profile of the syllable must slope outwards from the peak. In other words, the level of sonority must rise as wee proceed from the beginning of the syllable to the peak and fall as we proceed form the peak to the end, in accordance with **Sonority Hierarchy**. This principle is designed to block such putatively 'impossible' as [ndu] and [spidz].

## ② Key-points in this Section

→ **Phonotactics** is concerned with the possible sequences of sounds in a language.

→ **Sonority Sequencing Principle (SSP)**

In any syllable, there is a segment constituting a sonority peak that is preceded and/or followed by a sequence of segments with progressively decreasing sonority values.

→ Phonotactic constraints on double onsets

### Table 1. English Double Onsets

| C₁ \ C₂ | p | t | k | f | m | n | l | ɹ | w | j |
|---|---|---|---|---|---|---|---|---|---|---|
| p | ■ | | | | | | ✓ | ✓ | | ✓ |
| b | | | | | | | ✓ | ✓ | | ✓ |
| t | | ■ | | | | | ✓ | ✓ | | (✓) |
| d | | | | | | | ✓ | ✓ | | (✓) |
| k | | | ■ | | | | ✓ | ✓ | ✓ | ✓ |
| g | | | | | | | ✓ | ✓ | ✓ | |
| f | | | | ■ | | | ✓ | ✓ | | ✓ |
| v | | | | | | | | | | ✓ |
| θ | | | | | | | ✓ | ✓ | | |
| s | ✓ | ✓ | ✓ | ✓ | ✓ | ✓ | ✓ | | ✓ | (✓) |
| ʃ | | | | | | | | ✓ | | |
| h | | | | | | | | | | ✓ |
| m | | | | | | ■ | | | | ✓ |
| n | | | | | | | ■ | | | (✓) |
| l | | | | | | | | ■ | | (✓) |

NOTE　✓ Double onsets that are allowed in English
　　　(✓) Double onsets that are **not** found for **most speakers of American English**
　　　■ Impossible combination

→ Phonotactic constraints on double codas

**Table 2.** English Double Codas

| C1 \ C2 | p | b | t | d | k | g | tʃ | dʒ | f | v | θ | s | z | ʃ | m | n | l |
|---|---|---|---|---|---|---|---|---|---|---|---|---|---|---|---|---|---|
| p | ■ |  | ✓ |  |  |  |  |  |  |  | ✗ | ✓ |  |  |  |  |  |
| b |  | ■ |  | ✗ |  |  |  |  |  |  |  |  | ✗ |  |  |  |  |
| t |  |  | ■ |  |  |  |  |  |  |  | ✗ | ✗ |  |  |  |  |  |
| d |  |  |  | ■ |  |  |  |  |  |  | ✗ |  | ✗ |  |  |  |  |
| k |  |  | ✓ |  | ■ |  |  |  |  |  |  | ✓ |  |  |  |  |  |
| g |  |  |  | ✗ |  | ■ |  |  |  |  |  |  | ✗ |  |  |  |  |
| tʃ |  |  | ✗ |  |  |  | ■ |  |  |  |  |  |  |  |  |  |  |
| dʒ |  |  |  | ✗ |  |  |  | ■ |  |  |  |  |  |  |  |  |  |
| f |  |  | ✓ |  |  |  |  |  | ■ |  | ✗ | ✗ |  |  |  |  |  |
| v |  |  |  | ✗ |  |  |  |  |  | ■ |  |  | ✗ |  |  |  |  |
| θ |  |  | ✗ |  |  |  |  |  |  |  | ■ | ✗ |  |  |  |  |  |
| ð |  |  |  | ✗ |  |  |  |  |  |  |  |  | ✗ |  |  |  |  |
| s | ✓ |  | ✓ |  | ✓ |  |  |  |  |  |  | ■ |  |  |  |  |  |
| z |  |  |  | ✗ |  |  |  |  |  |  |  |  | ■ |  |  |  |  |
| ʃ |  |  | ✗ |  |  |  |  |  |  |  |  |  |  | ■ |  |  |  |
| ʒ |  |  |  | ✗ |  |  |  |  |  |  |  |  |  |  |  |  |  |
| m | ✓ |  | ✗ | ✗ |  |  |  |  | ✓ |  |  |  | ✗ |  | ■ |  |  |
| n |  |  | ✓ | ✓ |  |  | ✓ | ✓ |  |  | ✓ | ✓ | ✓ |  |  | ■ |  |
| ŋ |  |  | ✗ | ✓ |  |  |  |  |  |  | ✗ | ✗ |  |  |  |  |  |
| l | ✓ | ✓ | ✓ | ✓ | ✓ |  | ✓ | ✓ | ✓ | ✓ | ✓ | ✓ | ✗ | ✓ | ✓ | ✓ | ■ |
| ɹ | ✓ | ✓ | ✓ | ✓ | ✓ | ✓ | ✓ | ✓ | ✓ | ✓ | ✓ | ✓ | ✗ | ✓ | ✓ | ✓ | ✓ |

NOTE
✓ Non-suffixed double codas
✗ Suffixed double codas
■ Impossible combination

# General Stress Patterns

## KEY CONCEPT IN THIS CHAPTER

- Content Words and Function Words
- Noun and Adjective Stress
- Verb Stress
- English Stress and Affixes
  - stress-bearing (attracting) suffixes
  - stress-shifting (fixing) suffixes
  - stress-neutral suffixes
- Secondary Stress
- Trochaic Metrical Foot
- Eurhythmy
- Rhythm Reversal

**TIP**

- Stress in Nouns of at least three syllables (2018)
- Vowel Reduction in Unstressed Syllables (2017)
- Stress-Bearing, Stress-Shifting, and Stress-Neutral Suffixes (2016)

English is a Germanic language which has borrowed a huge amount of vocabulary from Latinate languages, notably French and Latin, many of them with Latinate suffixes and prefixes. The effect of this has been to make the word stress patterns more complex than they would otherwise have been, and nonnative speakers will testify to the difficulty they often experience in trying to master the stress patterns of English words.

Nonetheless, there is considerable regularity in English word stress patterns. Let us begin by considering words which clearly do not have prefixes or suffixes, in present-day English.

We will distinguish <u>words of a lexical category</u> from <u>words of a non-lexical category</u>. Words of a lexical category are nouns, verbs, adjectives and adverbs. Words of a non-lexical category include prepositions, determiners (such as *the, this, his*), pronouns (such as *he, her*) and the conjunction *and*. Words of a non-lexical category, often referred to as **function words**, are not normally stressed. Among the words of a lexical category, primary stress placement may vary, depending on <u>the syntactic category of the word</u>.

Monosyllabic words of a lexical category (such as *box, run, big*), are unproblematic: there is only one syllable for the primary stress to fall on. Let us therefore move on to morphologically simple bisyllabic words, and then proceed to morphologically simple polysyllabic words (words with three or more syllables).

## 9.1. Noun and Adjective Stress

There seem to be sufficient commonalities between the stress patterns of nouns and adjectives that they warrant a single grouping. <u>In **disyllabics**</u>, the default stress is on the penult. **In a 20,000-monomorphemic-word sample** reported by Hammond (1999), both disyllabic nouns and adjectives reveal penult stress over 80 percent of the time. More precisely, 81.7 percent of nouns and 81 percent of disyllabic adjectives followed this pattern. Below are some examples from both categories:

(1) 

| Noun | | Adjective | |
|------|------|------|------|
| ágent | cóokie | ábsent | sólid |
| bálance | cóuntry | árid | hónest |
| bállad | émpire | cómmon | réady |
| bóttom | dímple | flúent | súdden |
| bóttle | fáther | áctive | búsy |
| cábbage | húsband | éarly | ámple |
| cárrot | spínach | próper | vúlgar |
| chícken | zípper | pérfect | yéllow |

**The exceptions to the penult rule** fall into two groups.

The first contains examples with weightless (unstressable) penults, because they have [ə] nucleus, and thus are stressed on the final syllable (ult); for the reason, they might be considered exceptions:

(2)

| Noun | | Adjective | |
|------|------|-----------|------|
| appéal | giráffe | banál | compléte |
| ballóon | Japán | corrúpt | inténse |
| canóe | Tibét | corréct | seréne |
| Brazíl | machíne | precíse | secúre |
| canál | paráde | divíne | sincére |
| gazélle | | alíve | |

The second group constitutes the real exceptions because they are stressed in the final syllable (ult) despite the fact that they have stressable penults with branching rhymes:

(3)

| Noun | | Adjective | |
|------|------|-----------|------|
| typhóon | antíque | mundáne | robúst |
| sardíne | Julý | obscúre | obscéne |
| shampóo | | okáy | |

In trisyllabic and longer **nouns**, we formulate the following: stress penult if stressable (heavy/branching rhyme); if not stressable, then stress the next left syllable. We show this with the following examples:

(4)

| Three syllables | | More than three syllables |
|-----------------|------|---------------------------|
| tomáto | ábdomen | barracúda |
| aróma | álgebra | aspáragus |
| diplóma | ánimal | apócalypse |
| horízon | búffalo | basílica |
| compúter | cómedy | thermómeter |
| bonánza | vítamin | harmónica |
| diréctor | áccident | expériment |
| agénda | África | astrónomy |
| Decémber | pólicy | cémetery |
| enígma | órigin | hippopótamus |

The words in the leftmost group are stressed on the penult because their penults are stressable (the first five quality for their long vowel or diphthong nuclei, and the last five because of the closed rhyme).

The words in the second trisyllabic group receive their stresses on the antepenult <u>because their penults are not stressable (**all with [ə] nuclei**)</u>.

The rightmost group consists of words that have more than three syllables, but the stress rule remains the same. <u>The first word, barracúda, is stressed on the penult, as it contains a stressable penult, [u]. The remaining words</u> (eight with four syllables, and the last one with five syllables) <u>all have unstressable penults ([ə] nuclei)</u> and thus are stressed on the antepenult.

All for the frequency of such patterns, Hammond reports that this regularity accounts for over 90 percent of **nouns**. <u>The exceptions</u>, exemplified by the following, are below 10 percent:

(5)   clarinét        kangaróo        gasolíne        warrantée
      cavalíer        chimpanzée      cigarétte       mayonnáise
      enginéer        serenáde        magazíne

These examples, mostly **borrowings from French**, retain the original final stresses.

## 9.2. Verb Stress

If **nouns and adjectives** have **the penult** as their pivot, **verb** focus is on **the ult**. The general tendency is as follows: <u>stress ult if heavy (branching rhyme); if not, go to the next left syllable</u>, as shown in the following:

(6) **Heavy ult stressed**          **Unstressable ult, thus penult stressed**

| | | | |
|---|---|---|---|
| achíeve | inténd | bálance | púnish |
| admít | interfére | blóssom | fígure |
| agrée | impórt | bóther | súrface |
| annóunce | predíct | dístance | vísit |
| confíne | replý | fúrnish | díffer |
| digést | | hárvest | |

With the above generalization, we can account for over 99 percent of the stresses of disyllabic words. The few exceptions to the general tendency can be exemplified by the following, where penult is stressed **despite** the fact that the verb has **a heavy ult**:

(7)

| | | | |
|---|---|---|---|
| cópy | [i] | réscue | [u] |
| díagram | [æm] | stúdy | [i] |
| wórry | [i] | énvy | [i] |
| árgue | [u] | | |

English has dozens of orthographically identical word-pairs differentiated by stress as **nouns (penult stress)** or **verbs (ult stress)**, as exemplified in the following:

(8)

| | | | |
|---|---|---|---|
| abstract | convict | insert | refuse |
| address | discharge | insult | reject |
| ally | escort | permit | retard |
| combat | export | progress | subject |
| compress | extract | project | suspect |
| conduct | implant | protest | transfer |
| conflict | import | rebel | |
| contrast | increase | refund | |

Although noun-verb shift is accomplished by a shift in stressed syllable in some of these (e.g. import, insult), in many others, the difference of stress is also accompanied by vowel reduction in the stressed syllable, and thus these noun-verb pairs, although **homographs**, are **not homophonous**. For example:

(9)  abstract      N [ǽbstɹækt]      V [əbstɹǽkt]

conveict     N [kɑ́nvɪkt]      V [k̬ənvíkt]

protest      N [pɹóтɛst]      V [pɹətɛ́st]

refuse       N [ɹɛ́fjus]       V [ɹəfjúz]

However, **not all** two-syllable words that are both nouns and verbs follow the stress-switch rule. Some have the stress on the penult (e.g. sílence, tríumph, hárvest, prómise) and others have it on the ult (e.g. surpríse, deláy, resúlt) for both nouns and verbs.

**EXERCISE**

Consider the following English verbs. Those in column A have stress on the penultimate (next-to-last) syllable, whereas the verbs in column B and C have their last syllables stressed. ❷

| A | B | C |
|---|---|---|
| astónish | collápse | amáze |
| éxit | exíst | impróve |
| imágine | resént | surpríse |
| cáncel | revólt | combíne |
| elícit | adópt | belíeve |
| práctice | insíst | atóne |

a. Transcribe the words under columns A, B, and C phonemically. (Use a schwa for the unstressed vowels even if they can be derived from different phonemic vowels. This should make it easier for you.)

Examples: *astonish* /əstanɪʃ/, *collapse* /kəlæps/, *amaze* /əmez/

b. Consider the phonemic structure of the stressed syllables in these verbs. What is the difference between the final syllables of the verbs in columns A and B? Formulate a rule that predicts where stress occurs in the verbs in columns A and B.

c. In the verbs in column C, stress also occurs on the final syllable. What must you add to the rule to account for this fact? (*Hint:* For the forms in columns A and B, the final consonants had to be considered; for the forms in column C, consider the vowels.)

---

❷ Answer: a. A: short V + C     B: short V + CC     C: long V + C
　　　 b. If the final syllable has a consonant cluster, then the syllable is stressed. If, however, the final syllable has a short vowel and a consonant, then the preceding syllable is stressed.
　　　 c. If the final syllable has a long vowel, then the syllable is stressed.

## 9.3. English Stress and Affixes

If the basic rules of stress looked rather untidy and replete with exceptions, **the rules accompanying affixes** can easily be said to overshadow the mono-morphemic roots.

Since the addition of prefixes does not change word stress, our presentation will be on the varying effects of suffixes on word stress. We can classify the suffixes as:

(10)    a. stress-bearing (attracting) suffixes

       b. stress-shifting (fixing) suffixes

       c. stress-neutral suffixes

The common element between groups (10a) and (10b), when added to a root, is that they change the location of the stress from its original position. **Stress-bearing suffixes** attract the stress to themselves, while **stress-shifting suffixes** move the stress to some other syllable. Group (10b) and (10c) have the common element of not carrying stress.

### 9.3.1. Stress-bearing (attracting) suffixes

As stated above, these suffixes attract stress. Below are the **some** common **derivational suffixes**:

(11)    -ade          lémon — lemonáde

       -aire        míllion — millionáire

       -ation      réalize — realizátion

       -ee          ábsent — absentée (exception: commíttee)

       -eer        móuntain — mountainéer

       -ese        Japán — Japanése

       -esque     pícture — picturésque

       -ette       kítchen — kitchenétte

       -itis        lárynx — laryngítis

       -ific       hónor — honorífic

Expectedly, these stress-bearing suffixes **always** constitute **heavy syllables**. The items above with suffixes should **not** be confused with the same/similar-looking monomorphemic forms such as *brig__ade__*, *jambor__ee__*, *grot__esque__*, *brun__ette__*, *burs__itis__*, etc.

## 9.3.2. Stress-neutral suffixes

These suffixes never make any difference to the stress pattern of the resulting word. Such suffixes include all eight **inflectional suffixes** (plural; possessive; third person singular present tense __-s__; progressive __-ing__; past __-ed__; past participle __-en/-ed__; comparative __-er__; and superlative __-est__), and **several derivational ones**:

(12)

| | | | | |
|---|---|---|---|---|
| -al | arríve — arríval | | -ize | spécial — spécialize |
| -ant | ascénd — ascéndant | | -less | bóttom — bóttomless |
| -cy | célibate — célibacy | | -ly | fríend — fríendly |
| -dom | frée — fréedom | | -ment | aménd — améndment |
| -er | pláy — pláyer | | -ness | fránk — fránkness |
| -ess | líon — líoness | | -ship | fríend — fríendship |
| -ful | gráce — gráceful | | -some | búrden — búrdensome |
| -hood | nátion — nátionhood | | -wise | clóck — clóckwise |
| -ish | gréen — gréenish | | -th | grów — grówth |
| -ism | álcohol — álcoholism | | -ty | cértain — cértainty |
| -ist | húman — húmanist | | **-y** | **sílk — sílky** |
| -ive | submít — submíssive | | | |

We should point out that the last item, **adjective-forming suffix** __-y__, should **not** be treated in the same way as the **noun-forming** __-y__, which shifts the stress to the antepenultimate, as in **hómophone** — **homóphony**, **phótograph** — **photógraphy**, etc.

## 9.3.3. Stress-shifting (fixing) suffixes

A multiplicity of derivational suffixes, when added to a root, shift the stress from its original position to the syllable immediately preceding the suffix. Below are some of the common ones in this group:

(13)  -ian          Áristotle — Aristotélian

      -ial          súbstance — substántial

      -ian          líbrary — librárian

      -ical         geómetry — geométrical

      -icide        ínsect — insécticide

      -ic           périod — periódic (exceptions: Árabic, lúnatic)

      -ify          pérson — persónify

      -ious         lábor — labórious

      -ity          húmid — humídity

      -ometer       spéed — speedómeter

      -ual          cóntext — contéxtual

      -ous          móment — moméntous

      **-y          hómonym — homónymy**

If the original stress is on the last syllable of the root (the syllable immediately before the suffix), no change in location of the stress will result, because it is already where it should be (e.i. divérse — divérsity, absúrd — absúrdity, obése — obésity).

While the eight **inflectional suffixes**:

(14)  -s (third per. sing. present)      "she look**s** here"
      -s (plural)                        "two cat**s**"
      -s (possessive)                    "cat**'s** tail"
      -ed (past tense)                   "she look**ed** here"
      -en, -ed (past participle)         "she has eat**en**"
      -ing (progressive)                 "she is eat**ing**"
      -er (comparative)                  "she is short**er** than you"
      -est (superlative)                 "she is the short**est**"

do not have effect on the stress (i.e. the addition of these suffixes does not change the location of the stress), **derivational suffixes** have no such predictability. As we saw in several examples above, while they may stay neutral to the stress, e.g. bottom — bottomless [bɑ́rəm]-[bɑ́rəmləs], they can shift the stress, e.g. geography — geographic [dʒiɑ́gɹəfi]-[dʒiəgɹǽfək], or even carry the stress themselves, e.g. lemon — lemonade [lɛ́mən]-[lɛmənéd].

## 9.4. Secondary Stress

This book will treat <u>the difference between</u> **the primary stress** and **the secondary stress** as **a difference in pitch instead of stress**. The **major pitch change** is called the **tonic accent**.

Thus, we can say that (a) an English syllable is **either stressed (+stress) or unstressed (− stress)**; (b) if there is only one prominent syllable in the word, then it necessarily is the stressed syllable and has the tonic accent, while if there is more than one prominent (stressed) syllable, then **only one of them will have the major pitch-changing tonic accent**; and (c) a stressed syllable necessarily has a **full vowel** (no vowel reduction can take place in a stressed syllable); thus, **vowel reduction** <u>is a question relevant only for unstressed syllables</u>. We can illustrate these dependencies in the following diagram:

(15)

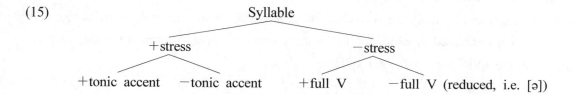

Thus, we have the following combinatory possibilities for English syllables:

Primary stressed syllable: +stress, +tonic accent, +full V.
Secondary stressed syllable: +stress, −tonic accent, +full V.
Unstressed syllable: −stress, −tonic accent, +/−full V.

Let us now look at the following examples:

(16)

|  | photograpy [fə.tɑ́.gɹə.fi] | | | | photographic [fò.tə.gɹǽ.fək] | | | |  |  |
|---|---|---|---|---|---|---|---|---|---|---|
| Stress | − | + | − | − | + | − | + | − | three pluses | ⟹ 1 |
| Tonic accent | − | + | − | − | − | − | + | − | two pluses | ⟹ 2 |
| Full V | − | + | − | + | + | − | + | − | one plus | ⟹ 3 |
|  | 4 | 1 | 4 | 3 | 2 | 4 | 1 | 4 | no pluses | ⟹ 4 |

We can now analyze the word *pronunciation* in light of what has been said so far:

(17)
|  | [pɹə.nʌn.si.e.ʃən] |
|---|---|
| Stress | − + − + − |
| Tonic accent | − − − + − |
| Full V | − + + + −    4 ⇐ reduced vowels |
|  | 4  2  3  1  4 |

## 9.5. More on the Trochaic Metrical Foot

We said that the rhythm of English is *trochaic*: the basic rhythmic pattern consists of a stressed syllable followed by zero or more unstressed syllables. For instance, in the phrase *made in a factory*, the metrical structure is ['meɪdɪnə'fæktəɹi]. The two trochaic feet here are ['meɪdɪnə] and ['fæktəɹi]. We assumed too that syllables with secondary stress also form trochaic metrical feet, as in the word *academic*: [ˌækə'dɛmɪk]. The two trochaic metrical feet here are [ˌækə] and ['dɛmɪk]: the secondary stress in [ˌækə] forms a trochaic metrical foot with the following unstressed syllable, and the primary stress in ['dɛmɪk] forms a trochaic metrical foot with the following unstressed syllable.

## 9.6. Representing Metrical Structure

We have represented primary stress with a superscript diacritic, as in ['dɛmɪk], and secondary stress with a subscript diacritic, as in [ˌækə] in the word academic. These conventions will suffice if we confine our interest to the level of the word. But they will not suffice if we wish to represent the way levels of stress and relative perceptual salience operate when words are combined into phrases. Take the phrase *kangaroo court*, for instance. When *kangaroo* appears in the phrase *kangaroo court*, the secondary and primary stresses in that word switch round. The single syllable of the word *court* has more stress than any of the stressed syllables in *kangaroo*, but in the word *kangaroo*, the [kʰæŋgə] foot is less salient than the [ɹuː] foot. So we are dealing here with three different levels of salience. That is not easy to represent using only the two diacritics we have used for word stress. We need a further mode of representation.

We represented syllable structure in terms of branching tree structures. Many phonologists also represent foot structure in terms of branching trees. We will represent any syllable which has any degree of stress with an 'S', indicating that it is strong with respect to weak unstressed syllables, which we label with a 'W'. A stressed syllable and any unstressed syllables with which it forms a foot may then be represented as follows:[3]

(18)
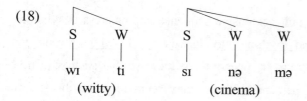

The bottom-most level of representation in this diagram is the level of the segment. The next level up is the syllable. At that level, the S labels represent strong (stressed) syllables and the W labels represent unstressed syllables. It is important to bear in mind that stress levels are *relational*: rather than a stressed syllable being definable in absolute terms, one syllable is more or less stressed *in relation to another*.

## 9.7. The Rhythm of English: Stress Timing and Eurhythmy

We saw that the rhythm of English is **stress-timed**. What this means is that the regular recurring beats found in the speech of English speakers (the rhythm of English speech) fall on stressed syllables. That is, stressed syllables in English occur at more or less equal intervals.

---

[3] The metrical trees we present here are abbreviated. Because metrical structure is determined by syllable structure, we ought, strictly speaking, to show metrical trees built upon syllable structure trees, as follows:

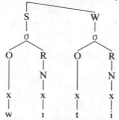

The abbreviated trees used in this section do not actually show that it is the structure of the rhyme, and not the entire syllable, which is crucial in determining metrical structure. However, they will suffice for our purposes.

One of the consequences of this kind of rhythm is that English feet may consist of a stressed syllable followed by a sequence of unstressed syllables, as in the phrase *heard in the park*, in which the stressed syllable in *heard* is followed by two unstressed syllables, or the phrase *heard it in the park*, where *heard* is followed by three, or the phrase *heard it in the announcement*, where it is followed by four.

Having said that English allows for really quite extensive sequences of unstressed syllables, it has to be said that **the 'ideal' or optimal rhythmic structure** is one in which strong and weak syllables alternate, in an S-W-S-W pattern. It appears to be the case that such sequences of 'alternating opposites' are optimal in a perceptual sense: they seem to make the speech signal more easily decoded. Such optimal rhythmic structures are often referred to as **eurhythmic** stuctures. It follows from this that the optimal, most eurhythmic, foot structure is a simple S-W structure, with only one unstressed syllable to the right of the stressed syllable. Foot structures with more than one W syllable are therefore **less eurhythmic**, **less optimal**, than those with only one, and the greater the number of unstressed syllables, the less eurhythmic or optimal the foot.

This preference for eurhythmy extends to sequences of feet: sequences of S and W feet are also more eurhythmic than other sequences. For instance, in the sentence *I want a cup of coffee*, there is an S-W-S sequence of three feet in the verb phrase, each of which is itself an S-W sequence of syllables; it is eurhythmic both at the level of sequences of syllables and at the level of sequences of feet:

(19)

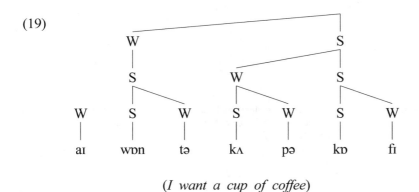

(*I want a cup of coffee*)

In many cases, however, a given combination of words may potentially create a phrase which is less than eurhythmic, and indeed may potentially result in **adjacent S-labelled feet**. This results from the fact that, in most English phrases, it is the final word which is most stressed, as in the phrase *black bird*. This **Phrasal Stress Rule** seems to hold for most types of phrase in English, as in *slowly ate* (verb phrase), *very yellow* (adjective phrase), *into London* (prepositional phrase) and *very slowly* (adverb phrase). It also seems to apply at the level of the sentence, as we can see from the example just given: the predicate verb phrase is more salient than the preceding subject noun phrase. Where the Phrasal Stress Rule brings about **adjacent S-labelled feet**, it appears that 'evasive action' can be taken.

Take the words *academic, Tennessee* and *champagne*. Clearly, *academic* has primary stress on the penultimate syllable and secondary stress on the first syllable; the other syllables are unstressed. The foot structure of the word is as follows:

(20)

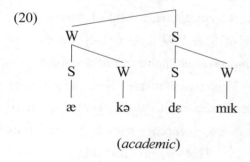

(*academic*)

*Tennessee* also contains two feet, the second stronger than the first. However, the second foot consists simply of a stressed syllable, with no unstressed syllables following it:

(21)

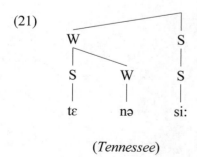

(*Tennessee*)

*Champagne* also has two feet, as we have already seen, the first of which consists of a syllable with secondary stress and the second of which consists of a syllable with primary stress:

(22)

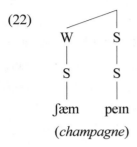

(*champagne*)

In each of these three cases, the word consists of two feet, the second of which is strong with respect to the first. However, when these words appear in phrases where the stronger of the two feet is immediately followed by the stressed syllable of another foot, and where that syllable must be more heavily stressed than the preceding one, a kind of 'stress clash' results, in which, rather than a eurhythmic sequence of S and W feet, an S-S sequence of feet occurs. In situations such as this, a rule of **rhythm reversal** applies. Consider some such phrases, e.g. *academic banter, champagne breakfast, Tennessee Williams*. Note that, in each case, the rule for phrasal stress assignment means that the second of the two words must have greater stress than the first. Note too that the primary and secondary stresses in the words *academic, champagne* and *Tennessee* have reversed. That is, the offending structure (exemplified in (23) below) is altered to the more eurhythmic structure exemplified in (24).

(23)

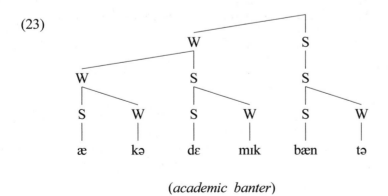

(*academic banter*)

(24)

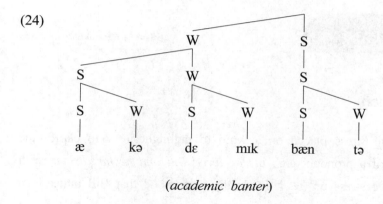

(*academic banter*)

This process of rhythm reversal is quite regular in English. Other examples are easily found; consider *Piccadilly* vs *Piccadilly Circus*, *Heathrow* vs *Heathrow Airport*, *Dundee* vs *Dundee marmalade*, *thirty four* vs *thirty four books*, *good-looking* vs *good-looking tutor*, and so on. As we have seen, in English phrases, it is the head, rather than a preceding modifier, which bears the most stress. **Rhythm reversal** occurs whenever a word containing a weak-strong sequence of feet is combined, to form a phrase or compound, with a word whose first syllable is the first syllable of a foot (i.e. is stressed). That is, rhythm reversal operates, within the context of phrases and compounds, on feet, not syllables, reversing weak-strong sequences of feet, rather than weak-strong sequences of syllables. Another way of putting this is to say that the reversal process reverses a sequence of a secondary stressed syllable and a primary stressed syllable when it is followed by a primary stressed syllable within a phrase.

# Check Up the Points

## 1 Glossary for this Section

**contrastive stress**
대조 강세

Additional stress placed on a word to highlight it or to clarify the referent of a pronoun: e.g., in *Joe hired Bill and he hired Sam*, with contrastive stress on *he*, it is usually understood that Bill rather than Joe hired Sam.

**dactylic foot**
강약약 음보

A metrical foot consisting of a stressed syllable followed by two unstressed syllables: e.g., *múrmuring* or *cápital*.

**eurhythmy**
운율적 균형

(also **eurythmy**) Metrical symmetry: the existence of a highly regular metrical structure in utterance. Adj. **eur(h)ythmic**.

**foot**
음보

1. The basic unit of rhythm in poetry, generally consisting of a group of two or more syllables in which one syllable bears the main stress. Among the commonest types of foot are the **iamb**, the **trochee**, and the **dactyl**. 2. The fundamental unit of rhythm in phonology, most typically consisting of a sequence of syllables one of which bears a stress or other prosodic element.

**iambic**
약강

Stress on the second syllable of a two-syllable word: e.g., *giráffe*.

**secondary stress**
제2강세

In English, a degree of stress which is less than primary stress but greater than that found on unstressed syllables, as in the first syllable of *kangaroo* or in the last syllable of *formaldehyde*.

**tonic accent**
억양 액센트

The emphasis given to the tonic syllable in any tone group.

**tonic syllable**
억양 음절

The syllable that carries the major pitch change.

**trochaic**
강약

Stress on the first syllable of a two-syllable word: e.g., *páper*.

## 2 Key-points in this Section

➡ English word stress is not random.

➡ English rhythm is trochaic, as in *woman* and *battery*.

➡ Primary stress is calculated from the end of the word, not the beginning.

➡ English words cannot begin with more than one unstressed syllable.

➡ When one English word is derived from another, and the primary stress shifts as a result of the derivation, there is a tendency to place the secondary stress on the syllable that had primary stress in the deriving word, as in *ˌcharacteriˈzation*.

➡ There is a tendency to avoid placing primary and secondary stresses next to each other, as in *ˌJapaˈnese*.

➡ While English nouns, adjectives and adverbs mainly follow the basic trochaic pattern, there are many verbs which do not.

➡ English suffixes may be divided into those which affect the primary stress (such as *-ese* and *-ity*) and those which do not (such as *-ness*).

➡ Among the suffixes which affect primary stress, some take the primary stress (such as *-ese*), while others do not (such as *-ity*).

➡ Separable prefixes normally take secondary stress, as in *ˌpre-ˈpay*.

➡ The basic pattern for two-part compounds is: the first element is the most prominent, as in *darkroom*.

# Intonation

(**TIP**)

- Sentence Types and Their Unmarked and Marked Intonation Patterns (2012)

**Intonation** is variation of pitch that is not used to distinguish words. Languages that are not tone languages, such as English or French, are called intonation languages. The pitch contour of an utterance may affect the meaning of the whole sentence, so that *John is here* spoken with falling pitch at the end is interpreted as a statement, but with rising pitch at the end, a question.

In English, pitch still plays an important role, but only in the form of **the pitch contour or intonation of the phrase or sentence**.

In English, intonation may reflect syntactic, semantic or pragmatic differences.

A sentence that is **ambiguous** in writing may be **unambiguous** when spoken because of **differences in the pitch contour**. Written, the following sentence is **unclear** as to whether Tristram intended for Isolde to read and follow directions, or merely to follow him:

(1)     Tristram  left  directions  for  Isolde  to  follow.          ⇐ ambiguous

Spoken, <u>if Tristram wanted Isolde to follow him</u>, the sentence would be pronounced with a rise in pitch on the first syllable of *follow*, followed by a fall in pitch:

(2)     <u>Tristram  left  directions  for  Isolde  to</u>  |*follow. ⟍        ⇐ unambiguous ("follow him")

In this pronunciation of the sentence, the primary stress is on the word *follow*.

<u>If the meaning is to read and follow a set of directions</u>, the highest pitch comes on the second syllable of *directions*:

(3)     <u>Tristram  left</u>  |*directions |  <u>for  Isolde  to  follow.</u>     ⇐   unambiguous
                                                    ("follow  the  directions")

The primary stress in this pronunciation is on the word *directions*.

## 10.1. Intonation Patterns

We defined **intonation** as <u>pitch variations that occur over a phrase or sentence</u>. Intonation contours can be described in terms of **tone groups** or **intonational phrases**. **A tone group** is <u>the part of a sentence over which an intonation contour extends</u>. Within a tone group, each stressed syllable has a minor pitch increase, but there is one syllable in which this pitch increase is more significant. <u>The syllable that carries the major pitch change</u> is called the **tonic syllable**. For example, in the following sentence:

(4)     The  'boy  'gave  the  'book  to  his  *teacher

the elements marked with a ' are stressed, but the major pitch increase is on *teacher*, which is marked with **an asterisk.**

Since in the usual cases in English, the **utterance-initial position** is reserved for **shared (old) information**, and the **new information** is placed in **utterance-final position**, the most common pattern is to put **the tonic accent** on **the last stressed lexical item** (noun, verb, adjective, adverb). cf. LLI

One should note, however, that this is merely a tendency, as we may easily find cases where the tonic accent is brought forward.

(5) a. He was **some**what *dis**cou**raged

   b. He was ***some**what dis**cou**raged

In (5b) the tonic accent on <u>somewhat</u> is a result of **emphasis (contrast)**.

Not all cases of placing the tonic accent earlier than the last stressed lexical item involve contrast/emphasis, as exemplified in (6):

(6)   I have *a **par**ty to plan

        ***let**ters to write

It is important to note that **a tone group** is **a unit of information** rather than a syntactically definable unit. Thus, the way the speaker shapes his or her utterance(s) depends on what he or she considers to be the important point(s) in the sentence. In (6), the speaker has the lexical item *party/letters* that has the greater importance.

Likewise, while the neutral expression of (7a) will assign the tonic accent to the last lexical word *vegetable* (talking about the category/characterization of *spinach*),

(7) a. Spinach is a *vegetable     ⇐ unmarked

we would be likely to bring the tonic accent on to *spinach* in a discussion of vegetables and considering what would fit into that group:

(7) b. *Spinach is a vegetable ⇐ marked ⇐ contrastive

※ other exceptions to the tonic accent falling on the last lexical item (LLI)

The **first** one of these relates to the tone group that has an **intransitive** verb or verb phrase **whose subject is non-human**:

(8) a. Our *town is on an upswing

b. The *bird flew away (cf. the man *swore)

The **second** involves certain types of adverbials in final position. **Sentential adverbials** (i.e. those that modify the whole sentence) and **adverbials of time** usually do **not** take the tonic accent:

(9) a. I don't watch *TV typically (cf. contrastive: I don't watch TV *typically)

b. It wasn't a very nice *day unfortunately.

### 10.1.1. Falling Intonation Contour

The sentences in (4)-(9) all are examples of "**falling intonation contour**," which is quite typical of **utterances that express finality**.

It may be useful, to make a distinction between **"full" (or "long") fall** versus **"low" (or "short") fall**.

<1> A **full fall** is **unmarked for declaratives** where there is **clear finality in the statement** (i.e. there is nothing more to be said).

(10)    I am leaving the house right now.

This pattern is common in expressing emotional involvement:

(11)    I'm so glad. (with genuine enthusiasm)

A falling contour is also typical of <u>wh</u>-questions (questions that start with a <u>wh</u>-word such as <u>what</u>, <u>which</u>, <u>where</u>):

(12)    Which way did she go?

<2> While a full (or "long") fall shows <u>a **definitive, involved** mood</u>, **a short (or "low") fall** is generally, an indication of <u>a **detached** mood in the speaker</u>. It displays <u>a rather **neutral, perfunctory** attitude</u>:

(13)    Whatever you say. (i.e. "I agree with it")

## 10.1.2. Rising Intonation Contour

If falling contour is indicative of "finality" or "completion," ***rising*** intonation represents <u>"**non-definiteness**,"</u> <u>"**lack of assurance**,"</u> or <u>"**incompletion**</u>." This pitch pattern is addressee-oriented, and the degree of "rise" is matched to the degree of **uncertainty** or **incompleteness**. Accordingly, we can describe this pattern as:

(a)  "high" (or "long") rise, or  (b)  "low" (or "short") rise.

## 10.1.2.1. Long Rise

**High (or long) rise** is a more marked pattern, which is indicative of an attitude of puzzlement or unbelieving:

In **yes-no questions** (typical order, or with statement order), such as:

(14) a. Is this a joke?              b. This is a joke?

the speaker has the attitude of asking "are you sure you know what you are saying?" or "this is hard to believe."

### 10.1.2.2. Short Rise

**A low (or short) rise**, on the other hand, is more common and is used in a variety of situations:

<1> In **yes-no questions** (typical order or with statement order), such as:

(15) a. Has your uncle left already?　　　b. Your uncle has left already?

<2> **Echo questions**, such as:

(16)　Where will I work? I haven't thought of that yet.

<3> **Repetition questions**, such as:

(17)　What are you doing? (I haven't heard you)

Note that this is different from (12), where the question in information-seeking.

<4> **Open-choice alternative questions**, such as:❹

(18)　Would you like a paper or magazine? (something to read)

<5> **Certain tag questions** that signal **uncertainty**, such as:

(19)　She usually comes at ten, doesn't she?

<6> Items in a list prior to the last item, such as:

(20)　I need to buy a shirt, a jacket, and a tie.

---

❹ Note the falling contour for the "closed choice" alternative:

Paper or magazine?

**&lt;7&gt; Questions that display readiness to present some new information**, such as:

(21) Do you know when the first kidney transplant was?

If this is uttered as **a neutral "information-seeking" question**, it will end in a falling pitch.

## 10.1.3. Falling-Rising Intonation Contour

Other than the falling and rising intonation discussed thus far, there are two other patterns that are combinatory. A *falling-rising* intonation is indicative of **an agreement with reservation**:

(22) You can do it that way.

The speaker accepts that it can be done the way the hearer suggested and at the same time expresses some reservation or hesitation (i.e. "I don't think you should").

## 10.1.4. Rising-Falling Intonation Contour

The opposite, a *rising-falling* intonation, which is the dramatic equivalent of a simple "fall," reveals strong feelings of approval or disapproval:

(23) a. That's wonderful. (cf. "That's wonderful" with simple fall)

   b. You can't do that. (cf. "You can't do that" with simple fall)

## 10.1.5. Level Intonation

Finally, mention should be made of a *level* intonation, which marks a bored or sarcastic attitude:

(24)   A: John will be at the party.
       B: Great.

## 10.2. Sentence Types and Their Unmarked and Marked Intonation Patterns

In English, a **sequence of pitch levels** can indicate the **intonation pattern** of an intonational phrase. In the following data, the numbers in parentheses at the end of each intonational phrase correspond to the pitch level as follows: 1 indicates a low pitch, 2 a normal pitch, and 3 a high pitch. Thus, the 2-3-1 pattern is what is known as rising-falling intonation, and 2-3 represents rising intonation. This kind of pitch change takes place around the **tonic syllable** depending on factors such as the pattern of a sentence and the intention of the speaker. Importantly, sentences that are **ambiguous** in writing may be **unambiguous** when spoken with different intonation patterns as in the following examples (CAPITAL letters indicate tonic syllables. Intonation is marked only for B's utterances.):

(a) A: Do you know him?

    B: Do I KNOW him? (2-3-2) He's my BROther. (2-3-1)

In dialog (a), B is not asking A to repeat what A said, but B is saying that certainly he knows him.

(b) A: Let's go back to the classroom.

    B: It's time for class to START? (2-3)

In dialog (b), B does not state that the class will resume very soon, but B states that he is unaware that the class will resume very soon.

(c) A: Let's go somewhere this summer!

    B: Where do you want to GO? (2-3-1)

      Do you want to go to LONdon, (2-3) or PAris? (2-3)

In dialog (c), it is not that B wants A to choose between London and Paris to visit, but that B wants to know just where A wants to go this summer.

(d) A: We might need to go that way to escape from this hazard.
　　B: Are you CERtain? (2-3-2)

In dialog (d), B does not think that A is certain at all.

(e) A: What time is it now?
　　B: What TIME is it now? (2-3)

In dialog (e), B is not asking A the correct time, but B is saying that A should not ask B what the time is.

Let's consider another example. Intonation in questions functions to differentiate normal information from contrastive or expressive intentions. In other words, intonation performs an important conversation management function, with the speaker being able to subtly signal to the interlocutor to respond in a particular fashion, or to pay particular attention to a piece of highlighted information.

There are two syntactic options for making yes/no questions. The first option, which is general or unmarked, involves the inversion of the subject and the auxiliary verb, as in (25).

(25)　Did Tom cook |DINer?

This unmarked option is accompanied by rising intonation. In this pattern, the speaker is asking about the truth of what he or she is saying.

The second option, which is less general or marked, takes the form of a statement with no subject-auxiliary inversion, as in (26).

(26)　Tom cooked |DINer?

In this marked pattern with rising intonation, the speaker is either asking the interlocutor to repeat or is making an assumption and wants the interlocutor to confirm it (i.e., the speaker has good reason to expect a *yes* answer).

Another prosodic pattern for the uninverted question has emphatic stress, high pitch, and exaggerated intonation on one or two of the constituents that lend themselves to focus, as in (27).

(27)     Tom | cooked | DINer?

In this pattern, the speaker is reacting with surprise or disbelief to certain information just received.

For learners of English, it does not make sense to practice the unmarked and marked versions of *Tom cooked dinner* in isolation and out of context. Learners must understand early on that one version is appropriate in one context, whereas the other is appropriate in another context.

Consider one more example. A foreign student is applying for a library card at a university library. He is handed a form by an overworked male assistant, who is a native speaker of English, but after looking at it, he realizes it is the wrong one. (\ means falling intonation. \\ means extra emphasis on stressed syllables. Capital letters mean stressed syllables.)

(28)     Foreign student: Excuse \ME. You have \GIVEn me the \\WRONG form.
         Library assistant: Sorry. I gave you what you \ASKed for [irritated, appeals to others in the queue for support].
         Foreign student: \\NO. It \IS the \\WRONG form.
         Library assistant: OK. There's no need to be rude.

Instead of the underlined section of the conversation, a native speaker of English might say the following:

(29)     Ex\CUSE me. You've given me the wrong \FORM.

Compared to the native speaker's utterance, the foreign student's pronunciation appears to give the impression of being rude (or impolite).

# Check Up the Points

## 1 Glossary for this Section

**intonation**
억양

The variation of pitch while speaking which is not used to distinguish words, though it may affect meaning. The pitch variation that occurs over a phrase or sentence.

**intonation phrase**
억양구

(also **intonation group**) The phonological unit of intonational structure, the longest stretch od speech to which a singel intonation pattern applies.

**pitch**
음정

The fundamental frequency of sound perceived by the listener.

**pitch contour**
음정변화

The intonation of a sentence.

**tone group**
억양군

The fundamental unit of intonation, the stretch of utterance to which a singel intonation contour applies.

## 2 Key-points in this Section

➡ A sentence that is **ambiguous** in writing may be **unambiguous** when spoken because of **differences in the pitch contour**.

➡ We defined **intonation** as pitch variations that occur over a phrase or sentence. Intonation contours can be described in terms of **tone groups** or **intonational phrases**.

➡ **A tone group** is the part of a sentence over which an intonation contour extends.

➡ Within a tone group, each stressed syllable has a minor pitch increase, but there is one syllable in which this pitch increase is more significant. The syllable that carries the major pitch change is called the **tonic syllable**.

➡ The most common pattern is to put **the tonic accent** on **the last stressed lexical item** (noun, verb, adjective, adverb).

➡ Intonation Patterns

| Intonation Patterns | | | | |
|---|---|---|---|---|
| Falling | long fall | finality or completion | clear finality in the statement (i.e. there is nothing more to be said) a definitive, involved mood | unmarked for declaratives |
| | short fall | | a detached mood in the speaker a rather neutral, perfunctory attitude | |
| Rising | long rise | non-definiteness, lack of assurance, uncertainty, or incompletion | an attitude of puzzlement or unbelieving | more marked pattern |
| | short rise | | used in a variety of situations | more common |
| Falling-Rising | | an agreement with reservation | | |
| Rising-Falling | | strong feeling of approval or disapproval strong conviction, strength of feeling, certainty, exclamation | | the dramatic equivalent of long fall, the emphatic kind of long fall |
| Level | | a bored or sarcastic attitude | | |

MEMO

# Chapter 04

# Morphology

# MEN
# TOR

# Morphological Processes

- Addition, Mutation, Conversion and Subtraction
- Morphological Processes
  - Compounding
  - Conversion
  - Clipping
  - Acronym
  - Word Coinage
  - Back-Formation
  - Affixation
  - Blending
  - Abbreviation

**TIP**

- Affixation (2017, 2016, 2014, 2013)

There are four different types of derivational relationship between words: **addition, mutation, conversion** and **subtraction**.

**Addition**: Some lexemes are formed by combining morphemes: those like *armchair* and *busybody*, which consist entirely of free morphemes; words like *violinist, disarm* and *blue-eyed*, which have partly free and partly bound morphemes; and the type represented by *astronaut* and *biology*, composed entirely of bound morphemes.

**Mutation**: The word *proud* and *pride* are systematically related and are related formally as well, but it is impossible to say that one is formed by adding something to the other. Rather, derivation is accomplished here by a change of vowel; in other pairs of words the change may be in consonants, as in *believe* and *belief*; or both vowel and consonant, as with *choose* and *choice*; or by change of stress: e.g. verbs *extráct, insúlt, progréss* in contrast to nouns *éxtract, ínsult, prógress*.

**Conversion** or **Zero Change**: This is the simple change of a word of one class to a word of another class with no formal alternation. Thus *clean, dry* and *equal* are adjectives and also verbs; the relation of adjective *clean* to the verb *clean* is the same as that of the adjective *long* to the verb *length*. *Fan grasp* and *hammer* are verbs and also nouns; *capital, initial* and *periodical* are nouns and adjectives.

**Subtraction** (or **Reduction**): By removing parts of certain lexemes new lexemes are formed. One kind of shortening is called **acronym**; another is called a **clipping**. An acronym is a word derived from the written form of a construction; a construction is a sequence of words that together have a meaning. Some acronyms are pronounced as a sequence of letters: *UK* for 'United Kingdom,' *USA* for 'United States of America.' In other acronyms the letters combine to produce something pronounceable: *AIDS* for 'Acquired Immune Deficiency Syndrome,' *UNESCO* for 'United Nations Educational, Scientific, and Cultural Organization.' As these examples show, the acronym is typically but not always formed from the first letter of each written word. The acronym may be formed from parts of a single word: *ID* for identification, *TB* for tuberculosis, *TV* for television; or it may include more than initial letters: *Nabisco* (National Biscuit Compony), *Sunoco* (Sun Oil Company). With a few exceptions, acronyms are essentially names.

Another process applied to existing words is **clipping**, the use of part of a word to stand for the whole word. *Laboratory* is abbreviated to *lab, telephone* to *phone, refrigerator* to *fridge*. Sometimes a vowel is added when other materials cut away, as in *Chevy* for *Chevrolet, divvy* for *dividend, ammo* for *ammunition*.

(from C. Kreidler (1998) *Introducing English Semantics*, London and New York: Routledge, pp. 269-270.)

## 1.1. Compounding

A compound is formed by combining two bases, which may be words in their own right, to form a new lexical item. This is shown in (1a) where the two bases are separated by a hyphen:

(1)  a.  shop-steward    ink-pot
       room-mate      road-show
       moon-light     shoe-string
    b.  strong-mind=ed  book-sell=er
       old-fashion=ed  market-garden=er
       time-honour=ed  muck-rak=er

Compounding and affixation are by no means incompatible. An affixed base may serve as input to a compounding process, and vice versa. In (1b), the suffix is separated by '=' from the base.

Compounds differ in their structure. The majority of English compounds are nouns. Common types of noun compounds include the following:

(2)

| *Noun* | *Noun* | *Noun* |
|---|---|---|
| *Adj.*  *Noun* | *Noun*  *Noun* | *Noun*  *Noun* (agent/instrument) |
| red tape | bathroom | schoolteacher |
| High Court | ball-point | head-hunter |
| blackberry | briefcase | speech writer |
| greenfly | bulldog | housekeeper |
| hothouse | ashtray | firefighter |
| White House | desktop | matchmaker |
| soft-ball | housewife | gamekeeper |
| easychair | inkwell | door-keeper |
| New Year | millstone | mine sweeper |
| blueprint | dustman | can opener |

Let us now turn to examples of adjectiveal compounds. Some are listed in (3):

(3)  *N + Ven*          *Adj. + Ving*        *Adj. + Ven*

    crestfallen          hard-working         clear-sighted

    waterlogged          good-looking         hard-featured

    heartbroken          easygoing            soft-hearted

    frost-bitten         fast-growing         new-born

> **NOTE** *Ven* is the past participial form of the verb. It is the verb form that ends *-en* or *-ed* after has in, e.g. *It has eaten* or in *It has wounded*.

An interesting property of most compounds is that they are headed. This means that one of the words that make up the compound is syntactically dominant. In English the head is normally the item on the right hand of the compound. The syntactic properties of the head are passed on to the entire compound. Thus in our examples above, if we have a compound like *easychair* which is made up of the adjective *easy* and the noun *chair*, syntactically the entire word is a noun. This applies to all the words in the left-hand column in (2).

Furthermore, the syntactic head is usually also the semantic head of the compound. The non-head element in the compound specifies more narrowly some characteristic of the head. So, an easychair is a type of chair, a bulldog is a kind of dog, a bedroom is a kind of room etc. If a compound contains a semantic head, it is called an **endocentric compound**.

(from F. Katamba (1994) *English Words*, London and New York: Routledge, pp. 72-73.)

## 1.2. Back-Formation

A new word may be formed from an existing word by "subtracting" an affix thought to be part of the old word; that is, ignorance sometimes can be creative. Thus, *peddle*, was derived from *peddler* on the mistaken assumption that *-er* was the "agentive" suffix. Such a word is called a **back-formation**. The verbs *hawk, stoke, swindle,* and *edit* all came into the language by this word-formation process.

## 1.3. Conversion, Function Shift, Zero Derivation

In English very often lexical items are created not by affixation but by **conversion** or **zero derivation**, i.e. without any alternation being made to the shape of the input base. The word-form remains the same, but it realizes a different lexical item.

Conversion of verbs into nouns and nouns into verbs is extremely productive in English. Usually the same word-form can be used as a verb or a noun, with only the grammatical context enabling us to know which category it belongs to. Thus, *jump* in the two sentences below is exactly the same in form but it belongs to two different lexemes. In (4a) *jump* is the non-finite form of the verb 'jump' while in (4b) it is the singular form of the noun *jump*.

(4)   a. The pig will jump over the stile!

   b. What a jump!

In *what a jump!* the verb is converted into a noun by 'zero derivation', i.e. without using any affix. What enables us to know whether the word is a noun or a verb is the position that it occupies in the sentence. If we see the subject *the pig* and the auxiliary verb *will* before the word *jump*, we know it must be a verb. But when *jump* occurs after the indefinite article *a* we know it must be a noun.

In (5) I have listed some common examples of forms that are subject to noun-to-verb or verb-to-noun conversion. It is not difficult to think of situations where these words may be used either as nouns or as verbs:

(5)

| light | bridge | seal | kick |
|-------|--------|------|------|
| fish | bus | dog | lift |
| farm | police | smear | finger |
| smell | skin | rain | paper |

(from F. Katamba (1994) *English Words*, London and New York: Routledge, pp. 70-71.)

## 1.4. Affixation

Adding affixes to an existing word is very common way of creating new words. English exploits this possibility by adding the agentive *-er* to the prepositions *up* and *down* to create the nouns *upper* and *downer*, which were invented in connection with drugs but have extended their meaning to anything that lifts or dampens one's spirits. More commonly, *-er* is suffixed to verbs (V) and means 'one who Vs' as in *runner* 'one who runs,' *campaigner*, and *designer*.

English takes advantage of two kinds of affixation: **prefixing** and **suffixing**. Prefixes like *un-, pre-,* and *dis-* serve to change the meaning of words, though not usually their lexical category. Thus the prefix *un-* added to an adjective creates a new adjective with the opposite meaning, as in *untrue, unpopular, unsuccessful,* and *unfavorable*. The prefix *dis-* added to a verb derives a verb with the opposite meaning, as in *disobey, disappear, dishonor,* and *displace*. *Pre-* serves as a prefix to several categories of words. It can be prefixed to verbs (*preaffirm, preallot, preplan, prewash,* and *premix*), adjectives (*pre-Copernican, precollegiate, precultural, presurgical*), or nouns (*preantiquity, preaffirmation, preplacement*). The prefix *pre-* has roughly the same sense in each of these words, and in each of them it create from an existing word a new word in the same lexical category.

Suffixes in English usually operate differently from prefixes. More often than not, they change a word's lexical category. The suffix *-ment*, for example, when added to a verb, makes a noun of it, as in *displacement, arrangement, agreement,* and *consignment*. The suffix *-ation* does the same thing: *resignation, organization, implementation, observation,* and *reformation*. *Discrimination* and *alienation*, which may look like the result of the same affix, are more accurately analyzed as coming from the verbs discriminate and alienate, the latter itself derived by suffixing *-ate* to the noun *alien*.

(from Finegan Edward (1989) *Language: its structure and use*, 2nd ed., Harcourt Brace, p. 97)

## 1.5. Clipping

Clipping is the abbreviation of longer words into shorter ones, such as *fax* for *facsimile*, the British word *telly* for *television*, *prof* for *professor*, *piano* for *pianoforte*, and *gym* for *gymnasium*. Once considered slang, these words have now become lexicalized, that is, full words in their own right. These are only a few examples of such clipped forms that are now used as whole words. Other examples are *ad, bike, math, gas, phone, bus,* and *van* (from *advertisement, bicycle, mathematics, gasoline, telephone, omnibus,* and *caravan*). More recently, *dis* and *rad* (from *disrespect* and *radical*) have entered the language, and *dis* has come to be used as a verb meaning "to show disrespect."

(from Fromkin et al. (2014) An Introduction to Language, 10th edition, Wadsworth, p. 355)

## 1.6. Blending

Blends are similar to compounds in that they are produced by combining two words, but parts of the words that are combined are deleted. *Smog*, from *smoke + fog*; *brunch*, from *breakfast* and *lunch*; *motel*, from *motor + hotel*; *infomercial*, from *info + commercial*; and *urinalysis*, from *urine + analysis* are examples of blends that have attained full lexical status in English. *Podcast* (*podcasting, podcaster*) is a relatively new word meaning "Internet audio broadcast" and recently joined the English language as a blend of *iPod* and *broadcast*. Lewis Carroll's *chortle*, from *chuckle + snort*, has achieved limited acceptance in English.

(from Fromkin et al. (2014) An Introduction to Language, 10th edition, Wadsworth, p. 354)

## 1.7. Acronym and Alphabetic Abbreviation

Acronyms are words derived from the initials of several words. Such words are pronounced as the spelling indicates: *NASA* [næsə] from National Aeronautics and Space Administration, *UNESCO* [yunɛsko] from United Nations Educational, Scientific, and Cultural Organization, and *UNICEF* [yunisɛf] from United Nations International Children's Emergency Fund. *Radar* from "radio detecting and ranging," *laser* from "light amplification by stimulated emission of radiation," *scuba* from "self-contained underwater breathing apparatus," and *RAM* from "random access memory" show the creative efforts of word coiners, as does *snafu*, which was coined by soldiers in World War II and is rendered in polite circles as "situation normal, all fouled up." Recently coined additions are *AIDS* (1980s), from the initials of acquired immune deficiency syndrome, and *SARS* (2000s), from severe acute respiratory syndrome.

When the string of letters is not easily pronounced as a word, the "acronym" is produced by sounding out each letter, as in *NFL* [ɛ̃nɛfɛl] for National Football League, *UCLA* [yusiɛle] for University of California, Los Angeles, and *MRI* [ɛ̃maraɪ] for magnetic resonance imaging. These special kinds of acronyms are sometimes called **alphabetic abbreviations**.

(from Fromkin et al. (2014) *An Introduction to Language*, 10th edition, Wadsworth, p. 355-6)

## 1.8. Word Coinage

Words may be created outright to fit some purpose. The advertising industry has added many words to English, such as *Kodak, nylon, Orlon,* and *Dacron.* Specific brand names such as *Xerox, Band-Aid, Kleenex, Jell-O, Brillo,* and *Vaseline* are now sometimes used as the generic name for different brands of these types of products. Some of these words were actually created from existing words (e.g., *Kleenex* from the word *clean* and *Jell-O* from *gel*).

The sciences have given us a raft of newly coined words over the ages. Words like *asteroid, neutron, genome, krypton, brontosaurus,* and *vaccine* were created to describe the objects or processes arising from scientific investigation.

(from Fromkin et al. (2014) *An Introduction to Language*, 9th edition, Wadsworth, p. 501)

# Check Up the Points

## ❶ Glossary for this Section

**accidental gap**
우연공백

Phonological or morphological form that constitutes possible but nonoccurring lexical items: e.g., *blick, unsad*.

**acronym**
두자어

Word composed of the initials of several words and pronounced as such: e.g., PET scan from positron-emission tomography scan. See **alphabetic abbreviation**.

**alphabetic abbreviation**
두자어

A word composed of the initials of several words and pronounced letter-by-letter: e.g., MRI from magnetic resonance imaging. See acronym.

**back-formation**
역형성

Creation of a new word by removing an affix from an old word: e.g., donate from donation; or by removing what is mistakenly considered an affix: e.g., edit from editor.

**blend**
혼성어

A word composed of the parts of more than one word: e.g., smog from smoke + fog.

**blocked**
파생차단

A derivation that is prevented by a prior application of morphological rules: e.g., when *Commun* + *ist* entered the language, words such as *Commun* + *ite* (as in *Trotsky* + *ite*) or *Commun* + *ian* (as in *grammar* + *ian*) were not needed and were not formed.

**borrowing**
차용

The incorporating of a loan word from one language into another: e.g., English borrowed buoy from Dutch. See **loan word**.

| | |
|---|---|
| **cognates**<br>동족어 | Words in related languages that developed from the same ancestral root, such as English *man* and German *Mann*. |
| **coinage**<br>신조어 | The construction and/or invention of new words that then become part of the lexicon: e.g., *vaccine*. |
| **compound**<br>복합어 | A word composed of two or more words, which may be written as a single word or as words separated by spaces or hyphens: e.g., *dogcatcher, dog biscuit, dog-tired*. |
| **derivation**<br>파생 | The steps in the application of rules to an underlying form that results in a surface representation: e.g., in deriving a syntactic s-structure from a d-structure, or in deriving a phonetic form from a phonemic form. |
| **derived word**<br>파생어 | The form that results from the addition of a derivational morpheme: e.g., *firmly* from *firm + ly*. |
| **folk etymology**<br>민간어원 | The process whereby the history of a word is derived from nonscientific speculation or false analogy with another word: e.g., *hooker* for 'prostitute' is falsely believed to be derived from the name of the U.S. Civil War general Joseph Hooker. |
| **head of a compound**<br>복합어의 핵 | The rightmost word: e.g., *house* in *doghouse*. It generally indicates the category and general meaning of the compound. |

**loan translations**
차용 번역어

Compound words or expressions whose parts are translated literally into the borrowing language: e.g., *marriage of convenience* from French *mariage de convenance*.

**loan word**
차용어

Word in one language whose origins are in another language: e.g., in Japanese, *besiboru*, 'baseball,' is a loan word from English. See **borrowing**.

**reduplication**
중첩

A morphological process that repeats or copies all or part of a word to produce a new word: e.g., *wishy-washy*, *teensy-weensy*, *hurly-burly*.

## ② Key-points in this Section

➡ A **compound** is formed by combining two bases, which may be words in their own right, to form a new lexical item.

➡ A new word may be formed from an existing word by "subtracting" an affix thought to be part of the old word. Such a word is called a **back-formation**.

➡ In English very often lexical items are created not affixation but by **conversion** or **zero derivation**, i.e. without any alternation being made to the shape of the input base.

➡ **Affixation**, by which affixes are added to an existing word, is very common way of creating new words.

➡ **Clipping** is the abbreviation of longer words into shorter ones, such as *fax* for *facsimile*.

➡ **Blends** are similar to compounds in that they are produced by combining two words, but parts of the words that are combined are deleted.

➡ **Acronyms** are words derived from the initials of several words.

➡ When the string of letters is not easily pronounced as a word, these special kinds of acronyms are sometimes called **alphabetic abbreviations**.

# Morphological Analysis

• The Process of Identifying Form-meaning Units
• Analyzing Words into Morphemes

Morphological analysis is the process of identifying form-meaning units in a language, taking into account small differences in pronunciation, so that prefixes *in-* and *im-* are seen to be variants of the "same" prefix in English (cf. *intolerable, impeccable*) just as *democrat* and *democrac* are stem variants of the same morpheme, which shows up in *democratic* with its "t" and in *democracy* with its "c."

Speakers of a language know the internal structure of words because they know the **morphemes** of their language and the rules for their combination. This is unconscious knowledge of course and it takes a trained linguist to make this knowledge explicit as part of a descriptive grammar of the language. The task is challenging enough when the language you are analyzing is your own, but linguists who speak one language may nevertheless analyze languages for which they are not native speakers.

Suppose you were a linguist from the planet Zorx who wanted to analyze English. How would you discover the morphemes of the language? How would you determine whether a word had one, two, or more morphemes, and what they were?

The first thing to do would be to ask native speakers how they say various words. (It would help to have a Zorxese-English interpreter along; otherwise, copious gesturing is in order.) Assume you are talented in miming and manage to collect the following forms:

(1)     **Adjective**          **Meaning**

ugly                  'very unattractive'

uglier                'more ugly'

ugliest               'most ugly'

pretty                'nice looking'

prettier              'more nice looking'

prettiest             'most nice looking'

tall                  'large in height'

taller                'more tall'

tallest               'most tall'

To determine what the morphemes are in such a list, the first thing a field linguist would do is to see whether some forms mean the same thing in different words, that is, to look for recurring forms. We find them: *ugly* occurs in *ugly, uglier,* and *ugliest,* all of which include the meaning 'very unattractive.' We also find that *-er* occurs in *prettier* and *taller,* adding the meaning 'more' to the adjectives to which it is attached. Similarly, *-est* adds the meaning 'most.' Furthermore by having our Zorxese-English interpreter pose additional questions to our native English-speaking consultant we find that *-er* and *-est* do not occur in isolation with the meanings of 'more' and 'most.' We can therefore conclude that the following morphemes occur in English:

(2)     ugly           root morpheme

pretty         root morpheme

tall           root morpheme

-er            bound morpheme 'comparative'

-est           bound morpheme 'superlative'

As we proceed we find other words that end with *-er* (e.g., *singer, lover, bomber, writer, teacher*) in which the *-er* ending does not mean 'comparative' but, when attached to a verb, changes it to 'a noun who "verbs,"' (e.g., *sings, loves, bombs, writes, teaches*). So we conclude that this is a different morpheme, even though it is pronounced the same as the comparative. We go on and find words like *number, somber, butter, member,* and many others in which the *-er* has no separate meaning at all—a *somber* is not 'one who sombs' and a *member* does not *memb*—and therefore these words must be monomorphemic.

# Words and Morphemes

---

**TIP**

• Trisyllabic Laxing is due to the attachment of a suffix. (2017)
• Stress-bearing, Stress-shifting and Stress-neutral Suffixes (2016)

The study of **word-formation** and **word-structure** is called **morphology**. Morphological theory provides a general theory of word-structure in all the languages of the world. Its task is to characterize the kinds of things that speakers need to know about the structure of the words of their language in order to be able to use them to produce and to understand speech.

In order to use language, speakers need to have two types of morphological knowledge. First, they need to be able to analyse existing words. Second, speakers need to be able to work out the meanings of novel words constructed using the word-building elements and standard word-constructing rules of the language.

## 3.1. Words

Word is the smallest linguistic unit capable of standing meaningfully on its own in the grammar of a language.

According to Leonard Bloomfield, 'a minimum free form is a word'. By this, he meant that the word is the smallest meaningful linguistic unit that can be used on its own.

### 3.1.1. Word Knowledge

Depth of word knowledge refers to a learner's knowledge of the different aspects of a given word. This knowledge has to do with extent of knowledge of the following categories:

(1) a. pronunciation and orthography;
   b. morphological properties;
   c. syntactic properties and collocations;
   d. semantic properties including connotations, polysemy, antonymy, and synonymy;
   e. register;
   f. and frequency.

A key concept in this notion of vocabulary depth is that as the word is known in a deeper manner, then the more words that are associated with that word are also known. It is also congruent with the view that lexical depth is incremental and there are degrees of word knowing. Knowledge of vocabulary is multidimensional, encompassing various types of knowledge. The relationships between words are connected on different dimensions. Words may be related

(2) a. thematically (*book-journal-manuscript*),
   b. phonologically (*dock-sock-rock*),
   c. morphologically (*indemnification-notification-intensification*),
   d. conceptually (*pan-pot-steamer*), and
   e. sociolinguistically (*dude-guy-man*)

**among others.**

The number of relations that are established between words is in part a function of the number of exposures to a word providing a variety of information about the item.

Understanding the richness of these connections represents the depth of knowledge of a particular word.

### 3.1.2. Content Words and Function Words

Languages make an important distinction between two kinds of words—**content words** and **function words**.

Nouns, verbs, adjectives, and adverbs are the **content words**. These words denote concepts such as objects, actions, attributes, and ideas that we can think about like *children, build, beautiful,* and *seldom.* **Content words** are sometimes called the **open class words** because we can and regularly do add new words to these classes, such as *Facebook* (noun), *blog* (noun, verb), *frack* (verb), *online* (adjective, adverb), and *blingy* (adjective).

Other classes of words do not have clear lexical meanings or obvious concepts associated with them, including

(3) **conjunctions** such as *and, or,* and *but*;
   **prepositions** such as *in* and *of*;
   the **articles** *the* and *a/an*, and
   **pronouns** such as *it*.

These kinds of words are called **function words** because they specify grammatical relations and have little or no semantic content.

For example, the articles indicate whether a noun is definite or indefinite—*the* boy or *a* boy. The preposition *of* indicates possession, as in "the book of yours," but this word indicates many other kinds of relations too. The *it* in *it's raining* and *the archbishop found it advisable* are further examples of words whose function is **purely grammatical**—they are required by the rules of syntax and we can hardly do without them.

**Function words** are sometimes called **closed class words**. This is because it is difficult to think of any conjunctions, prepositions, or pronouns that have recently entered the language.

### 3.1.3. Onomatopoeic Words

There is some **sound symbolism** in language—that is, words whose pronunciation suggests their meanings. Most languages contain **onomatopoeic words** like *buzz* or *murmur* that imitate the sounds associated with the objects or actions they refer to. But even here, the sounds differ from language to language and reflect the particular sound system of the language. In English *cock-a-doodle-doo* is an onomatopoeic word whose meaning is the crow of a rooster, whereas in Finnish the rooster's crow is *kukkokiekuu*.

### 3.1.4. Lexical Gaps

The words *bot* [bat] and *crake* [kʰɹek] are not known to all speakers of English, but they are words. On the other hand [bʊt] (rhymes with *put*), *creck* [kʰɹɛk], *cruke* [kʰɹuk], *cruk* [kʰɹʌk], and *crike* [kʰɹaɪk] are not words in English now, although they are **possible words**.

Advertising professionals often use possible but nonoccurring words for the names of new products. Although we would hardly expect a new product or company to come on the market with the name *Zhleet* [ʒlit]—an impossible word in English—we do not bat an eye at *Bic*, *Xerox* /ziɹaks/, *Kodak*, *Glaxo*, or *Spam* (a meat product, not junk mail), because those once nonoccurring words obey the phonotactic constraints of English.

A **possible word** contains phonemes in sequences that obey the phonotactic constraints of the language. An **actual, occurring word** is the union of a possible word with a meaning. Possible words without meaning are sometimes called **nonsense words** and are also referred to as **accidental gaps in the lexicon**, or **lexical gaps**. Thus "words" such as *creck* and *cruck* are **nonsense words** and represent **accidental gaps in the lexicon** of English.

Other gaps result when possible combinations of morphemes never come into use. Speakers can distinguish between **impossible words** such as *\*unsystem* and *\*needlessity* and **possible but nonexisting words** such as *magnificenter* or *disobvious* (cf. *distrustful*). The latter are blocked owing to the presence of *more magnificent* and *nonobvious*.

Words that conform to the **rules of word formation** but are not truly part of the vocabulary are called **accidental gaps** or **lexical gaps**. Accidental gaps are well-formed but nonexisting words.

## 3.2. Morphemes

The linguistic term for <u>the most elemental unit of grammatical form</u> is **morpheme**. The word is derived from the Greek word *morphe*, meaning 'form.'

<u>The study of the internal structure of words, and of the rules by which words are formed,</u> is **morphology**. This word itself consists of two morphemes, *morph* + *ology*. The suffix *-ology* means 'branch of knowledge,' so the meaning of morphology is 'the branch of knowledge concerning (word) forms.' Morphology also refers to our internal grammatical knowledge concerning the words of our language, and like most linguistic knowledge we are not consciously aware of it.

**A single word** may be composed of one or more morphemes:

(4)  One morpheme      boy

desire

meditate

two morphemes     boy + ish

desire + able

meditate + tion

three morphemes    boy + ish + ness

desire + able + ity

four morphemes    gentle + man + li + ness

un + desire + able + ity

more than four    un + gentle + man + li + ness

anti + dis + establish + ment + ari + an + ism

**A morpheme** may be represented by <u>a single sound</u>, such as the morpheme *a-* meaning 'without' as in *amoral* and *asexual*, or by <u>a single syllable</u>, such as *child* and *ish* in *child* + *ish*. A morpheme may also consist of more than one syllable: by <u>two syllables</u>, as in *camel, lady,* and *water*; by <u>three syllables</u>, as in *Hackensack* and *crocodile*; or by <u>four or more syllables</u>, as in *hallucinate, apothecary, helicopter,* and *accelerate*.

A **morpheme**—the minimal linguistic unit—is thus <u>an arbitrary union of a sound and a meaning (or grammatical function) that cannot be further analyzed</u>.

## Bound and Free Morphemes

Our morphological knowledge has two components: knowledge of the individual morphemes and knowledge of the rules that combine them. One of the things we know about particular morphemes is <u>whether they can **stand alone** or whether they must be attached to a base morpheme</u>.

Some morphemes like *boy, desire, gentle,* and *man* may constitute words by themselves. These are **free morphemes**.

Other morphemes like *-ish, -ness, -ly, pre-, trans-,* and *un-* are never words by themselves but are always parts of words. These affixes are **bound morphemes** and they may attach at the beginning, the end, in the middle, or both at the beginning and end of a word.

## 3.3. Affixes

Affixes like *-ing* or *-y* are called **bound morphemes** because they cannot stand alone. They always have to be attached to the stem or root of a word in order to be used. There are two types of affixes: **derivational** and **inflectional**.

## 3.3.1. Derivational and Inflectional Affixes

**Derivational affixes** are added to a stem or root to form a new stem or word, possibly, but not necessarily, resulting in a change in syntactic category or meaning. For example, the derivational affix *-er* is added to a verb like *kick* to give the noun *kicker*.

On the other hand, by the addition of **inflectional affixes**, forms with different grammatical functions are created as in *cats*. That is, **inflectional affixes** have a strictly grammatical function, marking properties such as tense and number.

English has eight inflectional suffixes:

| (5) | -s (third per. sing. present) | "she look**s** here" |
|---|---|---|
| | -s (plural) | "two cat**s**" |
| | -s (possessive) | "cat'**s** tail" |
| | -ed (past tense) | "she look**ed** here" |
| | -en, -ed (past participle) | "she has eat**en**" |
| | -ing (progressive) | "she is eat**ing**" |
| | -er (comparative) | "she is short**er** than you" |
| | -est (superlative) | "she is the short**est**" |

### 3.3.2. Prefixes and Suffixes

We know whether an affix precedes or follows other morphemes, for example that *un-*, *pre-* (*premeditate, prejudge*), and *bi-* (*bipolar, bisexual*) are **prefixes**. They occur before other morphemes.

Some morphemes occur only as **suffixes**, following other morphemes. English examples of suffix morphemes are *-ing* (*sleeping, eating, running, climbing*), *-er* (*singer, performer, reader*), *-ist* (*typist, pianist, novelist, linguist*), and *-ly* (*manly, sickly, friendly*), to mention only a few.

### 3.3.3. Suffixes and Word Stress

If the basic rules of stress looked rather untidy and replete with exceptions, **the rules accompanying affixes** can easily be said to overshadow the mono-morphemic roots.

Since the addition of prefixes does not change word stress, our presentation will be on the varying effects of suffixes on word stress. We can classify the suffixes as:

(6) a. stress-bearing (attracting) suffixes

    b. stress-shifting (fixing) suffixes

    c. stress-neutral suffixes

The common element between groups (6a) and (6b), when added to a root, is that they change the location of the stress from its original position. **Stress-bearing suffixes** attract the stress to themselves, while **stress-shifting suffixes** move the stress to some other syllable. Group (6b) and (6c) have the common element of not carrying stress.

### 3.3.3.1. Stress-bearing Suffixes

As stated above, these suffixes attract stress. Below are the **some** common **derivational suffixes**:

(7)  -ade          lémon — lemonáde

     -aire         míllion — millionáire

     -ation        réalize — realizátion

     -ee           ábsent — absentée (exception: committee)

     -eer          móuntain — mountainéer

     -ese          Japán — Japanése

     -esque        pícture — picturésque

     -ette         kítchen — kitchenétte

     -itis         lárynx — laryngítis

     -ific         hónor — honorífic

Expectedly, these stress-bearing suffixes **always** constitute **heavy syllables**. The items above with suffixes should **not** be confused with the same/similar-looking monomorphemic forms such as *brig_ade_, jambor_ee_, grot_esque_, brun_ette_, burs_itis_,* etc.

### 3.3.3.2. Stress-neutral Suffixes

These suffixes never make any difference to the stress pattern of the resulting word. Such suffixes include all **inflectional suffixes**, and **several derivational ones**:

(8)

| | | | | |
|---|---|---|---|---|
| -al | arríve — arríval | -ize | spécial — spécialize |
| -ant | ascénd — ascéndant | -less | bóttom — bóttomless |
| -cy | célibate — célibacy | -ly | fríend — fríendly |
| -dom | frée — fréedom | -ment | aménd — améndment |
| -er | pláy — pláyer | -ness | fránk — fránkness |
| -ess | líon — líoness | -ship | fríend — fríendship |
| -ful | gráce — gráceful | -some | búrden — búrdensome |
| -hood | nátion — nátionhood | -wise | clóck — clóckwise |
| -ish | gréen — gréenish | -th | gów — grówth |
| -ism | álcohol — álcoholism | -ty | cértain — cértainty |
| -ist | húman — húmanist | **-y** | **sílk — sílky** |
| -ive | submít — submíssive | | |

We should point out that the last item, **adjective-forming suffix** -*y*, should **not** be treated in the same way as the **noun-forming** -*y*, which shifts the stress to the antepenultimate, as in *hómophone — homóphony*, *phótograph — photógraphy*, etc.

### 3.3.3.3. Stress-shifting Suffixes

A multiplicity of derivational suffixes, when added to a root, <u>shift the stress from its original position to the syllable immediately preceding the suffix</u>. Below are some of the common ones in this group:

(9)

| | | |
|---|---|---|
| -ian | Áristotle — Aristotélian |
| -ial | súbstance — substánial |
| -ian | líbrary — librárian |
| -ical | geómetry — geométrical |
| -icide | ínsect — insécticide |
| -ic | périod — periódic (exceptions: Árabic, lúnatic) |
| -ify | pérson — persónify |
| -ious | lábor — labórious |
| -ity | húmid — humídity |
| -ometer | spéed — speedómeter |
| -ual | cóntext — contéxtual |
| -ous | móment — moméntous |
| **-y** | **hómonym — homónymy** |

If the original stress is on the last syllable of the root (the syllable immediately before the suffix), no change in location of the stress will result, because it is already where it should be (e.g. *divérse — divérsity, absúrd — absúrdity, obése — obésity*).

There is also a group of suffixes that put the stress on the syllable immediately before them if that syllable is heavy (i.e. has branching rhyme). The suffix -al in refusal, recital, and accidental is an example of this phenomenon. The stress falls on the syllable that is immediately before the suffix, because that syllable is heavy (long vowel, diphthong, and closed syllable, respectively). However, if the syllable in question is not heavy, then the stress moves one more syllable to the left (e.g. séasonal, práctical). The same is observable in the suffix -ency of emérgency and consístency on the one hand, and présidency and cómpetency on the other. While in the first two words the stress is on the syllable immediately before the suffix (closed syllable), it falls on the syllable one more position to the left in the last two words because the syllable before the suffix is light.

It is worth pointing out that there are some other endings that seem to vacillate between the different suffix types, of which -able is a good example. This suffix behaves like stress-neutral suffixes in most cases, as in quéstion — quéstionable, adóre — adórable, mánage — mánageable. However, in several disyllabic stems with final stress, it shifts the stress one syllable left (to stem-initial), as in admíre — ádmirable, compáre — cómparable, prefér — préferable (however, note the more recent tendency to stress-neutral behavior, e.g. compárable, admírable). To complicate things further, -able may also shift the stress one syllable to the right, as in démonstrate — demónstrable.

Another interesting case is the -ive suffix. When added to a monosyllabic root, the stress, expectedly, is on the root (-ive cannot bear stress) as in áct — áctive. However, in words with three or more syllables, we may see the stress falling on the syllable before it (e.g. decísive, offénsive), or moving one more to the left (e.g. négative, sédative), or even to one further left (e.g. génerative, méditative). There are attempts to separate cases such as decisive, offensive, etc. from others by stating that in these the roots are preceded by prefixes. Such explanations, although historically justifiable, are very dubious synchronically, and will not be followed here.

We can also point out that the classification has nothing to do with the morphological division of inflectional and derivational suffixes. While the eight **inflectional suffixes**:

| | | |
|---|---|---|
| -s (third per. sing. present) | "she looks here" | (cf. "you look here") |
| -s (plural) | "two cats" | (cf. "one cat") |
| -s (possessive) | "cat's tail" | (cf. "a cat tail") |
| -ed (past tense) | "she looked here" | (cf. "you look here") |
| -en, -ed (pat participle) | "she has eaten" | (cf. "eat your food") |
| -ing (progressive) | "she is eating" | (cf. "eat your food") |
| -er (comparative) | "she is shorter than you" | (cf. "a short book") |
| -est (superlative) | "she is the shortest" | (cf. "a short book") |

do not have effect on the stress (i.e. the addition of these suffixes does not change the location of the stress), **derivational suffixes** have no such predictability. As we saw in several examples above, while they may stay neutral to the stress, e.g. *bottom* − *bottomless* [bá ɾəm]-[bárəmləs], they can shift the stress, e.g. *geography* − *geographic* [dʒiágɹəfi]-[dʒiəgɹǽ fək], or even carry the stress themselves, e.g. *lemon* − *lemonade* [lɛ́mən]-[lɛmənéd].

## 3.4. Roots and Stems

**Morphologically complex words** consist of a morpheme root and one or more affixes. Some examples of English roots are *paint* in *painter*, *read* in *reread*, *ceive* in *conceive*, and *ling* in *linguist*. A **root** may or may not stand alone as a word (*paint* and *read* do; *ceive* and *ling* don't).

When a root morpheme is combined with an affix, it forms a stem. Other affixes can be added to a stem to form a more complex stem, as shown in the following:

(10)

| | | |
|---|---|---|
| **root** | Chomsky | (proper) noun |
| **stem** | Chomsky + ite | noun + suffix |
| **word** | Chomsky + ite + s | noun + suffix + suffix |
| | | |
| **root** | believe | verb |
| **stem** | believe + able | verb + suffix |
| **word** | un + believe + able | prefix + verb + suffix |
| | | |
| **root** | system | noun |
| **stem** | system + atic | noun + suffix |
| **stem** | un + system + atic | prefix + noun + suffix |
| **stem** | un + system + atic + al | prefix + noun + suffix + suffix |
| **word** | un + system + atic + al + ly | prefix + noun + suffix + suffix + suffix |

With the addition of each new affix, a new stem and a new word are formed. Linguists sometimes use the word **base** to mean <u>any root or stem to which an affix is attached</u>. In the preceding example, *system, systematic, unsystematic,* and *unsystematical* are bases.

## Bound Roots

**Bound roots** <u>do not occur in isolation and they acquire meaning only in combination with other morphemes</u>. For example, words of Latin origin such as *receive, conceive, perceive,* and *deceive* share a common root, *-ceive*; and the words *remit, permit, commit, submit, transmit,* and *admit* share the root *-mit*. For the original Latin speakers, the morphemes corresponding to *ceive* and *mit* had clear meanings, but for modern English speakers, Latinate morphemes such as *ceive* and *mit* have no independent meaning. Their meaning depends on the entire word in which they occur.

The morpheme *huckle*, when joined with *berry*, has the meaning of a berry that is small, round, and purplish blue; *luke* when combined with *warm* has the meaning 'somewhat.' Both these morphemes and others like them (*cran, boysen*) are bound morphemes that convey meaning only in combination.

# Check Up the Points

## 1 Glossary for this Section

**affix**
접사

A bound morpheme attached to a stem or root. See prefix, suffix, infix, circumfix, stem, root.

**bound morpheme**
의존형태소

A morpheme that must be attached to other morphemes: e.g., *-ly, -ed, non-*. Bound morphemes are prefixes, suffixes, and some roots such as *cran* in *cranberry*. See **free morpheme**.

**closed class**
닫힌 범주

A category, generally a functional category, that rarely has new words added to it: e.g., prepositions, conjunctions. See **open class**.

**content words**
내용어

The nouns, verbs, adjectives, and adverbs that constitute the major part of the vocabulary. See **open class**.

**free morpheme**
독립 형태소

A single morpheme that constitutes a word: e.g., *dog*.

**function word**
기능어

A word that does not always have a clear lexical meaning but has a grammatical function; function words include conjunctions, prepositions, articles, auxiliaries, complementizers, and pronouns. See **closed class**.

**functional category**
기능 범주

One of the categories of function words, including determiner, Aux, complementizer, and preposition. These categories are not lexical or phrasal categories. See **lexical category**, phrasal category.

**grammatical categories**
문법 범주

Traditionally called "parts of speech"; also called **syntactic categories**; expressions of the same grammatical category can generally substitute for one another without loss of grammaticality: e.g., noun phrase, verb phrase, adjective, auxiliary verb.

| | |
|---|---|
| **grammatical morpheme**<br>문법 형태소 | A function word or bound morpheme required by the syntactic rules: e.g., *to* and *-s* in *he wants to go*. See **inflectional morpheme**. |
| **inflectional affix**<br>굴절 접사 | See **inflectional morpheme**. |
| **inflectional morpheme**<br>굴절 형태소 | A bound grammatical morpheme that is affixed to a word according to rules of syntax: e.g., third-person singular verbal suffix *-s*. |
| **lexical category**<br>어휘 범주 | A general term for the word-level syntactic categories of noun, verb, adjective, and adverb. These are the categories of content words like *man, run, large,* and *rapidly*, as opposed to functional category words such as *the* and *and*. See **functional category**, **phrasal category**, **open class**. |
| **lexical gap**<br>어휘 공백 | A possible but nonoccurring word; a form that obeys the phonotactic constraints of a language yet has no meaning: e.g., *blick* in English. |
| **lexicon**<br>어휘부 | The component of the grammar containing speakers' knowledge about morphemes and words; a speaker's mental dictionary. |
| **monomorphemic word**<br>단일형태소어 | A word that consists of one morpheme. |
| **morphology**<br>형태론 | The study of the structure of words; the component of the grammar that includes the rules of word formation. |
| **nonsense word**<br>무의미어 | A permissible phonological form without meaning: e.g., *slithy*. |

| | |
|---|---|
| **onomatopoeia/ onomatopoeic** 의성어 | Words whose pronunciations suggest their meanings: e.g., *meow, buzz*. |
| **open class** 열린 범주 | The class of lexical content words; a category of words that commonly adds new words: e.g., nouns, verbs. |
| **polymorphemic word** 다형태소어 | A word that consists of more than one morpheme. |
| **possible word** 가능어 | A string of sounds that obeys the phonotactic constraints of the language but has no meaning: e.g., *gimble*. Also called a **nonsense word**. |
| **prefix** 접두사 | An affix that is attached to the beginning of a morpheme or stem: e.g., *in-* in *inoperable*. |
| **root** 어근 | The morpheme that remains when all affixes are stripped from a complex word: e.g., *system* from *un + system + atic + ally*. |
| **stem** 어간 | The base to which an affix is attached to create a more complex form that may be another stem or a word. See **root, affix**. |
| **suffix** 접미사 | An affix that is attached to the end of a morpheme or stem: e.g., *-er* in *Lew is taller than Bill*. |
| **syntactic category/class** 통사 범주 | See **grammatical categories**. |
| **word** 단어 | The smallest linguistic unit capable of standing meaningfully on its own in the grammar of a language. |

## ❷ Key-points in this Section

➡ Word Knowledge

➡ Function Words vs. Content Words

➡ Free Morphemes vs. Bound Morphemes

➡ Derivational and Inflectional Affixes (or Morphemes)

➡ Stress-bearing (attracting) Suffixes vs. Stress-shifting (fixing) Suffixes vs. Stress-neutral Suffixes

➡ Lexical Categories and Syntactic Categories

Chapter

04

# Word Formation Rules and Word Structure

> **KEY CONCEPT IN THIS CHAPTER**
>
> • Word Formation Rules
>   - Derivational Rules
>   - Inflectional Rules
> • Characteristics of Derivational and Inflectional Affixes
> • Hierarchical Structure of Words
> • Rule Productivity
> • Structural Ambiguity in Words

> **TIP**
>
> • Derivational Suffix —*al* (2014)
>   - A Denominal Adjective-forming Suffix vs. A Deverbal Noun-forming Suffix

## 4.1. Derivational Morphology

A characteristic of all human languages is the potential to create new words. The categories of noun, verb, adjective, and adverb are open in the sense that new members are constantly being added. One of the most common types of formation is **derivation**, which creates new words from already existing morphemes.

**Derivation** is the process by which a new word is built from a base, usually through the addition of an affix. However, derivation does not always apply freely to the members of a given category. Sometimes, for instance, a particular derivational affix is able to attach only to stems with particular phonological properties.

## I. The Suffix -*en*

A good example of this involves the English suffix -*en*, which combines with adjectives to create verbs with a causative meaning. However, there are many adjectives with which -*en* cannot combine, since the suffix -*en* is subject to a phonological constraint. In particular, it can only combine with a monosyllabic stem that ends in an obstruent.

## II. The Suffix -*able* and the Prefix *un*-

Words with more than one affix are formed by means of several steps. For example, consider the word *unusable*, which is composed of a prefix *un*-, a stem *use*, and a suffix -*able*. The prefix *un*-, meaning 'not', attaches only to adjectives and creates new words that are also adjectives such as *unkind*. The suffix -*able*, on the other hand, attaches to verbs and forms adjectives such as *countable*. Since *un*- cannot attach to *use*, the suffix -*able* attaches first to the stem *use*, creating *usable*. The prefix *un*- is then allowed to combine with *usable* to form *unusable*.

Now consider the word *reusable*, in which the prefix *re*- attaching only to verbs is used. Our understanding of how the affixes combine with other morphemes enables us to state the formation of *reusable* as a two-step process whereby *re*- attaches to *use* first, and then -*able* is added to *reuse*.

## III. The Suffix -*al*

There are two types of derivational suffix -*al*: the type that attaches to nouns and forms adjectives as in (1a), and the type that attaches to verbs and forms nouns as in (1b).

(1) a. central, coastal, musical
    b. refusal, proposal, recital

The second type, called a deverbal suffix, can derive well-formed nouns if a requirement are satisfied. The requirement is that the final syllable of the verb it attaches to has stress, and based on this requirement, English lacks nouns like *fidgetal, *promisal,* and *abandonal.*

## IV. The Suffix -self: Morphological Anaphora

One very important theme in current linguistic studies concerns *anaphora*. Anaphora involves a relation between, for example, a pronoun and an antecedent noun phrase whereby the two are understood as being used to refer to the same thing. The linguistic system utilizes various mechanisms to signal this phenomenon. Below we examine morphological data related to anaphora.

In English the morpheme *self* functions to signal when two phrases are being used to pick out one individual:

(1) Mary sees herself.

The person who is "seeing," Mary, is the same person who is being "seen." *Self* attaches not only to pronouns but also to other categories of words:

(2) admirer        self-admirer
    denial          self-denial
    amusement     self-amusement
    deceived       self-deceived
    employed      self-employed
    employable     self-employable
    closing         self-closing
    destructive      self-destructive
    inhibitory       self-inhibitory

The data in (2) illustrate that *self* may attach to a noun (*admirer, denial, amusement*) or an adjective (*deceived, employed, destructive*). However, *self* does not attach to just any noun or adjective:

(3) *seif-red
    *self-cat
    *self-chalk

In fact, notice that the nouns and adjectives in the left-hand column of (2) are all morphologically complex and that they are all based on verbs (*employable-employ, inhibitory-inhibit, amusement-amuse*). However, *self* does not attach directly to verbs:

(4) deceive         *self-deceive(s)

    employ        *self-employ(s)

    deny          *self-deny(s)

    admire        *self-admire(s)

Clearly, there is some kind of dependency between *self* and the verb, yet *self* cannot attach directly to the verb. We can make the following descriptive observation: the deverbal nouns and adjectives in (2) are all based on transitive verbs (note in contrast that *self-fidgety*, based on the intransitive verb *fidget*, is odd):

(5) admire the child

    deny the truth

    amuse the class

    deceive the public

    employ the elderly

    close the door

    destroy the argument

    inhibit the boy

This is not too surprising since *self* functions to indicate that, for example, the subject and the object refer to the same entity. Therefore, a *self-admirer* is someone who admires himself or herself, *self-destruction* involves someone destroying himself or herself, and so on. This is another instance of word formation where the properties of the base word are crucial.

In this case the relevant properties may have more to do with whether or not the word is "transitive" than with the category to which the word belongs (though there must be an explanation for why verbs—even though they may be transitive—do not allow *self* to be attached).

## Other Derivational Suffixes

Let us survey derivational suffixes. A representative sample of derivational suffixes is provided in (1) together with general meaning, the grammatical class of bases that they attached to and the grammatical class of the resulting word.

(1)  a.  **Verb → Noun**

*-ation*    'derives nouns of action from verbs':

don-ation, reconcili-ation, regul-ation, simul-ation

*-ant*    'person that does whatever the verb means':

inhabit-ant, celebr-ant, protest-ant, attend-ant

*-ant*    'instrument that is used to do whatever the verb means':

lubric-ant, stimul-ant, intoxic-ant

*-er*    'person that does whatever the verb means':

teach-er, runn-er, writ-er, build-er, paint-er

*-er*    'instrument that is used to do whatever the verb means':

cook-er, strain-er, drain-er, pok-er

*-ing*    'act of doing whatever the verb means':

learn-ing, read-ing, writ-ing, sav-ing, rid-ing, wait-ing

*-ist*    'derives agent nouns from verbs—one who does X':

cycl-ist, typ-ist, copy-ist

*-ion*    'derives nouns of condition or action from verbs':

eros-ion (from *erode*), persuas-ion (from *persuade*), promot-ion

*-ment*    'the result or product of the action of the verb; the instrument used to perform the action of the verb':

pave-ment, appoint-ment, accomplish-ment, govern-ment

*-ery*    'derives nouns indicating a place where animals are kept or plants grown':

catt-ery, pigg-ery, orang-ery, shrubb-ery

*-ery*    'derives nouns indicating a place where the action specified by the verb takes place':

bak-ery, cann-ery, brew-ery, fish-ery, refin-ery, tann-ery

b. **Verb → Adjective**

*-ing*      'in the process or state of doing whatever the verb means':

          waiting (as in *waiting car*), standing (as in *standing passengers*)

*-ive*      'having the tendency to X; having the quality character of X; given to the action of X-ing':

          act-ive, indicat-ive, evas-ive, product-ive, representat-ive

*-ing*      'the act of doing whatever the verb means':

          sail-ing, sing-ing, fight-ing, writ-ing

c. **Noun → Verb**

*-ate*      'derives verbs from nouns':

          regul-ate, capacit-ate, don-ate

*-ise/-ize*  'to bring about whatever the noun means':

          colon-ize, American-ize, computer-ize

*-ise/-ize*  'put in the place or state indicated by the noun':

          hospital-ize, terror-ize, jeopard-ize

d. **Noun → Adjective**

*-ate*      'derives adjectives denoting state':

          intim-ate, accur-ate, obdur-ate

*-ish*      'having the (objectionable) nature, qualities of character of X':

          lout-ish, freak-ish, child-ish

*-less*    'without X':

          joy-less, care-less, fear-less, child-less

*-ful*     'filled with X':

          joy-ful, care-ful, fear-ful, cheer-ful

*-(i)an*   'associated with whatever the noun indicates':

          Chomsky-an, suburb-an, Canad-ian

e. **Adjective → Verb**

*-ate*      'cause to become, do etc. whatever the adjective means':

          activ-ate, euq-ate (< equal)

*-ise/-ize*  'cause to become whatever the adjective means':

          tranquill-ize, modern-ize, stabil-ize, civil-ize, familiar-ize

f. **Adjective → Noun**

-*ness*     'forms a noun expressing state or condition':

good-ness, fair-ness, bitter-ness, dark-ness

-*ity*     'forms a noun expressing state or condition':

timid-ity, banal-ity, pur-ity, antiqu-ity

-*ery*     'having the property indicated by the adjective':

brav-ery, trick-ery, chican-ery

g. **Adjective → Adverb**

-*ly*     'forms adverbs from adjectives':

usual-ly, busi-ly, proud-ly, loud-ly, grateful-ly

h. **Noun → Noun**

-*acy*     'derives a noun of quality, state or condition from another noun or adjective (normally the base to which it is added also takes the nominal suffix -*ate*)':

advoc-acy, episcop-acy, intim-acy, accur-acy, obdur-acy

-*er*     'a person who practises a trade or profession connected to the noun':
marin-er, geograph-er, football-er, hatt-er

-*ery*     'derives nouns indicating general collective sense "-ware, stuff"':

machin-ery, crock-ery, jewell-ery, pott-ery

-*let*     'derives a diminutive noun':

pig-let, islet, rivu-let

-*ling*     'derives a diminutive noun from another noun':

duck-ling, prince-ling, found-ling

-*hood*     'quality, state, rank of being X':

boy-hood, sister-hood, priest-hood

-*ship*     'state or condition of being X':

king-ship, craftsman-ship, director-ship, steward-ship

-*ism*     'forms nouns which are the name of a theory, doctrine or practice':

femin-ism, capital-ism, structural-ism

-*ist*     'adherent to some -ism, a protagonist for X, and expert on X':

femin-ist, capital-ist, structural-ist

   i.   **Adjective** → **Adjective**

     *-ish*       'having the property of being somewhat X':

               narrow-ish, blu-ish, pink-ish

   j.   **Verb** → **Verb**

     *-er*       'adds frequent or iterative meaning to verbs':

               chatt-er, patt-er, flutt-er

## 4.2. Inflectional Morphology

Consider the forms of the verb in the following sentences:

(2)  a. I sail the ocean blue.

     b. He sails the ocean blue.

     c. John sailed the ocean blue.

     d. John has sailed the ocean blue.

     e. John is sailing the ocean blue.

In sentence (2b) the *-s* at the end of the verb is an agreement marker; it signifies that the subject of the verb is third-person and is singular, and that the verb is in the present tense. It doesn't add lexical meaning. The suffix *-ed* indicates past tense, and is also required by the syntactic rules of the language when verbs are used with *have*, just as *-ing* is required when verbs are used with forms of *be*.

Word-formation rules related to the verbs in (2) can be described like (3) and each of the corresponding word structures, like (4):

(3)  a. Verb  +  s  → Verb

     b. Verb  +  ed  → Verb

     c. Verb  +  ing  → Verb

(4)  a.     Verb       b.     Verb       c.     Verb

      Verb    -s         Verb    -ed       Verb    -ing

      sail              sail              sail

**Inflectional morphemes** represent relationships between different parts of a sentence. For example, *-s* expresses the relationship between the verb and the third-person singular subject; *-ed* expresses the relationship between the time the utterance is spoken (e.g., now) and the time of the event (past). If you say "John danced," the *-ed* affix places the activity before the utterance time. **Inflectional morphology** is closely connected to the syntax and semantics of the sentence.

English also has other inflectional endings, such as the plural suffix, which is attached to certain singular nouns, as in *boy/boys* and *cat/cats*.

(5)     Noun  +  s  →  Noun

(6)     a.

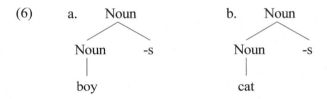

Inflectional morphemes in English follow the derivational morphemes in a word. Thus, to the derivationally complex word *commit + ment* one can add a plural ending to form *commit + ment + s*, but the order of affixes may not be reversed to derive the impossible *commit + s + ment = *commitsment*.

In distinguishing inflectional from derivational morphemes in Modern English we may summarize in the table below:

**Table 1.** Characteristics of Derivational and Inflectional Affixes in English

| Derivational | Inflectional |
| --- | --- |
| Lexical function | Grammatical function |
| May cause word class change | No word class change |
| Some meaning change | Small or no meaning change |
| Never required by rules of grammar | Often required by rules of grammar |
| Precede inflectional morphemes in a word | Follow derivational morphemes in a word |
| Some productive, many nonproductive | Productive |

## 4.3. Morphological Structure : Hierarchical Structure of Words

When we examine words composed of only two morphemes, a stem and an affix, we implicitly know something about the way in which the affix combined with its stem. That is, the word was formed via the addition of the affix to the stem. By itself, this fact seems neither particularly significant nor particularly interesting. After all, there are no other options. However, when a word comprises more than two morphemes, the order in which the morphemes are put together becomes a more significant question. In order to consider such questions, we first will note two facts about morphemes and lexical categories.

First, the stems with which a given affix may combine (its input) normally belong to the same lexical category. For example, the suffix -able attaches freely to verbs, but not to adjectives or nouns. Thus, we can add this suffix to the verbs *adjust, break, compare,* and *debate,* but not to the adjectives *asleep, lovely, happy,* and *strong,* nor to the nouns *anger, morning, student,* and *success.* Second, the words that are formed when an affix attaches to a stem (its output) also normally belong to the same lexical category. For example, the words resulting from the addition of *-able* to a verb are always adjectives. Thus, *adjustable, breakable, comparable,* and *debatable* are all adjectives.

It turns out that these two facts have an important consequence for determining the way in which words with more than one derivational affix must be formed. What it means is that you can trace the derivational history of words as though they were formed in steps, with one affix attaching to a stem at a time. Words with more than one affix can be represented as forming by means of several steps. For example, consider the word *reusable,* which is composed of a prefix *re-,* a stem *use,* and a suffix *-able.* One possible way this morphologically complex word might be formed is all at once: *re + use + able,* where the prefix and the suffix attach at the same time to the stem *use.* This cannot be the case, however, knowing what we know about how derivational affixes are restricted with respect to both their input and their output. Which attaches to *use* first, then: *re-,* or *-able?*

The prefix *re-,* meaning 'do again,' attaches to verbs and creates new words that are also verbs. (Compare with *redo, revisit,* and *rewind.*) The suffix *-able* also attaches to verbs, but it forms words that are adjectives. (Compare with *stoppable, doable,* and *washable.*) When working with problems such as those described in this file, you may find it helpful to anthropomorphize the affixes a bit in your mind. For example, you can think about *re-* as the sort of thing that says, "I am looking for a verb. If you give me a verb, then I will give you another verb," and *-able* as the sort of thing that says, "I am looking for a verb. If you give me a verb, then I will give you an adjective."

We learn from examining these two rules that *re-* cannot attach to *usable,* because *usable* is an adjective, but *re-* is "looking for" a verb. However, *re-* is able to attach to the root *use,* because *use* is a verb. Since *reuse* is also a verb, it can then serve as a stem to take *-able.* Thus, the formation of the word *reusable* is a two-step process whereby *re-* and *use* attach first, and then *-able* attaches to the word *reuse.* In this way, the output of one affixation process serves as the input for the next. The restrictions that each affix is subject to can help us determine the sequence of derivation.

Words that are "layered" in this way have a special type of structure characterized as **hierarchical**. This hierarchical structure can be schematically represented by a tree diagram that indicates the steps involved in the formation of the word. The tree for *reusable* appears in (1).

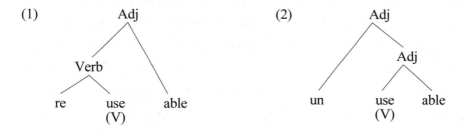

Now consider the word *unusable.* This word also contains three morphemes, so it is tempting to say that they will be put together in the same order as were the morphemes in *reusable.* However, notice that unlike *reuse, *unuse* is not a word, because in this case, *un-* needs to have its input be an adjective. (Compare with *unhappy, unkind,* and *untrue.*) Fortunately, when *-able* attaches to verbs, it forms adjectives! Once the adjective *useable* has been formed, the needs of *un-* are met, and it is able to attach in order to form the target word, *unusable.* A tree for this derivation showing the hierarchical structure of *unusable* appears in (2).

Notice that these two trees, that is, the ones in (1) and (2), do not have the same shape. The shape of the tree is particular to the order in which morphemes are combined. Using the tools you have been given, though, it is possible to deduce the hierarchical structures even for very complex words. In (3) there is an example of a word with four morphemes; try to determine for yourself why this is the correct structure for the word *dehumidifier*.

(3)

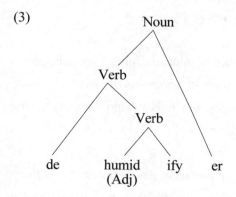

## 4.4. Rule Productivity

Another distinction between inflectional and derivational morphemes is that inflectional morphemes are **productive**: they apply freely to nearly every appropriate base (except "irregular" forms such as *feet*, not *\*foots*). Most nouns take an *-s* inflectional suffix to form a plural, but only some nouns take the derivational suffix *-ize* to form a verb: *idolize*, but not *\*picturize*.

Among derivational morphemes, the suffix *-able* can be conjoined with any verb to derive an adjective with the meaning of the verb and the meaning of *-able*, which is something like 'able to be' as in *accept + able, laugh + able, pass + able, change + able, breathe + able, adapt + able,* and so on. The productivity of this rule is illustrated by the fact that we find *-able* affixed to new verbs such as *downloadable* and *faxable*.

The prefix *un-* derives same-class words with an opposite meaning: *unafraid, unfit, un-American,* and so on. Additionally, *un-* can be added to derived adjectives that have been formed by morphological rules, resulting in perfectly acceptable words such as *un + believe + able* or *un + pick + up + able*.

Yet *un-* is **not fully productive**. We find *happy* and *unhappy*, *cowardly* and *uncowardly*, but not *sad* and *\*unsad*, *brave* and *\*unbrave*, or *obvious* and *\*unobvious*. It appears that the "un-Rule" is most productive for adjectives that are derived from verbs, such as *unenlightened, unsimplified, uncharacterized, unauthorized, undistinguished,* and so on. It also appears that most acceptable *un-* words have polysyllabic bases, and while we have *unfit, uncool, unread,* and *unclean*, many of the unacceptable *un-* forms have monosyllabic stems such as *\*unbig, \*ungreat, \*unred, \*unsad, \*unsmall, \*untall*.

The rule that adds an *-er* to verbs in English to produce a noun meaning 'one who does' is a **nearly productive** morphological rule, giving us *examiner, exam-taker, analyzer, lover, hunter,* and even *girlplayerwither,* as the cartoon illustrates, but fails full productivity owing to "unwords" like *\*chairer,* which is not 'one who chairs.'

The other *-er* suffix, the one that means 'more' as in *greedier,* also fails to be entirely productive. The more syllables a word has, the less likely *-er* will work and we will need the word *more,* as in more beautiful (but not *\*beautifuler*) compared with the well-formed *nicer* or *prettier.*

Even less productive to the point of rareness are such derivational morphemes as the diminutive suffixes in the words *pig + let* and *sap + ling.*

## 4.5. Exceptions to Word Formation Rules

The morphological rule that forms plural nouns from singular nouns does not apply to words like *child, man, foot,* and *mouse.* These words are exceptions to the rule. Similarly, verbs like *go, sing, bring, run,* and *know* are exceptions to the inflectional rule for producing past-tense verbs in English.

## 4.6. Structurally Ambiguous Words

The hierarchical organization of words is most clearly shown by structurally ambiguous words. Consider the word *unbuttonable.* The two meanings of the word correspond to different structures, as follows:

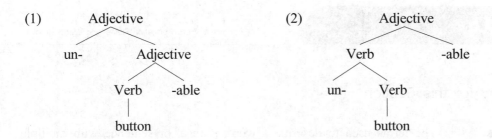

The ambiguity of this word arises because the prefix *un-* can combine with different grammatical categories.

In the first structure the verb *button* combines with the deverbal adjective-forming suffix *-able* to form an adjective *buttonable* ('able to be locked'). Then the prefix *un-*, meaning 'not,' combines with the derived adjective to form a new adjective *unbuttonable* ('not able to be buttoned'). In the second case, the prefix *un-* combines with the verb *button* to form a derived verb *unbutton*. Then the derived verb combines with the suffix *-able* to form *unbuttonable*, 'able to be unbuttoned.'

An entire class of words in English follows this pattern: *unlockable, unzippable,* and *unlatchable*, among others. The ambiguity arises because the prefix *un-* can combine with an adjective, as illustrated in the rule (3a), or it can combine with a verb, as illustrated in the rule (3b), as in *undo, unstaple, unearth, and unloosen.*

(3)  a.  un- + Adjective  →  Adjective
     b.  un- + Verb  →  Verb

If words were only strings of morphemes without any internal organization, we could not explain the ambiguity of words like *unbuttonable*. These words also illustrate another key point, which is that structure is important to determining meaning. The same three morphemes occur in both versions of *unbuttonable*, yet there are two distinct meanings. The different meanings arise because of the different structures.

# Check Up the Points

## 1 Glossary for this Section

| | |
|---|---|
| **ambiguous, ambiguity**<br>중의적, 중의성 | The terms used to describe a word, phrase, or sentence with multiple meanings. |
| **morphological rules**<br>형태 규칙 | Rules for combining morphemes to form stems and words. |
| **productive**<br>생산적 | Refers to morphological rules that can be used freely and apply to all forms to create new words: e.g., the addition to an adjective of *-ish* meaning 'having somewhat of the quality,' such as *newish, tallish, incredible-ish*. |
| **structural ambiguity**<br>구조적 중의성 | The phenomenon in which the same sequence of words has two or more meanings accounted for by different phrase structure analyses: e.g., *He saw a boy with a telescope.* |

## ❷ Key-points in this Section

**Table 1.** Characteristics of Derivational and Inflectional Affixes in English

| Derivational | Inflectional |
|---|---|
| Lexical function | Grammatical function |
| May cause word class change | No word class change |
| Some meaning change | Small or no meaning change |
| Never required by rules of grammar | Often required by rules of grammar |
| Precede inflectional morphemes in a word | Follow derivational morphemes in a word |
| Some productive, many nonproductive | Productive |

Two different *un-* prefixes in (1), structurally ambiguous words, *unbuttonable* and *undoable* in (2) and (3) and their related word-formation rules in (4):

(1)　a. *un-* 'negative' (with adjectives): unoriginal, unusual, unpleasant, ...

　　　b. *un-* 'reversive, i.e, doing the same action in the opposite direction'
　　　　　(with verbs): undo, unblock, unpack, unpick, unroll, ...

(2)　a.　Adjective　　　　　　　　　b.　　Adjective

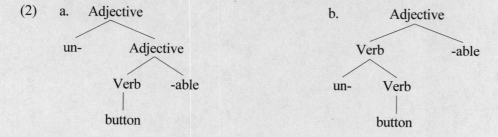

(3) a.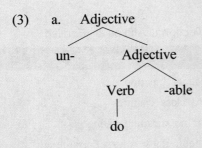

b.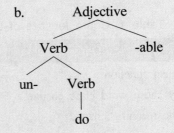

(4) a. Verb + able → Adjective
b. un + Adjective → Adjective
c. un + Verb → Verb

MEMO

**Chapter 05**

# Semantics

# MEN
# TOR

Mentor Linguistics
전공영어
멘토영어학

# Sentential Semantics : Truth-Conditional Semantics

---

**KEY CONCEPT IN THIS CHAPTER**

- **Truth**
- **Entailment**
- **Presupposition**
- **Tautology and Contraction**
- **Implicatives**

---

**TIP**

- Implicative Verb *refuse* (2018)

---

The study of the linguistic meaning of morphemes, words, phrases, and sentences is called **semantics**. Subfields of semantics are **lexical semantics**, which is concerned with the meanings of words and the meaning relationships among words; and **phrasal** or **sentential semantics**, which is concerned with the meaning of syntactic units larger than the word.

## 1.1. Introduction to Truth-Conditional Semantics

You know, or have the capacity to discover, when sentences are true or false. That is, if you know the meaning of a sentence, you know its truth conditions.

Linguistic knowledge permits you to determine <1> whether a sentence is true or false, <2> when one sentence implies the truth or falseness of another, and <3> whether a sentence has multiple meanings. One way to account for this knowledge is by formulating semantic rules that build the meaning of a sentence from the meanings of its words and the way the words combine syntactically. This is often called **truth-conditional semantics** because it takes **speakers' knowledge of truth conditions** as basic. It is also called **compositional semantics** because it calculates the truth value of a sentence by **composing, or putting together, the meanings of smaller units**.

## 1.1.1. Meaning Relations in Truth-Conditional Semantics

**Truth conditional semantics** studies lexical relations by comparing predications that can be made about the same referring expression. Its task is to account for the meaning relations between different expressions in a language. Three of such relations are **entailment**, **paraphrase** and **contradiction**.

**Entailment** is the relation between two propositions—let's label them 'p' and 'q'—such that if p is true, q must also be true, but if q is true, it does not necessarily follow that p is true.

**Paraphrase** is the relation between two propositions, p and q, such that if either is true, the other is necessarily true also, and if either is false, the other is false.

**Contradiction** is the relation between two propositions such that if either is true, the other is necessarily false.

Semantic relations may hold between sentences of a language. Sometimes these relations are the result of particular words in the sentences, but in other cases the relations are the result of syntactic structure. We will look at an approach to meaning based on the notion of **truth**, which has grown out of the study of logic. In particular we examine how successfully **a truth-based approach** is in characterizing the semantic relations of **entailment** and **presupposition**.

What kind of knowledge about the meaning of a language does the native speaker have? For sentence meaning, a semantic theory should reflect an English speaker's knowledge:

(1) That a and b below are **synonymous**:
   a. My brother is a bachelor.
   b. My brother has never married.

(2) That a below **entails** b:
   a. The anarchist assassinated the emperor.
   b. The emperor is dead.

(3) That a below **contradicts** b:

    a. My brother Sebastian has just come from Rome.

    b. My brother Sebastian has never been to Rome.

(4) That a below **presupposes** b, as c does d:

    a. The Mayor of Manchester is a woman.

    b. There is a Mayor of Manchester.

    c. I regret eating your sandwich.

    d. I ate your sandwich.

(5) That a and b are necessarily true, i.e. **tautologies**:

    a. Ireland is Ireland.

    b. Rich people are rich.

(6) That a and b are necessarily false, i.e. **contradictions**:

    a. ?He is murderer but he's never killed anyone.

    b. ?Now is not now.

We can give a rough characterization of each, as follows:

(7) A is **synonymous** with B: A has the same meaning as B.

(8) A **entails** B: we know that if A then automatically B.

(9) A **contradicts** B: A is inconsistent with B.

(10) A **presupposes** B: B is part of the assumed background against which A is said.

(11) A is a **tautology**: A is automatically true by virtue of its own meaning, but informationally empty.

(12) A is a **contradiction**: A is inconsistent with itself, i.e. asserts and denies the same thing.

The problem for semantics is to provide a more rigorous account of theses and similar notions.

A truth-based definition of entailment allows us to state the relationship more clearly below:

(13) Entailment defined by truth

A sentence p entails a sentence q when the truth of the first (p) guarantees the truth of the second (q), and the falsity of the second (q) guarantees the falsity of the first (p).

In other words,

If p is true, then q is automatically true. If q is false, then p is also false. If p is false, then q can be either true or false.

In the following example the a sentence is said to **presuppose** the b sentence:

(14) a. He's stopped turning into a werewolf every full moon.
     b. He used to turn into a werewolf every full moon.

(15) a. Her husband is fool.
     b. She has a husband.

(16) a. I don't regret leaving London.
     b. I left London.

(17) a. The Prime Minister of Malaysia is in Dublin this week.
     b. Malaysia has a prime minister.

(18) a. I do regret leaving London.
     b. I left London.

A truth-based definition of **presupposition** allows us to state the relationship more clearly below:

(19) Presupposition defined by truth

> A sentence p presupposes a sentence q when the truth of the first (p) guarantees the truth of the second (q), and the falsity of the first (p) also guarantee the truth of the second (q).

> In other words,

> If p is true then q is true. If p is false, then q is still true. If q is true, p could be either true or false.

(from John I. Saeed (2009) Semantics, 3<sup>rd</sup> edition, Wiley-Blackwell, pp.87-89, 99 & 102)

For most sentences it does not make sense to say that they are always true or always false. Rather, they are true or false in a given situation, as we previously saw with *Jack swims*.

But a restricted number of sentences are indeed always true regardless of the circumstances. They are called **tautologies**. (The term analytic is also used for such sentences.) Examples of tautologies are sentences like *Circles are round* or *A person who is single is not married*. Their truth is guaranteed solely by the meaning of their parts and the way they are put together.

Similarly, some sentences are always false. These are called **contradictions**. Examples of contradictions are sentences like *Circles are square* or *A bachelor is married*.

## 1.1.2. Entailment and Related Notions

If you know that the sentence *Jack swims beautifully* is true, then you also know that the sentence *Jack swims* must also be true.

This meaning relation is called **entailment**.

We say that *Jack swims beautifully* **entails** *Jack swims*.

More generally, one sentence **entails** another if whenever the first sentence is true the second one is also true, in all conceivable circumstances.

On the other hand, negating both sentences reverses the entailment. *Jack doesn't swim* entails *Jack doesn't swim beautifully*.

Omitting tautologies and contradictions, two sentences are **synonymous** (or **paraphrases**) if they are both true or both false with respect to the same situations.

Sentences like *Jack put off the meeting* and *Jack postponed the meeting* are synonymous, because when one is true the other must be true; and when one is false the other must also be false.

We can describe this pattern in a more concise way by using the notion of entailment:

(20) Two sentences are **synonymous** if they **entail** each other.

Thus if sentence A entails sentence B and vice versa, then whenever A is true B is true, and vice versa.

Two sentences are **contradictory** if, whenever one is true, the other is false or, equivalently, there is no situation in which they are both true or both false.

For example, the sentences *Jack is alive* and *Jack is dead* are **contradictory** because if the sentence *Jack is alive* is true, then the sentence *Jack is dead* is false, and vice versa. In other words, *Jack is alive* and *Jack is dead* have opposite truth values.

Like synonymy, **contradiction** can be reduced to a special case of entailment.

(21) Two sentences are **contradictory** if one **entails** the negation of the other.

## 1.2. Factive Predicates

The term '**factive verb**' is due to a pioneering study by Paul and Carol Kiparsky (1968). An illustrative sample of these verbs is provided in (22).

(22) Factive Verbs: be significant, be tragic, be relevant, be odd, regret, ignore, resent, know, realize, bear in mind, take into account, make clear, find out

What is common to them is that any simple assertion with a **factive predicate**, such as (23a), commits the speaker to the belief that the complement sentence, just by itself, is also true.

(23) a. It is odd that Bill is alone.

   b. Bill is alone.

   c. It is possible that Bill is alone.

It would be insincere for anyone to assert (23a) if he did not believe that (23b) is true. Intuitively, in uttering (23a) the speaker must take it for granted that Bill is alone; he is making a comment about that fact. The same relation holds between (24a) and (24b).

(24) a. Mary realized that it was raining.

   b. It was raining.

   c. Mary believed that it was raining.

Notice that these relations break down if we replace *odd* by *possible* and *realized* by *believed*. (23c) and (24c) do not carry a commitment to the truth of the complement sentence.

With factive verbs, it does not make a difference whether the main sentence is affirmative or negative. The negations of (23a) and (24a), which you find in (25), also obligate the speaker to accept the complement as true.

(25) a. It isn't odd that Bill is alone.

   b. Mary didn't realize that it was raining.

Even the illocutionary force of the main sentence is irrelevant. The question in (26) carries along the same commitment as (23a) and (25a).

(26) Is it odd that Bill is alone?

These facts about negation and questions become important when we have to distinguish between factive and implicative verbs.

## 1.3. Implicative Predicates

Some predicates do not presuppose the truth of a proposition that occurs as one of their arguments but carry some implication about the truth or non-truth of the proposition. We find an interesting variety of implications and can recognize different kinds of **implicative predicates**, first sketched by Karttunen (1971)[5] and sometimes called '**conditional factives**.' Consider first:

(27)   a. I managed to catch my bus, and I caught it.
       b. I managed to catch my bus, but I didn't catch it.

Sentence (27a) is as **redundant** as *I caught my bus, and I caught it*. Sentence (27b) is as **contradictory** as *I caught my bus, and I didn't catch it*.

If you hear someone say "I managed to catch my bus," you will no doubt **infer** that the speaker did catch the bus in question. Hearing the negative equivalent, "I didn't manage to catch my bus," you **infer** that the speaker did not catch the bus.

The verb *manage*, like some other verbs followed by a reduced clause, has a certain **implicative value**.

Different predicates have different implicative values, and we recognize **six groups of predicates** according to what they imply about the truth value of the included clause.

In our **first group**, which includes manage, if the predicate is affirmative, it implies that the following proposition is true, and if the predicate is negative, there is an implication that the following proposition is false. (The symbol '→' below should be read 'implies.')

(28)   a. I managed to catch my bus.  →  I caught my bus.
       b. I didn't manage to catch my bus.  →  I didn't catch my bus.

---

[5] Laurie Karttunen (1971) "Implicative Verbs," *Language* 47: 340-58.

More examples:

(29)   a. We happened/chanced to see your brother.   →   We saw your brother.
       b. We didn't happen/chance to see your brother. → We didn't see your brother.

(30)   a. He chose/condescended to wait for us.   →   He waited for us.
       b. He didn't choose/condescend to wait for us.   →   He didn't wait for us.

(31)   a. She remembered to stop at the post office.
          →   She stoped at the post office.
       b. She didn't remember to stop at the post office.
          →   She didn't stop at the post office.

With these verbs, Group 1, affirmative implies affirmative and negative implies negative.

(32)    $+ → +$    $- → -$

## Group 2 verbs occur in these sentences:

(33)   a. We neglected/failed to make reservations.   →   We didn't make reservations.
       b. We didn't neglect/fail to make reservations.   →   We made reservations.

(34)   a. I avoided/missed/escaped attending that party.   →   I didn't attend that party.
       b. I didn't avoid/miss/escape attending that party.   →   I attended that party.

With these verbs affirmative implies negative, that the embedded proposition is not true, and negative has an affirmative implication, that the embedded proposition is true.

(35)    $+ → -$    $- → +$

Both Group 1 and Group 2 verbs are followed only by clauses with tacit subject; the subject of the embedded proposition is the same as the subject of the main clause.

Verbs in some of the groups below are followed by clauses with tacit or overt subjects. When both kinds exists, both are illustrated here.

## Group 3:

(36)  a. Henry acknowledged/admitted starting the fire.  →  Henry started the fire.
      b. Henry didn't acknowledge/admit starting the fire.  →  ?

(37)  a. Circumstance forced us to cancel our plans.  →  We canceled our plans.
      b. Circumstance didn't force us to cancel our plans.  →  ?

We recognize that Henry's failure to admit starting the fire does not inform us whether he did or did not actually start the fire.

For Group 3 implicative verbs, affirmative implies affirmative but negative has no implication.

(38)  + → +     − → 0

## Group 4:

(39)  a. Mary pretended to be asleep.  →  Mary was not asleep.
      b. Mary didn't pretend to be asleep.  →  ?

(40)  a. A sudden storm prevented the men from completing the job.
          → The men didn't complete the job.
      b. A sudden storm didn't prevent the men from completing the job. → ?

(41)  a. We forgot to make reservations.  →  We didn't make reservations.
      b. We didn't forget to make reservations.  →  ?

In Group 4, affirmative implies negative but negative has no implication.

(42)   + → −     − → 0

## Group 5:

(43)  a. We tried to answer.  →  ?

  b. We didn't try to answer.  →  We didn't answer.

Affirmative has no implication, while the negative implies negative.

(44)  $+ \rightarrow 0$   $- \rightarrow -$

## Group 6:

(45)  a. We hesitated to accept the offer. →  ?

  b. We didn't hesitate to accept the offer.  →  We accepted the offer.

Affirmative has nothing, negative implies affirmative.

(46)  $+ \rightarrow 0$   $- \rightarrow +$

**Table 1.** Implications of the Six Groups With One Example for Each Group

| Group # | implicative verb | affirmative implies | negative implies |
|---------|------------------|---------------------|------------------|
| Group 1 | manage | $+ \rightarrow +$ | $- \rightarrow -$ |
| Group 2 | refuse | $+ \rightarrow -$ | $- \rightarrow +$ |
| Group 3 | force | $+ \rightarrow +$ | $- \rightarrow 0$ |
| Group 4 | prevent from | $+ \rightarrow -$ | $- \rightarrow 0$ |
| Group 5 | try | $+ \rightarrow 0$ | $- \rightarrow -$ |
| Group 6 | hesitate | $+ \rightarrow 0$ | $- \rightarrow +$ |

(from Charles W. Kreidler, *Introducing English Semantics*, pp. 233-239)

**Table 2.** A List of Implicative Verbs in the Six Groups

| Complement / Verb Group | Tacit Subject | | Overt Subject | |
|---|---|---|---|---|
| | infinitive complement | gerund complement | infinitive complement | gerund complement |
| Group 1 | chance<br>happen<br>choose<br>condescend<br>get<br>**manage**<br>remember | practice | | |
| Group 2 | decline<br>fail<br>neglect<br>**refuse**<br>forget | avoid<br>escape<br>keep from<br>miss<br>refrain from | | |
| Group 3 | | acknowledge<br>admit<br>remember | cause<br>compel<br>force<br>help<br>lead<br>oblige<br>**persuade** | find<br>leave<br>remember |
| Group 4 | pretend | | | deter from<br>dissuade from<br>excuse from<br>hinder from<br>keep from<br>**prevent from** |
| Group 5 | attempt<br>endeavor<br>**try**<br>undertake<br>venture | risk<br>undertake | consider | risk |
| Group 6 | **hesitate** | deny | | |

## 1.4. Presupposition Triggers

Some types of presupposition are produced by particular words or constructions, which together are sometimes called *presupposition triggers*. Some of these triggers derive from syntactic structures, for example the cleft construction in (47) and the pseudo-cleft in (48) share the presupposition in (49). In addition, a *wh*-question also serves as a presupposition trigger, but a *yes-no* question doesn't.

(47) It was his behavior with frogs that disgusted me.

(48) What disgusted me was his behavior with frogs.

(49) Something disgusted me.

Other forms of subordinate clauses may produce presuppositions, for example, time adverbial clauses and comparative clauses. In the following sentences, the (a) sentence has the presupposition in (b):

(50) a. I was riding motorcycles before you learned to walk.

    b. You learned to walk.

(51) a. He's even more gullible than you are.

    b. You are gullible.

Many presuppositions are produced by the presence of certain words. Many of these lexical triggers are verbs. For example, there is a class of verbs like *regret* and *realize* that are called *factive verbs* because they presuppose the truth of their complement clause. Compare sentences (52) and (53) below: only the sentence with the factive verb *realize* presupposes (54). There is no such presupposition with the non-factive verb *think* in (53).

(52) Sean realized that Miranda had dandruff.

(53) Sean thought that Miranda had dandruff.

(54) Miranda had dandruff.

Similarly compare (55)-(57):

(55) Sheila regretted eating the banana.

(56) Sheila considered eating the banana.

(57) Sheila ate the banana.

Some verbs of judgment produce presuppositions. Compare (58)-(60) below:

(58) John accused me of telling her.

(59) John blamed me for telling her.

(60) I told her.

Once again one verb, *blame*, produces the presupposition in (60), while another, *accuse*, does not.

### 1 Glossary for this Section

| | |
|---|---|
| **contradiction**<br>모순 | Describes a sentence that is false by virtue of its meaning alone, irrespective of context: e.g., *Kings are female*. See analytic, tautology. |
| **contradictory**<br>모순적 | Mutual negative entailment: the truth of one sentence necessarily implies the falseness of another sentence, and vice versa: e.g., *The door is open* and *The door is closed* are contradictory sentences. See **entailment**. |
| **compositional semantics**<br>조합 의미론 | A theory of meaning that calculates the truth value or meaning of larger units by the application of semantic rules to the truth value or meaning of smaller units. |
| **entail**<br>함의하다 | One sentence entails another if the truth of the first necessarily implies the truth of the second: e.g., *The sun melted the ice* entails *The ice melted* because if the first is true, the second must be true. |
| **entailment**<br>함의 | The relationship between two sentences, where the truth of one necessitates the truth of the other: e.g., *Corday assassinated Marat* and *Marat is dead*; if the first is true, the second must be true. |
| **factive verb**<br>사실 동사 | A verb that has a predication (a full clause, gerund clause or an abstract noun phrase) as one of its argument and that, whether affirmative or negative, presupposes the truth of that predication: *We forgot/didn't forget that the meeting was canceled* presupposes that the meeting was canceled. |

**implicative verb**
함의 동사

A verb that expresses something about the truth of the predication that follows in the sentence: *We didn't hesitate to accept the offer* implies that we accepted the offer.

**lexical paraphrases**
어휘적 동의문

Sentences that have the same meaning due to synonyms: e.g., She lost her *purse* and She lost her *handbag*.

**lexical semantics**
어휘 의미론

The subfield of semantics concerned with the meanings of words and the meaning relationships among words.

**paraphrases**
동의문

Sentences with the same truth conditions; sentences with the same meaning, except possibly for minor differences in emphasis, e.g., *He ran up a big bill* and *He ran a big bill up*. See **synonymy**.

**presupposition**
전제

Implicit assumptions about the world required to make an utterance meaningful or relevant, e.g., "some tea has already been taken" is a presupposition of *Take some more tea!*

**principle of compositionality**
조합성 원리

A principle of semantic interpretation that states that the meaning of a word, phrase, or sentence depends both on the meaning of its components (morphemes, words, phrases) and how they are combined structurally.

**semantic rules**
의미 규칙

Principles for determining the meaning of larger units like sentences from the meaning of smaller units like noun phrases and verb phrases.

| | |
|---|---|
| **semantics**<br>의미론 | The study of the linguistic meanings of morphemes, words, phrases, and sentences. |
| **sentential semantics**<br>문장 의미론 | The subfield of semantics concerned with the meanings of syntactic units larger than the word. |
| **tautology**<br>항진명제 | A sentence that is true in all situations; a sentence true from the meaning of its words alone: e.g., *Kings are not female*. Also called **analytic**. |
| **truth conditions**<br>진리조건 | The circumstances that must be known to determine whether a sentence is true, which are therefore part of the meaning, or sense, of declarative sentences. |
| **truth-conditional semantics**<br>진리조건 의미론 | A theory of meaning that takes the semantic knowledge of when sentences are true and false as basic. |
| **truth value**<br>진리값 | TRUE or FALSE; used to describe the truth of declarative sentences in context; the reference of a declarative sentence in truth-conditional semantics. |

## ❷ Key-points in this Section

➡ a rough characterization of sentential semantic relations:

(1) A is **synonymous** with B: A has the same meaning as B.

(2) A **entails** B: we know that if A then automatically B.

(3) A **contradicts** B: A is inconsistent with B.

(4) A **presupposes** B: B is part of the assumed background against which A is said.

(5) A is a **tautology**: A is automatically true by virtue of its own meaning, but informationally empty.

(6) A is a **contradiction**: A is inconsistent with itself, i.e. assets and denies the same thing.

➡ A truth-based definition of entailment and presupposition

(7) Entailment defined by truth

A sentence p entails a sentence q when the truth of the first (p) guarantees the truth of the second (q), and the falsity of the second (q) guarantees the falsity of the first (p). *If p is true, then q is automatically true. If q is false, then p is also false. If p is false, then q can be either true or false.*

(8) Presupposition defined by truth

A sentence p presupposes a sentence q when the truth of the first (p) guarantees the truth of the second (q), and the falsity of the first (p) also guarantee the truth of the second (q). *If p is true then q is true. If p is false, then q is still true. If q is true, p could be either true or false.*

➡ Describing paraphrase and contraction by using the notion of entailment:

(9) Two sentences are **synonymous** if they **entail** each other.

(10) Two sentences are **contradictory** if one **entails** the negation of the other.

➡ An example of **entailment**

(11) Jack swims beautifully. → Jack swims.

➡ An example of **presupposition**

    (12) a. I regret leaving London. → I left London.

        b. I don't regret leaving London. → I left London.

➡ An example of **tautology**

    (13) Circles are round.

➡ An example of **contraction**

    (14) A bachelor is married.

➡ An example of **paraphrases** (= sentential synonyms)

    (15) a. Jack put off the meeting.

        b. Jack postponed the meeting.

➡ An example of the factive verbs

    (16) Mary realized that it was raining. → It was raining.

➡ Six Groups of Implicative Verbs

**Table 1.** Implications of the Six Groups With One Example for Each Group

| Group # | Implicative Verbs | affirmative implies | negative implies |
|---|---|---|---|
| Group 1 | manage | + → + | − → − |
| Group 2 | refuse | + → − | − → + |
| Group 3 | force | + → + | − → 0 |
| Group 4 | prevent from | + → − | − → 0 |
| Group 5 | try | + → 0 | − → − |
| Group 6 | hesitate | + → 0 | − → + |

(17)   a. I **managed** to catch my bus. → I caught my bus.

       b. I didn't **manage** to catch my bus. → I didn't catch my bus.

(18)   a. Mary **refused** to visit the city. → Mary didn't visit the city.

       b. Mary didn't **refuse** to visit the city. → Mary visited the city.

(19)  a. Circumstance **forced** us to cancel our plans. → We canceled our plans.
      b. Circumstance didn't **force** us to cancel our plans. → ?

(20)  a. A sudden storm **prevented** the men **from** completing the job.
      → The men didn't complete the job.
      b. A sudden storm didn't **prevent** the men **from** completing the job. → ?

(21)  a. We **tried** to answer. → ?
      b. We didn't **try** to answer. → We didn't answer.

(22)  a. We **hesitated** to accept the offer. → ?
      b. We didn't **hesitate** to accept the offer. → We accepted the offer.

# Lexical Semantics

## KEY CONCEPT IN THIS CHAPTER

- Reference and Sense
- Lexical Semantic Relations
  - Synonymy
  - Hyponymy
  - Antonymy
  - Meronymy
- Semantic Features
- Broadening and Narrowing of Meaning
- Overextension and Underextension of Meaning

 **TIP**

- Complementary pairs, Gradable Pairs, Relational Opposites, and Reversives (2011)

The meaning of a phrase or sentence is partially a function of the meanings of the words it contains. Similarly, the meaning of a morphologically complex word is a function of its component morphemes.

However, there is a fundamental difference between word meaning—or lexical semantics— and sentence meaning. The meaning of entries in the mental lexicon—be they morphemes, words, or idioms—is conventional; that is, speakers of a language implicitly agree on their meaning, and children acquiring the language must simply learn those meanings outright.

In this section we will talk about word meaning and the semantic relationships that exist between words and morphemes.

## 2.1. Reference and Sense

The meaning of a word or expression is its **reference**, its association with the object it refers to. This real-world object is called the *referent*.

The meaning of a proper name like *Jack* is its reference: the link between the word Jack and the person named Jack, which is its referent.

On the other hand, not every NP refers to an individual. For instance, the sentence *No baby swims* contains the NP *no baby*, but your linguistic knowledge tells you that this NP does not refer to any specific individual. If *no baby* has no reference, but is not meaningless, then something about meaning beyond reference must be present.

There must be something more to meaning than reference alone. This is also suggested by the fact that speakers know the meanings of many words that have no real-world referents (e.g., *hobbits, unicorns,* and *Harry Potter*). Similarly, what real-world entities would function words like *of* and *by*, or modal verbs such as *will* or *may* refer to?

These additional elements of meaning are often termed **sense**. It is the extra something referred to earlier. *Unicorns, hobbits,* and *Harry Potter* have sense but no reference (with regard to objects in the real world). Conversely, proper names typically have only reference. A name like *Clem Kadiddlehopper* may point out a certain person, its referent, but has little linguistic meaning beyond that.

## 2.2. Lexical Semantic Relations

Lexical relations include synonymy, antonymy, hyponymy, and meronymy.

### 2.2.1. Synonymy

**Synonyms** are <u>words or expressions that have the same meaning in some or all contexts</u>. There are dictionaries of synonyms that contain many hundreds of entries, such as:

(1) apathetic/phlegmatic/passive/sluggish/indifferent
    pedigree/ancestry/genealogy/descent/lineage

## 2.2.2. Antonymy

Words that are opposite in meaning are **antonyms**.

Words are related in various kinds of antonyms such as complementary pairs, gradable pairs, relational opposites, and reversive pairs.

### 2.2.2.1. Complementary Pairs

**Complementary pairs**:

(2) alive/dead, present/absent, awake/asleep

They are complementary in that *alive* = *not dead* and *dead* = *not alive*, and so on.

### 2.2.2.2. Gradable Pairs

**Gradable pairs** of antonyms:

(3) big/small, hot/cold, fast/slow, happy/sad

The meaning of adjectives in gradable pairs is related to the objects they modify. The words do not provide an absolute scale. For example, we know that "a small elephant" is much bigger than "a large mouse." *Fast* is faster when applied to an airplane than to a car.

Another characteristic of certain pairs of gradable antonyms is that one is **marked** and the other **unmarked**.

The unmarked member is the one used in questions of degree. We ask, ordinarily, "How high is the mountain?" (not "How low is it?"). We answer "Ten thousand feet high" but never "Ten thousand feet low," except humorously or ironically.

Thus *high* is the unmarked member of *high/low*. Similarly, *tall* is the unmarked member of *tall/short*, *fast* the unmarked member of *fast/slow*, and so on.

## 2.2.2.3. Relational Opposites or Converse Antonyms

**Relational opposites**:

(4) give/receive, buy/sell, teacher/pupil

They display symmetry in their meanings. If X gives Y to Z, then Z receives Y from X. If X is Y's *teacher*, then Y is X's *pupil*. Pairs of words ending in *-er* and *-ee* are usually relational opposites. If Mary is Bill's *employer*, then Bill is Mary's *employee*.

The following sentences contain **converse predicates**, which necessarily have a valency of 2 or more.

(5) a. The map is above the chalkboard.
　　b. The chalkboard is below the map.

(6) a. Sally is Jerry's wife. (Sally is the wife of Jerry.)
　　b. Jerry is Sally's husband. (Jerry is the husband of Sally.)

Converseness is a kind of antonymy between two terms. For any two converse relational terms X and Y, if [a] is the X of [b], then [b] is the X of [a]. In (5a) *map* has the role of Theme and *chalkboard* the role of Associate; in (5b) the roles are reversed. The same is applies to *Sally* and *Jerry* in (6a) and (6b).

Common **converse pairs** include kinship and social roles (*husband-of/wife-of; employer-of/ employee-of*) and directional opposites (*above/below; in front of/behind; left-of/right-of; before/after; north-of/south-of; outside/inside*).

There are a few pairs of converse 3-argument predicates: give-to/receive-from; sell-to/ buy-from; lend-to/borrow-from.

(7) a. Dad lent me a little money.
　　b. I borrowed a little money from Dad.

If A gives X to B, B receives X from A. All three of these pairs of predicates are built around the relationship of **source** and **goal**.

Some conjunctions, or clause connector, like *before* and *after* form converse pairs.

(8) a. Herbert left the party before Jean (left the party).

   b. Jean left the party after Herbert (left the party).

In all these examples of sentences with converse pairs, (a) and (b) are paraphrases.

Consider these paraphrastic sentences:

(9) a. The dictionary is heavier than the novel.

   b. The novel is lighter than the dictionary.

Although *heavy* and *light* are non-binary (gradable) antonyms, the comparative forms are converse: more heavy = less light; more light = less heavy.

(10) a. The dictionary is more expensive than the novel.

    b. The novel is less expensive than the dictionary.

Factoring out the common term, *more* and *less* are converse.

There are practical **constraints on converseness**. Though we can say (11), it would be unusual to speak of the Grand Hotel as being behind a newspaper kiosk.

(11) #A newspaper kiosk is in front of the Grand Hotel.

Converseness requires the two arguments, theme and associate, to be of about the same size, rank, or importance. Talmy (1975) uses the terms **figure** and **ground** for entities of unequal rank like these. The figure, the newspaper kiosk in (11), is located with respect to the ground, the Grand Hotel in (11), but not the ground with respect to the figure.

A special kind of converseness is the use of a single term in a **symmetrical relationship**, as in (12):

(12) a. Line AB is parallel to Line CD.

   b. Line CD is parallel to Line AB.

This relationship can also be expressed as:

(12) c. Line AB and Line CD are parallel to each other.

or simply as:

(12) d. Line AB and Line CD are parallel.

To generalize, if X is a **symmetrical predicate**, the relationship *a X b* can also be expressed as *b X a* and *a and b X (each other)*. Here 'a' and 'b' interchange the roles of Theme and Associate. The features [sibling] and [spouse] are each symmetrical (C sibling-of D → D sibling-of C; E spouse-of F → F spouse-of E).

Other examples of symmetrical predicates appear in these sentences:

(13) a. The truck is similar to the bus.

   b. Line AB intersects Line CD.

   c. Hampton Road converges with Broad Street.

   d. Oil doesn't mix with water.

## 2.2.2.4. Reversive Pairs

Reversives include pairs of verbs such as *fold/unfold*. As unfold depicts the reverse process of *fold*, and vice versa, one member of a reversive pair describes the reverse process of the other member. Other examples of reversives are *tie/untie*, *enter/exit*.

## 2.2.3. Hyponymy

The words *red*, *white*, and *blue* are color words. Similarly, *lion*, *tiger*, *leopard*, and *lynx* are all felines.

**Hyponymy** is <u>the relationship between the more general term such as</u> *color* <u>and the more</u> <u>specific instances of it, such as</u> *red*. Thus *red* is a hyponym of *color*, and *lion* is a hyponym of *feline;* or equivalently, *color* has the hyponym *red* and *feline* has the hyponym *lion*.

### 2.2.4. Meronymy

The semantic relation between a lexical item denoting a part and that denoting the corresponding whole is termed **meronymy**; the relation between lexical items designating sister parts is termed co-meronymy.

X is meronym of Y if and only if sentences of the form *A Y has Xs/an X* and *an X is a part of a Y* are normal when the noun phrases *an X, a Y* are interpreted generically.

Virtually all word pairs which one would wish to recognize as having a meronymic relation will yield normal sentences in the test-frame *A Y has Xs/an X*:

(14) a. A hand has fingers.
     b. A piano has a keyboard.
     c. A car has wheels.
     d. A saw has teeth.
     e. A book has pages.

On its own, however, the frame is too generous, as it accepts any characteristic attributes, and not only parts:

(15) a. A wife has a husband.
     b. A sound has a pitch and a volume.

(It is possible that have is ambiguous.) The second frame, *An X is a part of a Y*, also leaks:

(16) a. A huge bank balance is a part of his attractiveness to women.
     b. Changing nappies/diapers is part of being a mother.

Only meronyms, however, will satisfy both frames:

(17) a. ?A husband is part of a wife.

　　 b. ?A volume is part of a sound.

(18) a. ?His attractiveness to women has a huge bank balance.

　　 b. ?Being a mother has changing nappies/diapers.

(19) a. A hand has fingers.

　　 b. A finger is a part of a hand.

A test-frame which does not leak, and which accepts all the above cases is: *The parts of a Y include the X/Xs, the Z/Zs, etc.*

(20) a. The parts of a flower include the sepals, the petals, ...

　　 b. The parts of a word include the root, ...

　　 c. The parts of a door include the handle, the lock, ...

**NOTE** Words like *bear* and *bare* are **homonyms** (also called **homophones**). Homonyms are words that have different meanings but are pronounced the same, and may or may not be spelled the same. (They're **homographs** when spelled the same, but when homographs are pronounced differently like *pussy* meaning 'infected' or *pussy* meaning 'kitten,' they are called **heteronyms** rather than homonyms.)

**NOTE** When a word has multiple meanings that are related conceptually or historically, it is said to be **polysemous**. For example, the word *diamond* (referring to a jewel and also to a baseball field) is polysemous.

## 2.3. Semantic Features

It is possible to look for a more basic set of **semantic features** or <u>properties that are part of word meanings and that reflect our knowledge about what words mean.</u>

Decomposing the meanings of words into semantic features can clarify how certain words relate to other words.

### 2.3.1. Evidence for Semantic Features

Semantic properties are not directly observable. Their existence must be inferred from linguistic evidence. One source of such evidence is the speech errors, or "slips of the tongue," that we all produce. Consider the following unintentional word substitutions that some speakers have actually spoken.

| (21) | **Intended Utterance** | **Actual Utterance (Error)** |
|------|------------------------|------------------------------|
|      | bridge of the nose | bridge of the neck |
|      | when my gums bled | when my tongues bled |
|      | he came too late | he came too early |
|      | Mary was young | Mary was early |
|      | the lady with the Dachshund | the lady with the Volkswagen |
|      | that's a horse of another color | that's a horse of another race |
|      | his ancestors were farmers | his descendants were farmers |
|      | he has to pay her alimony | he has to pay her rent |

### 2.3.2. Semantic Features and Grammar

Further evidence that words are composed of smaller bits of meaning is that semantic features interact with different aspects of the grammar such as morphology or syntax.

### 2.3.3. Semantic Features of Nouns

The same semantic feature may be shared by many words. "Female" is a semantic feature, sometimes indicated by the suffix -*ess*, that makes up part of the meaning of nouns, such as:

(22)

| tigress | hen | aunt | maiden |
|---------|-----|------|--------|
| doe | mare | debutante | widow |
| ewe | vixen | girl | woman |

The words in the last two columns are also distinguished by the semantic feature "human," which is also found in:

(23)

| doctor | dean | professor | teenager |
|--------|------|-----------|----------|
| bachelor | parent | baby | child |

Another part of the meaning of the words *baby* and *child* is that they are "young." The word *father* has the properties "male" and "adult," as do *uncle* and *bachelor*.

## 2.3.4. Semantic Features of Verbs

Verbs also have semantic features as part of their meaning. For example, "cause" is a feature of verbs such as *darken, kill, uglify,* and so on.

(24)
| *darken* | cause to become dark |
|----------|---------------------|
| *kill* | cause to die |
| *uglify* | cause to become ugly |

"Go" is a feature of verbs that mean a change in location or possession, such as *swim, crawl, throw, fly, give, or buy:*

(25)    Jack swims.

The baby crawled under the table.

The boy threw the ball over the fence.

John gave Mary a beautiful engagement ring.

Words like *swim* have an additional feature like "in liquid," while *crawl* has "close to a surface."

"Become" is a feature expressing the end state of the action of certain verbs.

For example, the verb *break* can be broken down into the following components of meaning: "cause" to "become" broken.

## 2.4. Broadening and Narrowing of Meaning in Language Change

When the meaning of a word becomes **broader**, it means everything it used to mean and more.

The Middle English word *dogge* referred to a specific breed of dog, but was eventually **broadened** to encompass all members of the species *canis familiaris*. The word *holiday* originally meant a day of religious significance, from 'holy day.' Today the word refers to any day that we do not have to work. *Picture* used to mean 'painted representation,' but now you can take a picture with a camera, not to mention a host of other electronic "toys." *Quarantine* once had the restricted meaning of 'forty days' isolation,' and *manage* once meant simply 'to handle a horse.'

More recent broadenings, spurred by the computer age, are *computer, mouse, cookie, cache, virus,* and *bundle. Footage* used to refer to a certain length of film or videotape, but nowadays it means any excerpt from the electronic video media, such as DVDs, irrespective of whether its length can be measured in feet. *Google* was broadened first from the name of a company to a verb meaning 'to use that company's search engine on the Internet,' and from there further broadened to simply 'search the Internet.' *Twitter* and *tweet* were once words confined to the aviary—need we say more.

In the King James Version of the Bible (1611 CE), God says of the herbs and trees, "to you they shall be for meat" (Genesis 1:29). To a speaker of seventeenth-century English, *meat* meant 'food,' and *flesh* meant 'meat.' Since that time, semantic change has **narrowed** the meaning of meat to what it is in Modern English. The word *deer* once meant 'beast' or 'animal,' as its German cognate *Tier* still does. The meaning of *deer* has been narrowed to a particular kind of animal. Similarly, the word *hound* used to be the general term for 'dog,' like German *Hund*. Today *hound* refers to a certain class of dog breeds. *Skyline* once meant 'horizon' but has been **narrowed** to mean 'the outline of a city at the horizon.'

## 2.5. Overextension and Underextension of Meaning in Language Acquisition

It is not surprising that children often **overextend** a word's meaning, as J. P. did with the word sock. A child may learn a word such as *papa* or *daddy*, which she first uses only for her own father, and then extend its meaning to apply to all men, just as she may use the word *dog* to mean any four-legged creature. On the other hand, children may also use a lexical item in an overly restrictive way. For example, they may first use a word like bird to refer only to the family's pet canary without making a connection to birds in the trees outside, as if the word were a proper noun. This is referred to as **underextension**. And just as overextended words eventually hone in on the adult meanings, **underextended** words will broaden their scope until they match the target language.

# Check Up the Points

## 1 Glossary for this Section

**antonyms**
반의어

Words that are opposite with respect to one of their semantic properties: e.g., tall/short are both alike in that they describe height, but opposite in regard to the extent of the height. See **gradable pair**, **complementary pair**, **relational opposites**.

**antonymic pair**
동음이철반의어

Two words that are pronounced the same (i.e., are homonyms) but spelled differently and whose meanings are opposite: e.g., *raise* and *raze*. See **autoantonym**.

**autoantonym**
자기반의어

A word that has two opposite meanings: e.g., *cleave*, 'to split apart' or 'to cling together.' See **antonymic pair**.

**broadening**
의미 확장

A semantic change in which the meaning of a word changes over time to become more encompassing: e.g., dog once meant a particular breed of dog.

**complementary pair**
상보적 반의어

Two antonyms related in such a way that the negation of one is the meaning of the other: e.g., *alive* means *not dead*. See **gradable pair**, **relational opposites**.

**connotative meaning/ connotation**
내포적 의미

The evocative or affective meaning associated with a word. Two words or expressions may have the same denotative meaning but different connotations: e.g., *president* and *commander-in-chief*.

**coreference**
동일지시

The relation between two noun phrases that refer to the same entity.

| | |
|---|---|
| **coreferential**<br>동일지시적 | Describes noun phrases (including pronouns) that refer to the same entity. |
| **denotative meaning**<br>외연적 의미 | The referential meaning of a word or expression. See connotative meaning. |
| **extension**<br>외연 | The referential part of the meaning of an expression; the referent of a noun phrase. See **reference**, **referent**. |
| **gradable pair**<br>등급적 반의어 | Two antonyms related in such a way that more of one is less of the other: e.g., *warm* and *cool*; more warm is less cool, and vice versa. See **complementary pair**, **relational opposites**. |
| **heteronyms**<br>동철이음이의어 | Different words spelled the same (i.e., homographs) but pronounced differently: e.g., *bass*, meaning either 'low tone' [bes] or 'a kind of fish' [bæs]. |
| **homographs**<br>동철이의어 | Words spelled identically, and possibly pronounced the same: e.g., *bear* meaning 'to tolerate,' and *bear* the animal; or *lead* the metal and *lead*, what leaders do. |
| **homonyms/ homophones**<br>동음이의어 | Words pronounced, and possibly spelled, the same: e.g., *to, too, two*; or *bat* the animal, *bat* the stick, and *bat* meaning 'to flutter' as in "bat the eyelashes." |

Chapter

05

**hyponyms**

하의어

Words whose meanings are specific instances of a more general word: e.g., *red, white,* and *blue* are hyponyms of the word *color*; *triangle* is a hyponym of *polygon*. A word whose referent is included in the referent of a more geneal word, called the **superordinate**: *rose* is a hyponym of *flower*, and *flower* is a superordinate of *rose*.

**intension**

내연

The inherent, nonreferential part of the meaning of an expression, also called **sense**. See **sense, extension**.

**lexical paraphrases**

어휘적 바꿔쓰기

Sentences that have the same meaning due to synonyms: e.g., *She lost her <u>purse</u>* and *She lost her <u>handbag</u>*.

**lexical semantics**

어휘 의미론

The subfield of semantics concerned with the meanings of words and the meaning relationships among words.

**marked**

유표어

In a gradable pair of antonyms, the word that is not used in questions of degree: e.g., *low* is the marked member of the pair *high/low* because we ordinarily ask *How high is the mountain?* not *\*How low is the mountain?* In a masculine/feminine pair, the word that contains a derivational morpheme, usually the feminine word: e.g., *princess* is marked, whereas *prince* is unmarked. See **unmarked**.

**meaning**

의미

The conceptual or semantic aspect of a sign or utterance that permits us to comprehend the message being conveyed. Expressions in language generally have both form—pronunciation or gesture—and meaning. See **extension, intension, sense, reference**.

**meronymy**
부분전체관계

The semantic relation between a lexical item denoting a part and that denoting the corresponding whole.

**narrowing**
의미 축소

A semantic change in which the meaning of a word changes in time to become less encompassing: e.g., *deer* once meant 'animal.'

**onomatopoeia/**
**onomatopoeic**
의성어

Words whose pronunciations suggest their meanings: e.g., *meow, buzz*.

**overextension**
과잉 의미 확장

The broadening of a word's meaning in language acquisition to encompass a more general meaning: e.g., using *dog* for any four-legged animals including cats or horses.

**polysemous/**
**polysemy**
다의적, 다의어

Describes a single word with several closely related but slightly different meanings: e.g., *face*, meaning 'face of a person,' 'face of a clock,' 'face of a building.'

**proper name**
고유어

A word or words that refer to a person, place, or other entity with a unique reference known to the speaker and listener. Usually capitalized in writing: e.g., *Nina Hyams, New York, Atlantic Ocean*.

**reference**
지시의미

That part of the meaning of a noun phrase that associates it with some entity. That part of the meaning of a declarative sentence that associates it with a **truth value**, either true or false. Also called **extension**. See referent, sense.

**referent**
지시체

The entity designated by an expression: e.g., the referent of *John* in *John knows Sue* is the actual person named John; the referent of *Raleigh is the capital of California* is the truth value *false*. Also called **extension**.

**relational opposites**
관계적 반의어

A pair of antonyms in which one describes a relationship between two objects and the other describes the same relationship when the two objects are reversed: e.g., *parent/child, teacher/pupil*; *John is the parent of Susie* describes the same relationship as *Susie is the child of John*. See **gradable pair**, **complementary pair**.

**semantic features**
의미 자질

Conceptual elements by which a person understands the meanings of words and sentences: e.g., "female" is a semantic feature of the nouns *girl* and *filly*; "cause" is a semantic feature of the verbs *darken* and *kill*.

**semantic network**
의미 연결망

A network of arcs and nodes used to represent semantic information about sentences.

**semantic priming**
의미적 마중물 효과

The effect of being able to recognize a word (e.g., doctor) more rapidly after exposure to a semantically similar word (e.g., nurse) than after exposure to a semantically more distant word. The word nurse primes the word doctor.

**semantic properties**
의미 속성

See semantic features.

| | |
|---|---|
| **semantic representation**<br>의미 표상 | A symbolic system suitable for the characterization of the meaning of natural language utterances in a computer: e.g., logic-based expressions or semantic networks. |
| **sense**<br>의의 | The inherent part of an expression's meaning that, together with context, determines its referent. Also called **intension**. For example, knowing the sense or intension of a noun phrase such as *the president of the United States in the year 2010* allows one to determine that Barack Obama is the referent. See **intension**, **reference**. |
| **synonyms**<br>동의어 | Words with the same or nearly the same meaning: e.g., *pail* and *bucket*. |
| **synonymy (synonymous)**<br>동의어 관계 | Having the same meaning in all contexts. More technically, in the semantic component of the grammar, two sentences are synonymous if they entail each other: e.g., *the cat ate the rat*; *the rat was eaten by the cat*. See **paraphrases**. |
| **underextension**<br>과잉 의미 축소 | The narrowing of a word's meaning in language acquisition to a more restrictive meaning: e.g., using *dog* for only the family pet and not for other dogs. |
| **unmarked**<br>무표적 | The term used to refer to that member of a gradable pair of antonyms used in questions of degree: e.g., *high* is the unmarked member of *high/low*; in a masculine/feminine pair, the word that does not contain a derivational morpheme, usually the masculine word: e.g., *prince* is unmarked, whereas *princess* is marked. See **marked**. |

Chapter

05

### ② Key-points in this Section

➡ **Synonyms** are words or expressions that have the same meaning in some or all contexts.

➡ Words that are opposite in meaning are **antonyms**. Words are related in various kinds of antonyms such as complementary pairs, gradable pairs, relational opposites, and reversive pairs.

➡ **Hyponymy** is the relationship between the more general term such as *color* and the more specific instances of it, such as *red*.

➡ The semantic relation between a lexical item denoting a part and that denoting the corresponding whole is termed **meronymy**; the relation between lexical items designating sister parts is termed **co-meronymy**.

➡ **Homonyms** are words that have different meanings but are pronounced the same, and may or may not be spelled the same.

➡ When a word has multiple meanings that are related conceptually or historically, it is said to be **polysemous**.

➡ **Semantic features** are part of word meanings and reflect our knowledge about what words mean.

# Ambiguity

**TIP**

• Scope Ambiguity (2018)
• Lexical Ambiguity and Structural Ambiguity (2015)

Our semantic knowledge tells us when words or phrases (including sentences) have more than one meaning: that is, when they are **ambiguous**.

The sentence *The boy saw the man with a telescope* was an instance of **structural ambiguity**. It is ambiguous because it can mean that the boy saw the man by using a telescope or that the boy saw the man who was holding a telescope. The sentence is structurally ambiguous because it is associated with two different phrase structures, each corresponding to a different meaning. Here are the two structures:

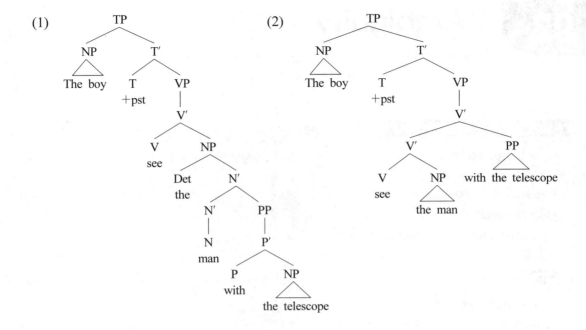

In (1) the PP *with the telescope* modifies the N *man*, so the interpretation is that the man has the telescope. In (2) the PP *with a telescope* modifies V-bar, the action of seeing the man, so the interpretation is that the boy saw the man by using the telescope.

**Lexical ambiguity** arises when at least one word in a phrase has more than one meaning. For instance the sentence *This will make you smart* is ambiguous because of the two meanings of the word *smart*: 'clever' and 'feel a burning sensation.'

Our knowledge of lexical and structural ambiguities reveals that the meaning of a linguistic expression is built both on the words it contains and on its syntactic structure.

## 3.1. Lexical Ambiguity

The occurrence of an ambiguous word—lexical ambiguity—when it combines with the other elements of a sentence can make the entire sentence ambiguous, as in *She can't bear children.*

Consider these sentences with:

(3) This will make you smart.

The two interpretations of this sentence are due to the two meanings of *smart*—'clever' and 'burning sensation.' Such lexical or word-meaning ambiguities, as opposed to structural ambiguities.

**Count nouns** can be enumerated and pluralized—*one potato, two potatoes*. They may be preceded by the indefinite determiner *a*, and by the quantifier *many* as in *many potatoes*, but not by *much*: *\*much potato*. They must also occur with a determiner of some kind. Nouns such as *rice, water,* and *milk*, which cannot be enumerated or pluralized, are **mass nouns**. They cannot be preceded by *a* or *many*, and they can occur with the quantifier *much* or without any determiner at all.

## 3.2. Structural Ambiguity

Consider the following sentence:

(4) The captain ordered all old men and women off the sinking ship.

This phrase *old men and women* is ambiguous, referring to either old men and to women of any age or to old men and old women. The ambiguity arises because the words *old men and women* can be grouped in two ways. If the words are grouped as in (5), *old* modifies only *men* and so the women can be of any age.

(5) [old men] and [women]

When we group them like (6), the adjective *old* modifies both *men* and *women*.

(6) [old [men and women]]

The rules of syntax allow both of these groupings, which is why the expression is ambiguous. The following hierarchical diagrams, also called tree diagrams, illustrate the same point:

(7)　　a.　　　　b.

In the first structure *old* and *men* are under the same node and hence *old* modifies *men*. In the second structure *old* shares a node with the entire conjunction *men and women*, and so modifies both.

This is similar to what we find in morphology for ambiguous words such as *unlockable*, which have two structures, corresponding to two meanings.

Many sentences exhibit such ambiguities, often leading to humorous results. Consider the following two sentences, which appeared in classified ads:

(8) For sale: an antique desk suitable for lady with thick legs and large drawers.
　　We will oil your sewing machine and adjust tension in your home for $10.00.

In the first ad, the humorous reading comes from the grouping [desk] [suitable for lady with thick legs and large drawers] as opposed to the intended [desk suitable for lady] [with thick legs and large drawers], where the legs and drawers belong to the desk. The second case is similar.

Because these ambiguities are a result of different structures, they are instances of structural ambiguity.

Syntactic rules reveal the grammatical relations among the words of a sentence as well as their order and hierarchical organization. They also explain how the grouping of words relates to its meaning, such as when a sentence or phrase is ambiguous.

The hierarchical organization of words is even more clearly shown by **structurally ambiguous words**, words that have more than one meaning by virtue of having more than one structure.

Consider the word *unlockable*. Imagine you are inside a room and you want some privacy.

You would be unhappy to find the door is *unlockable*—'not able to be locked.' Now imagine you are inside a locked room trying to get out. You would be very relieved to find that the door is *unlockable*—'able to be unlocked.' These two meanings correspond to two different structures, as follows:

(9)   a. 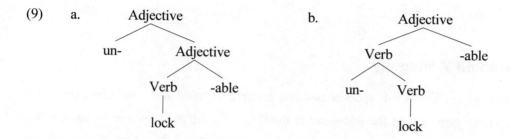   b.

In the first structure the verb *lock* combines with the suffix *-able* to form an adjective *lockable* ('able to be locked'). Then the prefix *un-*, meaning 'not,' combines with the derived adjective to form a new adjective *unlockable* ('not able to be locked'). In the second case, the prefix *un-* combines with the verb *lock* to form a derived verb *unlock*. Then the derived verb combines with the suffix *-able* to form *unlockable*, 'able to be unlocked.'

An entire class of words in English follows this pattern: *unbuttonable, unzippable,* and *unlatchable,* among others. The ambiguity arises because the prefix *un-* can combine with an adjective, or it can combine with a verb, as in *undo, unstaple, unearth,* and *unloosen.*

If words were only strings of morphemes without any internal organization, we could not explain the ambiguity of words like *unlockable*. These words also illustrate another key point, which is that structure is important to determining meaning. The same three morphemes occur in both versions of *unlockable*, yet there are two distinct meanings. The different meanings arise because of the different structures.

Like derived words, compounds have internal structure. This is clear from the **ambiguity of a compound** like *top + hat + rack*, which can mean 'a rack for top hats' corresponding to the structure in tree diagram (10a), or 'the highest hat rack,' corresponding to the structure in (10b).

(10)    a.

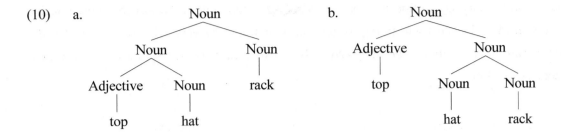

b.

## 3.3. Referential Ambiguity

Misunderstandings occur when a speaker has one referent in mind for a definite expression like *George* or *the papers*, and the addressee is thinking of a different George or some other papers. No doubt we have all experienced, and been troubled by, this kind of problem in reference. We can see other instances of referential ambiguity that are due to the nature of referring expressions, the vagueness that pieces of language necessarily have.

Referential ambiguity occurs when

( i ) an indefinite referring expression may be specific or not:

(11) I want to buy a newspaper.

Here *a newspaper* may refer to a specific news or some newspaper, any news paper. The ambiguity disappears if we add, on the one hand, *but I couldn't find it* or, on the other hand, *but I couldn't find one.*

( ii ) anaphora is unclear because a personal pronoun, *he, she, it,* or *they,* can be linked to either of two referring expressions:

(12) Jack told Ralph that a visitor was waiting for him.

(iii) the pronoun *you* is used generically or specifically:

(13) If you want to get ahead, you have to work hard.
       (Is *you* the addressee or is this sentence a general platitude?)

(iv) a noun phrase with *every* can have distributed reference or collected reference:

(14) I'm buying a drink for everybody here.

   (One drink for all or one drink for each?)

Referential ambiguity occurs when the context does not make clear whether a referring expression is being used specifically or not; when the interpretation of a referring expression can be collective or distributed; and when it is not clear to which of two or more referring expressions an anaphoric item is linked.

## 3.4. Scope Ambiguity

Some determiners, **quantifiers**, express the amount of or quantity of the entity denoted by the noun. Cardinal numbers are **specific quantifiers**: *one day, five people, 76 trombones*. **General quantifiers** are shown like theses phrases: *some eggs, a little milk, a few problems, much traffic, several accidents*. If a countable noun phrase expresses a total, it may be **collective** (*all donkeys*) or **distributive** (*every donkey*).

(15) I'm buying a drink for everybody here.

   (One drink for all or one drink for each?)

A noun phrase with *every* as in (15) can have distributed reference or collected reference.

Consider the following two sentences with a negative element. In (16a) the negative word *not* creates ambiguity, whereas in (16b) the negative prefix *un-* does not.

(16) a. Tom is not well because of the weather.
   b. Tom is unwell because of the weather.

Sentence (16a) is ambiguous: ( i ) Tom is sick because of the weather, and ( ii ) Tom is well, not because of the weather but for some other reason. Sentence (16b), in contrast, is not ambiguous. It means only: Tom is sick because of the weather. The negative word *not* and the negative prefix *un-* differ with respect to the ability to create ambiguity. Technically speaking, the negative word *not* is a scope-bearing element, while the negative prefix *un-* is not.

There are sentences in English, like (17), for example:

(17) Everyone admires someone.

These sentences are ambiguous depending on quantifier scope. The different readings of these sentences correspond to different formulas in predicate logic. The sentence in (17) has the following two readings. *A* stands for 'admire' in the formulas below.

(18) a. $\forall x \exists y\ A(x,\ y)$    'Everyone has someone whom he admires'
    b. $\exists y \forall x\ A(x,\ y)$    'There is someone whom everyone admires'

The scope ambiguities produced by sentences containing two quantifiers are interesting from a linguistic point of view.


## 3.5. Transformationally Induced Ambiguity

Transformations may delete elements. For example, the s-structure of the ambiguous sentence *George wants the presidency more than Martha* may be derived from two possible d-structures:

(19) a. George wants the presidency more than he wants Martha.
    b. George wants the presidency more than Martha wants the presidency.

A deletion transformation either deletes *he wants* from the structure of example (19a), or *wants the presidency* from the structure of example (19b). This is a case of **transformationally induced ambiguity**: two different d-structures with different semantic interpretations are transformed into a single s-structure.

# Check Up the Points

## 1 Glossary for this Section

**lexical ambiguity**
어휘적 중의성

Multiple meanings of sentences due to words that have multiple meanings: e.g., *He blew up the pictures of his ex-girlfriend*.

**structural ambiguity**
구조적 중의성

The phenomenon in which the same sequence of words has two or more meanings accounted for by different phrase structure analyses: e.g., *He saw a boy with a telescope*.

**transformationally induced ambiguity**
변형으로 인한 중의성

A situation in which different d-structures are mapped into the same s-structure by one or more transformations: e.g., the ambiguous *George loves Laura more than Dick* may be transformationally derived from the d-structure *George loves Laura more than Dick loves Laura* or *George loves Laura more than George loves Dick*, with the underlined words being deleted under identity by a transformation in either case.

**2** Key-points in this Section

➡ **Lexical ambiguity** arises when at least one word in a phrase has more than one meaning.

➡ The sentence is **structurally ambiguous** because it is associated with two different phrase structures, each corresponding to a different meaning.

➡ **Referential ambiguity** occurs when
( i ) an indefinite referring expression may be specific or not
( ii ) anaphora is unclear because a personal pronoun, *he, she, it,* or *they,* can be linked to either of two referring expressions
( iii ) the pronoun *you* is used generically or specifically
( iv ) a noun phrase with *every* can have distributed reference or collected reference

➡ The **scope ambiguities** are produced by sentences containing two quantifiers.

➡ **Transformationally induced ambiguity**: two different d-structures with different semantic interpretations are transformed into a single s-structure.

# Noncompositional Meaning

Semantic rules compute sentence meaning compositionally based on the meanings of words and the syntactic structure that contains them. There are, however, interesting cases in which **compositionality** breaks down, either because there is a problem with words or with the semantic rules. If one or more words in a sentence do not have a meaning, then obviously we will not be able to compute a meaning for the entire sentence. Moreover, even when the individual words have meaning, if they cannot be combined together as required by the syntactic structure and related semantic rules we will also not get to a meaning. We refer to situations of this sort as semantic **anomaly**. Alternatively, it might require a lot of creativity and imagination to derive a meaning. This is what happens in **metaphors**. Finally, some expressions—called **idioms**—have a fixed meaning: that is, a meaning that is not compositional. Applying compositional rules to idioms gives rise to funny or inappropriate meanings.

## 4.1. Anomaly

The semantic properties of words determine what other words they can be combined with. A sentence widely used by linguists illustrates this fact:

(1) Colorless green ideas sleep furiously.

The sentence obeys all the syntactic rules of English. The subject is *colorless green ideas* and the predicate *is sleep furiously*. There is obviously something semantically wrong with the sentence. The meaning of *colorless* includes the semantic feature 'without color,' but it is combined with the adjective *green*, which has the feature 'green in color.' How can something be both 'without color' and 'green in color'? Other semantic violations occur in the sentence. Such sentences are **semantically anomalous**.

Other English "sentences" make no sense at all because they include "words" that have no meaning; they are uninterpretable. They can be interpreted only if some meaning for each nonsense word can be dreamt up.

Semantic violations in poetry may form strange but interesting aesthetic images, as in Dylan Thomas's phrase *a grief ago*. *Ago* is ordinarily used with words specified by some temporal semantic feature:

(2)  a week ago          *a table ago
     an hour ago   but   not   *a dream ago
     a month ago          *a mother ago
     a century ago

When Thomas used the word *grief* with *ago*, he was adding a durational feature to grief for poetic effect, so while the noun phrase is anomalous, it evokes certain emotions.

## 4.2. Metaphor

When what appears to be an anomaly is nevertheless understood in terms of a meaningful concept, the expression becomes a **metaphor**. There is no strict line between anomalous and metaphorical expressions. Technically, metaphors are anomalous, but the nature of the anomaly creates the salient meanings that metaphors usually have. The anomalous *A grief ago* might come to be interpreted by speakers of English as 'the unhappy time following a sad event' and therefore become a metaphor.

Metaphors may have a literal meaning as well as their metaphorical meaning, so in some sense they are ambiguous. However, when the semantic rules are applied to *Walls have ears*, for example, the literal meaning is so unlikely that listeners use their imagination for another interpretation. The principle of compositionality is very "elastic" and when it fails to produce an acceptable literal meaning, listeners try to accommodate and stretch the meaning. This accommodation is based on semantic properties that are inferred or that provide some kind of resemblance or comparison that can end up as a meaningful concept.

To interpret a metaphor we need to understand the individual words, the literal meaning of the whole expression, and facts about the world. To understand the metaphor

(3) Time is money

it is necessary to know that in our society we are often paid according to the number of hours or days worked. In fact, "time," which is an abstract concept, is the subject of multiple metaphors. We "save time," "waste time," "manage time," push things "back in time," live on "borrowed time," and suffer the "ravages of time" as the "sands of time" drift away. In effect, the metaphors take the abstract concept of time and treat it as a concrete object of value.

Many expressions now taken literally may have originated as metaphors, such as "the fall of the dollar," meaning its decline in value on the world market. Many people wouldn't bat an eyelash (another metaphor) at the literal interpretation of saving or wasting time. Metaphorical use of language is language creativity at its highest. Nevertheless, the basis of metaphorical use is very much the ordinary linguistic knowledge that all speakers possess about words, their semantic properties, and their combinatorial possibilities.

## 4.3. Idioms

It turns out that languages also contain many <u>phrases whose meanings are not predictable on the basis of the meanings of the individual words</u>. These phrases typically start out as metaphors that "catch on" and are repeated so often that they become fixtures in the language. Such expressions are called **idioms**, or **idiomatic phrases**, as in these English examples:

(4) sell down the river

rake over the coals drop the ball

let their hair down

put his foot in his mouth

throw her weight around

snap out of it

give a piece of your mind

Here is where <u>the usual semantic rules for combining meanings do not apply</u>. The principle of compositionality is superseded by expressions that act very much like individual morphemes in that they are not decomposable, but have a fixed meaning that must be learned. <u>Idioms are similar in structure to ordinary phrases except that they tend to be frozen in form and do not readily undergo rules that change word order or substitution of their parts</u>.

Thus, the sentence in (5a) has the same structure as the sentence in (5b).

(5) a. She put her foot in her mouth.

b. She put her bracelet in her drawer.

But while the sentences in (6a) and (6b) are clearly related to (5b),

(6) a. The drawer in which she put her bracelet was her own.

b. Her bracelet was put in her drawer.

the sentences in (7a) and (7b) do not have the idiomatic sense of sentence (5a), except, perhaps, humorously.

(7) a. The mouth in which she put her foot was her own.

b. Her foot was put in her mouth.

Also, if we know the meaning of (5b) and the meaning of the word *necklace* we will immediately understand (8).

(8) She put her necklace in the drawer.

But if we try substituting *hand* for *foot* in sentence (5a), we do not maintain <u>the idiomatic meaning</u>, but rather have <u>the literal compositional meaning</u>.

Like metaphors, idioms can break the rules on combining semantic properties. The object of *eat* must usually be something with the semantic feature "edible," but in

(9) He ate his hat.

and

(10) Eat your heart out.

this restriction is violated.

Idioms, grammatically as well as semantically, have special characteristics. They must be entered into the lexicon or mental dictionary as single items with their meanings specified, and speakers must learn the special restrictions on their use in sentences.

### ❶ Glossary for this Section

| | |
|---|---|
| **anomalous**<br>의미변칙적 | Semantically ill-formed: e.g., *Colorless green ideas sleep furiously.* |
| **anomaly**<br>의미변칙 | A violation of semantic rules resulting in expressions that seem nonsensical: e.g., *The verb crumpled the milk.* |
| **idiom/idiomatic phrase**<br>숙어 | An expression whose meaning does not conform to the **principle of compositionality**, that is, may be unrelated to the meaning of its parts: e.g., *kick the bucket* meaning 'to die.' |
| **principle of compositionality**<br>조합성 원리 | A principle of semantic interpretation that states that the meaning of a word, phrase, or sentence depends on both the meaning of its components (morphemes, words, phrases) and how they are combined structurally. |
| **metaphor**<br>은유 | Nonliteral, suggestive meaning in which an expression that designates one thing is used implicitly to mean something else: e.g., *The night has a thousand eyes*, to mean 'One may be unknowingly observed at night.' |

## 2 Key-points in this Section

→ There are interesting cases in which **compositionality** breaks down, either because there is a problem with words or with the semantic rules.

→ Sentences in which semantic violations occur are **semantically anomalous**.

→ When what appears to be an anomaly is nevertheless understood in terms of a meaningful concept, the expression becomes a **metaphor**.

→ Phrases whose meanings are not predictable on the basis of the meanings of the individual words are called **idioms**, or **idiomatic phrases**.

# Event Semantics

## KEY CONCEPT IN THIS CHAPTER

- Events and States
- Telic vs. Atelic
- Activities and Accomplishments
- Achievement and Accomplishment

 TIP

- Two Kinds of Events: Telic and Atelic (2016)
- Types of Situations: Activities and Accomplishments (2011)

## 5.1. Events and States

Verbal features, like features on nouns, may have syntactic consequences. For example, verbs can either describe **events**, such as *John kissed Mary/John ate oysters*, or **states**, such as *John knows Mary/John likes oysters*.

The eventive/stative difference is mirrored in the syntax. Eventive sentences still sound natural <u>when passivized</u>, <u>when expressed progressively</u>, <u>when used as imperatives</u>, and <u>with certain adverbs</u>:

> **Eventives**
> Mary was kissed by John.
> Oysters were eaten by John.
> John is kissing Mary.
> John is eating oysters.
> Kiss Mary!
> Eat oysters!
> John deliberately kissed Mary.
> John deliberately ate oysters.

**Statives**

?Mary is known by John.

?Oysters are liked by John.

?John is knowing Mary.

?John is liking oysters.

?Know Mary!

?Like oysters!

?John deliberately knows Mary.

?John deliberately likes oysters.

## 5.2. Telic and Atelic

Vendler (1967) proposed a four-way classification of predicates as **stative**, **activity**, **achievement**, and **accomplishment** predicates. Stative and activity predicates are **atelic**, and achievement and accomplishment predicates are **telic**. Later research suggests that these terms should be applied to whole sentences because what a sentence expresses depends on more than the predicate alone.

Consider these sentences:

(1)  a.  George was waiting.          Sandra was holding the baby.
    b.  Sandra was swimming.         George was running.
    c.  George was leaving.          Sandra was dying.
    d.  Sandra was writing a letter.  George was cutting the rope.

The sentences in (1a) are stative and those in (1b) are activities. In contrast, (1c) contains achievement sentences and the sentences in (1d) are accomplishments. The predicates in (1a) and (1b) do not have an end or a goal; they are atelic. On the other hand, Achievements (1c) and accomplishments (1d) have an end result; they are telic.

Achievements differ from accomplishments in having an instantaneous result. Since achievement events are instantaneous, we can ask "When did George leave?" or "When did Sandra die?" but not "How long did George leave?" or "How long did Sandra die?" On the other hand, since accomplishment events are durative, we can ask "How long does/did it take Sandra to write a letter?" and we can say, for example, "It took George several minutes to cut the rope."

To summarize:

(2) a. States          : non-dynamic   durative        and   atelic
    b. Activities      : dynamic       durative        and   atelic
    c. Achievements    : dynamic       instantaneous   and   telic
    d. Accomplishments : dynamic       durative        and   telic

Activities and accomplishments are both dynamic and durative, and duration means the passage of a period of time. But there is a difference: activities occur throughout a period of time, in English most commonly introduced by the preposition *for*.

(3) Lucy wrote for half an hour/all afternoon.

Accomplishments require expenditure of effort during a period leading to the result accomplished. The period is most often introduced by the preposition *in*.

(4) Lucy wrote a letter in half an hour.

Sentence (3) is indefinite about what Lucy wrote and sentence (4) is specific. Note that sentence (5a) is indefinite like (3) and the sentences in (5b) are specific like (4).

(5) a. Lucy wrote letters for half an hour/all afternoon.
    b. Lucy wrote the letter/several letters/three letters in half an hour.

If a sentence tells of an unbounded activity, either because the verb has no object, as in (3), or because the object is itself an unbounded noun phrase, as in (4), the activity takes place throughout a measurable duration. When the object of a verb is a definite referring expression (*the letter, the letters,* for example) or a quantified referring expression (*several letters, three letters,* for example), the sentence is an accomplishment and we can express how long it takes for this to be accomplished.

A note about atelic and telic predicates: a verb that is atelic by itself may become telic with the addition of a particle such as *up, down* or *out*. Consider the two sentences in (6).

(6) a. The paper burned.
　　b. The paper burned up.

There are two kinds of events or situations that predicates describe in sentences: One is telic and the other atelic. A telic event is the kind of event that has a natural finishing point and once it is completed, it cannot go on any further as shown in (7). In contrast, an atelic event does not have a natural finishing point and it can go on and on as shown in (8).

(7) a. They built the barn.
　　b. They reached the summit.

(8) a. The room was sunny.
　　b. The choir sang.

One of the tests for telicity is modification of the event duration by an adverbial led by *in* or *for*. Telic predicates take in adverbials; atelic predicates take *for* adverbials, as shown in (9-11) below. In the sentences describing a telic event in (9-10), in adverbials have either the event duration interpretation as in (9a) or the event delay interpretation as in (10a). In the latter interpretation, the time which elapses prior to the event is specified by in adverbials, and the event occurs at the end of the stated interval. Meanwhile, in the sentences describing an atelic event as in (11), *for* adverbials have the event duration interpretation only.❻

(9) a. They built the barn in two days.
　　b. #They built the barn for two days.

---

❻ # indicates that the sentence is anomalous.

(10) a.   They reached the summit in half an hour.

    b. #They reached the summit for half an hour.

(11) a. #The room was sunny in an hour.

    b.   The room was sunny for an hour.

It is essential to use simple past tense sentences when we do the above adverbial test; if *in* adverbials occur in future tense sentences, they can modify any type of predicate, including atelic predicates, and produce the event delay interpretation, as shown in (12a). This in turn leads to the following; certain unambiguous sentences with *in* adverbials may become ambiguous in the future tense as in (12b).

(12) a. The room will be sunny in an hour.

    b. They will build the barn in two days.

# Check Up the Points

## 1 Glossary for this Section

**accomplishment verb**
성취동사

A verb that takes an object and denotes a change in the status or condition of what thtat object refers to: *I broke the window*.

**achievement verb**
도달동사

A verb that indicates a change in the status or condition of the referent of the subject: *We moved away*.

**activity verb**
활동동사

A verb that expresses action without expressing an end to the action: *They ran*.

**atelic predicate**
미종결술어

A predicate that does not have an end or a goal.

**event/eventive**
사건문

A type of sentence that describes activities such as *John kissed Mary*, as opposed to describing states such as *John knows Mary*. See **state/stative**.

**state/stative**
상태문

A type of sentence that describes states of being such as *Mary likes oysters*, as opposed to describing events such as *Mary ate oysters*. See **event/eventive**.

**stative verb**
상태동사

A verb that expresses some state of affairs, rather than an action or event.

**telic predicate**
종결술어

A predicate that has an end result.

## Check Up the Points

**2** Key-points in this Section

➡ Achievements and accomplishments have an end result; they are telic.

➡ Statives and activities do not have an end or a goal; they are atelic.

MEMO

**Chapter 06**

# Pragmatics

MEN
TOR

# Semantics and Pragmatics

The study of the linguistic meaning of morphemes, words, phrases, and sentences is called **semantics**. The study of <u>how context affects meaning</u>—for example, how the sentence *It's cold in here* comes to be interpreted as 'close the windows' in certain situations—is called **pragmatics**.

Literal meaning isn't the only sort of meaning we use when we use language to communicate with others. Some meaning is **extra-truth-conditional**: it comes about as a result of <u>how a speaker uses the literal meaning in conversation</u>, or as a part of a **discourse**. <u>The study of extra-truth-conditional meaning</u> is **pragmatic**s.

**Pragmatics** is the study of the <u>use of language in communication</u>, particularly the <u>relationships between sentences</u> and the **contexts** and **situations** <u>in which they are used</u>. This study is concerned with what people mean by the language they use, how they actualize its meaning potential as a communicative resource. It is sometimes contrasted with **semantics**, which deals with meaning without reference to the users and communicative functions of sentences.

Pragmatics is a branch of linguistics that is concerned with meaning. **Pragmatics** and **semantics** can be viewed as different parts, or different aspects, of the same general study. Both are concerned with people's ability to use language meaningfully. While **semantics** is mainly concerned with a speaker's competence to use the language system in producing meaningful utterances and processing (comprehending) utterances produced by others, the chief focus of **pragmatics** is a person's ability to derive meanings from specific kinds of speech situations—to recognize what the speaker is referring to, to relate new information to what has gone before, to interpret what is said from background knowledge about the speaker and the topic of discourse, and to infer or 'fill in' information that the speaker takes for granted and doesn't bother to say.

## 1.1. Deixis

### 1.1.1. Pronouns and Other Deictic Expressions

One way (in which **context** can supplement a less-than-explicit sentence meaning) is through words that receive part of their meaning via context and the orientation of the speaker. Such words are called **deictic** and include pronouns (*she, it, I*), demonstratives (*this, that*), adverbs (*here, there, now, today*), prepositions (*behind, before*) and complex expressions involving such words (*those towers over there*).

Imagine both sets of sentences in (1) being spoken by Arnold Schwarzenegger in Venice on December 11, 2012.

(1) a. Arnold Schwarzenegger really likes it in Venice. On December 11, 2012, there was a boat parade in the canals in Venice. On December 12, 2012, an art festival will be held. The art festival on December 12, 2012 will be extremely fun.

    b. I really like it in Venice. Today, there was a boat parade in the canals here. Tomorrow an art festival will be held. It will be extremely fun.

Even though the referent of a pronoun is lexically restricted, we need to look to the context in which the pronoun is uttered to determine the referent. This process is called **reference resolution**.

There are two types of context relevant for the resolution of a pronoun: **linguistic** and **situational**. Linguistic context is anything that has been uttered in the discourse prior to or along with the pronoun. Situational context is anything non-linguistic.

### 1.1.2. Pronouns and Situational Context

Situational context is anything non-linguistic.

*Next week* has a different reference when uttered today than a month from today.

Directional terms such as (2) are deictic insofar as you need to know the orientation in space of the conversational participants to know their reference.

(2) before/behind     left/right     front/back

The verbs *come* and *go* have a deictic aspect to their meaning. If someone says *A thief came into the house* versus *A thief went into the house*, you would assume the speaker to have been in the house in the first case, and not in the house in the second.

### 1.1.3. Pronouns and Linguistic Context

Linguistic context is anything that has been uttered in the discourse prior to or along with the pronoun.

A reflexive pronoun is a sort of pronoun that needs to receive its reference via linguistic context, and more specifically by sentence-internal linguistic context. In other words, it requires that the sentence contain another NP—an antecedent—that it can co-refer with. In English, reflexive pronouns end with -self or -selves, like himself or themselves. (3a) shows that a reflexive pronoun requires an antecedent in the sentence. (3b) shows that a reflexive pronoun must match the person, gender, and number of its antecedent.

(3) a. *Herself left.
    b. *John wrote herself a letter.

(4) a. *Himself washed John.

    b. *Jane said the boy bit herself.

Non-reflexive pronouns (which we'll refer to simply as pronouns) such as *he, she, him, her, it,* etc. also have their reference resolved via linguistic context.

(5) Sue likes pizza. She thinks it is the perfect food.

(6) Sue: I just got back from Rome.
    Mary: I've always wanted to go there!

(7) John: It seems that the man loves the woman.
    Bill: Many people think he loves her.

## 1.2. Presupposition in Pragmatics

Speakers often make implicit assumptions about the real world, and the sense of an utterance may depend on these assumptions. For example, the utterance of "Have you stopped hugging your sheepdog?" is only appropriate in the context in which the listener has at some past time hugged his sheepdog. Assumptions of this sort can be also used to communicate information indirectly. If someone says "My brother is rich," we assume that person has a brother, even though that fact is not explicitly stated. The assumptions in question are called **presupposition**.

A somewhat different consequence of the maxim of relevance arises for sentences like *I am sorry that the team lost*. To be relevant—to obey **the maxim of relevance**—it must be true that "the team lost." Else why say it? Situations that must exist for utterances to be appropriate are called **presuppositions**.

(8) a. I am sorry that the team lost. → The team lost.

    b. Have you stopped hugging your border collie? → You hugged your border collie.

Utterances like *Take some more tea* or *Have another beer* carry the presupposition that one has already had some.

Presuppositions hold up under negation. *I am NOT sorry that the team lost* still needs the team to have lost to adhere to **the maxim of relevance**.

(9) I am not sorry that the team lost. → The team lost.

**Presuppositions** are different from **implicatures**. To cancel a presupposition—oh, the team didn't lose after all—renders the entire utterance *I'm sorry that the team lost* inappropriate and in violation of Grice's Maxims. No such incongruity arises when implicatures are cancelled.

**Presuppositions** also differ from **entailments** in that they are taken for granted by speakers adhering to the cooperative principle. Unlike entailments, they remain when the sentence is negated. On the other hand, while Jon killed Jim entails Jim died, no such entailment follows from Jon did not kill Jim.

# Check Up the Points

## 1 Glossary for this Section

**context**
문맥, 상황

The discourse preceding an utterance together with the real-world knowledge of speakers and listeners. See **linguistic context**, **situational context**.

**deictic/deixis**
직시사

Refers to words or expressions whose reference relies on context and the orientation of the speaker in space and time: e.g., *I, yesterday, there, this cat*.

**demonstrative articles, demonstratives**
지시사

Words such as *this, that, those,* and *these* that function syntactically as articles but are semantically deictic because context is needed to determine the referents of the noun phrases in which they occur.

**linguistic context**
언어적 문맥

The discourse that precedes a phrase or sentence that helps clarify meaning.

**person deixis**
인칭 직시사

The use of terms to refer to persons whose reference relies entirely on context: e.g., pronouns such as *I, he, you* and expressions such as *this child*. See **deictic**, **time deixis**, **place deixis**, **demonstrative articles**.

**place deixis**
장소 직시사

The use of terms to refer to places whose reference relies entirely on context: e.g., *here, there, behind, next door*. See **deictic**, **time deixis**, **person deixis**, **demonstrative articles**.

**pragmatics**
화용론

The study of how context and situation affect meaning; the study of extra-truth-conditional meaning.

Chapter

06

**presupposition**
전제

Implicit assumption about the world required to make an utterance meaningful or relevant: e.g., "some tea has already been taken" is a presupposition of *Take some more tea!*

**proposition**
명제

The meaning of any sentence that is asserted to be true or false.

**pro-form**
대용어

A word that replaces another word or expression found elsewhere in discourse, or understood from the situational context. Pronouns are the best known pro-forms, but words like *did* may function as "pro-verb phrases" as in *John washed three sheepdogs and Mary did too.*

**situational context**
상황적 문맥

Knowledge of who is speaking, who is listening, what objects are being discussed, and general facts about the world we live in, used to aid in the interpretation of meaning.

**time deixis**
시간 직시사

The use of terms to refer to time whose reference relies entirely on context: e.g., now, then, tomorrow, next month. See **deictic**, **deixis**, **demonstrative articles**, **person deixis**, **place deixis**.

## ❷ Key-points in this Section

➡ Semantics and Pragmatics

The study of the linguistic meaning of morphemes, words, phrases, and sentences is called **semantics**. The study of how context affects meaning—for example, how the sentence *It's cold in here* comes to be interpreted as 'close the windows' in certain situations—is called **pragmatics**.

➡ Two Types of Context

Linguistic context is anything that has been uttered in the discourse prior to or along with the pronoun.

Situational context is anything non-linguistic.

➡ Deixis

The words that receive part of their meaning via context and the orientation of the speaker are called **deictic** and include pronouns (*she, it, I*), demonstratives (*this, that*), adverbs (*here, there, now, today*), prepositions (*behind, before*) and complex expressions involving such words (*those towers over there*).

➡ Presupposition

**Presuppositions are** Situations that must exist for utterances to be appropriate.

(1) I am sorry that the team lost. → The team lost.

# Maxims of Conversation

**KEY CONCEPT IN THIS CHAPTER**

- Cooperative Principle
- Grice's Maxims
  - Maxim of Quality
  - Maxim of Relation
  - Maxim of Quantity
  - Maxim of Manner
- Implicature
- Flouting Maxims

## 2.1. Grice's Maxims

In his article "Logic and Conversation," the philosopher Paul Grice (1975) proposes that conversations are governed by what he calls the **Cooperative Principle**: the assumption that participants in a conversation are cooperating with each other. This Cooperative Principle, in turn, consists of four conversational maxims:

(1) Maxim of Quality: Truth
- Do not say what you believe to be false.
- Do not say that for which you lack adequate evidence.

(2) Maxim of Quantity: Information
- Make your contribution as informative as is required for the current purposes of the exchange.
- Do not make your contribution more informative than is required.

(3) Maxim of Relation: Relevance
- Be relevant.

(4) Maxim of Manner: Clarity
- Avoid obscurity of expression.
- Avoid ambiguity.
- Avoid unnecessary wordiness.
- Be orderly.

**Maxim of Quality** states that each participant's contribution should be truthful and based on sufficient evidence. **Maxim of Quantity** states that each participant's contribution to a conversation should be no more or less informative than required. **Maxim of Relation** states that each participant's contribution should be relevant to the subject of the conversation. **Maxim of Manner** states that each participant's contribution should be expressed in a reasonably clear fashion; that is, it should not be vague, ambiguous, or excessively wordy.

These are not prescriptive rules but rather part of a strategy used by the community of language users to enable the use of **conversational implicature**. They tend to be violated only by uncooperative people.

So if John stops Mary on the street and asks her for directions to the library, and she responds "Walk up three streets and take a left," it's a successful discourse only because Mary is being cooperative (and John assumes Mary is being cooperative). In particular, John assumes that Mary is following the **Maxim of Quality**.

## 2.2. Implicature

### 2.2.1. Maxims of Conversation and Implicature

Grice pointed out that an utterance can imply a proposition (i.e., a statement) that is not part of the utterance and that does not follow as a necessary consequence of the utterance. He called such an implied statement an **implicature**.

Let us start with the following two examples of conversational implicatures:

(5) Sue: Does Mary have a boyfriend?
    Bill: She's been driving to Santa Barbara every weekend.

(6) John: Do you know how to change a tire?

   Jane: I know how to call a tow truck.

In (5), Bill asserts that Mary has been driving to Santa Barbara every weekend. But he implicates that Mary has a boyfriend (and that the boyfriend lives in Santa Barbara). In (6), Jane asserts that she knows how to call a tow truck. But she implicates that she doesn't know how to change a tire.

When one listens to everyday conversations, **implicatures** appear everywhere. It is often enough for a speaker to just hint at a certain piece of information; the addressee will interpret that information as relevant to the ongoing interaction and will infer the speaker's intention. This facilitates processing for the listener. It probably also does so for the speaker. Speakers manage to select just the relevant information for expression.

Consider the following example. John says to his wife, Mary, and she responds:

(7) John: Uncle Chester is coming over for dinner tonight.

   Mary: *I guess I'd better hide the liquor.*

Someone hearing this interchange might draw the inference that Uncle Chester has a drinking problem. In Grice's terms, we might say that Mary's utterance raises the implicature that Uncle Chester has a drinking problem.

There are three important points to note about this example. First, the implicature is not part of Mary's utterance. Second, the implicature does not follow as a necessary consequence of Mary's utterance. (A necessary consequence of an utterance is called an entailment and will be covered in the chapter on semantics.) Third, it is possible for an utterance to raise more than one implicature, or to raise different implicatures if uttered in different contexts. Thus, implicatures are heavily dependent upon the context of an utterance, including the participants.

A maxim is violated when a speaker chooses to be uncooperative for whatever reason. A maxim is obeyed in a literal discourse devoid of implicature, as in (8).

(8) Dad: Very nice girl. What do you think, Hon?

    Mom: Not really.

<u>Implicatures can arise when a maxim is flouted.</u> To flout a maxim is to choose not to follow that maxim in order to implicate something.

On the other hand, the discourse in (9) is an example of the **Maxim of Relevance** being **flout**ed.

(9) Dad: Very nice girl. What do you think, Hon?

    Mom: The turkey sure was moist.

Because Mom knows that the quality of the turkey isn't relevant to being a "very nice girl"—and because Dad is assuming that Mom knows it, too—Dad can pick up on the fact that Mom is implicating that she doesn't like the girl.

In the Hamlet discourse below, Hamlet is violating the maxim in order to sound insane. But we can easily imagine a slightly different context, one in which Polonius and Hamlet have more or less the same exchange, but one in which Hamlet is not trying to be insane.

(10) Polonius: What do you read, my lord?

    Hamlet: Words, words, words.

In this context, Hamlet is still not obeying the Maxim of Quantity—he's not saying enough to really answer Polonius' question—but he is instead flouting the maxim to implicate that he doesn't want Polonius to know what he's reading.

A blatant failure to respect a **conversational maxim** can convey some intention in a marked way. Here is an example of such exploitation: Arnold and Betty jointly attend a harpsichord performance. When it is over, the following conversation ensues.

(11) Arnold: How did you like it?

    Betty: It was a nice piano recital.

Chapter

06

Betty's answer **violates** the **maxim of quality**, since she knows perfectly well that the instrument was a harpsichord. This is in fact mutually known. Arnold therefore infers that Betty is flouting a maxim, and, on the assumption that Betty is cooperative, Arnold will try to find out what Betty intended to convey. The most likely interpretation here is that the performer played the harpsichord as if it were a piano—i.e., without real feel for the instrument. A less likely but possible interpretation is that the harpsichord was such an awful make that it sounded like a piano. Which interpretation Arnold will infer from the Betty's answer depends upon the mutually known context. There is no standard or conversational way to infer the intention in this case of **flouting a maxim**. A speaker who exploits a maxim, for instance, to produce irony, as in the above example, must estimate whether enough contextual conditions are fulfilled in order for the addressed interlocutor to make the inference. It should further be noticed that Betty's remark does not convey the same information that would have been conveyed if she had said *The performer played without real feel for the instrument*. That would not have been ironical; the breaking of the maxim creates the special effect of irony.

**Implicatures** are different than **entailments**. An entailment cannot be cancelled; it is logically necessary. The truth of *Jon killed Jim* entails that *Jim is dead* and nothing anyone can say will resurrect him. But further world knowledge or verbal clarification may cancel an implicature.

### 2.2.2. Other Examples of Implicature

<1> Suppose an undergraduate in a geography class says, in response to a question from the instructor, *Reno's the capital of Nevada*. The instructor, Mr. Barbados, then says, *Yeah, and London's the capital of New Jersey*. The instructor's utterance raises an implicature. The student reasons (unconsciously) as follows: Mr. Barbados said that London is the capital of New Jersey; he knows that is not true. He appears to be **flout**ing **the Maxim of Quality**; there must be a reason for him saying something patently false. The inference (i.e., the implicature) I draw is that my answer is false (i.e., Reno is not the capital of Nevada).

<2> Suppose Kenny and Tom are college roommates. Kenny walks into the living room of their apartment, where Tom is reading a book. Kenny asks Tom, *What are you reading?* Tom responds with *A book*, which raises an implicature. Kenny reasons (unconsciously) as follows: I asked Tom what he was reading, and my question required him to tell me either the title of his book or at least its subject matter. Instead, he told me what I could already see for

myself. He appears to be **flout**ing **the Maxim of Quantity**. There must be a reason that he gave less information than the situation requires. The inference (i.e., the implicature) that I draw is that he does not want to be disturbed, and thus is trying to end the conversation.

<3> Suppose a man wakes up in the morning and asks his wife, *What time is it?* She responds with *Well, the paper's already come*. Her statement raises an implicature. The husband reasons (unconsciously) as follows: I asked about the time, and she mentioned something seemingly unrelated—the arrival of the newspaper. She appears to be **flout**ing **the Maxim of Relation**; there must be some reason for her seemingly irrelevant comment. The inference (i.e., the implicature) I draw is that she doesn't know the exact time, but the arrival of the newspaper has something to do with the time, namely that it is now past the time of day that the newspaper usually comes (i.e., 7:00 A.M.).

<4> Suppose Mr. and Mrs. Jones are out for a Sunday drive with their two preschool children. Mr. Jones says to Mrs. Jones, *Let's stop and get something to eat*. Mrs. Jones responds with *Okay, but not M-c-D-o-n-a-l-d-s*. Mrs. Jones's statement raises an implicature. Mr. Jones reasons (unconsciously) as follows: She spelled out the word McDonald's, which is certainly not the clearest way of saying it. She appears to be **flout**ing **the Maxim of Manner**; there must be a reason for her lack of clarity. Since the kids cannot spell, the inference (i.e., the implicature) I draw is that she does not want the children to understand that part of her statement.

# Check Up the Points

## ❶ Glossary for this Section

| | |
|---|---|
| **cooperative principle**<br>협력 원리 | A broad principle within whose scope fall the various maxims of conversation. It states that in order to communicate effectively, speakers should agree to be informative and relevant. |
| **implicature**<br>함축 | An inference based not only on an utterance, but also on assumptions about what the speaker is trying to achieve: e.g., *Are you using the ketchup?* to mean "Please pass the ketchup" while dining in a café. |
| **maxim of manner**<br>방법의 격률 | A conversational convention that a speaker's discourse should be brief and orderly, and should avoid ambiguity and obscurity. |
| **maxim of quality**<br>질의 격률 | A conversational convention that a speaker should not lie or make unsupported claims. |
| **maxim of quantity**<br>양의 격률 | A conversational convention that a speaker's contribution to the discourse should be as informative as is required, neither more nor less. |
| **maxim of relevance/relation**<br>관련성 격률 | A conversational convention that a speaker's contribution to a discourse should always have a bearing on, and a connection with, the matter under discussion. |
| **maxims of conversation**<br>대화의 격률 | Conversational conventions such as the maxim of quantity that people appear to obey to give coherence and sincerity to discourse. |

## 2 Key-points in this Section

➡ **Grice's Maxims**

(1) Maxim of Quality: Truth
- Do not say what you believe to be false.
- Do not say that for which you lack adequate evidence.

(2) Maxim of Quantity: Information
- Make your contribution as informative as is required for the current purposes of the exchange.
- Do not make your contribution more informative than is required.

(3) Maxim of Relation: Relevance
- Be relevant.

(4) Maxim of Manner: Clarity
- Avoid obscurity of expression.
- Avoid ambiguity.
- Avoid unnecessary wordiness.
- Be orderly.

➡ Grice (1972) pointed out that an utterance can imply a proposition (i.e., a statement) that is not part of the utterance and that does not follow as a necessary consequence of the utterance. He called such an implied statement an **implicature**.

➡ Two examples of conversational implicatures:

(5) Sue: Does Mary have a boyfriend?
Bill: She's been driving to Santa Barbara every weekend.

(6) John: Do you know how to change a tire?
Jane: I know how to call a tow truck.

# Speech Acts

> **TIP**
> - Illocutionary Force (2012)
> - Indirect Speech Act (2008)
> - Speech Act, Locutionary Act, and Illocutionary Act (2007)

You can use language to do things. You can use language to make promises, lay bets, issue warnings, christen boats, place names in nomination, offer congratulations, or swear testimony. The theory of **speech acts** describes how this is done.

By saying (1), you can not only say something, you warn someone.

(1) I warn you that there is a sheepdog in the closet.

Verbs like *bet, promise, warn,* and so on are **performative verbs**. Using them in a sentence (in the first person, present tense) adds something extra over and above the statement.

(2) a. I bet you five dollars the Yankees win.

    b. I challenge you to a match.

    c. I dare you to step over this line.

    d. I fine you $100 for possession of oregano.

    e. I move that we adjourn.

    f. I nominate Batman for mayor of Gotham City.

    g. I promise to improve.

    h. I resign!

    i. I pronounce you husband and wife.

In all of these sentences, the speaker is the subject (i.e., the sentences are in first person), who by uttering the sentence is accomplishing some additional action, such as daring, nominating, or resigning. In addition, all of these sentences are affirmative, declarative, and in the present tense. They are typical **performative sentences**.

In studying speech acts, the importance of context is evident. In some situations *Band practice, my house, 6 to 8* is a reminder, but the same sentence may be a warning in a different context. We call this underlying purpose of the utterance—be it a reminder, a warning, a promise, a threat, or whatever—the **illocutionary force** of a speech act. Illocutionary force may accompany utterances without overt performative verbs, for example *I've got five bucks that says you're wrong* has the illocutionary force of a bet under appropriate circumstances. **Because the illocutionary force of a speech act depends on the context of the utterance**, speech act theory is a part of pragmatics.

The theory of **speech acts** tells us that people use language to do things such as lay bets, issue warnings, or nominate candidates. By using the words "I nominate Bill Smith," you may accomplish an act of nomination that allows Bill Smith to run for office. Verbs that "do things" are called **performative verbs**. The speaker's intent in making an utterance is known as **illocutionary force**. In the case of performative verbs, the illocutionary force is mentioned overtly. In other cases it must be determined from context.

Austin (1962, 1975) claimed that all utterances, in addition to meaning whatever they mean, perform specific acts via the communicative force of an utterance. Furthermore, he introduced a threefold distinction among the acts one simultaneously performs when saying something.

(3) **Three facets of a speech act**
  a. Locutionary act: the production of a meaningful linguistic expression.
  b. Illocutionary act: the action intended to be performed by a speaker in uttering a linguistic expression, by virtue of the conventional force associated with it, either explicitly or implicitly.
  c. Perlocutionary act: the bringing about of consequences or effects on the audience through the uttering of a linguistic expression, such consequences or effects being special to the circumstances of the utterance.

A **locutionary act** is the basic act of speaking, which itself consists of three related subacts. They are ( i ) a **phonic act** of producing an utterance-inscription, (ii) a **phatic act** of composing a particular linguistic expression in a particular language, and (iii) a **rhetic act** of contextualizing the utterance-inscription.

In other words, the first of these three subacts is concerned with the physical act of making a certain sequence of vocal sounds (in the case of spoken language) or a set of written symbols (in the case written language). The second refers to the act of constructing a well-formed string of sounds/symbols, be it a word, phrase or sentence, in a particular language. The third subact is responsible for tasks such as assigning reference, resolving deixis, and disambiguating the utterance-inscription lexically and/or grammatically. These three subacts correspond broadly to the three distinct levels and modes of explanation in linguistic theory, namely, phonetics/phonology, morphology/syntax, and semantics/pragmatics.

When we say something, we usually say it with some purpose in mind. This is the **illocutionary act**. In other words, an illocutionary act refers to the type of function the speaker intends to fulfil, or the type of action the speaker intends to accomplish in the course of producing an utterance. It is an act defined within a system of social conventions. In short, it is an act accomplished in speaking.

Examples of illocutionary acts include accusing, apologizing, blaming, congratulating, giving permission, joking, nagging, naming, promising, ordering, refusing, swearing, and thanking. The functions or actions just mentioned are also commonly referred to as the **illocutionary force** or **point** of the utterance. Indeed, the term 'speech act' in its narrow sense is often taken to refer specifically to illocutionary acts.

The same linguistic expression can be used to carry out a wide variety of different speech acts, so that the same locutionary act can count as having different illocutionary forces in different contexts. Depending on the circumstances, one may utter (4) below to make a threat, to issue a warning or to give an explanation.

(4) The gun is loaded.

Conversely, the same speech act can be performed by different linguistic expressions, or the same illocutionary force can be realized by means of different locutionary acts. The utterance in (5), for example, illustrate different ways of carrying out the same speech act of requiring.

(5) (At ticket office in railway station)
    a. A day return ticket to Oxford, please.
    b. Can I have a day return ticket to Oxford, please?
    c. I'd like a day return ticket to Oxford.

Finally, a **perlocutionary act** concerns the effect an utterance may have on the addressee. A perlocution is the act by which the illocution produces a certain effect in or exerts a certain influence on the addressee. A perlocutionary act represents a consequence or by-product of speaking, whether intentional or not. It is therefore an act performed by speaking.

For example, in an armed bank robbery, a robber may utter (4) to get the cashier to open the safe. This effect of the act performed by speaking is also generally known as the **perlocutionary effect**.

While there are unclear cases, the main differences between illocutions and perlocutions can be summed up as follows. In the first place, <u>illocutionary acts are intended by the speaker, while perlocutionary effects are not always intended by him or her</u>. Secondly, <u>illocutionary acts are under the speaker's full control, while perlocutionary effects are not under his or her control</u>. Thirdly, <u>if illocutionary acts are evident, they become evident as the utterance is made, while perlocutionary effects are usually not evident until after the utterance has been made</u>. Fourthly, <u>illocutionary acts are more, while perlocutionary effects are less conventionally tied to linguistics forms</u>.

# Check Up the Points

## 1 Glossary for this Section

| | |
|---|---|
| **direct speech act**<br>직접화행 | Speech act where a direct relationship exists between the structure and communicative function of an utterance, e.g. using an interrogative form ('Can you ...?') to ask a question ('Can you swim?'). cf. **indirect speech act**. |
| **felicity condition**<br>[on speech acts] 적절성 조건 | A condition that the world must meet for a performative or speech act to be felicitous or appropriate. |
| **illocutionary act**<br>언표내적 화행 | An act or action intended to be performed by a speaker in uttering a linguistic expression, by virtue of the conventional force associated with it, either explicitly or implicitly. |
| **illocutionary force**<br>언표내적 의미 | The intended effect of a speech act, such as a warning, a promise, a threat, or a bet: e.g., the illocutionary force of *I resign!* is the act of resignation. |
| **indirect speech act**<br>간접화행 | Speech act where an indirect relationship exists between the structure and communicative function of an utterance, e.g. using an interrogative form ('Can you ...?') not to ask a question, but to make a request ('Can you help me with this?'). cf. **direct speech act**. |
| **locutionary act**<br>언표적 화행 | An act of producing a meaningful linguistic expression. |

| | |
|---|---|
| **performative sentence**<br>수행문 | A sentence containing a performative verb used to accomplish some act. Performative sentences are affirmative and declarative, and are in first person, present tense: e.g., *I now pronounce you husband and wife*, when spoken by a justice of the peace in the appropriate situation, is an act of marrying. |
| **performative verb**<br>수행 동사 | A verb, certain usages of which result in a speech act: e.g., *resign* when the sentence *I resign!* is interpreted as an act of resignation. |
| **perlocutionary act**<br>언표외적 화행 | An act that produces consequences or effects on the audience through the uttering of a linguistic expression, such consequences or effects being special to the circumstances of the utterance. |
| **speech act**<br>화행 | The action or intent that a speaker accomplishes when using language in context, the meaning of which is inferred by hearers: e.g., *There is a bear behind you* may be intended as a warning in certain contexts, or may in other contexts merely be a statement of fact. See **illocutionary force**. |

Chapter

06

### ② Key-points in this Section

➡ You can use language to do things. You can use language to make promises, lay bets, issue warnings, christen boats, place names in nomination, offer congratulations, or swear testimony. The theory of **speech acts** describes how this is done.

➡ In typical **performative sentences**, the speaker is the subject (i.e., the sentences are in first person), who by uttering the sentence is accomplishing some additional action, such as daring, nominating, or resigning. In addition, all of the performative sentences are affirmative, declarative, and in the present tense.

➡ **Three facets of a speech act**
   a. **Locutionary act**: the production of a meaningful linguistic expression.
   b. **Illocutionary act**: the action intended to be performed by a speaker in uttering a linguistic expression, by virtue of the conventional force associated with it, either explicitly or implicitly.
   c. **Perlocutionary act**: the bringing about of consequences or effects on the audience through the uttering of a linguistic expression, such consequences or effects being special to the circumstances of the utterance.

➡ Main differences between illocutions and perlocutions
   (1) Illocutionary acts are intended by the speaker, while perlocutionary effects are not always intended by him or her.
   (2) Illocutionary acts are under the speaker's full control, while perlocutionary effects are not under his or her control.
   (3) If illocutionary acts are evident, they become evident as the utterance is made, while perlocutionary effects are usually not evident until after the utterance has been made.
   (4) Illocutionary acts are more, while perlocutionary effects are less conventionally tied to linguistics forms.

# Discourse Analysis

**TIP**

• Discourse Analysis, Cohesion, Coherence (2006)

The **analysis of discourse** is the study of how sentences in spoken and written language form larger meaningful units such as paragraphs, conversations, interviews, etc., and recent analyses have been carried out in the classroom. Such analyses can be useful in finding out about the effectiveness of teaching methods and the types of teacher-student relationships.

The term **discourse analysis** is very ambiguous. We will use it to refer mainly to the linguistic analysis of naturally occurring connected spoken and written discourse. Roughly speaking, it refers to attempts to study the organization of language above the sentence or above the clause, and therefore to study larger linguistic units, such as conversational exchanges or written texts. If follows that discourse analysis is also concerned with language in use in social contexts, and in particular with interaction or dialogue between speakers.

**Discourse analysis** covers an extremely wide range of activities, from the narrowly focused investigation of how words such as 'oh' or 'well' are used in casual talk, to the study of the dominant ideology in a culture as represented, for example, in its educational or political practices. When it is restricted to linguistics issues, discourse analysis focuses on the record (spoken or written) of the process by which language is used in some context to express intention.

Naturally, there is a great deal of interest in the structure of discourse, with particular attention being paid to what makes a well-formed text. Within this structural perspective, the focus is on topics such as the explicit connections between sentences in a text that create cohesion, or on elements of textual organization that are characteristic of storytelling, for example, as distinct from opinion expressing and other text types.

However, within the study of discourse, the pragmatic perspective is more specialized. It tends to focus specifically on aspects of what is unsaid or unwritten (yet communicated) within the discourse being analyzed. In order to do the pragmatics of discourse, we have to go beyond the primarily social concerns of interaction and conversation analysis, look behind the forms and structures present in the text, and pay attention to **psychological concepts** such as **background knowledge, beliefs, and expectations**. In the pragmatics of discourse, we inevitably explore what the speaker or writer has in mind.

## 4.1. Cohesion and Coherence

Cohesion and coherence are terms used in discourse analysis and text linguistics to describe the properties of written texts.

A text may be cohesive without necessarily being coherent: Cohesion does not spawn coherence. **Cohesion** is determined by lexically and grammatically overt intersentential relationships, whereas coherence is based on semantic relationships.

A text can be cohesive through the use of the following devices:

(1) a. **Repetition**. In sentence B (the second of any two sentences), repeat a word from sentence A.
   b. **Synonymy**. If direct repetition is too obvious, use a synonym of the word you wish to repeat. This strategy is call 'elegant variation.'
   c. **Antonymy**. Using the 'opposite' word, an antonym, can also create sentence cohesion, since in language antonyms actually share more elements of meaning than you might imagine.
   d. **Parallelism**. Repeat a sentence structure. This technique is the oldest, most overlooked, but probably the most elegant method of creating cohesion.

e. **Transitions**. Use a conjunction or conjunctive adverb to link sentences with particular logical relationships. There are many kinds of transitions.

The following text is superficially **cohesive** but makes no sense and is therefore not **coherent**:

(2) A puppy is sitting on a stool. A stool is often made of wood. Carpenters work with wood. A piece of wood can be bought from a lumber store.

In this text, the relationships between propositions are overtly signalled by means of lexical repetition, yet the propositions are not logically connected in terms of how we perceive the world. On the other hand, we can provide a good example of a short text that seemingly has no overt **cohesive devices** yet makes perfect sense:

(3) The picnic was ruined. No one remembered to bring a corkscrew.

This text is not **cohesive** but it is **coherent**. **Coherence** is created due to the fact that the writer and the reader share the knowledge that relates corkscrews to wine bottles and wine to picnics. The extratextual knowledge in this case is imperative for the perception of coherence in the text.

Generally, what language users have most in mind is an assumption of **coherence**, that what is said or written will make sense in terms of their normal experience of things. The 'normal' experience will be locally interpreted by each individual and hence will be tied to the familiar and the expected.

In the neighborhood where we live, the notice in (4a) means that someone is selling plants, but the notice in (4b) does not mean that someone is selling garages.

(4) a. Plant Sale
   b. Garage Sale

Although these notices have an identical structure, they are interpreted differently. Indeed, the interpretation of (4b), that someone is selling household items from their garage, is one that requires some familiarity with suburban life.

This emphasis on familiarity and knowledge as the basis of coherence is necessary because of evidence that we tend to make instant interpretation of familiar material and tend not to see possible alternatives.

For example, the question presented in (5) is easily answered by many people.

(5) How many animals of each type did Moses take on the Ark?

If you immediately thought of 'two', then you accessed some common cultural knowledge, perhaps even without noticing that the name used ('Moses') was inappropriate. We actually create a coherent interpretation for a text that potentially does not have it.

## 4.2. Background Knowledge: Schemata and Scripts

Our ability to arrive automatically at interpretations of the unwritten and the unsaid must be based on pre-existing knowledge structures. These structures function like familiar patterns from previous experience that we use to interpret new experience. The most general term for a pattern of this type is a **schema** (plural, schemata). A **schema** is a pre-existing knowledge structure in memory.

If theres is a fixed, static pattern to the schema, it is sometimes, called a **frame**. A frame shared by everyone within a social group would be something like a prototypical version.

For example, within a **frame** for an apartment, there will be assumed components such as kitchen, bathroom, and bedroom. The assumed elements of a frame are generally not stated, as in the advertisement in (6).

(6) Apartment for rent. $500. 763-6683.

A normal interpretation of the small fragment of discourse in (6) will be based on not only an 'apartment' frame as the bases of inference (if X is an apartment, then X has a kitchen, a bathroom, and a bedroom), but also an 'apartment for rent' advertisement frame. Only one the basis of such a frame can the advertiser expect the reader to fill in 'per month' and not 'per year' after '$500' here. If a reader of the discourse in (6) expects that it would be 'per week', for example, then that reader clearly has a different frame (i.e. based on a different experience of the cost of apartment rental). The pragmatic point will nevertheless be the same: the reader uses a pre-existing knowledge structure to create an interpretation of what is not stated in the text.

When more dynamic types of schemata are considered, they are more often described as **script**. A **script** is a pre-existing knowledge structure involving event sequences. We use scripts to build interpretations of accounts of what happened.

For example, we have **scripts** to build for what normally happens in all kinds of events, such as going to a doctor's office, a movie theater, a restaurant, or a grocery store as in (7).

(7) I stopped to get some groceries but there weren't any baskets left so by the time I arrived at the check-out counter I must have looked like a juggler having a bad day.

Part of this speaker's normal **script** for 'getting groceries' obviously involves having a basket and going to the check-out counter. Everything else that happened in this event sequence is assumed to be shared background knowledge (for example, she went through a door to get inside the store and she walked around picking up items from shelves).

The concept of a **script** is simply a way of recognizing some expected sequence of actions in an event. Because most of the details of a script are assumed to be known, they are unlikely to be stated. For members of the same culture, the assumption of shared scripts allows much to be communicated that is not said. However, for members of different culture, such an assumption can lead to a great deal of miscommunication.

Chapter

06

# Check Up the Points

## ① Glossary for this Section

**cohesion**
응집성

The connections between sentences. Cohesive ties are furnished by pronouns that have antecedents in previous sentences, by adverbial connections, by known information, and by knowledge shared by the reader.

**coherence**
일관성

The familiar and expected relationships in experience which we use to connect the meanings of utterances, even when those connections are not explicitly made.

**collocation analysis**
연어 분석

Textual analysis that reveals the extent to which the presence of one word influences the occurrence of nearby words.

**context**
문맥

The discourse preceding an utterance together with the real-world knowledge of speakers and listeners. See **linguistic context**, **situational context**.

**corpus**
말뭉치

A collection of language data gathered from spoken or written sources used for linguistic research and analysis.

**discourse**
담화

A linguistic unit that comprises more than one sentence; A continuous stretch of spoken or written language, consisting of at least one sentence and usually more than one.

**discourse analysis**
담화 분석

The study of broad speech units comprising multiple sentences.

**frame**
프레임

A pre-existing knowledge structure with a fixed static pattern.

**known-new contract**
구정보−신정보 규약

The common feature of sentences in which old, or known, information (information that is repeated from an earlier sentences or paragraph to provide cohesion, often in the form of a pronoun or related word) will appear in the subject slot, with the new information in the predicate.

**linguistic context**
언어적 문맥

The discourse that precedes a phrase or sentence that helps clarify meaning.

**metadiscourse**
초담화

Certain signals, such as connectors and hedges, that communicate and clarify the writer's attitude, the direction and purpose of the passage: *for example, in the first place, next.*

**schema**
스키마, *pl.* schemata

A pre-existing knowledge structure in memory typically involving the normal expected patterns of thing, e.g. an apartment schema has a kitchen, a bedroom, etc.

**script**
스크립트

A pre-existing knowledge structure for interpreting event sequences, e.g. a visit to the dentist has a script of specific events in sequence (which might start with giving one's name to the receptionist and finish with making a further appointment).

**situational context**
상황적 문맥

Knowledge of who is speaking, who is listening, what objects are being discussed, and general facts about the world we live in, used to aid in the interpretation of meaning.

Chapter

06

## Check Up the Points

### 2 Key-points in this Section

➡ The **analysis of discourse** is the study of how sentences in spoken and written language form larger meaningful units such as paragraphs, conversations, interviews, etc.

➡ Cohesion is determined by lexically and grammatically overt intersentential relationships, whereas coherence is based on semantic relationships.

➡ Devices for a cohesive text:
(1) Repetition, (2) Synonymy, (3) Antonymy, (4) Parallelism, (5) Transitions

➡ What language users have most in mind is an assumption of **coherence**, that what is said or written will make sense in terms of their normal experience of things. The 'normal' experience will be locally interpreted by each individual and hence will be tied to the familiar and the expected.

➡ A **schema** is a pre-existing knowledge structure in memory. If theres is a fixed, static pattern to the schema, it is sometimes, called a **frame**. A frame shared by everyone within a social group would be something like a prototypical version.

➡ A **script** is a pre-existing knowledge structure involving event sequences. The concept of a **script** is simply a way of recognizing some expected sequence of actions in an event.

MEMO

# Chapter 07

# Sociolinguistics

MEN
TOR

# Language in Use (1)

---

**KEY CONCEPT IN THIS CHAPTER**

- Use of Language
- Social Contexts
- Styles or Registers
- Formal and Informal
- Slang
- Jargon and Argot

## 1.1. Introduction to Socioliguistics

**Sociolinguists** study the relationship between language and society. They are interested in explaining why we speak differently in different social contexts, and they are concerned with identifying the social functions of language and the ways it is used to convey social meaning.

Examining the way people use language in different social contexts provides a wealth of information about the way language works, as well as about the social relationships in a community, and the way people convey and construct aspects of their social identity through their language.

(1) Ray: Hi mum.

　　Mum: Hi. You're late.

　　Ray: Yeah, that bastard Sootbucket kept us in again.

　　Mum: Nana's here.

　　Ray: Oh sorry. Where is she?

Ray's description of his teacher would have been expressed differently if he had realized his grandmother could hear him. The way people talk is influenced by the social context in which they are talking. It matters who can hear us and where we are talking, as well as how we are feeling. The same message may be expressed very differently to different people. We use different **styles** in different **social contexts**. Leaving school, Ray had run into the school principal.

(2) Ray: Good afternoon, sir.

Principal: What are you doing here at this time?

Ray: Mr Sutton kept us in, sir.

This response indicated Ray's awareness of the social factors which influence the choice of appropriate ways of speaking in different social contexts. **Sociolinguistics** is concerned with the relationship between language and the context in which it is used.

The conversation between Ray and his mother also illustrates the fact that language serves a range of functions. We use language to ask for and give people information. We use it to express indignation and annoyance, as well as admiration and respect. Often one utterance will simultaneously convey both information and express feelings. Ray's utterance

(3) Yeah, that bastard Sootbucket kept us in again.

not only tells his mother why he is late, his choice of words also tells her how he feels about the teacher concerned, and tells us something about his relationship with his mother (he can use words like *bastard* talking to her) compared to his grandmother and the principal (to whom he uses *sir*). The way Ray expresses himself indicates that his relationship with his mother is an **intimate** and **friendly** one, rather than a **formal**, **distant** or **respectful** one.

We also indicate aspects of our social identity through the way we talk. Our speech provides clues to others about who we are, where we come from, and perhaps what kind of social experiences we have had. Written transcripts provide no auditory clues to readers, and examples (1) and (2) are also too short to provide reliable clues to speaker gender or ethnicity, but we can make a reasonable guess at Ray's age on the basis of his linguistic choices (he is probably in his early teens), as well as his social background.

Chapter

07

You have a deep social knowledge of your language. You know the appropriate way to talk to your parents, your friends, your clergy, and your teachers. You know about "politically correct" language: to say "mail *carrier*," "fire*fighter*," and "police *officer*," and not to say "nigger," "wop," and "bitch." In short, you know <u>how to use your language appropriately</u>, even if you sometimes choose not to. This chapter discusses some of the many ways in which **the use of language** varies in society.

## 1.2. Styles or Registers

Most speakers of a language speak one way with friends, another on a job interview or presenting a report in class, another talking to small children, another with their parents, and so on. These "situation dialects" are called **styles**, or **registers**.

Nearly everybody has at least an **informal** and a **formal style**. In an **informal style**, the rules of contraction are used more often, the syntactic rules of negation and agreement may be altered, and many words are used that do not occur in the **formal style**.

**Informal styles**, although permitting certain abbreviations and deletions not permitted in formal speech, are also **rule-governed**. For example, questions are often shortened with the subject you and the auxiliary verb deleted. You can ask *Running the marathon?* or *You running the marathon?* instead of the more formal *Are you running the marathon?* but you cannot shorten the question to *\*Are running the marathon?* Informal talk is not anarchy. It is rule-governed, but the rules of deletion, contraction, and word choice are different from those of the **formal language**.

It is common for speakers to have competence in several styles, ranging between the two extremes of formal and informal. <u>The use of **styles** is often a means of identification with a particular group (e.g., family, gang, church, team), or a means of excluding groups believed to be hostile or undesirable (cops, teachers, parents).</u>

Social situations affect the details of language usage, but the core grammar remains intact, with a few superficial variations that lend a particular flavor to the speech.

## 1.3. Slang

One mark of an **informal style** is the frequent occurrence of **slang**. **Slang** is something that nearly everyone uses and recognizes, but nobody can define precisely. It is more metaphorical, playful, elliptical, vivid, and shorter-lived than **ordinary language**.

The use of slang has introduced many new words into the language by recombining old words into new meanings. *Spaced out*, *right on*, *hang-up*, *drill down*, and *rip-off* have all gained a degree of acceptance.

Slang also introduces entirely new words such as *barf*, *flub*, *hoodie*, and *dis*.

Finally, slang often consists of ascribing entirely new meanings to old words. *Rave* has broadened its meaning to 'an all-night dance party,' where *ecstasy* (slang for a kind of drug) is taken to provoke wakefulness; *crib* refers to one's home and posse to one's cohorts. *Weed* and *pot* widened their meaning to 'marijuana'; *pig* and *fuzz* are derogatory terms for 'police officer'; *rap*, *cool*, *dig*, *stoned*, *split*, and *suck* have all extended their semantic domains.

## 1.4. Jargon and Argot

Practically every conceivable science, profession, trade, and occupation uses specific slang terms called **jargon**, or **argot**.

Linguistic jargon, some of which is used in this book, consists of terms such as *phoneme*, *morpheme*, *case*, *lexicon*, *phrase structure rule*, *X-bar schema*, and so on.

Part of the reason for specialized terminology is for clarity of communication, but part is also for speakers to identify themselves with persons with whom they share interests.

Because the jargon used by different professional and social groups is so extensive (and so obscure in meaning), court reporters in the Los Angeles Criminal Courts Building have a library that includes books on medical terms, guns, trade names, and computer jargon, as well as street slang.

Chapter

07

The computer age not only ushered in a technological revolution, it also introduced a slew of jargon, called, slangily, computerese, used by computer "hackers" and others. So vast is this specialized vocabulary that *Webster's New World Computer Dictionary* has four hundred pages and contains thousands of computer terms as entries. A few such words that are familiar to most people are *modem* (from ***modulator-demodulator***), *bit* (from ***binary digit***), and *byte* ('eight bits'). Acronyms and alphabetic abbreviations abound in computer jargon. *ROM* ('read-only memory'), *RAM* ('random-access memory'), *CPU* ('central processing unit'), and *DVD* ('digital video disk') are a small fraction of what's out there.

Some jargon may over time pass into the standard language. Jargon, like all types of slang, spreads from a narrow group that originally embraced it until it is used and understood by a large segment of the population.

# Check Up the Points

## ❶ Glossary for this Section

**argot**
전문어

The specialized words used by a particular group, such as pilots or linguists: e.g., *morphophonemics* in linguistics.

**jargon**
전문어

Special words peculiar to the members of a profession or group: e.g., *glottis* for phoneticians. See **argot**.

**register**
어역, 언어사용역

A stylistic variant of a language appropriate to a particular social setting. Also called **style**.

**slang**
속어

Words and phrases used in casual speech, often invented and spread by close-knit social or age groups, and fast-changing.

**style**
문체

A situation dialect: e.g., formal speech, casual speech; also called register.

Chapter

07

## 2 Key-points in this Section

➡ **Sociolinguists** study the relationship between language and society. They are interested in explaining why we speak differently in different social contexts, and they are concerned with identifying the social functions of language and the ways it is used to convey social meaning.

➡ **Style**, which is also called **register**, is a situation dialect: e.g., formal style, informal style.

➡ **Slang**, one mark of an **informal style**, is something that nearly everyone uses and recognizes, but nobody can define precisely. It is more metaphorical, playful, elliptical, vivid, and shorter-lived than **ordinary language**.

➡ Practically every conceivable science, profession, trade, and occupation uses specific slang terms called **jargon**, or **argot**.

# Language in Use (2)

## 2.1. Taboo

How can language be filthy? In fact, how can it be clean? The filth or beauty of language must be in the ear of the listener, or in the collective ear of society.

Nothing about a particular string of sounds makes it intrinsically clean or dirty, ugly or beautiful. If you say that you *pricked* your finger when sewing, no one would raise an eyebrow, but if you refer to your professor as a *prick*, the judge quoted previously would undoubtedly censure this "dirty" word.

You know the obscene words of your language, and you know the social situations in which they are desirable, acceptable, forbidden, and downright dangerous to utter. This is true of all speakers of all languages. All societies have their taboo words. (*Taboo* is a Tongan word meaning 'forbidden.') People everywhere seem to have a need for undeleted expletives to express their emotions or attitudes.

Words relating to sex, sex organs, and natural bodily functions make up a large part of the set of taboo words of many cultures. Often, two or more words or expressions can have the same linguistic meaning, with one acceptable and the other taboo. In English, words borrowed from Latin sound "scientific" and therefore appear to be technical and "clean," whereas native Anglo-Saxon counterparts are taboo. Such pairs of words are illustrated as follows:

(1)

| Anglo-Saxon Taboo Words | Latinate Acceptable Words |
|---|---|
| cunt | vagina |
| cock | penis |
| prick | penis |
| tits | mammaries |
| shit | feces, defecate |

There is no grammatical reason why the word *vagina* is "clean" whereas *cunt* is "dirty," or why *balls* is taboo but *testicles* acceptable. Although there is no grammatical basis for such preferences, there certainly are sociolinguistic reasons to embrace or eschew such usages, just as there are sociolinguistic reasons for speaking formally, respectfully, disrespectfully, informally, in jargon, and so on.

## 2.2. Euphemisms

The existence of taboo words and ideas motivates the creation of **euphemisms**. A euphemism is a word or phrase that replaces a taboo word or serves to avoid frightening or unpleasant subjects. In many societies, because death is feared, there are many euphemisms related to this subject. People are less apt to *die* and more apt to *pass on* or *pass away*. Those who take care of your loved ones who have passed away are more likely to be *funeral directors* than *morticians* or *undertakers*. And then there's *feminine protection.* ...

These euphemisms, as well as the difference between the accepted Latinate "genteel" terms and the "dirty" Anglo-Saxon terms, show that a word or phrase has not only a linguistic **denotative meaning** but also a **connotative meaning** that reflects attitudes, emotions, value judgments, and so on. In learning a language, children learn which words are taboo, and these taboo words differ from one child to another, depending on the value system accepted in the family or group in which the child grows up.

In his book *The Language Instinct*, the psychologist Steven Pinker uses the expression **euphemism treadmill** to describe how the euphemistic terms that are created to replace negative words often take on the negative associations of the words they were coined to replace. For example, *handicapped* was once a euphemism for the offensive term *crippled*, and when *handicapped* became politically incorrect it was replaced by the euphemism *disabled*. And as we write, *disabled* is falling into disrepute and is often replaced by yet another euphemism, *challenged*. Nonetheless, in all such cases, changing language has not resulted in a new worldview for the speakers.

### 1 Glossary for this Section

**euphemism**

완곡어법

A word or phrase that replaces a taboo word or is used to avoid reference to certain acts or subjects: e.g., *powder room* for *toilet*. An expression used in place of one considered unpleasant: *pass away* instead of *die*.

**euphemism treadmill**

완곡어법 재지정

The process whereby a euphemism takes on the taboo characteristics of the word it replaced, thereby requiring another euphemism: e.g., *crippled—handicapped—disabled—challenged*.

**taboo**

금기어

Words or activities that are considered inappropriate for "polite society," e.g., *cunt, prick, fuck* for *vagina, penis,* and *sexual intercourse*, respectively.

MEMO

# REFERENCES

• Aarts, B. (2018) *English Syntax and Argumentation*. Palgrave Macmillan.

• Avery, P and S. Ehrlich (1992) *Teaching American English Pronunciation*. Oxford University Press.

• Baker, C. L. (1995) *English Syntax*. Cambridge, MA: MIT Press.

• Burton-Roberts, N. (2013) *Analysing Sentences: An Introduction to English Syntax*. Routledge.

• Carnie, A. (2013) *Syntax: A Generative Introduction*. Wiley-Blackwell.

• Carr, P. (1999) *English Phonetics and Phonology*. Blackwell Publishing.

• Celce-Murcia, M., D. Brinton and J. Goodwin (2010) *Teaching Pronunciation*. Cambridge University Press.

• Celce-Murcia, M. and D. Larsen-Freeman (2016) *The Grammar Book*. National Geographic Learning.

• Cowan, R. (2008) *The Teacher's Grammar of English*. Cambridge University Press.

• Fromkin, V., R. Rodman and N. Hyams (2014) *An Introduction to Language*. Wadsworth Cengage Learning.

• Griffiths, P. (2006) *An Introduction to English Semantics and Pragmatics*. Edinburgh University Press.

• Grundy, P. (2008) *Doing Pragmatics*. Hodder Education.

• Haegeman, L. (1994) *Introduction to Government and Binding Theory*. Blackwell.

• Huddleston, R. and G. Pullum (2005) A *Student's Introduction to English Grammar*. Cambridge University Press.

• Katamba, F. (1989) *An Introduction to Phonology*. Longman.

• Katamba, F. (2004) *English Words*. Routledge.

• Lobeck, A. and K. Denham (2013) *Linguistics for Everyone: An Introduction*. Wadsworth Cengage Learning.

- McMahon A. (2002) *An Introduction to English Phonology*. Edinburgh University Press.

- Napoli, D. (1993) *Syntax: Theory and problems*. New York: Oxford University Press.

- O'Grady, W. and J. Archibald (2012) *Contemporary Linguistics Analysis*. Pearson, Canada.

- Paker, F and K. Riley (2014) *Linguistics for Non-Linguists*. Pearson Allyn and Bacon.

- Quirk, R., S. Greenbaum, G. Leech, and J. Svartvik (1985) *A Comprehensive Grammar of the English Language*. Longman, London.

- Quirk, R. and S. Greenbaum (1990) *A Student's Grammar of the English Language*. Longman, London.

- Radford, A. (1988) *Transformational Grammar: A First Course*. Cambridge University Press.

- Saeed, J. (2016) *Semantics*. Wiley-Blackwell.

- Yavas, M. (2020) *Applied English Phonology*. Wiley-Blackwell.

**Mentor Linguistics**

# 전공영어
# 멘토영어학

---

**초판인쇄** | 2024. 1. 5.　**초판발행** | 2024. 1. 10.
**편저자** | 앤드류 채　**발행인** | 박 용　**발행처** | (주)박문각출판
**표지디자인** | 박문각 디자인팀　**등록** | 2015년 4월 29일 제2015-000104호
**주소** | 06654 서울특별시 서초구 효령로 283 서경 B/D　**팩스** | (02)584-2927
**전화** | 교재 주문 (02)6466-7202, 동영상 문의 (02)6466-7201

저자와의
협의하에
인지생략

ISBN 979-11-6987-656-8
정가 42,000원